The Conservative Case for Class Actions

The Conservative Case for Class Actions

BRIAN T. FITZPATRICK

THE UNIVERSITY OF CHICAGO PRESS   CHICAGO AND LONDON

The University of Chicago Press, Chicago 60637
The University of Chicago Press, Ltd., London
© 2019 by Brian T. Fitzpatrick
Published 2019
Paperback edition 2021
Printed in the United States of America

30 29 28 27 26 25 24 23 22 21   1 2 3 4 5

ISBN-13: 978-0-226-65933-6 (cloth)
ISBN-13: 978-0-226-81673-9 (paper)
ISBN-13: 978-0-226-65947-3 (e-book)
DOI: https://doi.org/10.7208/chicago/9780226659473.001.0001

Library of Congress Cataloging-in-Publication Data

Names: Fitzpatrick, Brian T. (Brian Timothy), 1975–author.
Title: The conservative case for class actions / Brian T. Fitzpatrick.
Description: Chicago ; London : The University of Chicago Press, 2019. |
    Includes bibliographical references and index.
Identifiers: LCCN 2019015604 | ISBN 9780226659336 (cloth : alk. paper) |
    ISBN 9780226659473 (e-book)
Subjects: LCSH: Class actions (Civil procedure)—United States.
Classification: LCC KF8896 .F58 2019 | DDC 347.73/53—dc23
LC record available at https://lccn.loc.gov/2019015604

FOR RICHARD NAGAREDA

Contents

Acknowledgments

This is my first book, and I owe many people many debts of gratitude for their help. Let me begin with Vanderbilt Law School. Many of my colleagues read drafts of chapters, and all of them offered wise counsel and encouraging support. In addition, Deborah Schander in the Law Library tirelessly tracked down research paper after research paper. To say that she was invaluable would be an understatement. Last but not least were my students, many of whom read drafts of the manuscript, and two of them, Alex Carver and Nigel Halliday, spent countless hours as my research assistants helping me prepare the notes.

Many people outside Vanderbilt contributed mightily to this project as well. I did a workshop with the faculty at Pepperdine Law School. Likewise, the Charles Koch Foundation awarded me a grant to bring a number of people together at New York University Law School to discuss a draft of the first half of the book. The participants at these events included Robert Anderson, Babette Boliek, Trey Childress, Michael DeBow, Donald Elliott, Ted Frank, Michael Greve, David Han, Thomas Lambert, John McGinnis, Geoffrey Miller, Mark Moller, Walter Olson, Robert Pushaw, Victoria Schwartz, Ahmed Taha, Stephen Ware, and Maureen Weston. I also presented ideas from the book at gatherings of the Federalist Society for Law and Public Policy around the country. The feedback in all these places—as challenging as it was—was outstanding.

A number of scholars and friends read full drafts of the manuscript and gave me valuable comments. They included Jonathan Adler, David Engstrom, Rachael Fajardo, Marc Gross, Alexandra Lahav, Kenneth Lee, and Bill Rubenstein as well as three anonymous reviewers for the University of Chicago Press.

Thank you to you all.

Introduction

This is a book about conservative principles. I hope this is a matter
I know something about. I have been a conservative my entire life.
As an adolescent, I subscribed to the *National Review* and read books by
Dinesh D'Souza. Ever since my first semester of law school, I have been
a member of a notorious conservative and libertarian legal organization
called the Federalist Society. After law school, I worked for the most conservative judges as well as for one of the most conservative members of
the US Senate. I have never voted for a Democrat for president in my
entire life.

One thing I have learned over the years is that what is good for conservative principles is not always what is good for big corporations. It often
is, but not always. This has been a theme of conservative academics like
myself for a very long time. Consider what perhaps the most famous conservative academic of them all—the economist Milton Friedman—says
on this question:

> Over and over again you have the big businessman who talks very effectively
> about the great virtues of free enterprise and, at the same time, he is off on a
> plane to Washington to push for special legislation or some special measures
> for his own benefit. I don't blame him from the point of view of his business,
> but . . . I do blame the rest of us for not recognizing that [the free enterprise]
> system is not going to be saved by the advertisements of General Electric,

General Motors, or Mobil Oil. It will be saved, if it is saved, by the fact that the ordinary people recognize what is happening and the intellectuals in this country change their attitudes and move in a different direction. . . . [But t]he National Association of Manufacturers, the Chamber of Commerce—you name them—the big organizations and big business—they are almost always on the wrong side.[1]

In other words, "being pro–free enterprise may sometimes require that we be anti–existing business."[2]

We see examples of the difference between conservative principles and the interests of big business all the time. Consider states' rights. Conservatives like to decentralize power by divesting it to the states, yet big corporations often lobby the federal government to start regulating things in order to override state laws the corporations don't like.[3] Or consider price controls. Conservatives *hate* government-imposed price controls on goods and services because we believe the market knows better than any government bureaucrat what the right prices are, yet only last year, big corporations lobbied Congress for a price control on what lawyers could charge their clients in many personal injury cases, asking to cap lawyers' fees at 20% of recoveries.[4]

The question I address in this book is whether we should add one more item to the list of things that may be good for conservative principles even though they may be bad for big corporations: class action lawsuits.

What is a class action lawsuit? It is a special lawsuit that permits one person to sue, not only for himself or herself, but for everyone who has been injured by the same wrongdoing. It does not matter if that means hundreds of people, thousands of people, or even millions of people: if only one injured person comes forward, everyone else who was injured can be redressed at the same time. It is the most effective means private citizens have to enforce the law.

Although class actions lawsuits can be filed against anyone—including the government—my focus in this book is on class action lawsuits that are filed against corporations. Why? Because these are the class actions that have become controversial in recent years. It should come as no surprise that corporations don't like class action lawsuits. They cost them a lot of money—billions of dollars every year.[5] For this reason, big corporations have been trying to get rid of class action lawsuits ever since we put them on the books in 1966. (Why they didn't stop them from being put on the books in the first place is an interesting story I tell in chapter 1.)

I like corporations. I happily represented corporations every day during my years as a practicing lawyer, and I still thank them frequently for all the prosperity they bring our country. But they are wrong about class actions. As I explain in this book, class action lawsuits are not only the most effective way to hold corporations accountable; they are also the most *conservative* way to hold them accountable. In fact, there are only two alternatives, and neither of them should be the least bit appealing to us conservatives.

The first alternative is to rely entirely on market feedback loops. If a company does something bad, won't it lose customers? If so, then shouldn't the fear of losing customers be enough to keep companies in line and thus render legal recourse unnecessary? Conservatives do like market feedback loops, but, as I explain in chapter 2, almost no conservatives think they are sufficient to keep companies in line. Although conservatives are often caricatured as against all regulation of the market, this caricature is not true. Almost all conservatives know that markets need at least *some* rules. At the very least, we support rules requiring companies to honor their contracts, rules preventing companies from committing fraud, and rules prohibiting companies from forming cartels to fix prices. No one really thinks companies ought to be able to do whatever they can get away with in the marketplace.

But someone has to enforce these rules. Who will do it if there are no class action lawsuits? Relying on each person a company steals from to enforce the rules is unrealistic: people sometimes don't know about the theft, and, even when they do, the theft might not be worth enough to hire a lawyer. Class actions overcome these problems by letting one person sue for everyone else; this transforms an unprofitable lawsuit for a small amount of money into a profitable lawsuit for a lot of money.

This brings me to the second alternative to the class action: the government. The government could file lawsuits against companies to disgorge all their ill-gotten gains. But when is the last time conservatives thought the government was the best solution to a problem? It has been so long ago that I don't even remember it! I thought conservatives believed that the private sector is better at doing most everything than the government is. We favor private schools, private highways and railroads, private prisons, private parks, private retirement accounts, private venture capitalists, and private insurers—just to name a few—rather than public ones. But that's exactly why we should like class action lawsuits: they are *privatized* enforcement of the law. That's why we often refer to class action lawyers as *private attorneys general.*[6] As I explain in chapters 3–5, as with just about everything else, we should favor the *private* attorney general over the public one.

The funny thing is that, for most of American history, what I have said thus far was not particularly controversial. It was liberals who thought the government should police the marketplace and conservatives and libertarians who thought that it should be private lawyers representing private citizens. Hence, in 1940, perhaps the most liberal president in American history, Franklin Delano Roosevelt, vetoed a bill because he thought that it tilted enforcement of the law too far in favor of private lawyers over government agencies.[7] As late as 1978, perhaps the second most liberal president in American history, Jimmy Carter, proposed abolishing most private class action lawsuits and replacing them with government lawsuits instead.[8] During all this time, it was conservative Republicans in Congress and elsewhere who argued that, if laws were to be created, they should be enforced by the private bar, not the government.[9]

Something changed in recent years. Today, most conservatives seem to want to get rid of class action lawsuits just like Jimmy Carter did in 1978.[10] Hence, when a major class action case called *AT&T Mobility v. Concepcion* came before the US Supreme Court a few years ago, many conservatives wrote to the Court and urged it to allow companies to insulate themselves from class action lawsuits entirely by adding fine print to their contracts; they said the government could enforce the law instead.[11] The five conservatives on the Supreme Court did not need much convincing: they readily agreed and, as I explain in chapter 1, have now put the class action lawsuit on the road to its demise. The same anti–class action sentiments reign supreme among Republicans in Congress, where proposals to abolish or seriously curtail class action lawsuits against corporations are frequently introduced and sometimes enacted.

Why the change of heart? Why are today's conservatives taking advice from Jimmy Carter? This is a complicated story that I try to tell later in this book, and part of the answer is the cozy relationship between today's Republican Party and big corporations. But some of the opposition is more principled. Some conservatives complain that the underlying rules we have adopted in the market go way too far and that, if the underlying rules go too far, then those who are trying to enforce them must be going too far as well. I completely understand this. We regulate companies way too much—well beyond the simple rules I mentioned above against breach of contract, fraud, and price fixing. But the solution to this problem is not to kill *all* class action lawsuits. The solution is to get rid of the rules we don't like — or, if that is not possible, to kill *only* the class actions that seek to enforce rules that we don't like. We should not throw the class action out with the bathwater. But, as I explain in chapter 1, that is exactly what the Supreme Court's *Concepcion* decision threatens to do.

Other conservatives oppose class actions because they don't like that the lawyers who file these cases are motivated by making money. I find this remarkable. We normally love the profit motive! Indeed, it is one of the reasons why we want to privatize everything in the first place. Profit-motivated private citizens do a better job than salaried, tenured government bureaucrats do, and relying on private citizens to do things reduces the size of government and the taxes we have to pay to support it. So why have we turned our backs on the profit motive here? Some conservatives say that the profit motive has led the lawyers to abuse the system. Some of these claims are based on common myths about class actions; I devote chapters 6–8 to debunking these myths by drawing on actual data about our class action system. But it is certainly true that an unbridled profit motive can lead to destructive consequences. But this is true of any profit motive, including the profit motives of corporations. We aren't afraid of corporate profit motives, and we shouldn't be afraid of lawyers' profit motives either. The challenge is to put rules into place to harness the good of the profit motive without the bad. We do this for corporations by regulating them. We can do the same for class action lawyers.

What would the rules for class action lawyers look like? Many of them are already in place: judges already have the power to dismiss meritless class action lawsuits as soon as they are filed, and they already must scrutinize the lawsuits before they go to trial, approve any settlements, and award the fees the lawyers earn. Most judges exercise these powers wisely, but I have a few suggestions that I hope they might consider to make our system even better. I describe these suggestions in chapters 7 and 9.

But I think we also need some new rules altogether. Conservatives and our corporate friends have some valid concerns about class actions. Right now, you can bring a class action lawsuit for almost any violation of the law. But, as I noted, we don't like a lot of the laws that we make companies comply with. Perhaps we should reserve the class action only for the good laws like breach of contract, fraud, and horizontal price fixing? Right now, class actions are too expensive and risky for companies to defend — one jury can resolve hundreds, thousands, or even millions of claims all at once — and class action lawyers know it; this leads them to demand settlements from companies that sometimes may be more than the companies should have to pay. Perhaps we should make it even easier to dismiss meritless cases, break up class action trials into smaller pieces to reduce the risks, and require class action lawyers to share more of litigation expenses than they do now? In chapter 9, I discuss these possibilities.

Before I continue, I should say a word about what I mean by *conservatives*. In general, I mean people who are associated with the political right in the United States, people who identify themselves as "conservatives" or "libertarians" (or, as some prefer, "classical liberals") and who vote for Republican and Libertarian political candidates. For shorthand, I will often refer to all of us as *conservatives*.

Needless to say, libertarians do not agree with conservatives on some things, nor do libertarians and conservatives agree among themselves about everything.[12] Libertarians tend to favor government intervention in our lives only when it is necessary to protect our freedoms from infringing on the freedoms of others. Conservatives tend to favor a bit more intervention, but not much more: we tend to favor government intervention only when it is needed to ensure that resources find their way to their highest uses. Both groups tend to favor smaller government and greater reliance on private sector solutions, which, as I will show, should lead both groups to embrace class action lawsuits. Nonetheless, when our differences bear on the questions I confront in this book, I will try to note it. But, as I show, the differences are overshadowed by the similarities: almost all of us should be able to embrace class action lawsuits.

To do all this, I will draw on libertarian and conservative legal academics such as Richard Epstein and Richard Posner. I will draw on libertarian economists associated with the so-called Austrian school (popular with public officials like Rand Paul and Ron Paul) such as Friedrich Hayek[13] and the Virginia school such as James Buchanan[14] as well conservative economists associated with the so-called Chicago school (popular with mainstream Republican public officials) such as Milton Friedman and Gary Becker. I will also draw on conservative public intellectuals,[15] those who write for conservative magazines,[16] and those who belong to the Federalist Society, that organization of conservative and libertarian lawyers that I have belonged to since law school.[17]

I focus this book on conservatives because, if the class action is to survive, it is conservatives who need to be persuaded. We are the ones who are killing it. But, if I can be persuaded, I think others can be as well. We conservatives can mend the class action; we don't have to end it.

CHAPTER ONE

The Ironic History of Class Actions

A class action is a special lawsuit. Most of the time you file a lawsuit, you are suing only for yourself. You are not allowed to sue, say, for your neighbor, too, unless your neighbor has given you the power of attorney over him or her. If you have ever written a will, you know that giving someone power of attorney over you is a big deal and involves lots of paperwork. The class action cuts through all this red tape. It permits you to sue, not just for yourself, but for *everyone else* who was injured by the same wrongdoing. It does not matter if that means hundreds of people, thousands of people, or even millions of people: one person can sue for *all of them*. If a corporation steals $100 from one thousand people, the class action permits one person to sue the corporation for *all one thousand*. No power of attorney is needed.

We don't let just anyone file a class action lawsuit. There are special procedures in place to make sure the person who filed it and his or her lawyer are qualified to represent all the other class members.[1] In addition, we let most class members exit the lawsuit if any of them want to.[2] Moreover, the person who sues on behalf of everyone else is not allowed to keep all the money; he or she has to share it with the others. Still, it is not hard to see the special power of the class action lawsuit. In the example just given, it transformed someone's measly $100 lawsuit into a $100,000 lawsuit. A $100,000 lawsuit is a lot scarier to a defendant than a $100 lawsuit is. It is hard to find a lawyer who will file a lawsuit for $100. It is not hard to find a lawyer willing to file one for $100,000.

Although many class action lawsuits are filed against governments and government officials, most of the defendants in class actions are corporations.[3] Class actions against corporations will be the focus of this book because those are the class actions that conservatives love to hate the most. Suing the government is not as unpopular on the right; indeed, we are often the ones bringing *those* lawsuits.

As you can imagine, big corporations hate class actions. Honestly, I don't blame them. They have literally paid out *hundreds of billions of dollars* in class action judgments over the last fifty years.[4] If the class action had never been invented, they would have kept almost all that money for themselves. As I said, no one is going to sue a corporation for $100 on his or her own; without the class action, corporations would keep all the hundreds of dollars they take from us.

And that is not all. As I will explain in a later chapter, many class actions force companies, not to cough up money, but to change their behavior, relief that we lawyers call an *injunction*. Most injunctive class actions are filed against governments, but many of them are brought against companies, too. Companies don't like these class actions either.

But being forced to defend themselves when they do something wrong is not the only reason corporations don't like class actions. Corporations complain that class actions force them to pay up or change their behavior even when they *don't* do something wrong: because class actions are so expensive and risky to defend, they say they have no choice but to settle them. And there's some truth to that. No one thinks the class action lawsuit is perfect, least of all me.

The Invention of the Modern Class Action

You would think, then, that big corporations would have had a lot to say when the class action was invented in 1966. I say *invented* in 1966 because that's when the class action of today was created. There was a class action device before then, but it was not as powerful: class members either could win *only* injunctive relief or had to go through the trouble of *opting in* to the action in order to win money damages. Since 1966, class members have been included unless they go through the trouble of opting out.[5] Because so few people bother to opt in *or* opt out when they have lost only small amounts of money, the change from opt in to opt out transformed class actions from lawsuits that no one joined to lawsuits in which everyone was joined.

It seems pretty obvious that this change would increase the liability corporations face for their misdeeds. As I said, you'd therefore think corporations would have had their lobbyists out in full force to stop it. You'd think they would have run commercials on television and taken advertisements out in newspapers and magazines declaring that America would go down the drain if the new class action wasn't stopped. Those are the things big corporations do today when they don't like something. Remember the Harry and Louise commercials they ran to stop Bill Clinton's health care plan?

So what did the corporations say back in 1966 when the new class action was created? Very little. The class action became the law without much more than a whimper.[6] What happened?

It's hard to say exactly because so much time has passed now, but we know a few things. The first thing we know is that the advent of the new class action was not a well-publicized affair. It was not created by Congress or by a state legislature. There were no public hearings, no newspaper editorials, no marches on Washington. The class action was created by an obscure committee of lawyers, law professors, and judges.[7] The committee was appointed by the chief justice of the US Supreme Court to propose to the Court new procedural rules for the federal court system.[8] One of the committee's proposals was to overhaul the class action. The overhaul was controversial among the committee members because it was a new idea to allow someone to represent you without your explicit permission.[9] The opt-in class action had required such permission; the opt-out class action does not. After all, if your representative does a bad job and loses the class action case, you lose your right to sue on your own; you rise or fall with some stranger you may not know and may not ever have heard of. Although the committee included safeguards in the new class action—you have the right to be notified and to opt out[10]—what if you never received the notice and didn't know someone else was controlling your rights? The new class action binds you to whatever happens in the case just the same. Many of the members of the committee did not like this. They thought this new class action rule would be an affront to people's autonomy, to people's right to control their own legal claims.[11]

But most of the committee members thought this was not that big of a problem, and they submitted their proposal to the Supreme Court without much fanfare. They sent copies of it to some law schools, law firms, and judges.[12] But they didn't widely advertise it. They never published it anywhere. As a result, not many people may have known about it.[13] A few lawyers and lawyers' groups sent letters to the committee—most of them opposing the new class action—but not many.[14] As far as I can tell, corporate America had little to nothing to say. Maybe the business community didn't stop the new class action because it didn't know about it?

Or maybe the business community knew about it but didn't understand what it would do to it? As obvious as it seems today, the truth of the matter is that not many people seemed to understand what the new class action would do, including the members of the committee. It didn't occur to many of them that there was a big difference between opt in and opt out for people who had been harmed only a small amount because, as I said, such people would not bother going through the trouble to opt in *or* out of a class action. The old system basically excluded all such people from class action lawsuits; the new system would include all such people. Moving from opt in to opt out was like flicking on a light switch of corporate liability for small harms. But not many people seemed to understand that back then.[15]

In fairness, I can see why. There were not a whole lot of laws back in 1966 that people could use to sue corporations in a class action even if they had wanted to. There were antitrust laws and some fraud laws that shareholders and consumers could use, but it was not until later that many of the laws we use today were put on the books.[16] Thus, even if people *had* appreciated the significance of the new class action for small harms, there weren't that many small-harm legal claims to bring back then.[17]

I have never found these conventional hypotheses fully satisfying. For one thing, it is hard to believe that there weren't at least *some* corporations aware of the new class action proposal; after all, their law firms were aware of it and wrote letters to the committee about it. Moreover, although corporate America didn't have the lobbying apparatus back then that it has today, it knew how to fight legal changes it didn't like even then (and, indeed, it was involved in other legal fights around this time).[18] Finally, although it is true that much of the grist for the class action mill arose after 1966, as I noted, there were several laws that everyone at the time understood would form the basis for class actions against corporations.[19]

I have always wondered whether some corporations may have suspected that the new class action was going to be a *good* thing for them and that is what stayed their hand. Although it seems hard to fathom today, there is at least a bit of evidence pointing in that direction in 1966: several members of the committee that proposed the new rule said as much.[20] That's one of the reasons I call this chapter the *ironic* history of class actions.

Why did some people think the new class action might be good for corporations? Class actions provide companies something academics call *global peace*—they can resolve their liabilities to a bunch of people in one fell swoop. Some thought corporations would take advantage of class actions to obtain global peace on the cheap by *colluding* with the class action lawyers who sue them; some feared corporations would bribe class action lawyers into accepting a lowball settlement offer in exchange for the promise of a big fee award.[21] The committee put a mechanism in the rule to stop sweetheart deals like this: no class action can be settled and no fees awarded without the approval of a judge.[22] But the dissenters worried that wasn't good enough because corporations could collude with class action lawyers to bring the cases in favorable courts with pushover judges.[23] There were even some cases back then in which corporations had apparently attempted to do such things under the old class action rule but were stymied by the opt-in requirement: who would opt in to a bad settlement?[24] But, once the class action became opt out, the dissenters worried corporations could trap class members into bad settlements if they were not paying close attention to what was going on. As fanciful as all this might seem, it's not so fanciful that people don't still worry about collusive settlements even today.[25]

But whatever the reasons, letting the new class action become law was no doubt the biggest mistake corporate America has ever made with regard to our system of civil justice. If there have been any collusive settlements over the last fifty years, they have been far, far, far outnumbered by noncollusive ones.

Almost immediately, too, corporations realized their mistake. Only six years after the new class action became law, one of the lobbying organizations for corporate defense lawyers sent the committee that proposed the new class action a scathing report criticizing what it had done.[26] All the complaints we hear today about class actions can be found in the 1972 report: "judgments of astronomical size"; "legalized blackmail"; "ransom"; "no reasonable alternative other than settlement . . . regardless of the merits"; "[no] procedural and substantive fairness to the party opposing the class"; "the [class] attorney's potential fee."[27] The lobbyists begged the committee to change the class action rule back to opt in.[28]

The committee took these complaints seriously, and it studied its new class action rule for several years.[29] But, in the end, it decided to keep the opt-out class action. Still, every few years since then, lobbyists for corporate America have asked the rulemaking committee to go back to opt in—and, every few years, those requests are refused.[30] Indeed, even though no one anymore really expects the committee to ever go back to opt in,[31] to this day, corporate lobbyists still ask for it.[32] These efforts have not been entirely for naught; committees have tweaked the class action rule a bit over the years to benefit corporate defendants.[33] But the big change— the 1966 change—has survived intact.[34]

The Class Action in Congress

With little success to show before the rulemaking committees, corporate America has gone to Congress. Congress has the power to change or even eliminate the class action rule in federal court. Hence, corporate lobbyists have asked Congress over and over again to return the class action to opt in or, short of that, to weaken the class action in all sorts of other ways.[35] But, like the rulemakers, Congress has done little to help.[36] In 1995, Congress enacted a law making it easier for courts to throw out meritless securities fraud class actions.[37] And, in 2005, it enacted a law moving more class action lawsuits from state court (where the judges are often thought more anticorporation) to federal court.[38] But that's pretty much it. Even in the most conservative and Republican of Congresses, no one seriously considered going back to opt in.

Indeed, there is something interesting to note about these conservative Republicans in Congress. Until the 1980s, they didn't seem to have much of a beef with class actions at all.[39] Indeed, during the 1970s, most of the bills to weaken class actions were introduced by *Democrats* and *not Republicans*.[40] For example, in 1978, a bill was introduced that would have *ended* small-harm class actions altogether.[41] It was introduced by *Ted Kennedy*.[42] At the behest of the *Carter Administration*.[43] What happened?

As I explain in a later chapter, there had been a long tradition among conservative intellectuals and politicians in favor of private enforcement of the law over government enforcement of the law. As late as the 1960s and 1970s, it was not uncommon to see Republicans in Congress support new legal rules *on the condition* that they would be enforced only by private lawsuits and not the government.[44] Democrats, as is their wont, were more interested in government.[45] Hence, the Carter administration's 1978 bill would have not just abolished small-harm class actions; it would have replaced them with government enforcement.[46]

Things changed in the 1980s. Republicans finally came to the realization that we regulate the economy way too much; they stopped going along with new legal rules. But what to do about the old laws that went too far? It was not politically feasible to get rid of them. Instead, Republicans set their sights on the next best thing: rolling back their *enforcement*.[47] Since that time, Republicans have tried to weaken, not only class action lawsuits, but all manner of private lawsuits that enforce the law.[48] Many of these Republicans say they would rather have the *government* enforce the law—not because they love the government, but because they know the government won't enforce the law as much as the private bar does. As these efforts came to fruition, the lawyers who make their livelihoods bringing the private lawsuits fled to the Democratic Party, thereby moving that party into the embrace of private enforcement.[49] Hence, the partisan divide we have today: we have now come to the unlikely place where Democrats advocate for the *private sector* and Republicans advocate for the *government sector* when it comes to enforcement of the law. This is another reason why I have entitled this chapter the *ironic* history.

As I noted in the introduction, much of the conservative opposition to class actions stems from this second-best strategy of deregulating our economy by neutering enforcement of the legal rules. But, as I also noted, I think the second-best strategy paints with far too broad a brush. Even if it is indeed true that we still cannot roll back the substantive laws we do not like, it does not follow that we should throw out the class action altogether. At the very least we should preserve it for the laws we *do* like. And, as I explain in the next chapter, we do like some laws!

Moreover, unlike getting rid of the substantive laws we don't like, getting rid of the class actions we don't like *is* a politically feasible position. If we want to keep only some parts of the class action and not others, liberals have no choice but to go along with us. We hold all the class action cards.

The Class Action in the Supreme Court

Why do I say that? I say it because, when corporations got nowhere with the rulemaking committees and Congress, they turned to their last hope: the US Supreme Court. And the Court delivered. At first it didn't look like corporations would be any more successful there than they had been elsewhere. In case after case, they asked the Court to interpret the class action rule to make it harder and harder for plaintiffs to bring cases.[50] Yet, for decades, corporations had met with little success.[51] But then, in 2011, they hit the jackpot: a 5–4 decision in a case called *AT&T Mobility v.*

Concepcion.[52] The case was not about the class action rule but about an obscure statute called the Federal Arbitration Act that Congress enacted in 1925—*forty years* before the opt-out class action was even invented. As you can imagine, then, the statute says *absolutely nothing* about class actions. Instead, it says this: "A written provision . . . to settle [a controversy] by arbitration . . . shall be valid, irrevocable, and enforceable."[53]

Arbitration is a now-popular alternative to court. It is a way for parties to resolve their disputes in private. Who decides the dispute and what procedures are followed are up to the parties; they often specify such things by contract before a dispute even arises between them. In the 1920s, arbitration was not popular at all.[54] The only people who tried to arbitrate their disputes were merchants; regular people like you and me never used it.[55] Even still, courts didn't like it; many courts refused to enforce arbitration contracts and permitted parties to weasel out of them when the arbitration didn't go well.[56]

Congress enacted the Federal Arbitration Act in 1925 to force federal courts to enforce arbitration contracts. But it did not force federal courts to enforce all arbitration contracts; only those in a "maritime transaction or a contract evidencing a transaction involving commerce."[57] Congress was clear that it understood this language to cover only the people who were trying to use arbitration in the 1920s: merchants.[58] It expressly disavowed touching contracts between merchants and consumers or contracts between employers and employees.[59] Moreover, Congress did not say federal courts could *never* refuse to enforce arbitration contracts between merchants; it said courts couldn't refuse only if their reason was they didn't like arbitration. It explicitly said that courts could still refuse for any of the usual reasons courts refused to enforce any other contract.[60]

It was therefore quite shocking to most people when the Supreme Court handed down its decision in *Concepcion.* The case arose when Vincent and Liza Concepcion purchased a cell phone plan from AT&T that was supposed to come with a "free" cell phone. It turned out, however, that the phone was not quite free. Rather, AT&T charged them $30 for the sales tax it would have to pay the state of California on the phone. Unhappy with this turn of events, the Concepcions brought a class action lawsuit for false advertising and fraud against AT&T on behalf of themselves and all others who had been charged for the "free" phone.[61]

But AT&T said this lawsuit had to be dismissed. Buried deep in the contract the Concepcions had signed at the cell phone store was an arbitration clause. The clause said that all disputes with AT&T had to be brought in arbitration and that the arbitration had to be resolved individually—no class actions were allowed.[62]

The courts in California refused to enforce this arbitration clause. They said the clause was "unconscionable."[63] Unconscionability is a longstanding doctrine of contract law; it permits courts to refuse to enforce contracts that are fundamentally unfair, usually because one party did not realize what was in the contract and what was in the contract shocks the conscience.[64] The courts in California said that any fine-print contract that prevents people from becoming part of a class action was unconscionable because, when people are harmed small amounts, the class action is the only way they can seek redress.[65] That is, a no-class-action clause is tantamount to a you-can-never-sue-us-at-all clause. That's not fair, the courts said. None of this was especially controversial.

What was controversial was AT&T's next argument: that the Federal Arbitration Act overrode California's unconscionability law. It is true that federal laws can override state laws; this is what we lawyers call *preemption*. But using the Federal Arbitration Act to preempt here was controversial for the very reasons I noted above: the act was not supposed to apply to merchant-consumer contracts at all, and, even if it did, it explicitly said courts could refuse to enforce arbitration contracts if the reason was any of the usual reasons courts normally refuse to enforce contracts—and unconscionability was certainly one of those.

Yet, the five conservative justices on the Supreme Court agreed with AT&T. Part of the reason they did so was because, whatever Congress intended in 1925, the Federal Arbitration Act had been interpreted to do much more than that over the years by previous Supreme Courts; the five conservatives said they were bound by those decisions.[66] But part of the reason was that the five conservatives really seemed to want to help corporations out.[67] They openly worried in the opinion about whether it would be too risky for corporations to have to defend class actions in arbitration proceedings and whether corporations would have to abandon their arbitration programs altogether if they had to defend class actions in court instead.[68]

But what about the people who had been defrauded of $30 and would be left without recourse if they could not be included in a class action? The five conservatives said it was not allowed to worry about them because all they had going for them were "policy arguments." AT&T, they said, had "the law" on its side.[69]

As should be apparent by what I have said thus far, it was hardly clear in *Concepcion* that AT&T had the law on its side. As much as I love the author of the *Concepcion* decision—he was one of the judges I clerked for after law school and one of the finest justices to serve on the Supreme Court—it is hard for me see how "the law" forced the Court's hand.[70] After all, "the law" explicitly said courts could refuse to enforce arbitration contracts on grounds like unconscionability. Indeed, if there were any ambiguity about all that, you would have thought that conservative judges would have broken the tie in favor of states' rights: we conservatives normally don't like the federal government telling states what they can and cannot do, including, I would have thought, with their contract laws.[71]

The End of Class Actions?

Whether right or wrong, *Concepcion* has been a game changer. Now, any time a corporation can get you into a contract, it can get you to waive your right to be part of a class action. Do you sign forms when you take a new job? Sign something when you buy an item? Click on an "I agree" box when you purchase on the Internet? Then you probably are now or soon will be bound to an arbitration agreement with a class action waiver.[72] But it is important to realize that you do not even have to sign or click something to be bound by what it says. When your employer sends you revisions to your employment contract? When a merchant includes contractual language on the product packaging or even inside the packaging itself? You are bound if you do not quit your job or return the product.[73] Needless to say, there is now little to stop corporations from ensnaring all of us in class action waivers for pretty much everything we do. It is true that a federal agency, the Consumer Financial Protection Bureau, has the authority to prohibit class action waivers in consumer financial products, and it recently attempted to do just that—but its efforts were stymied once Donald Trump became president.[74]

There is really only one space where corporations have not yet been allowed to ensnare us in class action waivers: corporate-shareholder disputes. Although shareholders do not sign agreements when they buy shares in a company, they are bound by the terms of the corporation's charter and its bylaws. Corporations have not yet been permitted to put arbitration clauses into those documents, but the writing is on the wall: it is only a matter of time until they will be.[75] All this means that the class action lawsuit is really on the ropes. As dramatic as it sounds, it is not an overstatement to say that, if the *Concepcion* decision is not overruled by the Supreme Court or overturned by Congress, then class action lawsuits could be all but dead in a decade or less.

That's why I say we conservatives hold all the cards. If we want the class action to die, all we have to do is nothing; the work has already been done for us by the Supreme Court. But, if we think there is something worth preserving about the class action, then now is the time to preserve it. Because the status quo is the impending demise of class actions, liberals have little choice but to go along with any changes we want to make to the system; as far as liberals are concerned, some class actions are better than no class actions.

As I explain in the rest of this book, there is indeed something worth preserving about the class action. And, now, with *Concepcion* in our back pocket, we have no excuse not to.

CHAPTER TWO

The Conservative Case for Regulation

If you look around the world, you see that most countries regulate the market differently than we do here in the United States.[1] Most countries rely on government agencies to regulate the market. Companies must go to the government and ask for permission to do things, and, if the permission is granted, the company is insulated from legal liability if anyone is harmed. What happens to the people who are harmed? They are compensated, but not by the company: most other Western countries have generous social insurance programs—like universal, government-provided health care, unemployment benefits, etc.—to make people whole who are injured for any reason, including injury caused by perfectly legal corporate activity.[2]

In the United States, we sometimes employ this go-to-the-government-for-permission model (see, e.g., the Food and Drug Administration's requirement that companies seek its approval before they sell new drugs or many of our environmental laws),[3] but mostly we do not. For the most part, we let companies do what they want, but, if they injure people, then they get sued and have to pay compensation through our litigation system. We do not have the generous social insurance systems to pick up the tab.

Take but a small example: gender discrimination in employment. Employers are prohibited from discriminating on the basis of gender both in the United States and in Iceland. In the United States, we enforce this law by relying mostly on individuals who believe they have been discriminated against to file a lawsuit against their employer after the discrimination manifests itself. In Iceland, by contrast, employers must *turn their entire payrolls over to the government every three years* to get a "certificate of compliance" that says they are paying men and women equally.[4]

Or what about air purifiers? In the United States, you are mostly allowed to sell what you want when you want, subject only to lawsuits after the fact if you mislead or harm someone. In Russia, they put you in jail if you do not seek approval from state regulators before you sell a new device.[5]

That America is different from the rest of the world in this way is well-known. The legal scholar Robert Kagan puts it well when he says: "It is only a slight oversimplification to say that in the United States lawyers, legal rights, judges, and lawsuits are the functional equivalent of the large central bureaucracies that dominate governance in high-tax, activist welfare states."[6]

So which of these systems sounds more conservative to you? Go to the government for permission to do things and have "high-tax, activist welfare states" pick up the tab when something goes wrong? Or let people do what they want and rely on self-help (i.e., private litigation initiated by injured parties) to hold them accountable? The answer seems obvious to me: the American system of self-help.

Consider how another legal scholar, John Coffee, puts the choice:

> The United States [i]s different (and unique) in that it believe[s] in litigation, the role of the courts as an agent of social change, and individual action through private enforcement. Socialist governments were not sympathetic to such ideas, believing instead that the welfare of the common man was best protected by the state through political action and regulatory oversight. Private enforcement of law was not a relevant tool in the Socialist toolbox, in large part because the state saw itself as the champion of the masses. . . . [L]etting citizens sue was a regulatory answer that uniquely resonated in the United States, because ultimately the United States believed much more in the individual citizen's capacity to fend for himself.[7]

That's right: it's either private litigation or socialism! And there's nothing conservative about socialism!

The Conservative Core of Regulation

But wait a minute. I thought conservatives were for free markets. Why do we need to choose between private litigation and socialism at all? Why can't we have none of the above? Why not simply let the customers, employees, or shareholders of companies take their business, labor, and capital elsewhere if they don't like what companies do to them?

It is true that conservatives are sometimes caricatured as being opposed to all regulation of the market. But these are not serious characterizations. Virtually everyone—liberals and conservatives alike—believes that *some legal rules* in the market are necessary. The difference between conservatives and liberals is over *how many* rules they believe are needed. Conservatives believe in fewer rules, not no rules.

How *many* rules you want depends on what kind of conservative you are. Libertarians want fewer than do other conservatives. But both groups want some, and there is plenty of overlap between them.

Consider what the father of the libertarian Austrian school of economics, Friedrich Hayek (the favorite economist of Ron Paul and Rand Paul), says on the question: "In order that competition should work beneficially, a carefully thought-out legal framework is required."[8] "An effective competitive system needs an intelligently designed and continuously adjusted legal framework as much as any other."[9] "A functioning market economy presupposes certain activities on the part of the state."[10] Or consider what the father of the conservative Chicago school of economics, Milton Friedman, says on the matter: "Th[e] role of government also includes facilitating voluntary exchanges by adopting general rules—the rules of the economic and social game that the citizens of a free society play."[11] "A government which maintained law and order, defined property rights, served as a means where we could modify property rights and other rules of the economic game, adjudicated disputes about the interpretation of the rules, enforced contracts, promoted competition, provided a monetary framework, engaged in activities to counter technical monopolies and to overcome neighborhood effects widely regarded as sufficiently important to justify government intervention . . . such a government would clearly have important functions to perform. The consistent liberal is not an anarchist."[12] (This reference to "liberal" is a reference to *classical liberal*, a term generally associated with the right in academic circles.)

What legal rules do both libertarians and conservatives think we need in the market? Although they start from different places, at the very least both groups favor laws against theft, breach of contract, and fraud. Many would go further, favoring antitrust laws, and some would go even further than that.

But let's start with libertarians. They believe that government exists to protect our liberty from being infringed by others.[13] Thus, libertarians favor laws against theft: it obviously infringes on my autonomy if I invest millions of dollars in a factory and you come in and take my factory from me without my consent. But libertarians don't stop there. Breach of contract and fraud are closely related to theft. If I give you $100 to buy a product and you take my money and don't give me the product, you have essentially stolen my money. Likewise, if I give you $100 to buy a product and the product you give me is not the same one you told me I was buying, you have, again, essentially stolen my money. Almost all libertarians I know of believe that government should create laws against theft,[14] against breaching contracts,[15] and against fraud.[16]

It is true that, on rare occasion, one encounters a libertarian who takes the view that the government is not needed for any of these things. We do not need the government to forbid theft; people can just hire private security guards.[17] We do not need the government to prohibit breach of contract or fraud; people can just not do business with merchants who have a reputation for mistreating customers.[18] Although this sounds plausible in theory, in reality a world like this would be very costly. How much would each person have to spend to hire his or her own security guards? How much would we spend to research the track record of every merchant we might do business with? The answer most libertarians give is too much.[19] Even if it is theoretically possible to have a market without government, it is not a good market.[20]

If you do not believe me, take a look around at places where people do not have access to legal redress for theft, breach of contract, or fraud. The libertarian magazine *Reason* recently ran a story about why people continue to be so hungry in the African nation of Uganda despite decades of aid from Western nations. The article noted that the Western nations have correctly identified the problem in Uganda: the seeds the farmers plant there are not productive.[21] But, it went on, the problem cannot be solved because the farmers in Uganda are not willing to buy productive seeds rather than replant their unproductive seeds from the previous year.[22] Why not? Because there are so many fraudulent seeds on the market that the farmers are afraid to buy any seeds at all.[23] Although fraud is against the law in Uganda, it is too expensive to bring suit,[24] so, instead, no one buys seeds.

The current idea to solve the problem is to have the government inspect every bag of seeds before they are sold and to attach to the bags a lottery-style, scratch card that farmers can rub off to reveal a code that can be entered via text message to verify the bag is a good one.[25] That is not a very libertarian solution to the problem, of course, but, even if the government inspector were replaced by a private inspector, asking some-one to inspect everything we sell before we sell it does not lead to a nimble marketplace. As the *Reason* journalist concluded: "Outside of the context of rule of law and property rights, markets can go into [a] death spiral."[26]

Other conservatives agree that we need laws against theft, breach of contract, and fraud. They get there less as a matter of protecting liberty from infringement and more as a matter of making the market work bet-ter. These conservatives, like Milton Friedman and others from the Chi-cago school, are more utilitarian than the libertarians: their goal is to en-sure that society allocates resources to their highest uses. But this goal, too, requires laws against theft, breach of contract, and fraud.

For example, in order for markets to work well, people need to be able to trust each other. If I invest millions of dollars in a factory, I need to be able to trust that my competitor cannot simply come in and take the fa-cility from me. If I enter into a contract with you to sell me a product for $100, I need to be able to trust that you will deliver the product. If you tell me that the product will cure cancer, I need to be able to trust that you are not lying to me. If we cannot trust each other, then we will be reluctant to invest and to buy. If we are reluctant to invest and to buy, then the market is crippled. It might still be around, but it does not move very fast.

How do we inspire trust in the market? The answer is to create legal ground rules.[27] One rule says, You can't steal other people's things. An-other rule says, You have to honor your contracts. Another rule says, You cannot fraudulently represent your products. If you violate these rules, the government stands ready to force you to pay up through the court sys-tem. If you do not pay the court judgment, the government stands ready to help again by sending the sheriff to seize your property. This is not just an article of faith: there is empirical evidence showing that markets flour-ish when the participants must follow these basic legal rules.[28]

Of course, it is not enough to create rules and a court system. Someone has to bring the rule violators to court. Much of this book is about who is best to do this: private parties or the government? But, whoever brings the enforcement action, it is clear that we need at least a few rules. Mar-kets cannot form without rules already in place to govern transactions. Who would buy anything if there were no contract law in place to give you recourse if your product was never delivered? Not many of us.

Sometimes I hear skeptics say: "What is the point of making companies pay for their wrongdoing? They will just pass the costs on to consumers in the form of higher prices." This is true, but this is actually a good thing:

our markets for goods and services are more efficient if prices reflect all the costs those goods and services impose on consumers. Companies that do bad things will have to raise their prices to cover their legal costs; that will make them less competitive in the market. Over time, the bad companies will go out of business, and the good companies will be left standing.

Indeed, competition in the market is so important to conservatives that many of them do not stop with simple contract and fraud laws. Many of us believe that it is not enough to give people confidence that, if they buy something, they will receive what they thought they bought. Rules of that sort will create a good market, but not a great one. Why? Because, in order to have a great market, there must be, not only confidence, but also competition. Buyers and sellers must have options. If there is only one option, we do not have much of a market.

Consider the recent thoughts of a right-leaning economist at the University of Chicago, Luigi Zingales: "The true genius of the capitalist system is not private property, not the profit motive, but competition. Private property without competition leads to abusive monopolies, while competition can work wonders to maximize welfare even when private property is less than secure. . . . [A]s Adam Smith taught us . . . competition is the ultimate reason why free markets bring such abundant economic benefits. For competition to work its wonders, though, we need rules."[29] It is for this reason that many conservatives also believe in antitrust laws. These laws are not designed to facilitate trust; they are designed to facilitate competition. This can be seen most easily with price fixing. If merchants are permitted to collude on prices with one another, then customers don't have much of a choice; all products cost the same. We lose competition. The same is true if merchants are permitted to collude on other aspects of their products. Most conservatives believe that the government cannot allow this.[30] Many conservatives go even further and believe that the government should also prevent merchants from becoming monopolies or exploiting their monopolies.[31] Again the reason is clear: if there is only one provider of a product, we don't have any competition; indeed, we don't really have a market at all.

Some conservatives would go even further. Some, for example, would reduce transaction costs in the market even more than fraud and contract laws do by forcing merchants to internalize all the costs of their products in their prices through tort and environmental laws or by leveling information asymmetries through mandatory disclosure laws.[32] Others would promote liquidity in the market by prohibiting things like covenants not to compete.[33]

Libertarians leave the train well before all this.[34] So this is one area where libertarians and conservatives disagree with one another: how many ground rules we need. But the important point is that both groups agree we need some ground rules, and they agree on many of what those rules should be: laws against theft, laws against breach of contract, laws against fraud, and, for many, laws against price fixing. Almost no one believes in no rules at all.

Liberals, of course, would go further still. Unlike us conservatives, who wish to regulate the market only to prevent infringement on autonomy or to ensure the market allocates resources to their highest uses, liberals wish to regulate it for all sorts of other social goals.[35] Many favor legal rules for little reason other than that they redistribute wealth from rich to poor.[36] Others favor legal rules for paternalistic reasons: to override consumers' choices because policymakers know better what people want than the people themselves do.[37] The list goes on and on.[38] Many of our laws reflect liberal policy preferences and go well beyond the market ground rules conservatives support. Indeed, I believe that much of the conservative opposition to class action lawsuits is opposition to the underlying laws that class actions are seeking to enforce.[39] We do not like the laws, so of course we do not like the lawyers who are enforcing them.

But one point of this chapter is to show that this line of reasoning gets us only so far. There are some laws that even we conservatives like. Indeed, some conservatives may not realize this, but many—if not most—lawsuits seek to enforce our kind of laws. A majority of lawsuits filed in state court, for example, are breach of contract cases.[40] Indeed, even if we look only at class action lawsuits, most lawsuits may well fall within the conservative core I describe above. In 2010, I published an empirical study that examined every class action settlement in federal court over a two-year period. I found that more than half of all settlements were from breach of contract, fraud, and antitrust lawsuits.[41]

I say *may* fall within the conservative core because not every law that is labeled *breach of contract, fraud,* or *antitrust* is a law that is supported by conservatives. As I noted, there is disagreement among conservatives over whether some of our antitrust laws go too far. There is also disagreement over whether some antifraud laws go too far. For example, many conservatives believe that the California consumer antifraud statute prohibits much more than fraud;[42] others believe that federal securities fraud laws are undesirable.[43]

But my goal in this chapter is not to show that most class action lawsuits are good lawsuits. Rather, it is simply to show that even conservatives believe in some rules in the market. We do not believe that the market can be left entirely to its own devices. For at least the laws we like, we should want vigorous enforcement based on conservative principles. As the famous conservative Chicago school economists Gary Becker and George Stigler once put it: "The view of enforcement and litigation as wasteful in whole or in part is simply mistaken. They are as important as the harm they seek to prevent."[44]

The Enforcement Choice

In fairness, however, there are other ways to enforce the rules of the market besides litigation and the socialism of Europe. To that end, consider table 1. This is how legal scholars map the possible ways to enforce the law. On one axis, we see a choice between enforcing the law before a company acts (ex ante) or after a company acts (ex post). This is the choice between requiring permission before you act and being permitted to do whatever you want (but having to pay up later if things don't turn out well). On the other axis, we see a choice between who does the enforcement: the government or a private party.

All these models seek to do the same two things: discourage companies from harming people in the first place but compensate people if they nonetheless end up getting harmed. These two regulatory goals are often called *deterrence* and *compensation*.[45] Much of this book is about which one of these boxes best accomplishes these two goals.[46]

As I said at the outset of this chapter, most developed countries around the world fall into something like box 1: you have to ask permission before you do something new, and you go to the government for that permission. If the government tells you that what you want to do is lawful, then you are good to go. These countries deal with any fallout through social insurance programs. Deterrence comes from forcing companies to ask for permission before they act; compensation comes from the social insurance programs.

TABLE 1 **Enforcement Choices around the World**

	Ex Ante	Ex Post
Government	1	2
Private	3	4

The United States mostly falls into box 4: you don't have to ask anyone permission, but you do have to pay for any fallout you cause, and the mechanism to collect those payments is initiated by whoever is injured. We don't need social insurance programs to pick up the tab. Deterrence comes from the companies themselves when they figure out whether they should act by weighing whether they might be sued if they do and how much it would cost if they are; compensation comes from the companies when they lose those lawsuits.

As I intimated above, the choice between box 1 and box 4 is not difficult for a conservative. Many conservatives have said as much in the past.[47] They have included academics like the libertarian law professor Richard Epstein[48] and the conservative economist Milton Friedman[49] as well as politicians like the libertarian Republican Gary Johnson.[50] Indeed, a terrific new book by a libertarian research fellow at George Mason University's Mercatus Center is devoted entirely to this question; its conclusion could not be clearer: "*Ex post* (or after the fact) solutions should generally trump *ex ante* (preemptive) controls."[51] What kind of ex post solutions are these? "Contract" and other private "common law" lawsuits, including "class-action activity."[52]

It is therefore surprising that these days many companies—the same ones that generally support conservative politicians—say they prefer box 1. Indeed, many companies today *beg* Washington to regulate them. Without any prompting by the government, these companies go to the federal government *asking for permission* to do things.[53] Why would companies do this? Because they are hoping that the government's blessing will insulate them from private lawsuits (something that, as I noted in the previous chapter, we lawyers call *preemption* of state law).[54] But we don't have the European-style social insurance programs to compensate people who are injured from corporate activity; who will compensate injured persons? Incredibly, many corporations say they want more social insurance programs, too.[55]

Again, this is not usually thought of as the conservative way to run a country. So why do the companies want it? Why would companies trade away the freedom to innovate and the lower taxes that go along with fewer government programs? I will take up this question in more detail later, but the corporations say that they have no choice: the lawsuits they would otherwise face are out of control, and more government is the lesser of evils.[56] As I will use much of this book to explain, I do not believe that the lawsuits are really out of control. I suspect that there is another reason big companies turn to the federal government: they are able to use campaign contributions, lobbyists, and the revolving door of personnel between government and industry to influence the federal government in ways they cannot influence private lawyers and the courts. It is not so much that the lawsuits are that bad as that the government can be good—very good, indeed—for powerful corporations. Conservatives sometimes call this *crony capitalism.*[57] And it further reinforces why conservatives should prefer box 4 to box 1.

But boxes 1 and 4 are not our only boxes. We also have boxes 2 and 3. Box 3 has not been tried much,[58] and it suffers from the same threat to innovation and need for vast social insurance that box 1 does. Thus, the real choice for conservatives is between box 2 and box 4. Both these boxes take advantage of the innovation and energy that comes from letting companies do what they want without asking for permission first. Both seek to deter wrongdoing by giving companies incentives to be careful about what they do by insisting that they pay for any harm they cause later on. Neither requires the creation of social insurance programs to compensate people when the permitted corporate activities injure people; the companies themselves pay the compensation when they are sued later on. The only difference is who brings the lawsuit when the companies cause harm: government lawyers or private lawyers. In the next chapter, I explain why I believe conservatives should prefer private lawyers.

Before I do so, however, I should note that there was a time when this notion would not be as controversial as it is today. Although it has been largely forgotten, for most of our history, conservatives preferred legal enforcement by private lawyers because they thought private enforcers of the law were better than public enforcers. For example, in the 1970s, prominent conservative economists—Richard Posner, William Landes, Gary Becker, and George Stigler—engaged in a famous debate on the question, Who is better suited to enforce the criminal and the civil law: private parties or the government?[59] Becker and Stigler said it was private parties,[60] and Posner and Landes said it was sometimes private parties and sometimes the government.[61] But even Posner and Landes thought private parties were best for the civil laws that conservatives support (e.g., breach of contract, fraud, and antitrust) as well as the lawsuits that give rise to class actions.[62] Other conservative thinkers in this era came to the same conclusion.[63]

It was not just in the academy that conservatives had these thoughts. They manifested themselves in the political world as well. As Robert

Kagan[64] and Sean Farhang[65] have chronicled, many of the statutory regimes Congress enacted in this era could win Republican support only on
the promise that they would be enforced by private lawsuits rather than
government bureaucrats. Indeed, for much of the twentieth century, it
was *liberals* and *not conservatives* who objected to private lawsuits to enforce the law.[66] One of the reasons liberals built the administrative state
during the Progressive and New Deal Eras was to wrest enforcement of
the law away from the private sector.[67] Franklin Delano Roosevelt went
so far as to veto New Deal legislation when it relied too heavily on private
enforcement instead of government agencies.[68] Similarly, decades later,
it was the liberal Carter administration that sought legislation to *abolish*
small-claim class actions brought by the private bar and replace them with
government lawsuits.[69] As I noted, the sponsor of the administration's bill
in the US Senate was the liberal lion from Massachusetts: Ted Kennedy.[70]

Times have really changed![71]

CHAPTER THREE

The Conservative Case for Private Enforcement

In the last chapter, I showed that even conservatives believe that the market needs rules. This raises the question that is at the heart of this book: Who should enforce the rules? As I also showed in the last chapter, there are really only two choices: government lawyers or private lawyers. In this chapter, I explain why a good conservative should prefer the private lawyers. In a later chapter, I explain why, even better, it should be *class action* lawyers.

The Theory of Privatization

As I noted at the end of the last chapter, it was not so long ago that conservatives were the ones who liked to enforce the law with private lawyers. In this book, I try to reclaim this conservative tradition, but I do so by drawing on a new—and, I hope, an especially appealing—perspective: the theory of privatization of government. Since at least the 1970s, the theory of privatization has been a central tenet of the conservative theory of government. As I explain, there are few government functions that conservatives do *not* think should be turned over to the private sector. For many of the same reasons we want to privatize nearly everything else, I think we should want to privatize the enforcement of market rules as well.

TABLE 2 **One Possible Spectrum of Privatization**

Most privatized							Least privatized
Market	Voucher	Grant	Franchise	Government contracting	Government vending	Intergovernment agreement	Government

Source: Emanuel S. Savas, *Privatization and Public-Private Partnerships* (New York: Chatham House, 2000), 88, table 4.6.

The conservative theory of privatization is often traced to Margaret Thatcher's British government in the late 1970s,[1] but Robert Poole, the founder of the libertarian Reason Foundation (and leading privatization think tank),[2] is said to have coined the term in the 1960s.[3] Whatever its origin, it has been a staple of Republican politics and conservative and libertarian thought in the United States since Ronald Reagan.[4] The basic idea is that much of what the government does should be done by the private sector.[5] The theory encompasses a spectrum of efforts to transition government work to private parties.[6] At one end, the government entirely divests itself of assets or industries, as Britain did with many of its industries under Thatcher, and as many conservatives want the United States to do with Amtrak.[7] On the other end, more commonly in the United States, the government retains financial control but outsources the delivery of goods or services to private parties.[8] There are numerous arrangements in between. Table 2 shows how one conservative scholar orders the arrangements from more privatized to less.

There is almost no end to the government services that conservatives want to privatize in one form or another. Here is a just a sample, in alphabetical order:

Airports and air traffic controllers[9]

Ambulances[10]

Amtrak[11]

Debt collection[12]

Education[13]

Fire protection[14]

Government office space[15]

Health care for veterans, the poor, and the elderly[16]

Health- and building-code inspection[17]

Highways[18]

International development programs[19]

Low-income housing[20]

Mass transit[21]

Mortgage financing and other government loan programs[22]

Parks and other public lands[23]

Petroleum reserves[24]

Postal services[25]

Power generation[26]

Prisons[27]

Social Security and other pensions[28]

Space exploration[29]

Waste collection and management[30]

Water supply and treatment[31]

Why do we love to privatize? As I explain below, different conservatives have different reasons. But, as I also explain, no matter which of these reasons appeal to you, they apply with equal force to the enforcement of the rules of the market.

Let's start with the reasons.

Smaller government. Many conservatives—especially the libertarian-minded ones—want to privatize because they like less government rather than more.[32] Not only is a big government more expensive to maintain, but it is also a threat to our freedoms and liberties—if not today, then tomorrow. Once all the government agents we hired to do the good things are done doing them, we are afraid they might turn to taking away our freedoms.[33] This is all the more worrisome in a world of crony capitalism, where, as I explain in more detail below, government agents can be influenced by campaign contributors or other political supporters. Better to minimize the risk by minimizing the number of government agents. This is why, of course, those who founded our nation wanted the federal government to be of "limited and enumerated" powers.[34]

Self-help. Libertarian-minded conservatives have a special reason to prefer private solutions to many problems: they enable us to help ourselves instead of creating dependence on the government to do things for us. When we let government provide things for us, it becomes too easy to stop trying to provide things for ourselves. Over time, the government does not even need to take our liberties away: we freely hand them over. In order to forestall becoming wards of the state, we should minimize the number of instances where government does things that we could do for ourselves.[35]

Better incentives. Utilitarian-minded conservatives tend to favor privatization for a more pragmatic reason: they believe that the private sector will do a better job at most things than the public sector can.[36] Why? First and foremost because private sector workers have better incentives than do government workers. In particular, they believe that the profit motive drives private actors to do a better job than their government counterparts.[37] As the father of privatization, Robert Poole, noted: "Private firms tend to be efficient precisely *because* they have to make a profit."[38] For the most part, public officials make the same government salary no matter whether they do a good job or a bad job. Civil service protections make it harder to fire them for doing a bad job, too. Without financial "carrots" and "sticks,"[39] we have to depend on the professionalism of public officials to spur their performance. Although that is not nothing, we can do even better in the private sector: private actors have the same desire for professional success, but they also make more money when they do a good job and get fired when they do a bad job.[40] This is why, as the Yale law professor Peter Schuck summarized in his *Why Government Fails So Often*, "studies indicate that . . . services can usually be provided better and more cheaply by private groups" and that "the market almost always performs more cost-effectively."[41] What's not to like about that?

Better resources. A closely related reason we like to privatize is this one: the government is always strapped for cash. Frankly, this is the way we conservatives (especially libertarians) like it. We don't want to raise taxes, and, as a result, budgets are always limited in the public sector. This makes it hard for the government to make timely investments. Take a look at our infrastructure in this country. By all accounts, it is crumbling.[42] Or take a look at the Internal Revenue Service. No one likes the IRS, but, if it doesn't audit people every once in a while, no one will pay their taxes. Every dollar of enforcement brings in many dollars of additional tax revenue.[43] Yet Congress still slashes the IRS's enforcement budget because it is politically popular to do so.[44] The private sector doesn't have this problem.[45] The resources of the private sector are virtually unlimited. If there is a profitable venture, the private sector will fund it. If the proprietors of the goods or services themselves don't have the money, they can borrow it or find an investor. They don't have to worry about the political repercussions.

Less bias. Another popular reason why conservatives favor the private sector is that the public sector is unduly influenced by campaign contributions,[46] lobbying,[47] and the revolving personnel door between government and industry.[48] This, again, is the crony capitalism I mentioned above. Academics call it something that sounds nicer: *public choice theory*[49] or *agency capture*.[50] But the idea is the same. The private sector has its eye on one thing and one thing only: making a profit, something it should be able to earn only if it does a good job. By contrast, the government has its eye on other things,[51] many of which do not help its performance: Who gave us campaign contributions? Who will give us campaign contributions? Isn't that lobbyist or corporate executive our former colleague and friend? Didn't our colleague work for that lobbyist or corporation at some point? Campaign money, lobbying, and the revolving door make the government beholden to special interests in a way that the private sector simply is not.[52] For obvious reasons, we think this negatively affects public sector performance relative to its private sector counterparts.[53]

Less centralization. The last reason most conservatives favor the private sector over the public sector is because the private sector is less centralized.[54] We have only one federal government, for example, whereas we can have an infinite number of private providers of goods and services. As the godfather of the Austrian school of economics, Friedrich Hayek, explains, decentralization is good because it leads to "experimentation" and "competition."[55] Experimentation and competition produce information about what works and what doesn't; they are how we innovate, how we improve.[56] Government offers us one solution, for better or for worse. The private sector can offer us an infinite number of solutions; we can find the best solution over time, and keep one eye open to see if we might find an even better one someday. It is the difference between a monopoly and the market.[57] And it is another reason why we think the private sector generally does a better job than the public sector.

The Theory of Privatization and Enforcement of the Law

Do these reasons in favor of privatization tell us anything about using private lawyers to enforce the rules of the market? That is, is the so-called private attorney general better for these reasons than the public one? I think the answer is a big yes.

I should note that I am not the first scholar to see the connection between privatization and the private attorney general. Professor Margaret Lemos of Duke University has written about one type of privatization of civil law enforcement: when the government hires private lawyers to file the government's lawsuits instead of using government lawyers to do so. Along the spectrum of privatization in table 2 above, this might be considered in the middle of the spectrum: "government contracting." Lemos notes that "the potential benefits of contracting out government litigation work are fairly straightforward, and correspond neatly to themes stressed by proponents of privatization more generally." In particular: "Competition and market discipline will drive private attorneys to perform the same work at lower cost than salaried government employees."[58]

I think Lemos is right, but her analysis only skimmed the privatization literature and did not focus on conservative arguments for privatization. As would be expected, liberal scholars tend to be more tepid in their support for privatization,[59] which may explain why Lemos analyzed only a more tepid form of privatized law enforcement. The private attorney general I am describing in this chapter is much bigger than the government substituting private lawyers for public ones when the government itself is a plaintiff. The private attorney general is the private bar suing on behalf of private plaintiffs whenever the bar and the plaintiffs deem it desirable to do so. The government does not have to bless a suit for it to happen; it happens whenever participants in the private sector themselves think it makes sense. It is a purer form of privatization, more like the divestment of assets that I discussed above than like outsourcing. We might put it at the far left end of the spectrum in table 2 under "market" rather than in the middle under "government contracting." Lemos did not try to analyze whether this purer form of privatized civil law enforcement is supported by the privatization literature.

But I do. And, as I explain now, I think it is—and for all of the reasons we conservatives love to privatize everything else.

Smaller government. Obviously, this reason for privatizing favors privatizing the enforcement of market rules, too.[60] If we did not rely on the private bar to enforce the law, we would have to hire thousands on thousands of government lawyers to replace them—or, even worse, we would have to start regulating the economy ex ante like Europe does.

Self-help. Again, this reason for privatizing obviously favors privatizing the enforcement of the law. Indeed, many libertarians are especially keen on private enforcement because many of them believe that we have an innate right to protect ourselves from infringements on our liberty but that we had no choice but to surrender our right to protect ourselves by force to the government (which exercises a monopoly on force through the criminal law). As a consequence, they believe that the government has an *obligation* to give us a substitute form of self-help, such as the civil lawsuit. Yet it is not much of a substitute if the government has to file the lawsuit for us; it is not *self*-help if we have to depend on the whim of government bureaucrats.[61]

Better incentives. There is little question that the profit motive gives the private bar better incentives to enforce our market rules than those that government lawyers have. Government lawyers, like all government employees, generally earn the same salary no matter how much money they recover against wrongdoers. They also enjoy the same civil service protection from termination as many government employees. Whether they bring one lawsuit or ten, whether they win or lose, they still have a job, and they still make the same salary. This is not so for the private plaintiffs' bar. Much of the time—indeed, almost all the time in class action litigation—the private bar is paid only on what is known as *contingency*. This means that private lawyers are paid only when their clients recover; if their clients get nothing, they get nothing, too. Moreover, contingency lawyers are usually paid a percentage of what their clients recover. Thus, the more their clients get, the more they get, too.

This means that we would expect private lawyers to file more lawsuits, resolve those lawsuits for more money when they do file, and resolve those lawsuits more quickly than government lawyers. In short, it means that we would expect to get more deterrence and more compensation from the private bar. Indeed, this is why even rich corporations—clients that can afford to pay their lawyers by the hour—sometimes choose instead to pay their lawyers with a contingency percentage.[62]

It is true that the contingency-fee system is not perfect. Because lawyers earn only a percentage of their clients' recoveries but bear all the cost of going forward in the case, it is rational for lawyers to want to settle cases for less money than their clients would want them to if they can do so quickly.[63] But is there any doubt that even a dampened profit motive lights a hotter fire under the belly of the private bar than what burns under the government lawyer? No. Scholars from all walks of political life think that the profit motive gives the private bar a leg up over government lawyers,[64] including scholars affiliated with the conservative Chicago school of economics.[65] Indeed, even the most vocal critics of the private attorney generally concede this point. Consider Walter Olson, who authored the famous antilawsuit book *The Litigation Explosion*: "There is no point denying that contingency fees have certain productivity advantages. Paying people only if their efforts culminate in success definitely coaxes more effort out of them."[66]

It is true that government lawyers can be motivated by political ideology and that this can induce them to do a good job even without financial rewards. But it can also induce them to do a bad job. Ideological lawyers might enforce only the laws they like and not the ones they don't. It is another species of the bias that affects government enforcement that I discuss below.

Indeed, when conservatives criticize the private attorney general, it is not because they think the private bar does not have more fire under the belly than government lawyers; it is because they think the profit motive gives the private bar *too much* fire under the belly. They think the private bar creates too much deterrence and recovers too much compensation.[67] I will address this concern later. But, for now, it is enough to say yes—yes, the profit motive gives the private bar better incentives than government lawyers.

Better resources. There is also little doubt that the private attorney general outshines the public attorney general with respect to resources. Government enforcement budgets are just as strapped as other government budgets—if not more so because enforcement is a lot less sexy than other government expenditures (like those that send people checks in the mail or deliver other goodies). As the Yale law professor Peter Schuck summarizes: "Congressional appropriations for enforcement . . . tend to be woefully inadequate."[68] Other scholars agree.[69] Consider, for example, what scholars (including one who was Securities and Exchange commissioner!) have had to say about the Securities and Exchange Commission (SEC), one of the federal government's *best* funded and *most* active civil law enforcers:

> The SEC is underfunded, resource-constrained, and cannot afford to litigate the complex case. Undermanned and underfunded, the SEC must settle cases cheaply, because it cannot afford costly trials and lacks the experienced manpower to handle them.[70]

> The [SEC] does not have the resources to investigate every instance in which a public company's disclosure is questionable, . . . [and] [t]his would continue to be the case even if the Commission's resources were substantially increased.[71]

> [F]or most of its history the [SEC] has been plagued by poor funding. . . . It has also tended to be poorly staffed with notoriously high rates of staff turnover.[72]

> It's no secret that the [SEC] is terrifically understaffed and wildly underfunded compared with the populous and wealthy Wall Street world it is supposed to police.[73]

Scholars from across the political spectrum agree that the private sector can throw more resources into enforcing the law.[74] The reason is simple, and it goes back to the profit motive. The private sector invests in enforcement like it does everything else: as far as profit allows. Because the private bar is usually paid a one-third percentage of any recovery through the contingency fee system, this means that the private bar will invest in any lawsuit where the expected recovery is at least three times what it would cost in time and money to litigate the case.[75] If a given lawyer does not have enough time or money to do it on his or her own, he or she will borrow time and money from someone who does. As Posner and Landes, two of the economists associated with the conservative Chicago school, put it: "The assumption of a budget constraint would be unrealistic as applied to a private enforcer, for assuming reasonably well functioning capital markets he would be able to finance any enforcement activities where the expected monetary return exceeded the expected costs."[76] As we know, the government does not work this way; it works under a budget that is constrained by politics. That's why pretty much everyone thinks, in the words of Lemos, that the government "can rarely keep pace with . . . private-sector spending."[77]

But lawsuits cost money. You have to pay lawyers, paralegals, and experts. You have to pay travel expenses and for technology to sift through millions of pages of records. The more constrained your resources, the fewer lawsuits you can file. The more constrained your resources, the less you can do in the lawsuits you do file. This means, again, that we would expect the government to enforce the law less frequently and recover less when it does try to enforce it; it means, again, that there will be less compensation for victims of wrongdoing and less deterrence of misbehavior.[78]

Less bias. Government enforcers are beset by the distractions of special interest campaign money, lobbying, and the revolving door just as much as other government officials are. Indeed, government enforcers may be the government officials *most* affected by this crony capitalism. Businesses have every incentive to influence the government to look the other way when they do something wrong or to give them a sweetheart deal if it doesn't look the other way. The government has enormous discretion in deciding when to enforce the law and when not to, in deciding when to settle a case and when not to. Who's to say the decision wasn't made on the merits as opposed to past election support? The promise or even hope of future election support? The fact that the wrongdoer is run by a former colleague and friend from government? No one.

Scholars agree: government enforcers are often "captured" by the businesses and industries against which they are supposed to be enforcing the law.[79] Indeed, it is conservative scholars who are often the *most* agitated about government capture—hence, again, our focus in recent years on crony capitalism. As one scholar notes: "Libertarians and conservatives have been particularly critical of the progressive state because of its propensity to special interest capture."[80] Some trace this entire field of inquiry to the conservative Chicago school[81] or the libertarian Virginia school of economics.[82] Again, we would expect capture to lead to fewer enforcement actions and lower recoveries even when an enforcement action is brought.

These concerns with capture are not only theoretical. You can open the newspaper on any given day and find examples of it. Why did the federal Food and Drug Administration not crack down on dangerous chemicals in dietary supplements? Perhaps it was because "two of the agency's top officials overseeing supplements . . . were former leaders of the largest supplement industry trade and lobbying group."[83] Why did the federal National Highway Transportation and Safety Administration do nothing as automobile airbags were exploding and killing people year after year after year?[84] Perhaps it was because, "from 1999 to 2010, forty officials left NHTSA for industry jobs [and] twenty-three auto industry executives were appointed to top agency jobs."[85] The examples are just as numerous—if not more numerous—in our state governments.[86]

Indeed, there is now even empirical evidence that government enforcers are captured by special interests. In his exhaustive study of private and government enforcement of the federal False Claims Act, the Stanford law professor David Engstrom found that the Department of Justice was more likely to aid lawsuits filed by former government colleagues despite the fact that these lawsuits were less important than the lawsuits filed by other private lawyers.[87] It is much more difficult for wrongdoers to capture the private bar like this. Scholars from across the political spectrum agree with me.[88] There are three reasons for this.

The first reason is that it is hard for a wrongdoer to buy off a private lawyer without breaking the law. One way a defendant could try to do it is to offer to pay the plaintiff's attorneys' fees as part of the settlement of a case; the defendant could offer the lawyer more lucrative fees in exchange for a smaller overall settlement. This would be unethical, if not illegal, in most cases. Nonetheless, it might be easier to pull off in class actions because the clients are so diffuse—hence the concern with the collusive settlements that I said in chapter 1 people were worried would result from the modern class action rule. But in class action cases, which will be the focus of later chapters, any fee—no matter who pays it—must be approved by a judge. Thus, the judge can scrutinize the deal to make sure the lawyer has not traded higher fees for a smaller settlement.

The second reason goes to something that is discussed later in this chapter: the private bar is incredibly decentralized; there are thousands upon thousands of private lawyers who can sue any given wrongdoer. By contrast, there is usually only one or a small number of governments that wrongdoers must influence. This makes it impossible for wrongdoers to buy off the private bar.[89]

The third reason goes back, again, to something that was discussed earlier in this chapter: the profit motive. The private bar is focused on profits, and, because of the contingency-fee system, it can make profits only if their clients do. The private bar simply cannot afford to care about political campaigns or whether their former colleagues and friends work for their adversaries; they have payroll to make.

It is true that the private bar cannot bring wrongdoers to account all on their own; they have to bring their cases in court. But aren't courts run by judges, and aren't judges government officials? Can't the judges be captured by businesses and industries like other government officials? If so, what difference does it make whether a private lawyer or a government one brings the lawsuit?

It makes a big difference in federal court. Federal judges are not like other government officials. They never have to run in an election, and they do not work for people who have to run in elections. Unlike other public officials in America (and, indeed, almost the entire world), they can keep their jobs for life if they want to. Short of the improbable act of impeachment, a federal judge cannot be threatened. This was the entire reason the founding generation of our country conferred such job protection on them; it was obsessed with guaranteeing federal judges "independence." Moreover, the staff of a federal judge—so-called law clerks—turns over frequently (every year or two), and it is extraordinarily rare for someone to leave the staff for industry and come back again. That is, the doors of a federal judge's chambers do not revolve; they slam shut as you leave. For these reasons, few people think they can be captured like other government officials.[90]

I must admit that the same is not true of state judges (and most lawsuits are brought in state courts, not federal courts). Unlike federal judges, most state judges have to run for office—sometimes in partisan, contested elections, sometimes in nonpartisan, contested elections, and sometimes in unopposed retention referenda. Although these races are different from one another, they all have one thing in common: the judges can raise campaign contributions. This makes capture of state judges possible in a way it is not of federal judges.[91] Indeed, some people worry even more about capture of state judges than other government officials because it is thought that they can be captured by either side: not only do businesses and industries try to influence them with campaign contributions, but the private bar does, too.

The fact that many lawsuits brought by our private attorneys general are brought in state court undermines to some extent the conservative case for private enforcement. But it does not fatally undermine it.

First, less bias is only one of my six reasons for arguing that the private bar might be preferable to government lawyers; even if we throw this one out as a wash, I still have five others.

Second, the fact that both sides try to influence state judges with campaign contributions may be *less* reason rather than more reason to be concerned with capture because the special interests may cancel each other out in state court. The traditional concern with capture is that only the business side tries to influence the government because the consumer or employee side is too diffuse to organize.[92] If both sides can organize, then there is less reason to think that the government will be biased one way or the other over the long run.

But perhaps the most important reason capture of state judges does not undermine my argument here goes back to the focus of this book: class actions. Today, virtually any class action of significance ends up in *federal court*. This is because big businesses pressed Congress to enact a law in 2005 called the Class Action Fairness Act that requires most class actions seeking more than $5 million to be filed in federal court. As a result, state judges are now largely irrelevant to this book.

Less centralization. Finally, it is obvious that the private bar is less centralized than government enforcement,[93] and it is equally clear that less centralization in enforcement reaps the same benefits of less centralization in other areas. Lawyers can innovate just like anyone else. Private lawyers who come up with better legal theories or more skillful presentations of evidence attract more clients and make more money. Thousands of private lawyers bringing thousands of cases can try new things out in the way that the federal government's lawyers—and even the lawyers of the fifty states—cannot. Over time, we would expect this to lead to better compensation for victims and better deterrence of wrongdoing.

Indeed, the trial and error of the private attorney general model is one of the things that has made what lawyers call the *common law* approach to legal enforcement so attractive among conservative and libertarian scholars. What is the common law approach? Decentralized private lawyers persuading decentralized judges to try this or that. Over time, we learn what makes sense and what does not. If we had the same law firm—or even the same fifty law firms—litigating all our cases, we would miss out on all this.[94] As the conservative legal scholar Todd Zywicki noted of Friedrich Hayek, the father of the libertarian Austrian school of economics: "Hayek . . . clearly came to believe that the . . . common law uniquely embodied the rule of law . . . [because] the rules that emerge from the decentralized decision making of the common law, like the prices that emerge from the decentralized decision making of markets . . . emerge from . . . spontaneous order."[95] An even more extended libertarian defense of the common law method can be found in Georgetown law professor Randy Barnett's book *The Structure of Liberty*.[96]

We find much the same view among economists from the conservative Chicago school. Consider how Becker and Stigler put it: "Free competition among enforcement firms may seem strange. . . . But society does not pretend to be able to designate who the bakers should be. . . . Why should enforcers of the law be chosen differently? Let anyone who wishes enter the trade, innovate, and prosper or fail."[97] Indeed, utilitarian conservatives have often argued that the common law process will inevitably lead to the rules of law that produce the most wealth for our society.[98] That's obviously hard to prove, and a lot of people disagree.[99] But there is no doubt that the common law has innovated in many ways that conservatives favor. Consider a few examples:

- At one time, if two horse-drawn buggies crashed into one another and one person was really negligent and one person was only slightly negligent, the common law of torts would not let the slightly at fault person recover from the severely at fault person in light of a doctrine called *contributory negligence*.[100] The major change in the common law of torts over the last one hundred years has been to switch to *comparative negligence* instead: the party more at fault pays, but with a discount for however much at fault the other party was.[101] Many conservative scholars approve.[102]
- At one time, the common law of contracts required a subjective "meeting of the minds": both parties had to know what the terms of the contract were before an agreement formed.[103] Requiring people to read a contract before they buy something obviously slows down commerce. When we had horse-drawn buggies, maybe that was acceptable, but, today, we want transactions at the click of a button; we read the terms later, if at all. The major change in the common law

of contracts over the last one hundred years has been to embrace a doctrine of *objective consent*: whether you know what's in the contract or not, it's binding.[104] Conservative scholars like this, too.[105]

- At one time, the common law prohibited people from investing in lawsuits. This was called *champerty* or *maintenance*.[106] Indeed, these doctrines prevented even lawyers from investing in lawsuits; they could not give their clients legal services in exchange for a share of any recovery—that is, even contingency fees were prohibited. The major change in the common law of litigation financing over the last two hundred years is that we figured out that this made no economic sense. We figured it out for lawyers first, and, now, we are figuring it out for other investors, too.[107] Again, many conservative scholars agree.[108]

It is not only conservatives who praise decentralization in enforcement of the law. Scholars on the left and the right agree that the private bar is more innovative than the government.[109] Indeed, decentralization not only gives the private bar an advantage over the government with regard to innovation in prosecuting misconduct; it often gives the private bar an advantage over the government with regard to detection of misconduct. Private lawyers are often closer to the misconduct because they are closer to the people who are actually injured by it: their clients.[110] As the legal scholar Myriam Gilles puts it: "The massive government expenditures required to detect and investigate misconduct are no match for the millions of 'eyes on the ground' that bear witness to . . . violations."[111]

Consider, for example, who first discovered the famous Volkswagen diesel engine scandal, perhaps the worst example of corporate misconduct in modern history. For almost a decade, Volkswagen inserted computer code into its diesel engines that turned off the cars' pollution controls unless the cars sensed they were being tested for their emissions. Over this decade, some half a million cars in the United States emitted up to *forty-four times* more pollutants than legally allowed. Did the federal Environmental Protection Agency discover this scandal? No. Did a state government agency, like the environmentally active California Air Regulation Board? Wrong again. Who did? A private organization called the International Council on Clean Transportation.[112]

Or what about the infamous General Motors' ignition switches that suddenly shut off and led to fatal crashes? Did the government discover that problem? Nope. It was the automotive expert hired by the lawyer representing one of the victims.[113]

Indeed, three economists studied who first brings to light corporate securities fraud. The Securities and Exchange Commission—the government body assigned to police this fraud—was the answer less than 7 percent of the time. It is true that private law firms fared even worse (3 percent), but when you add up all the *other* profit-motivated private actors—short sellers, competitors, etc.—the private parties beat the government *many* times over.[114]

There is one way in which government enforcement might be better suited to detection of misconduct: if the government suspects a company of criminal misconduct, it can wield the awesome investigatory powers of the grand jury. It is not uncommon to see private lawsuits follow on a criminal investigation by the government for this reason (although, as I explain below, not as common as many people think). On the other hand, these powers are awesome only if they are used; many people have criticized government enforcers because they so infrequently use their criminal powers against corporations.[115] Moreover, even if these powers sometimes do give the government a leg up in detection, it does not mean that private enforcement is still not better suited to prosecuting wrongdoers once the misconduct has been detected. Indeed, in light of the reluctance of the government to pursue criminal charges against corporations, it is all the more imperative that someone is available to hold corporations accountable under the civil law. But my view is not that we should get rid of government enforcement; as I explain below, sometimes government enforcers are needed. But nor should we get rid of private enforcers.

Indeed, there is one way in which enforcement of our market rules makes an even stronger case for privatization than the other things conservatives want to privatize. One of the challenges of privatizing is developing metrics by which we can judge whether the private sector is doing a good job—metrics needed to exploit the profit motive of the private sector by tying compensation to results.[116] How do we measure, for example, whether a private prison is doing a good job? The number of inmates? How happy the inmates are? How nonviolent they are? How infrequently they are imprisoned again after their release? It's a challenge. But, with enforcement of the law, this job is easier. We have a ready-made measure of success: how much money private lawyers recover for their clients. So long as our laws set damages equal to the harm corporate violations cause—and they mostly do (but, as I note in the final chapter, improvements can be made)—then all we have to do is pay private lawyers a percentage of what they recover to tie their compensation to good work. As I note in a later chapter, we mostly do this already by paying class action lawyers with contingency-fee percentages, but, to the extent that we do not, I advocate there for doing it more often. But the important point is this one: paying for good private sector performance is much easier to do for law enforcement than it is for almost anything else.

Let me close this section by acknowledging that I understand why big businesses do not like the innovativeness that comes with decentralized enforcement of the law. Innovation makes things less certain.[117] When you are on top, you want certainty; big businesses have obviously mastered the existing rules. But locking incumbent businesses into their positions is not the goal of our legal system. For conservatives, the goal is fostering the conditions of competition, conditions that could very well lead to the displacement of incumbent businesses. Although it is hard to prove, scholars who try conclude that the economies in countries like ours that rely on decentralized lawmaking like the common law outperform countries like those in continental Europe that rely on centralized lawmaking.[118]

The Data on Private Enforcement

Thus far, I have tried to make the case for the private attorney general only at a theoretical level. In theory, we would expect the private attorney general to do a better job at enforcing market rules than the public attorney general would. In particular, the conservative theory of privatization teaches us that we should expect private lawyers to recover more compensation for injured persons and generate more deterrence of misconduct in a more cost-effective manner than the government would. That's the theory. But is there any proof?

There is. There is actually quite a bit of data to support the theory: as far as we can tell, private lawyers bring more lawsuits than government lawyers do, and, when they do, they recover a lot more money—money that delivers a lot more compensation and a lot more deterrence.

Consider, for example, the recent book *Entrepreneurial Litigation* by the legal scholar John Coffee. Coffee calculated how much money private lawyers recovered against corporations that made fraudulent representations to shareholders versus how much money the government recovered from corporations. The government enforcer for almost all securities frauds is a federal agency I mentioned earlier, the Securities and Exchange Commission. How does the SEC stack up against the private bar? Not well. Coffee found that in recent years the private bar has recovered *ten times as much* money as the SEC.[119]

Much of this difference comes from the fact that, as theory predicts, the private bar brings many more lawsuits than the SEC does.[120] But some of it comes from the fact that the private bar recovers more money than the SEC does even when the SEC does sue. Sometimes that is because the private bar pursues bigger cases.[121] But sometimes it is because the private bar simply does a better job. The best way to see this is to examine the cases where the private bar and the SEC both pursue the same wrongdoer for the same misconduct. Every once in a while, the SEC sues to recover government penalties and losses suffered by shareholders and the private bar sues the same defendant to recover any losses suffered by shareholders that the government did not recoup. What do we find when the private bar and the government go head to head? We find that the private bar still recovers a lot more. Coffee found that "damages paid in [private] securities class actions are usually (but not always) a multiple of those paid to the SEC."[122] Other studies have found the exact same thing. Perhaps the most exhaustive study found that private lawyers recover four times as much as the SEC when both pursue the same wrongdoers.[123]

Perhaps you are thinking that something is wrong with the SEC. Perhaps other government enforcers do a better job. They do not. We do not have data on every government enforcer, of course, but the ones we do have data on look much like the SEC. Thus, for example, the leading study of antitrust enforcement found that, between 1990 and 2007, the private bar recovered more than four times as much money as the "acclaimed anti-cartel program of the DOJ Antitrust Division" (the most meaningful government enforcer of antitrust law).[124] Industry-specific studies have found even more dramatic differences between private and government antitrust recoveries.[125]

Indeed, the empirical evidence in favor of the private attorney general is even stronger than it first appears. This is because we are assuming that one dollar recovered by the private bar is worth as much as one dollar recovered by the government. This is true for deterrence: so long as the wrongdoer pays, it does not matter who the wrongdoer pays; the wrongdoer will take care to avoid liability in the first place just the same. But this is not true for compensation. The government is woefully inferior to the private bar when it comes to delivering money to the people who have been injured. This might be obvious in individual litigation because little stands between the plaintiff in a private lawsuit and any recovery awarded to that plaintiff. But it is even true in class action litigation. Despite all the criticism of how little of class action recoveries is delivered to injured class members—something I discuss in a later chapter—the government often does not even try to distribute its recoveries to injured persons; the law often requires "all civil penalties must be paid to the U.S. Treasury."[126]

But, even when the law does allow the government to compensate people, I have found no evidence that it is any better than private lawyers. This stands to reason: both private lawyers and the government tend to rely on the same companies to find injured persons and send them the money.[127] For example, the SEC has "the most extensive and sustained effort by a public agency to compensate the victims of misconduct."[128] Although in recent years the SEC "has distributed between 75% and 90% of all collected sanctions,"[129] as I explain in the later chapter, private lawyers who sue companies for the same securities frauds have distributed roughly 85 percent of their settlements to victims, too. Moreover, in some respects the private lawyers are better than the SEC: as scholars have noted, the government does not extend the same procedural protections and participation rights to victims that the court system does in private class action litigation.[130] This may be why many victims complain that the government is often slow and inept at compensating them.[131]

Some critics of the private attorney general complain that the private bar free rides off government enforcement. These critics contend that the government spots the misconduct and puts together the case through its investigatory powers and that then the private bar swoops in to collect the money. As I noted above, even if this accurately described the typical lawsuit filed by the private bar, I am not sure that there would be anything wrong with it: perhaps the government is better at identifying misconduct and the private bar is better at litigating the cases.

But, as I also noted above, many scholars do not think this critique accurately describes the typical case. Many scholars believe that the private sector is often better at spotting misconduct than the government is. Why? It should be obvious why in the run-of-the-mill case where a corporation injures only one person: the person who is actually injured by misconduct knows that he or she has been injured much sooner than some government bureaucrat does.

But, although it is less obvious, it is true even when a corporation injures a large group of persons. How do we know that? Because, again, we have data. There have been a number of studies of the free-riding question, and they all show the same thing: only a small percentage of private securities fraud class action lawsuits,[132] private antitrust mass action lawsuits,[133] and private consumer financial class action lawsuits[134] accompanied government enforcement actions. Indeed, the studies find that "free riding" is a two-way phenomenon to the extent it is a phenomenon at all: just as often—if not more so—the government files suit *after* the private bar does so.[135]

Of course, just because private enforcement is more intense than public enforcement does not mean it is better. It may be that private enforcement is too intense—as we will see, many conservatives argue that the private bar files *too many* lawsuits and recovers *too much* money. But, whether the private bar recovers too much or too little, there are data showing that the private bar gets us closer to where we should be than the government does. In a study of forty-nine countries, a number of finance professors compared the two types of enforcement, and this is what they found: "We find little evidence that public enforcement benefits stock markets, but strong evidence that laws . . . facilitating private enforcement . . . benefit stock markets."[136] Not all studies confirm these findings,[137] but many do.[138] I personally do not put too much stock in these studies because comparisons across countries are so hard to study empirically—it is hard to control for all the ways in which countries might differ from one another. Moreover, all these studies in particular rely on rather crude proxies for intensity of enforcement and for healthy markets. But I note them to make my argument here as comprehensive as possible: the critics of private enforcement have not only theory to overcome but data as well.

CHAPTER FOUR

The Conservative Case against Private Enforcement

As I have shown, both conservative theory and the available data support the efficacy of private enforcement of the ground rules of the market. Why then do so many conservatives despise plaintiffs' lawyers? Why then are corporations begging for public enforcement instead? As I noted in a previous chapter, one reason is because these conservatives think we regulate the market way too much; our laws go well beyond the ground rules I discussed. They agree that the government is not as effective in enforcing our laws, but that is precisely what they want because they think we have too many laws. Sometimes the government is not as effective because it lacks the motives and resources; other times it is not as effective because it is captured by some or all of the corporate interests it is supposed to enforce the law against. As I also noted, I agree with this critique of our substantive law, but I do not think it follows that we should throw out private enforcement. Rather, as I said, I think we should roll back our substantive law or neuter private enforcement only for the substantive laws we don't like. Neutering *all* private enforcement is akin to throwing out the baby with the bathwater; let's just throw out the bathwater.

Is there anything else conservatives might say in response to what I have said here in favor of the private attorney general? There is, but I do not think you will find the responses very compelling.

Too much profit motivation. Ironically, the most popular reason conservatives oppose the private attorney general is because private lawyers *are* motivated by profits. Sometimes the criticism is that the profits have made private lawyers too wealthy. For example, in his *The Litigation Explosion*, Walter Olson complains that "contingency-fee law has made more overnight millionaires than just about any business one could name."[1] But, of course, as good conservatives, we can't be against people earning an honest dollar, even millions or billions of dollars. If someone is doing well by society, why shouldn't they do well by themselves? Isn't the lawyer who brings corporate wrongdoing to light and wins redress for its victims doing well by society? So what if the lawyer makes a good living in the process? With great respect to Olson, that's not a very conservative thing to be worried about. This concern is better placed among those on the left, which is why the more socialist democracies in Europe refuse to let lawyers work for contingency fees like we do; to the extent that these countries have class actions, they usually require them to be handled by nonprofit organizations rather than private lawyers.[2]

But other times the concern is that the profit motive leads lawyers astray. The concern is that profits can be made not only pursuing egregious corporate misconduct; they can also be made pursuing conduct that is neither egregious nor even in violation of the law. For example, some right-leaning critics complain that the profit motive leads lawyers to file lawsuits against companies for no reason but to exploit tiny technicalities in the law.[3] Perhaps the most famous instances involve so-called statutory damages laws. These laws make it illegal to do things like print more than four credit card digits on a receipt; if a corporation does this to you, you are automatically entitled to statutory damages of between $100 and $1,000.[4] Congress passed this law to help cut down on theft of credit card numbers. But, when corporations slip up and print too many numbers, lawyers can make a lot of money suing them if enough people have been affected.

Others—and not just right-leaning critics—complain that the profit motive leads lawyers to file lawsuits against corporations when it is not clear they violated the law; what the corporation did is close to the line.[5] These critics complain that debatable violations of the law are not the best use of our court system.

Finally, some right-leaning critics complain that the profit motive leads lawyers to sue corporations even when *no one* thinks the company has done something wrong.[6] How can this be profitable? Because sometimes it is so expensive for a company to defend itself in court that it is cheaper to settle with the lawyers who brought the suit—even if the lawyers had no chance to win in the end. In the academy, we call these *nuisance settle-ments* (but I'm sure corporate executives call them something else!).

Truth be told, all these criticisms are plausible. It makes sense that the pursuit of profits leads the private bar to exploit technicalities, to push the envelope on what is illegal, and to file meritless lawsuits. It also makes sense that, because government bureaucrats cannot pursue profits and have more limited resources, they do these things less often.[7] On the other hand, turning enforcement over to the government is not the only way we can inject more discretion into the enforcement of the law. In order for private plaintiffs to win lawsuits, they must convince a judge to interpret the law in their favor; if judges think that the lawsuits are nitpicky techni-calities not worthy of the court's time, they can dismiss them.

Indeed, to the extent that we have data on this question, they do not support the notion that the private bar pursues less meritorious cases than the government does. Two law professors, Stephen Choi at New York University Law School and Adam Pritchard at Michigan Law School (who, it should be noted, is no fan of the securities fraud class action), conducted an ingenious study to compare how "meritorious" government securities fraud investigations were relative to private securities fraud class actions.[8] They excluded cases where both the Securities and Exchange Commis-sion and the private class action lawyers went after the same companies; instead, they focused on investigations the SEC pursued on its own versus class actions the private bar pursued on its own. What did they find? On four different metrics of merit—including whether the corporate execu-tives alleged to have committed the fraud ended up resigning—the class action lawyers pursued either better cases or no worse cases than the gov-ernment did.[9] As they themselves put it: "Our findings offer little support to commentators who call for a shift from private actions to greater public enforcement."[10]

But the Choi and Pritchard study is only one study. What if their find-ings are not representative of most private enforcement? Does that mean we should reject the profit motive and run to the government to enforce the law instead? Absolutely not. It is a well-known problem of the profit motive that, if not pointed in the right direction, it can drive people to do bad things.[11] Many liberals complain about corporate profit motives for these same reasons. Corporate profit motives can lead corporations to cut corners when they make products, to deceive customers about what they are buying, and to conspire with their competitors to fix prices. As good conservatives, our response to these problems is not, as it has been in other countries, to nationalize all our industries. It is to acknowledge that profit motives can lead to both good and bad and to put laws in place that point corporate motives more toward the good than toward the bad.

Our answer should be the same when it comes to profit-motivated lawyers. Profit-motivated lawyers are no different than profit-motivated anything else. Because they are profit motivated, they will enforce the law more thoroughly than government lawyers will. This means that they will bring more lawsuits against egregious corporate misconduct. But it also means that, if we let them, they will bring more lawsuits that we are not so keen on. A rising tide lifts all lawsuits, so to speak. What we have to do is, not cast the private lawyer aside, but regulate, just as we have to regulate the corporate profit motive.[12]

It is true that some are pessimistic that we can regulate lawyers' profit motives well enough. The concern is that it is hard to calibrate lawyers' fee awards so that we achieve the socially optimal level of enforcement[13] or that the legislature or judges are not up to the task. But the same is true of every profit motive, including the corporate ones. It is hard to calibrate the rules of the market to ensure that corporate motives are pointed in the right direction, and corporations have big lobbying budgets to try to resist regulation. But we would rather try our best than to turn our industries over to the government. The same is true of the enforcement of legal rules.[14]

This is why I am not persuaded by what may be the most compelling concern with profit-motivated private enforcement. The concern is that, profit-motivated enforcers will not just push to enforce the law too frequently but push the law itself—the underlying market rules—in a more and more liberal direction. The private bar will push judges to interpret the law to encompass more and more corporate activity; they will lobby the legislature to do the same. The more market behavior that is illegal, the more misconduct private enforcers can remedy, and the more profits they will earn. If we dangle profits in front of enforcers, not only may we get too much enforcement, these critics worry, but we may get too much law to begin with—legal rules well beyond the ground rules of the market that I argued even conservatives favor.

This is a strong objection. But I do not think it kills the case for private enforcement. It does not even come close. The reason is that we already have profit-motivated actors pushing the law in directions we conservatives do not like. They are called *big corporations*. Corporations push judges and legislatures to eliminate even the necessary ground rules of the

market, for laws punishing their competitors, and for laws giving themselves special treatment that their competitors do not enjoy. All these
things should make conservatives blanch. In other words, corporations
already lobby judges and legislatures to push the law in one direction;
all the private bar does is counteract their efforts by seeking to push the
law in the other direction. Frankly, without the private bar pushing back
on corporate lobbying, it is not clear who would; consumers are not well
enough organized—and probably never could become well enough organized—to raise the money necessary to go toe to toe with corporate
lobbyists. In the academy, we call this a *collective action problem*; indeed,
it is the *classic* collective action problem: "one shots" like consumers versus "repeat players" like corporations. I made the same point when I re-
sponded to conservative critics who worry about the influence the private
bar exercises over the election of judges in states that elect them; corporations already try to influence these same elections. Thus, the point turns
out to be doubly important: if we neuter the private bar, not only does this
clear the playing field for corporations to lobby government enforcers not
to enforce the law (or to selectively enforce it against their competitors),
but it also clears the field for them to lobby judges and legislatures to eliminate the underlying laws in the first place.

Too little profit motivation. Paradoxically—in light of the previous
paragraphs—many conservatives complain that the profit motive does
not drive private lawyers far enough. They complain that private lawyers
will not enforce the law when it is not profitable enough. For example, if
a corporation has caused only a small harm, no private lawyer will bother
bringing a lawsuit; the one-third fee won't be worth his or her time.[15] Or,
if the best relief for the victim of corporate wrongdoing is not money but
an injunction reforming the corporation's future practices, private lawyers
may not take those cases; it is hard for a lawyer to eat one-third of an
injunction.[16] Or, if the best way to deter wrongdoing is not to sock the corporation with a big judgment but to sock the individuals who run the corporation with smaller but more painful judgments, the profit-motivated
lawyer will of course pursue the former before the latter.[17]

Again, all these concerns are well taken, but, again, they do not get
us very far. My position is not that the private attorney general is always
better than the public attorney general; it is that it is usually better. I do
not oppose keeping government enforcement around for the occasions
(including, perhaps, those listed above) when government enforcement is
superior to private enforcement. We should have the best of both worlds:

private enforcement when private enforcement is best and government enforcement when government enforcement is best. Indeed, retaining private enforcement enables government enforcers—with their limited budgets—to focus their efforts on the things they *can* do best.[18] Privatization is not all or nothing.

Some right-leaning scholars believe the best of both worlds is, not government lawyers and private lawyers pursuing their own cases, but government lawyers and private lawyers pursuing cases together. These scholars advocate what we might call *hybrid enforcement*: before private citizens and their lawyers can initiate certain lawsuits like class actions, a government agency would have to sign off on the lawsuit as being in the public interest.[19] This way, the government could take advantage of the resource and incentive advantages of the private bar but at the same time police the private bar to ensure that it does not go too far and overenforce the law.

I do not think this would be the best of both worlds. Rather, I think it would be the best of the private world with the worst of the government world. The hybrid model might well offer some advantages over pure government enforcement, but the price for those advantages is to introduce all the government's politically influenced bias into the private world. Under the hybrid model, campaign contributors and friends of the government bureaucrats will be able to influence the government to block private lawsuits against them—and to give the green light to lawsuits against their competitors. If there were no other way to stop private lawyers from overenforcing the law, perhaps this sort of crony capitalism would be worth bearing. But, as I explained above and as I explain in more detail in later chapters, we do have another way: rules that channel the profit motive of the private bar in the right directions.[20]

A better way to involve the government is to allow it merely to opine on big lawsuits like class actions rather than to allow it to block them. If the government thinks a suit is misguided or a settlement unfair, there is nothing to stop it from making its views known to judges who can then consider them on their merits. Indeed, the Class Action Fairness Act enacted by Congress in 2005 sought to promote this sort of participation by requiring litigants to notify the government of pending class action settlements.[21] For whatever reason—maybe because class actions are not as bad as some would have us believe!—the government has not taken advantage of the notices it now receives.[22] But that may change.[23]

Duplication. Some people worry that, if we have both public and private enforcers, then they will not coordinate but duplicate each other's efforts; these people worry that dual enforcers inevitably lead to over-enforcement of the law. But, as I noted above, the data do not bear this out: there is little overlap between public and private enforcement efforts. Moreover, it is not so clear that overlap is all that bad to begin with. An interesting analysis in this regard comes from a scholar at Cornell Law School named Zachary Clopton. Drawing on design principles from the hard sciences like engineering, he explained that redundant legal enforcement schemes offer many of the same benefits as redundant circuits on a microchip: fewer errors, greater resources, more information, and better monitoring.[24] Thus, it is not clear that this worry has much basis either in theory or in fact.

Undemocratic. Some critics[25]—and, again, not just conservatives[26]—worry that private enforcement lacks so-called democratic accountability. The image here is something like Frankenstein's monster; we created it, but now we have no control over it. Private lawyers are running around suing left and right, and, if the public does not like it, there is not much to be done about it. Government enforcers, by contrast, are always ultimately accountable to the public because the public elects their bosses. In other words, private enforcement means enforcement run amok. There are two problems with this notion.

The first is that we can in fact control private enforcers; we control them with judges, and we control them with legislatures. If there is too much private enforcement, the legislature can pass a law reining them in; judges can interpret laws to do the same.[27] This is especially true, as I will explain, in class action cases: judges, in particular, have enormous discretion over the fee awards that private lawyers earn in those cases; their fees can be slashed in any given case and often are. And, again, even if we were concerned about the private bar lobbying judges and legislatures for favorable treatment,[28] as I just explained, corporate defendants are doing the exact same thing on the other side. If anything, lobbying by the private bar is more antidote to corporate lobbying than illness.

Second, the fact that the private bar is not as accountable to the political process as government enforcers are (but still somewhat accountable) is more virtue than vice. As I explained, the independence of the private bar is what helps the private bar avoid what I call *agency capture* or *crony capitalism*. That is, the private bar's single-minded focus on profits means that it is not concerned, as government enforcers sometimes are, with who gave whom campaign contributions and who used to work with whom. I think the legal scholar John Coffee may sum it up best when he says:

"Interesting as this idea seems, it runs up head first against probably the central virtue of the private attorney general model, namely, its ability to protect against agency 'capture.' "[29]

Inconsistency. The last argument conservatives sometimes raise against the private attorney general is that private enforcement is less consistent than public enforcement.[30] Thousands of private lawyers left to their own devices poke and prod corporations from different angles in different places; this makes it difficult for corporations to know how to conduct their affairs. Wouldn't it be better if we had one enforcement entity—like the federal government—that could set a clear and consistent standard for everyone to follow? In a word, no. For all the reasons I state above, centralization is our enemy, not our friend. One-size-fits-all enforcement stifles the innovation and information that come from trial and error. We learn something from all that poking and prodding—and we can keep learning as time goes on. If we have one enforcer, by contrast, we get consistency, but we might get something that is consistently bad.

We could give corporations clarity in their affairs by doing what they do in Europe and insisting that corporations get permission from the government before they do something new. This was box 1 way back in table 1. The price we pay for giving corporations the freedom to innovate is the loss of certainty. That's the nature of innovation: no one is ever sure how it is all going to turn out. But that's a price we usually think is worth paying. Some people like command-and-control regulatory solutions, but we do not usually consider those people conservatives. We of all people should understand the virtues of uncertain yet flexible decentralized law enforcement:

> Free market philosophers such as Hayek and Leoni praised judge-made law for
> its role in preserving freedom. To them, decentralized evolution of law through
> primarily apolitical judicial decisions is vastly preferable to centralized yet ar-
> bitrary lawmaking by legislatures. [B]eck, Demirguc-Kunt, and Levine argue in
> the Hayek tradition that judge-made law is more adaptable than statutes. They
> suggest such adaptability benefits financial markets, and find evidence that rec-
> ognition of judge-made law predicts financial development and might account
> for the . . . finding of the superior development of financial markets in common
> law compared to civil law countries.[31]

This is probably why this particular concern with private enforcement is more popular on the left than it is on the right.[32]

Final Thoughts

Before I leave this chapter, I wish to make two more points. The first is that there are plenty of other reasons to oppose private enforcement of market rules, but these reasons sound more in the political theory of the left than that of the right. As such, I do not think that they are important to address in this book. For example, some scholars have voiced concerns about private enforcement on account of "procedural"[33] or "distributive" "fairness."[34] As Lemos put these worries: "In a world with severe wealth inequality, rationing government services according to ability to pay will mean that some citizens must go without."[35]

Likewise, the Yale law professor Nicholas Parrillo has written an entire book called *Against the Profit Motive* wherein he expertly chronicles our turn against the for-profit tax collectors, criminal prosecutors, and the like that government officials deputized in the United States in the nineteenth century. As he explains it, the vast regulatory state of the twentieth century could not be sustained with profit-motivated government officials.[36] Why not? The zealousness of the profit motive alienated citizens and reduced their willingness to comply with the law voluntarily.[37] As the regulatory ambitions of the government expanded, we could no longer deputize enough enforcement officials to coerce people to comply. Thus, we shifted responsibility to salaried government officials instead in order to induce citizens to more easily accept—and comply with the demands of—the modern regulatory state.[38] Needless to say, inducing the American people to more easily accept the modern regulatory state is not a conservative reason to reject private enforcement.[39] And, indeed, the privatization movement begun under Ronald Reagan has been understood as an attempt to turn the clock back to the world that Parrillo wrote against.[40]

It is worth asking, however, whether Parrillo's thesis that private enforcement undermines voluntarily compliance with the law—and, perhaps, overall compliance with the law if we cannot enlist enough private enforcers to coerce compliance—is a reason to cast doubt on the efficacy of private enforcement despite the case I have made for it. I do not think so. Parrillo's focus was on "laypeople,"[41] and, whatever may motivate them to comply with the law, corporations are motivated by one thing and one thing alone: profits. For better or for worse—and, like many on the right, I think it is probably for the better—shareholder value has become the only metric by which we judge the performance of corporate executives.[42]

It would be incredibly naive to believe that these executives would be more willing to forgo profits and be "good citizens" when the law is enforced by government officials than when it is enforced by the private bar.[43] In other words, given how profit motivated corporations have become, only equally profit-motivated enforcers may be able to keep them at bay.

If all this is not enough to persuade you of the efficacy of private enforcement, I saved the best for last. We know that private enforcement is better than government enforcement because of the revealed preferences of the government itself: when the government is the victim of fraudulent misrepresentation by a corporation, even it does not rely only on government lawyers to remedy the fraud. Instead, it permits private actors *to sue on its behalf* and keep a percentage of what is recovered. These are called *qui tam* lawsuits, and they have been around for centuries.[44] The modern embodiment is found in a federal statute called the False Claims Act.[45] Under the False Claims Act, the government is given a chance to take the lawsuit over from the private citizens who initiated it, but, when it refuses to do so, the private lawsuit still goes forward. That's right: a private citizen can represent the government without the government's permission.[46] In other words, the government itself has rejected both government enforcement and the hybrid model when its own rights are at stake. The False Claims Act is an open acknowledgment that even the government believes that the private bar does a better job than it itself does at enforcing the law.

Indeed, there was a period in our history when Congress cut back the False Claims Act to shrink private enforcement, but the government lost so much money to fraud during this period that the statute was restored to its previous form.[47] Which president signed the legislation reinvigorating private enforcement when the federal government was the one that had lost the money? None other than Ronald Reagan.

If private enforcement is good enough for the government,[48] surely it is good enough for the rest of us, too!

CHAPTER FIVE

Why Private Enforcement Needs Class Actions

In the previous chapters, I explained why conservatives should prefer private enforcement of our market rules over government enforcement. In this chapter, I explain why private enforcement needs the class action device to be effective.

Why We Need Class Actions

As I have said, a class action is a special type of private lawsuit. In a class action, one person who has been harmed by the defendant represents the interests of all the other people who have been harmed by the defendant in the same way. We call this person the *representative plaintiff*. Whatever happens to the representative plaintiff binds the other people who have been harmed by the defendant. Win, lose, or settle, all the rest of us sink or swim right along with the representative plaintiff.

That's a lot of responsibility on the representative plaintiff's shoulders. For this reason, we take special care in class action cases to make sure the representative plaintiff is up to the task. Courts are required to scrutinize the representative plaintiff to ensure that he or she will adequately represent the class before the case can proceed as a class action.[1] And the representative plaintiff obviously does not go it alone: he or she has a lawyer. Courts are also required to scrutinize whether this lawyer is up to the task of representing the entire class.[2]

But that is not all: when money is at stake, we require the lawyer to do his or her best to notify all the members of the class to tell them about the class action, and we permit anyone who wishes to opt out of the class to do so; the opt outs retain all their rights to sue on their own.[3]

Even with these safeguards in place, it is obviously not ideal to empower one person to speak for others without their affirmative permission. Although class members can opt out of the representation, they may have never gotten the notice the lawyer tried to send them so they may not know they need to opt out. Even worse, the judge might do a bad job determining whether the lawyer and the representative plaintiff are up to the task of representing everyone. Almost no country in the rest of the world allows class action lawsuits in the way we do in the United States.[4] So why do we?

We do it because it is hard to see how private enforcement can work without it. Recall that few places in the rest of the world rely on private enforcement like we do; most other places regulate the economy by requiring companies to get permission from the government before they do things. Private enforcement is what makes America different, and, as I have explained, it is also what makes America better. But, to make private enforcement work here, we need the class action.

Think back to the example I gave in chapter 2 about the fraudulent seeds that are sold to farmers in Uganda. We said that the farmers couldn't sue the seed merchants in court because the cost of bringing the lawsuit was more than the seeds were worth. That would be true in the United States, too, if not for the class action. Let's say the seeds cost $100. No one will pay a lawyer to help him or her recover a measly $100. And no lawyer will take the case to be paid only a contingency-fee percentage of $100.

But things change if the lawyer can bring the case as a class action. Why? Because now the lawsuit is brought on behalf of *every person* who bought the bad $100 seeds. Let's say there were one thousand such people. Now the lawsuit is worth $100,000. If we permit the lawyer to take the case on a contingency percentage, now we are talking about real money: one-third of $100,000 is $33,000. The class action transforms a case that is not profitable for the lawyer into a case that may be profitable.

Consider a recent class action lawsuit against Bank of America that I worked on as an expert witness. In this lawsuit, Bank of America was accused of ordering how it deducted debit card transactions from its customers' bank accounts to maximize the number of overdraft fees it could charge the customers.[5] Rather than deduct the transactions chronologically as they were made, the bank held all transactions in abeyance for a day or two and then processed them all at once in order from the biggest transaction to the smallest.[6] The bank did this because deducting the biggest transactions first meant that its customers would hit a zero balance more quickly if they were going into overdraft anyway. Fewer transactions to get to zero left more transactions in negative balance territory. The more transactions in negative balance territory, the more overdraft fees the bank could charge. Ingenious.

And also probably illegal.[7] But how much would any one customer lose from this scheme? Not that much. Each overdraft fee was only $35. One or two or even ten extra overdraft fees here or there are hardly worth anyone's time to sue about, let alone worth a lawyer's time paid on contingency. Yet, over several years, Bank of America skimmed *billions* of dollars out of its customers' accounts in this way.[8] A potential billion-dollar recovery *is* worth someone's time to sue about. Thus, thanks to the class action, Bank of America *was* sued and ended up paying $410 million for what it did.[9] Thirty percent of that sum was awarded to the lawyers who sued on behalf of the class, and the rest was distributed to the class members who were charged overdraft fees they would not have been charged if the bank had simply deducted their transactions in chronological order.[10]

Thanks to that 30 percent, customers could find lawyers who were willing to invest their time and money trying to repay victims—what we have called the *compensation goal* of private enforcement. Thanks to that 30 percent, companies have to worry what might happen to them if they wrongly skim even small sums from their customers' accounts—what we have called the *deterrence goal* of private enforcement.

Some people think that giving class action lawyers 30 percent is way too much. In the Bank of America case, 30 percent came to $123 million. That's a lot of money by any measure. I will have more to say about this in a later chapter, but, for now, the important point is that private enforcement of small harms is not possible without the class action device. As the famous libertarian University of Chicago legal scholar Richard Epstein puts it, without the class action, the "real risk is that serious wrongdoing at the corporate level will go unchecked for want of a champion to respond to a common problem."[11]

Some conservatives deny this. They think that private enforcement of small harms *is* possible on an individual basis. They say that this is possible because people can go to arbitration.[12] As I explained in chapter 1, companies love arbitration: many of them now ask most of the people they interact with to sign agreements to arbitrate any disputes that may arise between them. Some of these arbitration agreements may be generous; they may say things like, "If you bring a claim against us and win, we will pay your attorney for you," or, "If you bring a claim against us and win, we will pay you twice what we owed you."[13] Some conservatives say that, with such generous terms in arbitration, any claim is profitable, even a small one.

But this is a *gross* exaggeration. You get these generous terms only if you win the arbitration. What if you lose? Then you still have to pay your lawyer. Who's going to take that risk for a $5 loss? As we will see, not many people. And this assumes that you even know the company stole the $5 from you to begin with. Sometimes corporate schemes are so crafty it is difficult to figure out you've been wronged. One of the virtues of the class action is that one person who figured it out can represent all the other people who haven't. This virtue is lost in individual arbitration.

But we don't have to speculate that individual arbitration is a poor substitute for class actions. We have data. In fact, we have some of the best kind of data: data coming from what academics like to call a *natural experiment*, a happenstance that puts people into different groups so we can compare them in the same way as if we had randomly assigned them there. We had just such an experiment in the Bank of America case. Bank of America was not the only bank that reordered debit card transactions in the way that it did; some thirty banks did so.[14] But, by happenstance, some of the banks had arbitration agreements with their customers that banned class actions, and some did not. Thus, we can look to see what happened to customers in each group and thereby determine how effective individual arbitration is compared to class action litigation for the same wrongdoing. In fact, we don't even have to make this comparison ourselves because the Consumer Financial Protection Bureau has already done it for us.[15] And what did it find? There were eighteen banks that had to endure class actions: they ended up paying out *$1 billion* to *twenty-nine million customers*.[16] What about the other banks that didn't have to endure class actions? How much did they pay out? *Almost nothing.* Out of millions upon millions of debit card customers, only twenty per year in the entire country—twenty!—filed any sort of arbitration dispute regarding their cards—whether related to overdrafts or not—during the same time period.[17] Which system would you rather be stuck with? A system where there is a one-in-a-million chance you might get justice when a company wrongs you? Or a system where it is almost certain that a company that wrongs you will be brought to justice? Arbitration is simply no competition for the class action.

I think that even most conservatives know this. As the right-leaning economist Luigi Zingales puts it: "What speculation is for finance, class actions are for the law: the profit motive benefitting everyone, in the best tradition of Adam Smith."[18] The libertarian research fellow Andrew Thierer at George Mason's Mercatus Center agrees: "To the extent that any corrective action is needed to address harms, ex post measures" like "class-action activity" are the way to do it.[19] As even the frequent class action critic Martin Redish, a Northwestern law professor, concedes: "A class action may well perform a law enforcement function by both punishing and deterring unlawful private or governmental behavior."[20]

But perhaps no one says it better—as is often the case—than the famous University of Chicago libertarian legal scholar Richard Epstein:

> The class action is here to stay. And so it should, for there is no question that in some contexts it allows plaintiffs with sound but small substantive claims to gain access to the courthouse that would be denied to them without some method of amalgamation. The class action offers the key for taking the disorganized business of life and structuring it in simplified ways that permit mass adjudication. How could anyone such as myself, who authored a book entitled *Simple Rules for a Complex World*, be opposed to that development? [T]he class action is a boon to private contract when it permits large numbers of individuals to gain refunds of small sums to which they are entitled under contract. It is also a boon when it allows property holders to recover damages for wrongful conversion of their property.[21]

Class Actions and Privatization Theory

Thus, if private enforcement is a good thing, then class actions are a good thing, too. But, if you doubt me, let's return to the virtues of privatization that I discussed in the previous chapters: smaller government, self-help, better incentives, better resources, less bias, and less centralization. It is clear that class action lawsuits best government enforcement on all but one of these criteria:

- *Smaller government.* If we did not have class action lawyers to take small-stakes cases, either we would be unable to enforce the law, or we would have to hire a bunch of government lawyers to take the cases instead—or, even worse, create more administrative agencies to regulate more companies ex ante.

- *Self-help*. As I noted in a previous chapter, many libertarians believe that the government is all but obligated to permit us to take legal redress into our own hands because it took from us our ability to do so by force.
- *Better incentives*. Class action lawyers have the same profit motive as other private lawyers: they usually get a percentage (albeit a lower one) of their class action recoveries just like other plaintiffs' lawyers.[22]
- *Better resources*. Class action lawyers have even better resources than most contingency-fee lawyers. Because their cases are so lucrative, class action firms tend to be bigger and better capitalized than other plaintiff-side law firms, and they tend to have access to generous bank credit and other financing if they need it.[23]
- *Less bias*. Class action lawyers are just as independent of influence from corporations as other private lawyers are. As with other plaintiffs' lawyers, they are single-mindedly focused on profit and not who gave to whose campaign or who used to work for whom. As scholars note: "Since courts are less likely to be captured by industry than a regulatory agency . . . class actions can represent a check on the ability of industry to determine regulatory policy."[24]

The one virtue that class action lawsuits do not offer in the same way as other private lawsuits is *less centralization*.[25] By definition, the class action includes all the people who were injured by the defendant in the same way; by definition, corporate misconduct redressed by class action lawsuits is misconduct redressed by only one lawsuit. We don't get the same trial-and-error and enforcement experimentation that we might get if every person who was injured by the defendant sued on his or her own. Once a class action lawsuit is resolved, it forecloses individual lawsuits by any of the class members. In this sense, harking back to table 2 above, the class action lawsuit is therefore somewhat more like enforcement through a judicially awarded franchise than it is through the market. That's still pretty good on the privatization spectrum, but not all the way there.

To be sure, the class action still offers *some* decentralization benefit over government enforcement: although each class action is a centralization of what might have been individual lawsuits, each class action is prosecuted by a different private attorney before a different court. Thus, although the class action does not offer diversity of enforcement against a particular defendant, it does still offer diversity of enforcement against a particular industry. It is true that the class action bar is more concentrated than the plaintiffs' bar as a whole; there are only so many law firms that can handle a big, expensive, complex class action. But even the class action bar is less centralized than the government. If we had the government do all this enforcement work instead, we would get the same US Department of Justice—or perhaps, if state governments got involved, the same fifty state attorneys general—*every single time*. We would have little to no diversity of enforcement in *the entire economy*, let alone in a particular industry. So class action lawsuits are still better than the government. It might be *even better* if we could enforce the law through individual lawsuits, but, as I explained, when the injuries people suffer are small, this is simply not possible.

This is an important point. It means that conservative privatization theory shows us that class action lawsuits are a good thing when private enforcement by individual lawsuits is not profitable. But there is a flip side: it also suggests that, if private enforcement by individual lawsuits *is* profitable, then class actions might *not* be such a good thing; we'd rather have the individual lawsuits.

Many scholars dissent on this point and believe that private enforcement needs class actions even when individual lawsuits *would be* profitable. None of them are especially conservative,[26] but, still, it is worth asking why they think this because their reasons may appeal to us. They think this because class actions level the playing field between plaintiffs and defendants.[27] Consider a situation in which a defendant has harmed a bunch of people $100,000 each. Things like this do happen: there was a class action against the National Football League for hiding the risks of concussions from its players for decades.[28] Those players now fear that they will have serious risk of life-threatening conditions later in life; indeed, some have already manifested those conditions and died.[29] Almost all these players have *at least* $100,000 of harm to remedy.[30]

Now suppose that you are a lawyer who is representing one of these players. If your client suffered $100,000 in injuries and you took the case on the standard one-third contingency, you would stand to gain $33,000 if you win. That's pretty good money, but this case could be difficult. You have to prove that concussions from playing football cause complications later in life, that your client has complications that were caused by concussions, that it was the concussions your client sustained while playing in the NFL—not the ones he sustained while playing football in high school or college—that caused his complications, and that the NFL knew or should have known that these concussions were dangerous.[31] It could take a lot of time and energy to prove that stuff; indeed, you will probably have to hire medical experts to help you. How much time and money are you willing to spend to do it? It's hard to say for certain, except to this extent: you will not spend more than $33,000. Any more, and you are losing money on this case.

Now how much is the NFL willing to spend? Well, if the NFL loses this case, then it loses $100,000; so, right off the bat, it is willing to spend up to $100,000 in time and money—three times as much as you are. But things are even worse than that for you. Many of the questions that arise in your case—Do concussions cause complications later in life? Did the NFL know this, or should it have known?—will recur in every case brought by a former player. Thus, any money the NFL spends to develop *this* case is money that will help *all* its cases. So how much is the NFL willing to spend to defend your case? Up to whatever its total liability might be in all the concussion cases. It will simply reuse much of the defense it prepared in your case in the next case. Thus, if we assume that there are ten thousand former players each of whom suffered $100,000 in injury, this means that the NFL is willing to spend up to $1 billion to defend itself in your case.

Now, what do you think happens when a lawyer who is willing to spend up to $33,000 to litigate a case goes up against a defendant willing to spend $1 billion to defend the case? It's not pretty. The plaintiff is outmatched. He might not win even though he should. Or he might win but get a smaller damage award than he should. If either of these things happens, then the twin goals of enforcement—compensation and deterrence—are both undermined. This is the problem of the unlevel litigation playing field.

The class action helps with this problem, too. How? Because a class action that includes all ten thousand of the former players gives the lawyer representing the class much the same financial incentive to invest in the case that the NFL has. Instead of looking at a case worth $100,000, the class action lawyer is looking at a case worth the same $1 billion the NFL sees. If the lawyer could get a third of $1 billion by winning the case, then he or she could reap $333 million in fees. Now that's a reason to invest money in a case! It's not quite the same incentive the NFL has—the lawyer reaps only a fraction of any recovery, whereas the NFL suffers the entirety of any loss—but it's a heck of a lot closer. This is why many scholars endorse the class action when people have suffered big harms as well as small harms.[32]

I am not so sure. Although big-harm class actions may be preferable to individual lawsuits on one of our privatization criteria (better resources), they are also worse on one of them (less centralization). As a matter of theory, it is impossible to say whether the upside to resources outweighs the downside to centralization. As such, I am not sure we should permit class actions when individual lawsuits could be brought instead.

But we should have no such doubts about small-harm class actions. In small-harm situations, it is either the class action or no private enforcement at all. And, as I have shown, like other private enforcement, class-action private enforcement is better than asking the government to do it. On this point I am not alone. Other conservative scholars support small-harm class actions.[33]

Conservative Arguments against Class Actions

Yet there are a lot of conservatives and their friends in the business community who want to replace small-harm class actions with government enforcement.[34] Why? As I said in the previous chapters, I suspect that some of business's motivation for this comes from the influence that corporate America enjoys over our government—that is, crony capitalism. That is, I suspect some corporate interests believe that they can persuade the government to look the other way when they commit misconduct. Moreover, I suspect some businesses believe that, as a practical political matter, government enforcement will never expand to fill the void left by class actions. Who's going to vote for that? Thus, when we hear people say, "Let the government do it," I suspect what a lot them really mean is, "No one will do it." Needless to say, permitting corporations to get away with more misconduct is not a principled reason to oppose class actions.

But, of course, no one ever *says* that's why he or she opposes class actions. And many conservative scholars who oppose class actions do so for less self-serving reasons. Many of these reasons dovetail with the reasons I tried to refute in the previous chapter: many conservatives oppose class actions for the same reasons they oppose private enforcement altogether. But some of their reasons are special to class actions. In the remainder of this chapter, I discuss the special reasons. As we will see, four of these arguments are serious enough that I will treat them with full chapters later on. But some of the arguments I can respond to here.

Don't sweat the small stuff. Some conservatives argue that we should not bother rectifying small harms at all.[35] So what if some company stole $5 from you? Is it literally worth making a federal case out of it? Isn't this the normal friction of everyday life that all of us have to put up with when we coexist with other people? I think there is something to this point: I don't think we should run to court every time someone injures us in the slightest little way; our court system is an expensive way to solve problems. But here's the difficulty: if companies know that they can steal $5 from us with impunity, then they will steal $5 from us over and over again. And a lot of companies will do it, not just one. And, when you add up all these $5 thefts, at some point it becomes real money to most of us. That is, in the aggregate, it's no longer small harm at all.

But, even if it were, I really don't understand why we would want to give companies the incentive to steal even small amounts from us. As I showed in chapter 2, conservatives don't like theft. Why would we want to give a green light to theft of our property when we could deter it from happening through the threat of a class action?

I should add that, when we talk about small harms and class actions, we are actually talking about pretty big sums of money. As I explained above, the small harms we are talking about are the harms people won't file a lawsuit over on their own. That threshold is a heck of a lot higher than $5. It's probably thousands upon thousands of dollars. As Richard Posner, the conservative federal judge, once said famously: "Only a lunatic or a fanatic sues for $30."[36] Do we really want to give companies permission to steal thousands upon thousands of dollars from us? It is true that we can always take our business elsewhere, but, as I explained in chapter 2, conservatives and libertarians have never thought that was an adequate remedy for the fundamental rules of the market like breach of contract, fraud, and horizontal price fixing. This is all the more true because we may not even realize the companies have stolen from us. As I noted above, one of the virtues of the class action is that one person who finds out about misconduct can sue on behalf of all of us who don't know about it.

Class actions take away liberty. A more fundamental complaint that some conservatives have with class actions is that they are antiliberty.[37] What I have just described as a feature of class actions—one person representing others—some conservatives see as a bug. Class actions bind class members to whatever happens in the lawsuit—win, lose, or draw—*whether or not they actually consent.* Yes, class members usually get the opportunity to opt out—thus, class members consent to be part of the class action to some extent by not doing so—but there is no guarantee that we will be able to find every class member to notify them that they are part of a class action and have an opportunity to opt out. Doesn't this violate a fundamental tenet of libertarian philosophy that people should not infringe on the autonomy of others?[38]

I think this objection may present one of the few areas in this book where conservative principles do not all point in the same direction; harking back to the dichotomy I created in previous chapters, it may make a difference if you are a libertarian-minded conservative or a utilitarian-minded conservative. Utilitarian-minded conservatives should not find the antiliberty objection persuasive. What is the alternative for the small-harm class member besides the class action? As I said above, there is no alternative; it is the class action or nothing. Thus, class members can be made better off only by the class action. If the class action fails, they are in the same position they would have been in had there been no class action: they will have to suffer the small loss. But, if the class action succeeds, they will have more than they would have had: they will be entitled to a cash distribution or some other relief. This situation is what economists call *Pareto efficient*[39]— this means that no class members are made worse off by the class action, that people are either made better off or left in the same position. Pareto efficiency is a good thing to utilitarians.[40] But that's not all that a class action offers the utilitarian. Even better still are what economists call *positive externalities*: the benefits that flow to others (non–class members) from the class action.[41] Even if we are not part of a class action, we are made better off by it because, every time one company is sued, others know that they, too, could be sued; this fear deters companies from stealing from us in the first place.[42]

Libertarian-minded conservatives will not be persuaded by any of this so-called social welfare analysis.[43] They frankly don't care if class actions make society or even individuals better off; they care only about autonomy.[44] They don't like any government officials—including the judges who oversee class actions—taking away our freedom because those officials think something is best for us. Because the class action violates these principles, I can understand why hardcore libertarians might be inclined to oppose it.

But we should not forget the narrow scope of what we are talking about here. We are talking only about claims for small amounts of money, and we are talking only about people who did not get notice that they could opt out of the class action.[45] I really wonder how many libertarians are so hardcore that they find unacceptable a small-stakes infringement on liberty that nonetheless could only make the infringed better off. It is one thing to sacrifice liberty for the greater good when the sacrifice imposes burdens on some people. But when the sacrifice imposes no burden at all? When people lose nothing because they would never sue on their own? When liberty is of no use because you can't do anything with it anyway? When it comes to Pareto-efficient solutions, it seems to me that any objection from the perspective of liberty is more about symbolism than it is about substance.[46] I doubt that many of us on the right are really willing to make our economy and ourselves worse off for symbols. Even the famous libertarian legal scholar Richard Epstein seems unconcerned: "Who is likely to complain about the mandatory inclusion, when the alternative is to get nothing at all?"[47]

This is probably why, truth be told, I rarely hear conservatives voice this objection. Rather, the antiliberty objection is most often voiced from the left, not the right. It is usually liberal scholars, not conservatives, who oppose the class action because it denies class members their own day in court, because it treats them like a cog in a wheel rather than their own person, because it denies them their "autonomy."[48]

Class actions alter the substantive law. Occasionally, I hear conservatives complain that courts use class actions as an excuse to change the underlying substantive laws that companies must comply with. For example, some conservatives complain that courts change the law of fraud or prevent companies from presenting defenses in class action cases to make the cases easier to litigate.[49] Richard Epstein, in particular, has lodged these complaints at length.[50] There is little point to a class action if the individual circumstances of each class member must be litigated; these lawsuits make sense only if the questions that are identical for all class members dominate the case; otherwise, the whole thing would be an unmitigated mess. These conservatives complain that courts change the substantive law in order to get rid of all the individual questions in the case, matters that each class member would have to prove in order to win or defenses companies might have to the claims of individual class members. As Epstein puts it "The need to preserve a class action at all costs drives a court to distort the underlying theory of substantive liability beyond all recognition."[51] This doesn't sound like a good thing to do, and I do not know how often courts are really doing it. But, when they are, it is already against the law. There is a federal statute that says federal courts can't do this.[52] The US Constitution may prohibit state courts from doing this.[53] If a company sees a court do this, it should point out that this is against the law. In other words, we already have a way to stop this if it is happening—filing a legal brief in court and appealing until someone listens to you—but I am happy to cooperate with any ideas to beef up the laws we already have. As much as I respect Epstein and the others who have lodged this complaint, it is hardly reason to scrap our class action system (as even they concede).[54]

Class actions have special underenforcement problems. In the last chapter, I explained that, although most conservatives worry that the profit motive will overheat private enforcement, sometimes conservatives have the opposite worry: that it will underheat private enforcement. There is a special reason why some conservatives think this is a problem in class actions: collusion between the class action lawyer and the defendant.[55] I discussed this concern in chapter 1. It was one reason why people did not want to create the modern class action at all: they worried that corporations would take advantage of the system. As I noted, the concern here is that the class action lawyer and the defendant will structure a settlement in a way that *minimizes* total liability for the defendant in exchange for *maximum* attorney fees for the class action lawyer.[56] For example, perhaps the class action lawyer will agree to a settlement under which the defendant pays $10 million instead of $20 million but with a fee to the lawyer of $3 million instead of $2 million. This collusion is special to class action cases because the class action lawyer is more divorced from his clients than other lawyers are: as I have said, many class members many not even be aware of—let alone participate in—class actions. Although the representative plaintiffs participate, they, too, can be part of the collusion with so-called service or incentive payments to thank them for doing the extra work that goes into being a representative plaintiff.[57]

I do not doubt that class action lawyers are tempted to do things like this. That's the thing about the profit motive: if there is a sneaky way to make more money, a lawyer might well take it, just like corporations cut corners if they can make more money that way. But how big of a problem is this, and is it reason to scrap the system? I don't think it is very big and certainly not big enough to scrap the system.

To begin with, no settlement can be approved and no fees awarded in a class action unless a judge blesses the arrangement.[58] This is different than other lawsuits. So, in order to pull something like this off, the lawyers, the defendant, and the representative plaintiff would have to fool the judge overseeing the case. How likely is that? On the one hand, there are admittedly reasons to doubt the efficacy of judicial review of class action settlements: unless a class member objects to the settlement, the judge does not receive an adversary presentation about the settlement, and this can be hard for our judges, who normally hear both sides of every argument.[59] This is why some scholars favor appointing a "devil's advocate" to oppose every settlement so the judge can hear two sides.[60] On the other hand, people have been worried about collusive settlements for a long time.[61] As a result, we've been able to shut down some of the most popular schemes and educate judges to spot the telltale signs.

For example, class action lawyers and defendants once upon a time settled cases where the only relief the class would get were coupons to buy products from the defendants again.[62] The class action lawyer would tout the millions and millions of dollars in coupons the defendant was sending out to the class as reason to approve the fee the class action lawyer negotiated with the defendant.[63] But few class members ever used their coupons.[64] So the defendant got off without paying much, and the class action lawyers still got a big fee. It was a sneaky scheme, and judges let them get away with it because they were ignorant of what was unfolding: they were accustomed to awarding class action fees as soon as a case settled rather than waiting for the settlement to be distributed to class members, so they did not realize so few class members used their coupons.[65] So why don't lawyers and defendants do this as often anymore? Because Congress discouraged it in 2005.[66] Now there is a federal law that says that, if a settlement includes coupons and the lawyers want a fee equal to a percentage of them, then the judge has to wait to see how many coupons are redeemed and base the fee on that.[67] Problem solved.

Judges these days know to look for similar warning signs. For example, sometimes class action settlements will require class members to send in a form or go online to receive their money. But what if they don't do that? What happens to their money? Most of the unclaimed money is either distributed to the class members who *did* file claim forms—this is what is known in the business as a *pro rata* settlement: the money is distributed proportionally—or distributed to charity—this is known in the business as a *cy pres* provision; *cy pres* means "next best" in French[68]—but sometimes the unclaimed money goes back to the defendant. This poses the same opportunity as the coupon scheme: if the fee is based on how much might have been claimed rather than how much was actually claimed, the lawyer might get a big fee even though the defendant didn't end up paying much. These days, most courts spot this kind of thing and wait to see how many class members file claim forms before they award fees in such settlements.[69] These settlements may have been a problem at some point, but they are not today.

Nonetheless, new problems crop up all the time, and courts need to be vigilant. For example, some critics worry that lawyers try to take credit for things that corporate defendants would do anyway to justify a big fee award or that they inflate the value of nonmonetary relief they win for the class, like changes the defendant is required to make to its business practices. Nonmonetary relief is much more difficult to put a number on than a pot of cash is, and lawyers may give the court rosy numbers to justify big fee awards. Letting lawyers take credit for things companies would have done anyway or for inflated estimates of changes in their businesses costs defendants nothing, so, if it is an easy way out of a lawsuit, I don't doubt for a minute that they will take it. Truth be told, I don't know how often these things really happen, but I think that we should do whatever we can to stamp them out nonetheless. For this reason, in a later chapter I propose making all fee awards turn on how much the defendant actually ends up paying out as a result of the class action lawsuit; lawyers should not get a percentage of money that reverts back to corporations, a percentage of money that corporations would have spent even had there been no class action lawsuit, or a percentage of fantastic projections of how valuable nonmonetary relief is.

This brings me back to a point I made in previous chapters. Yes, the profit motive will give class action lawyers incentives to do sneaky things, just like it gives businesses incentives to do sneaky things. But we don't think this is a reason to give up on the profit motive for businesses, and we shouldn't think it is a reason to give up on the profit motive for lawyers; we can put rules in place to channel profit motives in the right direction. And, with regard to collusion, we've done a lot of that already, but I am happy to do even more.

Those are the conservative objections that I can respond to here. But, as I said, there are four more serious reasons some conservatives don't like class actions. These four reasons are the most popular arguments against class actions I hear from conservatives, and I will spend the rest of the book addressing them. But I want to give at least a preview here. The first three arguments are largely based on myths about class actions that can be refuted with data, but the last cannot be dismissed so easily.

Class actions are often meritless. Many conservatives think that lawyers file bogus class action cases. As I explain in the next chapter, why profit-motivated lawyers who get paid only if they win would want to file bad cases is hard to understand as a matter of theory, but, whatever the reason, the data do not bear this out. To the extent that there are meritless class actions, they are a small minority, and they are dismissed without much expense. Nonetheless, to the extent that we are not still satisfied, there are easy changes we can make to our system to discourage meritless lawsuits even further. I explain these changes in the last chapter.

Class action lawyers end up with all the money. This may be an even more popular argument that conservatives raise against class action cases: the class members don't end up with much of the money, and the lawyers get it all instead. As I explain in chapter 7, the data do not bear this out:

class action lawyers end up with a small fraction of what the class gets, a much smaller fraction than what most contingency-fee lawyers get from the cases they resolve. It is true that the *percentage* of class members who receive money in most small-harm cases is not high, but, as I noted above, when people don't send in their claim forms, their money is usually given to other class members or to charity; the lawyer does not get it. Nonetheless, it must be admitted that not many class members end up getting compensated through small-harm class actions. But, as I noted in a previous chapter, the class action is still better at compensating than the government is. Moreover, it is important to remember that compensation is only one of the reasons we need class actions: we also need them for deterrence. So long as defendants pay *someone*—and a charity counts just as well as class members—we gain deterrence. And deterrence is reason enough to keep class actions.

Class actions don't deter misconduct. Because class actions don't compensate well, much of the defense of class actions over the years has rested on deterrence. But the latest conservative attack on class actions is that they don't deter either. As I explain in chapter 8, this argument is especially ironic because conservative legal scholars *invented* the entire theory of deterrence through lawsuits. But, like the last two arguments, this one does not hold up under the weight of the data: the lion's share of academic studies has found that lawsuits, including class action lawsuits, deter misconduct.

Class actions overdeter misconduct. At the same time as many conservatives question whether class actions deter corporate misconduct, other conservatives—or even the same conservatives!—argue that class actions *overdeter* corporate misconduct. But this time the concern is real: our current class action system *does* put undue pressure on defendants to settle cases, and sometimes defendants may settle cases for more than the cases are worth. This is not a good thing: it is in no one's interest to force companies to pay more money out than they should have to; that's simply a meaningless tax on useful economic activity. But does this mean that we ought to get rid of class actions? No. We can make several changes to our system to mitigate and even eliminate the overdeterrence problem. I explain these changes in the last chapter.

The short of it is this: we need class actions if we want to enforce the market rules that even we conservatives want. Nothing else compares. Not the government, and not arbitration. To the extent the class action is not perfect, we can mend it. We don't have to end it.

CHAPTER SIX

Are Class Actions Meritless?

One of the most frequent criticisms of class action lawsuits that we hear from corporate America and some conservatives is that they are often meritless.[1] One form of this criticism is the argument that class action lawyers do not sue bad companies; they sue big companies, companies with lots of money.[2] This is an important component of the campaign against class actions. If most class actions are meritless, then many of the virtues of private enforcement that I described become moot: even if private lawyers are more effective than government bureaucrats at enforcing the law, if most of the enforcement efforts are misguided, why would we *want* them to be effective? The profit motive would simply be giving us more of something we don't want. Better to have someone ineffectual than someone effectual when it comes to delivering bad stuff.

Unfortunately for the critics, however, there is little reason to think that most or even many class action lawsuits are meritless. Moreover, businesses have a cheap and effective way to deal with the meritless class actions that are filed—it's called a *motion to dismiss*. In other words, meritless class actions are not such a big problem that it would justify crippling the entire class action system, as corporate America and some conservatives want to do.

As a matter of theory, this should not be particularly surprising. As I explained in chapter 3, it is one of the virtues of private enforcement that class action lawyers do not make any money unless their lawsuits succeed.

How can a lawyer succeed if his or her cases have no merit? Won't the company win every case, leaving the lawyer impoverished? Yes. As the Columbia law professor John Coffee concludes: "The existing theory and empirical evidence do not provide support for the claim that plaintiff's attorneys have strong incentives to bring nonmeritorious actions."[3]

Let me begin by acknowledging that, *of course*, every once in a while a lawyer will file a stupid class action lawsuit. There are one million lawyers in the United States. Occasionally, one of them does something stupid. This is true not only of class action lawsuits but also of all kinds of lawsuits: there are stupid lawsuits filed of every stripe. And it is not only true of lawyers: every profession includes in their ranks some individuals who sometimes do stupid things—including, I might add, corporate managers.[4]

But when lawyers do stupid things, companies have at their disposal a cheap and easy way to get relief: they can file that motion to dismiss that I mentioned above. What's a motion to dismiss? It's a legal maneuver a company can make *at the very beginning of the case* to ask the judge to dismiss it. If the company can show that the lawsuit has no legal basis or no plausible factual basis, then the judge will dismiss the case—no ifs, ands, or buts.[5] These motions are inexpensive to file.

Companies take advantage of the motion to dismiss all the time. Statisticians at the Federal Judicial Center twice examined a large sample of class actions in federal court—once in 1996 and once in 2008—and both times they found that, in the vast majority of cases, the defendants filed a motion to dismiss the case.[6] How often did courts grant them and dismiss the case? Less than 20 percent of the time. Scholars of securities fraud class actions have found similar dismissal rates, 20–30 percent.[7]

What do these numbers mean? They mean that only a *small minority* of class action cases could possibly be described as meritless. Why? Because the number of meritless cases is surely much *lower* than the number of dismissed cases. After all, not every dismissed case is meritless.[8] Sometimes the law is unclear and litigants have a good faith disagreement about how it should be interpreted; sometimes courts decide not to interpret the law your way. It is hard to call a lawsuit like that *meritless*.

But the more important point is that, whatever the number of meritless class actions, companies have a cheap and easy way to get rid of them—and they use it all the time. Nonetheless, some people will tell you that this is not good enough. They say sometimes judges make mistakes on the motion to dismiss and do not dismiss meritless cases. Thus, companies end up having to fight the lawsuits, and this costs money. They say companies end up settling these meritless cases to avoid the expense, distraction, and risks of litigation.[9]

It is true that, if it will cost less money to settle a meritless case than to fight it, then it is rational for a company to settle it instead.[10] It is also true that it is rational for a company to settle a case if there is even a small chance a crazy jury will award a huge sum of money at trial—even if the company would win at trial ninety-nine times out of a hundred.[11]

But it is rational for a company to do these things even when the case is *not* meritless. Companies are willing to pay extra to settle even *good* cases to avoid litigation expenses[12] and litigation risk.[13] Indeed, I worry enough about these oversettlements that I've devoted a big chunk of the last chapter of this book to reforms to mitigate them. But in this chapter the question is, How often does this happen in *meritless* cases? How often do judges let cases unlikely to succeed slip past the motion to dismiss? All the available data point to one answer: not often.

First, if cases are unlikely to succeed, companies will not be willing to pay much to settle them. After all, litigation expenses to fight the case will amount to only so much. Our best estimate for the most a company might be willing to pay in what we call a *nuisance settlement*—a settlement to avoid the nuisance of litigating—is $1–$3 million.[14] Any settlement above these amounts is unlikely to come from a meritless case, and even settlements below that amount do not necessarily come from meritless cases; there are some cases with small damages.[15] How often do class actions settle for such small amounts? A fraction of the time. In my empirical study of all class action settlements over a two-year period, I found that the median settlement was *over $5 million*; only 40 percent of settlements were for $3 million or less, one-third were for $2 million or less, and 20 percent were for $1 million or less.[16] And remember: not every settlement below these thresholds is meritless. In other words, no matter how you slice the data, the vast majority of class action settlements are *not* nuisance settlements.

Second, many times companies settle cases that have survived not only a motion to dismiss but also other tests of the merits. For example, in many cases, companies do not settle until after the judge denies what is known as a *motion for summary judgment*. This is another pretrial motion that companies can use to dismiss cases, but this one happens later on, after the parties have gathered evidence in the case. After examining all the evidence, the judge can dismiss the case if no reasonable jury could find for the plaintiff. It is even *more difficult* for a case to survive summary judgment than it is to survive a motion to dismiss. Yet, in the Federal Judicial Center studies mentioned earlier, most class action settlements followed a judge's decision to deny a motion to dismiss or to deny a motion for summary judgment or both.[17] Likewise, two scholars who studied settlements in antitrust class actions found that "most of the cases . . . were validated in whole or in part" either by criminal penalties, government recoveries, or favorable rulings on motions to dismiss, rulings on summary judgment, or even at trial.[18]

Third, the judges who should be *most concerned* by companies being forced to settle meritless cases do not appear concerned at all. Who are these judges? Conservative judges, of course. If companies had been forced to settle meritless class action cases, you would think that conservative Republican judges would be saying or doing something about it. Yet, when the antitrust scholars mentioned earlier examined class action settlements, they found that "a large number of the opinions [by the judges handling the cases] contain[ed] generous and gratuitous praise for the plaintiffs' counsel handling the case," including opinions by Republican judges.[19] I found something similar when I examined the attorneys' fees awarded in my empirical study of every class action settlement in federal court over a two-year period. As I have alluded to already and will discuss in more detail in a later chapter, judges have a great deal of discretion over the fee awards that class action attorneys receive when they settle their cases. Surely, then, Republican judges would punish the lawyers who brought meritless cases with low fee awards. If so, there must not be many meritless cases that end in settlement: no matter how I ran the data, Republican judges awarded the same fees as Democratic judges.[20] In other words, if meritless class actions are such a big problem, apparently the judges who hear the cases are unaware of it.

But even more telling than all these data is something else: despite ample opportunity and incentive to do so, corporate critics have never identified very many meritless class actions. There are probably around seven hundred class action settlements every year in the United States, and those are just the settled cases; there are probably several times that many class action cases filed every year.[21] If meritless class actions were such a big problem, surely the critics would have hundreds and hundreds of examples to share with us, right? Wrong.

I looked and looked for the list of hundreds of meritless class action cases maintained by the class action critics, but I could not find it. Instead, I found only two things. The first was a famous study from 1991 by the

Stanford law professor Janet Alexander in which she argues that securities fraud class actions were filed and settled without regard to whether there was any fraud but, rather, with regard only to how far a company's stock price had dropped; all companies with big drops were sued, and, when they were sued, the cases almost invariably settled for 25 percent of the drop.[22] If it were true that securities fraud class actions were all meritless, it would be saying something: there *are* hundreds of securities fraud class actions filed every year; this would go a long way toward proving the critics' claims. But it is not true. Alexander's study relied on a *very* small sample size, and her methodology has been criticized extensively by other scholars.[23] Moreover, there have been countless studies of securities fraud class actions since hers, and they suggest quite the contrary: these class actions are filed and settled with *ample* regard for the merits, especially after Congress made it more difficult to file securities fraud class actions by enacting the Private Securities Litigation Reform Act of 1995.[24]

The second thing I found are lists published by the US Chamber of Commerce of the "ten most ridiculous lawsuits" filed every year.[25] The lists go back many years, and I did not examine all of them, but I did examine five recent lists (2013–17) to see how many class action lawsuits were on them. The answer? Ten.[26] Of the thousands upon thousands of class actions filed over that five-year period, the Chamber has identified only ten "ridiculous" ones. That's not many.

Maybe there were many other ridiculous class actions that the Chamber wanted to put on these lists but they got bumped because there were so many *even more* ridiculous *non*–class action lawsuits that it had to put on the lists instead? It's impossible to know. But we can at least take a look at the ten that made it to learn what corporate America considers the worst of the worst of our class action system. If these ten aren't that bad, then we might conclude that there probably aren't hundreds and hundreds of *other* meritless ones out there:

- A lawsuit against Subway for false advertising because its "foot long" sandwiches were sometimes only eleven inches long.[27] (In fairness to the Chamber, a number of copycat lawsuits were filed as well, so this entry might be counted as several lawsuits instead of just one.) Subway did not file a motion to dismiss, and the case settled.[28]
- A lawsuit against Jimmy John's for consumer fraud because its menus said certain sandwiches included alfalfa sprouts even though they did not.[29] Jimmy John's did not file a motion to dismiss, and the case settled.[30]

- Two lawsuits against Starbucks for consumer fraud because it underfilled its drinks. One lawsuit was because it put too much milk in its drinks, and the other was because it put in too much ice.[31] Both lawsuits were dismissed.[32]
- A lawsuit against a lip balm company, Fresh, Inc., for deceiving consumers because not all the lip balm in the tube was accessible on account of how the twist-up mechanism in the tube works. This lawsuit was dismissed.[33]
- A lawsuit against the College Board for breach of contract (among other things) because a misprint led some students to get more time than others on a section of the SAT. The College Board ended up throwing out the section for all test takers.[34] This lawsuit was dismissed, too.[35]
- A lawsuit against Mastercard for fraud for continuing to advertise a promotion where a portion of every credit card purchase would go to charity even though the company's donation had hit its maximum for that year.[36] This lawsuit, too, was dismissed.[37]
- A consumer fraud lawsuit against Jelly Belly for listing the primary ingredient on some of its jellybean packages as "evaporated cane juice" instead of "sugar."[38] This lawsuit survived Jelly Belly's motion to dismiss and is ongoing.[39]
- A lawsuit against Starbucks for unpaid wages because the chain clocked out its employees before they locked up the store (which takes about four minutes).[40] Starbucks did not file a motion to dismiss, but it did file a motion for summary judgment, and the court granted that motion. The case is currently on appeal.[41]
- A lawsuit against several Dunkin' Donuts franchises for advertising butter on the menu but serving margarine instead.[42] The franchises did not file a motion to dismiss and settled the case.[43]

The first thing to take away from this list is that many of these lawsuits were dismissed at the beginning: four of ten (with a fifth dismissed before trial on summary judgment). Isn't this a pretty good indication that our system is working? When people file meritless lawsuits, companies can dismiss them without spending much money.

The second thing to note about this list is that many of these cases are not particularly meritless. I agree with the Chamber that the Subway lawsuit is ridiculous (which makes it all the more baffling that Subway didn't move to dismiss it): Subway uses the same ball of dough for every sandwich; some of them just bake a little differently than the others. In other words, consumers get the exact same amount of bread no matter what.[44] I also agree with the Chamber that the lip balm lawsuit is a stretch; as the court dismissing the case pointed out, it is obvious to anyone who uses the lip balm that the twist-up mechanism renders some of the balm inaccessible.[45] I also agree with the Chamber about the Starbucks consumer fraud lawsuits: if you don't like how your barista is making your drink, tell him or her to make it differently.

But the other lawsuits? I am not so sure. Why should Jimmy John's and Dunkin' Donuts be permitted to tell people on their menus that items include certain ingredients when they don't? If, by analogy, a menu says a hamburger with cheese and the hamburger does not come with cheese, I think you have every right to be unhappy. I feel much the same way about Jelly Belly: the only reason it uses the words *evaporated cane juice* in the list of ingredients is to try to trick customers who are trying to avoid sugary products. (On the other hand, the nutrition information elsewhere on the package does use the word *sugar*, so I am not sure if consumers would ever ultimately get tricked.) The Starbucks unpaid wages lawsuit is also a close call in my mind: four minutes does not seem like much time to complain about, but, if you lose four minutes of compensation every day and work five days a week, fifty weeks a year, that's one thousand minutes or almost seventeen hours—half a workweek. That's real money.

The other lawsuits don't strike me as even remotely ridiculous. The College Board messed up. They tried to make the best of it by throwing out the section of the exam with the misprint, but what if some students thought they did really well on that section? Why should they be punished because the College Board messed up? The SAT is traumatizing enough; why shouldn't the College Board refund some or all of the test-taking fee? And Mastercard? It promotes these charitable campaigns because it wants you to use its cards more often so it can make more money; it shouldn't be allowed to keep promoting the campaign when the campaign is really over. (It is not surprising to me that the reason the court dismissed this case had nothing to do with the merits; it was because the plaintiff could not show he was injured.)[46]

But you don't have to agree with my conclusions on any of these lawsuits. My point is simply that, if this is the *worst of the worst* of our system and many of these lawsuits are even *debatable*, then isn't our system in pretty good shape?

Fair enough, you might be thinking, but do I have a list of hundreds and hundreds of *meritorious* class actions? How can I criticize the Chamber for not having a list of all the bad class actions if I don't have a list of all the good ones? As the saying goes, "You can't beat something"—even if the Chamber's something is not very good—"with nothing."

Truth be told, I don't think I need a list. As I demonstrated above, I have something even better on my side: data. Data that say that the vast majority of class action cases survive a motion to dismiss, a motion for summary judgment, or both before they are settled. But, in order to give the data a bit of color, I will share with you some real-life examples of good cases. This is not a best-of-the-best list like the Chamber's worst-of-the-worst list; I have not scoured our entire court system to find the most meritorious class actions. It is simply a list of some of the lawsuits that I happened to be personally involved with as an expert witness over the same years covered by the Chamber's lists. But I think you'll find that these are some pretty worthwhile lawsuits nonetheless:

- As I have mentioned throughout this book, Bank of America and a number of other banks held their customers' debit card transactions for a day or two before processing them so they could change the order in which the transactions were processed from chronological to an order in which the biggest transactions were processed first and the smallest transactions last. Why? Because the big-to-small order would make customers go into overdraft more quickly and maximize the number of overdraft fee transactions the banks could charge. Customers of each bank brought class action lawsuits on behalf of all the other customers for fraud and breach of contract.[47]

- What happens when you try to send someone money through Western Union and the transaction is not completed for some reason? Western Union didn't tell you and kept your money instead. (At least until the law required it to turn your money over to the government years later; by then, of course, the address they had for you was probably no longer any good.) Several customers brought a class action lawsuit on behalf of all the others for fraud and breach of contract.[48]

- Ten different Asian manufacturers of flat-screen monitors agreed with one another not to compete on the prices they charged. Needless to say, this made devices with flat screens like computers and televisions more expensive. Several customers sued the companies on behalf of other customers for antitrust violations. Even the US Department of Justice got into this one, investigating the companies for criminal conduct.[49]

- Remember when the quasi-government home loan company Fannie Mae lied to its shareholders about its financial health by engaging in some tricky accounting? When it came to light, heads rolled, and Fannie Mae was eventually taken over by the government. When its stock became worthless, several shareholders sued Fannie Mae and its corporate executives—including one of Bill Clinton's cronies, Franklin Raines—on behalf of other shareholders.[50]

- Have you ever heard of a leveraged buyout? It is when private investors decide to borrow a bunch of money to buy a public company and take it private. They then try to improve the company and later take it public again, hoping to sell it for more than they bought it for.[51] There are not many private investors who have the means and wherewithal to do this, so it was easy for the few of them to agree among themselves not to bid against each other when one of them wanted to buy a company. That meant that companies were bought up for less than they might have been. Several shareholders of the target companies sued on behalf of all the shareholders for antitrust violations.[52]

- I am not Jewish, but I understand that many Jews take seriously the sanctity of those who have passed away: bodies are not supposed to be disturbed once they are buried.[53] That's why the Eden Memorial Jewish cemetery in Los Angeles sold burial plots with plenty of room between them. But the cemetery started to run out room. So what did it do? It decided to try to squeeze in a few more burial plots here and there. After all, how would the dead know if Eden encroached on the plots they and their loved ones had purchased? Well, they found out the hard way: when Eden dug the new plots with backhoes, it breached the concrete burial chambers in the adjacent plots. Many of those who had bought the plots sued on behalf of the others for breach of contract and fraud.[54]

- The largest oil spill in American history occurred when BP's Deepwater Horizon offshore drilling platform exploded off the coast of Louisiana in 2010. Businesses all along the Gulf were devastated because vacationers did not travel there for years. Many of them sued BP for their lost profits on behalf of all the other businesses. Again, even the federal and state governments got in on this one.[55]

- To those of us on the right side of the political spectrum, some of our favorite parts of federal and state constitutions are the so-called takings clauses. They say that the government cannot take your property without paying you compensation. Thank goodness it says so because a public utility in Missouri that had a legal right to run electrical wires across private land decided one day that it wanted to start a telecommunications business. Without telling any of the landowners, the utility started running telecommunications cable across their properties as well. Several landowners sued on behalf of all the others for takings and trespass.[56]

- The federal government is legally obligated to enter into contracts with Native American tribes who want to perform services that the federal government would otherwise provide for their tribe members. Yet, for many years, Congress never appropriated enough money to pay the tribes all the monies they were due on their contracts. Several tribes sued on behalf of all the others for breach of contract.[57]

- The heads of all the major technology companies on the West Coast were tired of competing with one another for talent. So what did they do? They agreed to stop trying to hire each other's employees away from one another. With no one competing over them anymore, employees' salaries were depressed. Some of the employees sued on behalf of all the others for antitrust violations.[58]

- This one you definitely remember (if for no other reason than I mentioned it earlier in the book). For nearly a decade, Volkswagen secretly inserted software into some of its diesel engines that turned off the emission controls on the cars unless the cars were being tested for emissions. Some of the cars were spewing forty times the legal limit of various toxins. Many of these cars were marketed to consumers as environmentally friendly. After the cheating was discovered by a private organization, both the government and several consumers (on behalf of all the others) sued for fraud.[59]

- Here's another well-known one. Former football players sued the NFL for hiding the brain-injury dangers associated with playing football. The NFL knew for years that the concussions the players suffered were more dangerous than they let on. Several former players sued on behalf of all the others for physical injuries caused by the NFL's breach of legal duties owed to them.[60]

- Did you know that FedEx charges you more when you send a package to a home versus a business? Well, it does. What happened if you didn't check a box on the part of the delivery slip that said "home or business"? FedEx ran the address through an inaccurate database and picked one for you. If the database couldn't find it, FedEx assumed that it was the more expensive option (a home address)—even if the delivery person could see when he or she arrived that it was a business. Several customers sued on behalf of the others for breach of contract.[61]

I think you'd be hard-pressed to find many people who think there's a single stinker in this bunch. Not only were these meritorious cases, but they also all sought to stop the kinds of things we conservatives think are important to stop: breach of contract, fraud, and horizontal price fixing. Yet most of these lawsuits would not have been possible but for the class action device; most of us either were unaware that this stuff was going on or wouldn't have been able to find a lawyer willing to bring the lawsuit for us because, on our own, the case wouldn't have been worth much. It is true that, as I noted, in some of the cases the government got involved, but not in many. Most of the time, it was either a class action or nothing at all.

Indeed, I think the truth of the matter is probably this: far from there being too many class action lawsuits in our country, there are *too few*. As I have told you, there are only around seven hundred settlements every year in state and federal courts combined. How many companies are there in this country? Hundreds of thousands, if not millions.[62] How often are they stealing small amounts from people every year? Seven hundred times? I don't know about you, but I suspect that those hundreds of thousands, if not millions, of companies are doing things that they shouldn't be doing many, many more than seven hundred times every year. Consider, for example, how many class actions are filed every year in Israel: if you control for the relative population of the two countries, lawyers there file *six times* the number of class action lawsuits that lawyers here do.[63] Is there more corporate wrongdoing in Israel than there is here? I doubt it. Sophisticated academic studies confirm this point. For example, three economists have estimated that 15 percent of major, publicly traded companies commit securities fraud every year, yet only 4 percent of them face a class action lawsuit.[64]

With so many good cases still unfiled, why would lawyers waste their time with meritless ones? The simple answer is that they don't. Whatever the number of meritless cases, they are not so numerous that we should throw the class action system out with the bathwater.

Nonetheless, if we are still worried about meritless cases, there are easy changes that we can make to our system to discourage them even further: require judges to stay class action litigation until they decide a company's motion to dismiss and then allow the company to take an immediate appeal if the judge denies its motion. I discuss these changes in the last chapter.

CHAPTER SEVEN

Do Class Action Lawyers Get All the Money?

D espite the importance of the meritlessness argument I addressed in the last chapter to the campaign against class actions, an even more common critique of class actions that I hear from some conservatives is this one: the only people who end up getting any of the class action money are the class action lawyers.[1] We hear this over, and over, and over again: Class members get nothing. Only the lawyers make money on these things.

Is this true? Not really—and I have the data to prove it.

As I have mentioned throughout this book, a few years ago I sat down and examined every single class action settlement in federal court over a two-year period—688 settlements in all.[2] One of the things I examined was how much the judges awarded to the class action lawyers. The answer? $5 billion.[3]

Now that sounds like a lot of money to give a bunch of lawyers in only two years. But it turns out that it was only a small fraction of all the money the lawyers extracted from the defendants in these settlements. The settlements extracted *over $33 billion*.[4] So that means that the *lawyers ended up getting only 15 percent*.[5] You heard that right: *15 percent*! Figure 1 is the graphic from my study showing how often judges awarded fees of various percentages.

As you can see, the fee awards varied quite a bit, ranging from 3 to 47 percent.[6] The average and median percentages were 25 percent,[7] but,

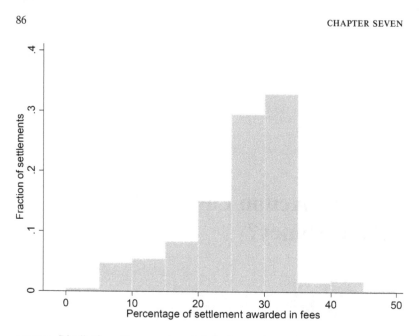

FIGURE 1. Distribution of fee percentages in federal court class actions

Source: Brian T. Fitzpatrick, "An Empirical Study of Class Action Settlements and Their Fee Awards," *Journal of Empirical Legal Studies* 7, no. 4 (2010): 811–46, 834, fig. 4.

because courts awarded the *smallest* percentages in the *biggest* cases[8] (a practice I will address in more detail below), if you add up all the fees, the lawyers ended up with *only 15 percent of the money*.

Now, I must make an important point about this 15 percent figure. There are very few data on how class action settlements are distributed once judges approve them. The parties do not often go back to the judges with a report that says: "This many class members received this much, and that many class members received that much, so on, and so on." So, when I calculated the 15 percent figure, I had to use the face value of the settlements rather than the actual monies paid out by the defendant. Thus, if a judge approved a settlement of $75 million and awarded the attorneys $7.5 million of it, I counted that as the lawyers receiving 10 percent of the settlement, no matter what happened to the other $67.5 million.

Isn't this a problem? What if not all the class members applied for their money, for example, and some of the $67.5 million was unspent? Wouldn't that money go back to the defendant? If so, haven't I *understated* what percentage ended up going to the class action lawyers? For example, let's say that class members applied for only $15 million of the $67.5 million.

Wouldn't the lawyers have ended up getting 33 percent ($7.5 million of $22.5 million) rather than 10 percent? The answers to these questions are no, no, and no.

First, the vast, vast, vast majority of class action money is distributed by what is known as the *pro rata* method.[9] This means that the company administering the settlement takes the pot of money and divides it among *however many class members applied for money*. If only a few class members apply, each of them gets more money; if many class members apply, each of them gets less. The good thing about the pro rata method is that it *guarantees* that class members end up getting everything other than what goes to the lawyers and to the other transaction costs (like notifying the class of the settlement and paying the settlement administrator). Thus, with only minor exceptions, the face value of settlements reflects what class members actually end up receiving.

Second, even when settlement money is not distributed pro rata—and therefore money might be left over after all class member claims have been paid—*the money rarely goes back to the defendant*.[10] As I noted in a previous chapter, there was a day when it did, but courts caught on to that scheme a long time ago. These days, if there is any money left over, it is almost always redistributed to the class members who did file claims or sent to a charity in some way connected to the class members.[11] We call the charity option *cy pres*, which, as we have seen, is French for "second best."[12] The idea is this: if we can't get the money to the class members, let's do the next best thing and get it to a charity that will indirectly benefit them. Now, some people complain that the class action lawyers and corporate defendants who write the settlement agreements—and the judges who approve them—are not good at picking these charities.[13] Some of this criticism is valid.[14] But that criticism does not take away from my point here: the face amount of class action settlements is almost always the same amount of money the defendant ultimately pays out.

Finally, even in the rare case when the settlement money is *not* distributed pro rata and any leftover money *would* go back to the defendant, these days many courts wait to see how many class members apply for money before awarding fees.[15] The courts then award fees based on the actual amount of money known to be claimed by the class rather than the theoretical amount that might have been claimed. Thus, no matter how you slice it, the 15 percent figure is an accurate reflection of what portion of class action money is going to the lawyers. And 15 percent is a far cry from everything.

It is important to emphasize that, when a settlement distributes money in cy pres, it means that class members are not getting that portion of the settlement. Although, again, this is an issue in only some cases, it must be admitted that—especially in consumer cases—it is often hard to find class members and not many of them end up getting compensated. Consider a class action lawsuit against a company that sells bottles of natural spring water. Let's say the company defrauded its customers because it put tap water in the bottles instead. How are we supposed to find the class members, that is, all the people who bought a bottle of water? No one keeps a record of that kind of thing. We can put advertisements in the newspaper, on television, and online, but it's going to be hard to get people to pay attention. And, even when they do, it's going to be hard to get them to respond to the advertisement and file a claim.

This is not the fault of the class action. It's the fault of the small harms we are trying to rectify with the class action—things that, as I explained in a previous chapter, we should want to rectify. How much does a bottle of water cost? $2? How much trouble should we go through to find people who lost $2? How much trouble are *they* willing to go through to collect the $2? Probably not much. As it is, we spend oodles and oodles of dollars every year in this country trying to get small checks like this to people in class action cases—I once heard a class action lawyer joke that his settlement checks were single-handedly responsible for keeping the US Postal Service in business—and, even so, few people end up getting paid in some cases. Sometimes it is because it is too expensive to find people.[16] Sometimes it is because it is not worth it for people to do much work to collect the money even when we can find them.[17] Sometimes it is because, when we make it too easy for people to collect the money, people do not take it because they are afraid they are being scammed.[18] It turns out to be harder to give away money than you think it would be.

As I noted above, we don't really have good data on how often we have trouble distributing class action money because no one goes back to the judge after a case is over to tell him or her what happened. But the data we do have in consumer cases are not inspiring: when class members are required to fill out claim forms to get paid, it may well be that less than 10 percent of class members end up receiving the payments they are entitled to.[19] Consumer cases are only one type of class action, but, still, that's not good.

This is starting to change. Indeed, in a few years I think we will see compensation rates that are much higher than we see now. In the Bank of

America overdraft fee case I discuss throughout this book, the rate was much higher because many of the class members were still customers of the bank; the bank could deposit their compensation directly into their accounts without asking them to file claim forms.[20] More and more corporations are keeping data on who their customers are, including their contact information; this data can be used to deliver compensation to class members without asking them to fill out forms.[21] Indeed, given that so many people now use electronic money-transfer services like PayPal and Venmo, I think the day when most class members receive automatic payments credited straight to their electronic accounts is on the horizon.[22]

In the meantime, however, we have to concede that at least one part of the lawyers-are-getting-everything critique rings true: not many class members are made whole in some cases.[23] Of course, as I noted in an earlier chapter, class actions are still better than the government in this regard—but, then again, beating the government is not a high bar. Nonetheless, as I have explained, the rest of the critique is not true: just because class members are not being compensated does not mean that the only ones getting any money are the class action lawyers. As I said, either the class members who do apply share the money, or the money goes to charity; the money does not typically go back to the defendant.

If we know that the best we can do is to give the class's money to charity, should we even fool with the class action to begin with? Some conservatives say no, but I beg to differ. Even if sometimes the class action doesn't do a good job compensating class members, cy pres still enables it to do a good job deterring corporate misconduct. How? Because, so long as corporations know they will have to pay *someone* when they do something wrong, then they will be discouraged from engaging in the wrongdoing all the same. Paying $67.5 million to charity makes the same dent in your bank account as paying $67.5 million to anyone else. If conservatives want to stop corporate misconduct—and, as I explained, we do (at least when it's breach of contract, fraud, and horizontal price fixing)—then we should want the class action even when it cannot serve its compensatory function. This is why the earliest defenses of the class action lawsuit by *conservative* law and economics scholars were on deterrence grounds, not compensation grounds.[24] Indeed, as I show in the next chapter, the entire theory of deterrence through lawsuits was invented by conservatives. (This makes it all the more bizarre that the final argument that conservatives raise against class action lawsuits is that they do not deter. I take up this argument in the next chapter.)

In any event, no matter what your view of cy pres, its existence means that class action lawyers are not gobbling up all the class action money. They are getting only 15 percent of it. The rest is going to class members, charity, or other transaction costs (like notifying the class and paying the settlement administrator).

Does that sound like too much to you? That's less than half of the 33 percent that contingency-fee lawyers normally get! It is true that it is more than real estate agents get—when you sell a house, you pay your agent 6 percent of the sale price—but, with due respect to real estate agents, many more people can sell a house than can sue a big company with $1,000-an-hour lawyers defending it. Indeed, if we *really* wanted to be good conservatives, we would probably want judges to give the lawyers *more* than 15 percent. Why do I think that? A little thing called *conservative economic theory*.

Consider first that some judges refuse to pay class action lawyers a *percentage* of what they recover despite the fact that every other contingency-fee lawyer in America is paid his or her fees as a percentage of what he or she recovers. Rather, some judges pay class action lawyers based on the number of hours they work on a case rather than the amount of money they recover from the corporate defendant.[25] They are doing this because they think that paying lawyers a percentage gives them too much money.[26]

Recall the Bank of America overdraft-fee case. The judge who heard the case was in Miami, Florida, and when the case concluded—recall that Bank of America settled for $410 million—he awarded the lawyers 30 percent of what they had recovered.[27] That was a lot of money, but the judge didn't care: the lawyers delivered, and they should be rewarded for it.[28] But a nearly identical case was filed against Wells Fargo Bank in San Francisco because the bank engaged in the same scheme of reordering its customers' debit card transactions. When that case was over—it did not settle; it went to trial, and the judge awarded $203 million to the class[29]— the judge decided *not* to give the lawyers a percentage but, instead, to pay the lawyers for the hours they had worked on the case.[30] He was worried, that if he awarded the standard percentage, then the lawyers would end up with a "windfall."[31] What is a windfall? The judge didn't quite say, but the gist of his opinion was that the fees the lawyers would earn if he gave them the standard percentage would be so far out of whack with how many hours they worked that it would be unseemly.[32] So he paid them for the number of hours they worked plus a small enhancement to compensate them for the risk they took of not getting paid if they had lost the case.[33] This is known as the *lodestar method*. The lawyers ended up getting $42 million less under the lodestar method than they would have received if they had been paid like the lawyers in Miami—even though they won the exact same case.

Now, if you were a class member who had been swindled out of some overdraft fees by a bank and you had to decide how to pay the class's lawyer, how would you do it? Maybe if you were doing it at the end of the case, you would think to yourself, Well, the lawyer has already recovered all this money for me, so perhaps I should give him as little as possible so I can keep as much as possible for myself! That would be perfectly rational until you were swindled the next time and couldn't find a lawyer to represent you because the lawyer knew what you would do at the end of the case. Unfortunately, our judges almost always set the fee award at the end of the case, and, as the Wells Fargo case shows, they sometimes succumb to this same sort of short-term thinking that we academics call *hindsight bias*: taking money away from the lawyers seems easy after they have already done all the work.[34]

But what if you had to hire the lawyer at the *beginning* of the case? What if you had to convince the lawyer to invest his or her time and money in this endeavor? What if you didn't know yet whether the lawyer would succeed or how much the lawyer would recover? Would you think it would be best to pay the lawyer on the basis of the number of hours worked? Or would you think it best to pay the lawyer on the basis of how much money was recovered?

Maybe if you could monitor the lawyer's work closely, you would consider paying on the basis of the number of hours because you could make sure the lawyer did a good job for you and ensure he or she didn't bill too many hours. But what if you couldn't monitor the lawyer? What if you wouldn't know if he or she was doing a good job or not—after all, what do most of us know about consumer fraud law?—or what if you didn't want to spend the time to monitor him or her because you had only $100 worth of overdraft fees at stake in the case anyway? Under the circumstances where you couldn't or wouldn't monitor your lawyer, how would you want to pay? The answer is easy: with the percentage method. The percentage method aligns the interests of your lawyer with your own interests: the more the lawyer recovers, the more he or she gets. Moreover, the percentage method incentivizes him or her to resolve the case quickly: the quicker the resolution, the more he or she can make per hour of work. The lodestar method, by contrast, incentivizes the lawyer to drag cases

along and work more hours. Indeed, the lodestar method makes the lawyer *indifferent* to how much is recovered; he or she gets paid *the same* no
matter what is recovered.

In other words, all this is easily explained by one of conservatives' favorite things: the "invisible hand" of incentives. Indeed, all this has been
known since the 1970s. Before that time, most judges used the lodestar
method to award fees in class action cases just like some conservatives
want them to do today. But then something happened: the conservative
Chicago school law and economics movement.[35] Conservative scholars
pointed out that no one in the free market for legal services who could not
monitor his or her lawyer ever hired a lawyer using the lodestar method;
they all hired lawyers using the percentage method.[36] That is, again, why
every other contingency-fee lawyer in America is paid that way. And you
know what happened? The judges listened to the conservative scholars.
All over America, they stopped using the lodestar method.[37] Today, most
judges use the percentage method.[38]

It should be noted that the percentage method is not perfect. Because
lawyers receive only a fraction of the benefit of their efforts but suffer the
full cost of their efforts, scholars have shown that they have an incentive
to settle cases quickly for less money than class members would prefer.[39]
The solution to this problem is to pay lawyers a percentage of what they
recover *plus* their lodestar.[40] Although clients indeed sometimes choose
to pay lawyers this way—I remember handling a case like this for a large
energy company when I practiced law, and lawyers who sue under statutes
where they can recoup their fees from the defendant if they win can also
collect a percentage of their clients' recoveries—I have never seen a judge
use it in a class action case. But, with or without this embellishment, there
is no doubt that the percentage method gives lawyers *much* better incentives than the pure lodestar method.

This is why it is such a shame that some judges are still using the lodestar method. Not many do, as I said, but enough of them do that class
action lawyers can't help but worry whether they need to drag cases out
for fear judges will reward them by the hour rather than by the result. Indeed, this fear is all the more acute because a lot of judges sneak the lodestar method in the back door even though they are ostensibly using the
percentage method: they often slash the percentage so that it is not too
far out of whack with class counsel's lodestar.[41] They call this the *lodestar
crosscheck*. It's the same thing as the lodestar method, just dressed up in
nicer clothing.[42] Why do I say this? Because every time a judge caps class

action fees on the basis of how many hours the lawyers worked, it sends a bad message to future class action lawyers: don't resolve cases too quickly; drag them out to beef up your lodestar so your fee percentage isn't cut. We shouldn't send that message.

It is important to note that the lodestar crosscheck is different from the formula I mentioned above according to which lawyers are paid a percentage *plus* their lodestar: the lodestar crosscheck *caps* the lawyers' percentage at some multiple of their lodestar. As I noted, scholars have shown that the percentage-plus formula creates the incentive to get the most for the class; it corrects the temptation to settle early for less that the pure percentage method creates. The percentage-capped formula, by contrast, creates perverse incentives, to be indifferent as to how much the class recovers and to want to drag cases out to build up more lodestar. As I noted, people in the real world sometimes contract for percentage plus lodestar; no one ever contracts for percentage-capped lodestar. We should not foist a compensation scheme on class members that people refuse to choose for themselves in the real world.

It is true that, in rare cases, we have no choice but to use the lodestar method. Sometimes the law mandates it.[43] Sometimes there is no other money in the settlement because the only remedy is nonmonetary relief like an injunction stopping the defendant from doing something. But most of the time we have a choice, and conservative economic theory tells us what the right choice is: the percentage method, preferably percentage *plus* lodestar. If judges used this method more often, class action lawyers would be paid a tad more than the 15 percent they are today.

There's something else that some judges do to suppress class action fee awards that is inconsistent with conservative economic theory: as I noted above, they award *smaller* fee percentages when class action cases settle for *more* money.[44] Now, again, if you were a class member, would you do this at the outset of a case? Tell your lawyer that you will give him a *smaller* fraction if he gets you *more*? That doesn't sound like a good idea, does it? Won't it discourage him or her from getting you more? That's exactly what it does, and, again, the conservative Chicago school tells us so: "Private parties would never contract for such an arrangement, because it would eliminate counsel's incentive to press for more [money] from the defendants."[45] Let me give you an example just to show you how irrational this practice is. Many courts award class action lawyers 25 percent of settlements when they are under $100 million but only 20 percent of settlements when they are above $100 million.[46] Let's say that a lawyer in front of one of these courts could extract $110 million out of the corporate defendant if he really tried. That would give him a fee of $22 million. That's good money. But why would he do it? If the lawyer settled the case for, say, $95 million instead—$15 million less—he would get $23.75 million in fees, $1.75 million more. You can do the math yourself: if you pay the lawyer a bigger percentage of smaller sums, he or she is better off sometimes resolving cases for smaller sums. That's obviously not good for class members. Yet courts do it every day.

Now, some in the Chicago school say that this practice wouldn't be so bad if it were done on a marginal basis—if courts slashed fee percentages only for those amounts over the $100 million threshold.[47] That is, for the $110 million settlement mentioned above, the court would give the lawyer 25 percent of the first $100 million and then 20 percent of the $10 million above that. The marginal approach always gives the lawyer more if he or she recovers more—to that extent, it is an improvement over the haphazard way courts usually do things. But I am not so sure even marginal reductions in fee percentages are a good idea. Why would we want to give lawyers lesser incentives to go after the bigger bucks?[48] Sometimes I hear people say: "Once the lawyers have invested enough time in a case to get a $100 million recovery, they don't have to do as much work to get the next $100 million, so we shouldn't have to pay them as much to get it."[49] Some in the Chicago school confirm this reasoning by pointing to corporate clients in the free market who, when they are plaintiffs, hire lawyers using declining contingency percentages.[50] But this reasoning is foreign to my experience. It is also foreign to the experience of the famous libertarian legal scholar Richard Epstein, who writes: "It has been suggested that the fee . . . be 'tapered,' so that the percentage take is reduced with an increase in the size of the class settlement. . . . In general, however, this does not seem to be the right approach."[51]

To the contrary: my experience is that it is usually easiest to get to *first* dollars in the case; companies are happy to settle on the cheap if they can. It is the *last* dollars in the case that you really have to turn screws to get.[52] And we see this in the free market, too: indeed, *even more* companies pay *increasing* contingency percentages when they are plaintiffs than pay *decreasing* percentages.[53] Usually these percentages increase on the basis of how mature the case is rather than how much money is recovered,[54] but sometimes they increase based on recovery, too.[55] If we pay lawyers a lesser return on later dollars, all we do is incentivize them to settle old cases quickly and invest their time instead in new cases that will allow them to reap a better return on their time. In short, I tend to agree with my right-leaning colleague at Vanderbilt Law School, Amanda Rose: if we are going to use marginal rates at all in class actions, they should probably increase with the recovery rather than decrease with it.[56] If judges would at least stop *decreasing* the percentages, class action lawyers would be paid a lot more than they are today—something closer to 25 percent of what they recover instead of 15 percent.

There is one final thing that judges sometimes do to suppress class action fee awards that is inconsistent with conservative economic theory: they don't pay class action lawyers for certain types of relief that they extract from the defendants. According to some courts, there is first-class relief and second-class relief, and the lawyers get only a percentage of the former and not the latter. What counts as second-class relief? The money the defendants pay for transaction costs and cy pres: for example, the money that goes to pay to notify the class, the money that goes to process class members' claim forms, and the money that goes to charities.[57] But it is not consistent with the conservative Chicago school to pay class action lawyers a percentage of only a portion of what they recover from the defendant.[58]

Courts do this because they think transaction expenses and cy pres payments don't compensate class members.[59] "Why should the lawyers be rewarded for money that doesn't go to class members?" these courts ask. The answer is because this money is needed in order to get money to class members. These are not unnecessary transaction costs; they are necessary transaction costs. How can you file a claim form if you don't know about the settlement? How can you get your money if no one processes your claim form? Even the cy pres payments compensate class members in an indirect sense: the charities judges send these payments to are supposed to benefit the class members in some way.[60] For example, in some financial fraud cases, when class members have not claimed all their compensation and there is leftover money, that money is sent to financial literacy organizations that help educate class members and others about how to avoid misleading financial solicitations in the future.[61]

But, even more importantly, every dime the defendant pays is important because it furthers the deterrence function of the class action. As I explain in the next chapter, the entire theory of deterrence through lawsuits was invented by the conservative Chicago school theory. And, as I explained above in connection with cy pres, deterrence does not care who gets the money; it cares only that the defendant pays the money. When defendants know that they will have to pay, they pay attention. Because every dime that class action lawyers extract from defendants furthers this deterrent function, class action lawyers should be rewarded for every dime they extract. What will happen if they are not? They will not spend the effort in settlement negotiations to try to get the defendants to pay for these things; they will let leftover money, for example, go back to the defendant. After all, why would you spend your time and money trying to extract something from the defendant if the court will ignore it when it sets your fee percentage? You wouldn't. I can understand why corporations would want to deincentivize class action lawyers like this, but I can't understand why conservatives who want the law enforced would. Not many courts are doing this yet—so I doubt stopping it would affect the 15 percent figure much—but I don't want these practices to grow.

A related question involves what I have called *injunctive relief*: provisions in class action settlements or judgments that require defendants to change their behavior. For example, many banks in the overdraft fee litigation that I mention throughout this book agreed that, in addition to compensating customers for past overdraft fees, they would also stop reordering debit card transactions in the future; those promises should save class members a lot of money going forward. Should class action lawyers receive a percentage of future savings as well? From a conservative Chicago school perspective focused on incentives, it is hard to see why not. If we don't reward class action lawyers for stopping bad practices just as we reward them for recovering money, then why would they spend their time stopping bad practices? They will only spend their time collecting money. With that said, courts need to be careful here. Cash is easy to value for purposes of giving class action lawyers a portion of it; injunctive relief is not. We can make estimates, for example, of how many overdraft fees class members will be saved in the future, but we don't know for sure. Courts shouldn't let class action lawyers inflate these numbers to pad their fees; they should insist on reliable estimates of the value of injunctive relief before they add some of it to the attorneys' fees they award. If it is not possible to estimate the value of injunctive relief reliably, courts should consider rewarding class action lawyers through other means, such as increasing the percentage they give of the cash relief the lawyers recover in the same cases. If more courts were open to things like this, it would modestly increase the fees class action lawyers collect from their successful cases.

So the truth of the matter is that courts are probably paying class action lawyers too little rather than too much. But there is one way in which courts are paying class action lawyers too much, and it must be addressed in this same vein: courts sometimes award class action lawyers a percentage of the settlement monies that end up *going back* to the defendant. I know that sounds crazy—why would we pay class action lawyers for *not* extracting money from the defendant?—but the Supreme Court has authorized this practice,[62] and some courts still do it. (Most don't, as I noted above, but some do.) The theory behind this practice is that class counsel have conferred a benefit on the class in the form of the *opportunity* to apply for money from the settlement; why should class counsel be punished because you did not take advantage of the opportunity?[63] There is something to this theory, but not much. Why on earth would we want to incentivize lawyers to generate *potential* compensation and deterrence when we could incentivize them to generate *actual* compensation and deterrence instead? It is much easier to negotiate settlements where defendants get to keep leftover money; if we don't pay lawyers for doing better than that, then they won't do better than that. That means less compensation and less deterrence. Even corporate America doesn't like this practice despite the fact that it would probably reduce how much they end up paying out to settle class action cases.[64] Again, not many courts follow this practice—so I doubt that it would affect the 15 percent figure much if they stopped—but stop they should.

Let me close by making one last point here: it is a shame we have to ask judges to do all this Chicago school economic theorizing to try to figure out what class members would want if they were hiring class action lawyers in the free market. It's complicated, and I don't blame them for not doing it.[65] Ideally, class action lawyers would be paid the same way we conservatives want to pay everyone else in society: by asking consenting adults in the market to decide for themselves what they want to pay and what they want to be paid. But, as I have explained in a previous chapter, we don't have that luxury in class actions. The harms we are trying to rectify are so small that there is no market for legal representation. If we want a private remedy—and, as I have explained, we should!—we need to bundle all the class members together into a package and give it to a lawyer. In other words, class members do not pick their lawyers; their lawyers pick them. That's not the free market. As I said in chapter 5, class actions are more akin to a bunch of small, government-sanctioned monopolies or franchises. If you recall the privatization chart that I reproduced in table 2 above, that's still better than asking government bureaucrats to do the law enforcement, but it's certainly not ideal.

If judges really wanted to, they could figure out the market fee percentage in every class action case that comes before them. Two conservative law professors, Geoffrey Miller of New York University and Jonathan Macey of Yale University, figured out how to do this several years ago: by holding a reverse auction at the beginning of every case and inviting class action lawyers to bid against each other for the right to represent the class.[66] A reverse auction would *create* a competitive market for the class's legal representation and drive down the winning fee percentage to the lowest possible price just like auctions drive the winning bid up to the highest possible price. It's a brilliant idea. And a few courts have tried it.[67] But the auctions didn't work out well. Not many class action firms were willing to bid against one another.[68] And, even when they were, it was hard for courts to decide which bid was better: sometimes the cheapest firm is not the best firm.[69]

I wish courts would try harder to implement the reverse auction idea. But the truth is that I don't have any clever ideas for making auctions work better than they have in the past. We may, therefore, be stuck trying to figure out fee percentages as best we can. That means that we ought at least to stop using class counsel's lodestar to cap their fees and stop cutting class counsel's fee percentages when they recover more from the defendant. If anything, we should pay class counsel their lodestar *plus* a percentage and *increase* the percentage as they recover more. We should stop excluding stuff from what class counsel gets paid for, and we should stop paying them for stuff they didn't even recover. Yes, these changes will mean class action lawyers probably get paid more. But if the lawsuits they are bringing are meritorious—which as I show in the previous chapter they largely are—and if the lawsuits are for things that we think should be stopped—like breach of contract, fraud, and horizontal price fixing—then we should not be afraid of paying them any more than we are afraid to pay other entrepreneurs. And, the last time I checked, we conservatives were not afraid of paying other entrepreneurs. Remember how the famous Chicago school economists Gary Becker and George Stigler put it: "The view of enforcement and litigation as wasteful in whole or in part is simply mistaken. They are as important as the harm they seek to prevent."[70]

CHAPTER EIGHT

Do Class Actions Deter Wrongdoing?

I love my fellow conservatives. But we are schizophrenic when it comes to deterrence and class actions. As I explained in a previous chapter, one of the principal conservative complaints about class actions is that they deter too much: the profit motive overheats enforcement, and corporations are thereby discouraged from many socially useful activities for fear of lawsuits. As I have also explained, to the extent that this is true—and I think to some extent it is—we can tweak our system to deal with it; we don't need to throw the class action out with the bathwater. I address these tweaks in the next chapter.

But some conservatives complain about class actions for the exact opposite reason: not that they deter too much, but that they don't deter at all. This argument is a curious one because it flies in the face of decades of economic theory that was pioneered by *conservative* academics. Nonetheless, it is the latest conservative attack on class actions, and, in this chapter, I try to explain why it does not hold up.

Specific versus General Deterrence

Let me begin by making an important distinction that is sometimes overlooked in the discussion about class actions and deterrence. There are two types of deterrence, and it is impossible to deny that class actions *do* achieve one of them.

One type of deterrence is known in the academic world as *specific de-terrence*. *Specific deterrence* refers to how an *actual* wrongdoer responds to an *actual* lawsuit against it. Does that wrongdoer stop the misbehavior after it gets caught?[1] The other type is known as *general deterrence*; it re-fers to how *potential* wrongdoers respond to a *potential* lawsuit. Do poten-tial wrongdoers decide not to commit misconduct to begin with because they are afraid of lawsuits against them?[2]

There is no doubt that class action lawsuits generate specific deter-rence. How do we know this? We know this because, when class action lawsuits are resolved, they often include a court order obligating the de-fendant to change its behavior. This is sometimes called *injunctive relief*, as I noted in previous chapters. When I examined every single class action settlement in federal court over a two-year period for the empirical study I have relied on throughout this book, I found that almost one-quarter of the time, the settlement included a provision requiring the defendant to change its behavior in some way. In some types of class action law-suits, I found behavior-modification provisions as often as 75 percent of the time.[3] That's a lot of specific deterrence! But even these numbers *un-derstate* how much specific deterrence is caused by class actions because many times corporations drop offending practices as soon as they get sued for them; they don't wait for a settlement.[4]

Some conservatives complain that the behavior-modification provi-sions in class action settlements are cosmetic and do not impose real restrictions on corporations.[5] For example, the well-known class action critic who worked at the conservative Competitive Enterprise Institute, Ted Frank, says that he has "yet to see one single case with valuable injunctive relief for the class."[6] Remember that there are roughly 350 class action settlements every year in federal court alone, and I found that roughly 80 of these include behavior-modification provisions.[7] Although our data on state courts are not as good, I suspect that there are at least as many settlements with behavior-modification provisions in state courts as well. Are these provisions as toothless as Frank suggests?

This charge is admittedly difficult to evaluate; it would require someone with knowledge about each lawsuit to make an educated judgment about how well the modification prevents future misconduct. Someone has indeed done this—the federal judge who approved each of the settlements—but critics are skeptical that judges do a good job of it because class action settlements often have no opposition and it is more difficult for judges to find flaws when no one is pointing them out.[8] There is something to this skepticism.[9] So what can we do to assess how good these behavior-modification provisions are?

As I argued in chapter 6 when I addressed the charge that class actions are meritless, we can at least ask critics to tell us what they think a bad behavior-modification provision looks like. And, if they have trouble coming up with many good examples, we might be skeptical of their skepticism. How many provisions have critics identified?

Not many. The most comprehensive list comes from an article coauthored by Erin Sheley and Ted Frank.[10] This is what they came up with:

- In lawsuits filed by shareholders objecting to mergers between their companies, the lawsuits often settle with the companies agreeing to disclose more information to shareholders about the merger; these disclosures have been found to be wholly irrelevant to shareholders as measured by how they vote on the mergers.[11] Sheley and Frank rightly criticize these provisions as toothless,[12] and courts have begun to reject them.[13] Although there have indeed been a large number of these settlements in the years after my empirical study,[14] I am not sure how many will escape judicial scrutiny in the future. In any event, merger litigation is obviously a *very* specialized area of the law; it does not tell us much about the rest of our class action system.[15]
- In a lawsuit against Gillette for making misrepresentations about a battery, the settlement included a provision forbidding the company from making the same misrepresentations in the future. Sheley and Frank say that the provision did not forbid the misrepresentations if Gillette changed the name of the battery.[16] I do not know if they are right or wrong about this, but, even if they are right, this would simply be bad lawyering. Most fraud lawyers know that you bar your adversary from repeating, not only the same misrepresentations, but also any misrepresentations that are functionally equivalent. Countless class action settlements follow the latter approach.[17]
- In a lawsuit against Facebook for violating the privacy of rights of customers by tracking the links they sent in their private messages, the settlement included a provision requiring Facebook to disclose this practice to its customers on its Web site. Sheley and Frank say that the disclosure was ineffective,[18] and, again, I do not know if they are right or wrong—Facebook says a lot of people have visited the Web site, and the courts haven't weighed in on the matter yet—but I will give them the benefit of the doubt.
- In three consumer fraud lawsuits against companies that made or sold vitamins and other health products, the settlements included provisions requiring the companies to disclose more information to consumers about their products.

Sheley and Frank say that the disclosures were hollow (or even counterproductive),[19] and, again, their claims are hard for me to evaluate, but, in two of the settlements, the courts agreed with them,[20] and, in the other one, the parties renegotiated the settlement.[21] Thus, I will side with them in these cases as well.

- In a lawsuit against a drug company by its shareholders, the settlement ordered the company to make corporate governance changes similar to changes that a committee convened by the company had already recommended.[22] Sheley and Frank said that the settlement therefore added nothing, but, as the court that rejected this argument noted, the corporate governance changes recommended by the committee had been suggested *because of the class action lawsuit*.[23] I think Sheley and Frank are wrong on this one.

- In a lawsuit against a company by some of its employees for racial discrimination, the settlement included a provision requiring the company to come up with unspecified reforms to its hiring and promotion practices.[24] The settlement required the company to meet periodically with an expert and class counsel to assess the efficacy of the reforms, but, if the expert or class counsel were unimpressed, the company was not obligated to do anything more.[25] Although the trial court thought this was good enough, the court of appeals disagreed,[26] and I think Sheley and Frank are right to criticize this behavior-modification provision, too, as weak.

Although Sheley and Frank seem right to criticize many of these settlements, outside the specialized world of merger litigation, that's only six bad examples—six out of hundreds upon hundreds of settlements with behavior-modification provisions over this same time period. That's not many. Outside merger litigation, I see no reason to doubt the efficacy of specific deterrence in class actions.

In a previous chapter, I noted that I have served as an expert witness in many class action cases over the last few years. In that chapter, I offered a list of some of the cases I worked on to show examples of what I think are the many meritorious class actions that are filed every year. Many of these cases ended in settlements that included provisions requiring the defendants to change their behavior, and, in my view, none of these provisions were illusory. I do not want to take the time here as I did earlier to describe each of these provisions in detail, but, if you are interested, I describe some of them briefly in this note.[27]

The reason I do not want to take the time to engage the topic of specific deterrence further is because, in my mind, the more interesting debate in class action circles is about general deterrence: as noted above, some conservatives today cast doubt on the theory of general deterrence when it comes to class actions. This is interesting because *conservative academics invented the entire theory of general deterrence*! I take up this surprising turn of events now.

The Theory of General Deterrence

In the first semester of the first year in every law school in America, the students are taught that the threat of a lawsuit deters misbehavior.[28] Law students have been taught this for almost fifty years. They are taught it because the conservative Chicago school of law and economics told us that it is true.[29] That this has become such an article of faith in the academic world is one of the most resounding successes of conservative intellectualism in the law.

It is easy to see why the theory is so powerful. All we have to do is assume that people are rational. A rational person does not want to get sued. Lawsuits cost money. You have to pay lawyers, and, if you lose, you have to pay the plaintiff. This means that lawsuits are a great way to stop people from misbehaving when we don't want them to: all you have to do is set the damages awarded in a lawsuit equal to an amount related to the harm the misbehavior inflicts on the injured party.[30] If the misbehavior benefits the corporation less than the harm it inflicts on others, then the corporation will rationally choose not to engage in the misconduct. Indeed, the only time the corporation will rationally choose to engage in the misconduct is when the benefits outweigh the harm, but that's OK: we want people to do things that generate more benefits than costs if we can make the injured party whole in the process. This is what we in the academy call *internalization of costs*.[31] The rational actor model of cost internalization is part of what is known as *classical law and economics*.[32] Classical law and economics was pioneered by conservative Chicago school giants.[33] Class action litigation has always been a hallmark of the conservative deterrence-through-litigation school of thought.[34]

It is important to note that lawsuits are not the only way we can deter misbehavior. Another way to do so is simply to rely on word of mouth in the marketplace: if a company mistreats its customers, employees, or shareholders, then the customers, employees, and shareholders can tell others to go elsewhere. We conservatives love market feedback loops like this, but, as I explained in chapter 2, most conservatives do not think that consumer, employee, and shareholder boycotts are sufficient to stop corporations from misbehaving; we think we also need market rules and someone to enforce the rules. Indeed, enforcing market rules through lawsuits *enhances* the market feedback loops we love so much: lawsuits publicize wrongdoing to consumers, employees, and shareholders in a way that word of mouth does not on its own.[35]

Many liberals do not like classical law and economics. Some don't like it because they do not like the utilitarianism that underlies it—who cares if the benefits outweigh the costs if what is going on is unfair?[36] But some don't like it because they think that the underlying model of human behavior is inaccurate: people, it turns out, are not very rational.[37] There are now countless studies[38] and even popular books[39] showing how all of us make the same types of mistakes over and over again when we try to process information; we do not simply add up the costs and compare them to the benefits before we act. Thus, a new branch of law and economics has formed called *behavioral law and economics*; behavioralists seek to update the classical rational actor model with findings from these studies.[40]

The behavioral findings are admittedly powerful, but none of them suggest that the teams of people who run corporations are systematically irrational in the same way the rest of us are.[41] Indeed, we often refer to corporate executives as *bean counters* for a reason: if anyone is counting up the costs and benefits of things, it's they. Moreover, the behavioral findings are not why some conservatives think that class actions do not facilitate general deterrence; conservative critics of class actions accept that corporations behave in a rational way in response to incentives just like conservative classical economists do.

So why do some conservatives think that the conservative theory of general deterrence through lawsuits is wrong when the lawsuits are class action lawsuits? There are two reasons. The first reason is what we in the academy call *principal-agent costs*.[42] This is the price a principal pays when his agent is unfaithful to him. For example, the people who run a corporation are agents of the corporation (or, better yet, agents of the owners of the corporation, the shareholders). Yet sometimes what is rational for the corporate executives to do is not what is best for the corporation.

Consider an example. Let's say that a given corporate executive has to decide whether to put a falsehood on the package of a product—something like, "Can cure cancer in two weeks!" Let's say that the he thinks that this new packaging will sell $10 million of additional product, leading to additional profits of $2 million. But let's say he thinks that there is a fifty-fifty chance that the corporation will get sued in a class action over the new packaging and lose the lawsuit and that, if it loses, it will have to pay $10 million. The corporation's owners would not want to use the new packaging: the expected initial gain is $2 million, but then come the expected losses of $5 million (50 percent chance of a $10 million loss). But let's say that the executive is planning to stay only one more year at the company and that, by the time any lawsuit is resolved, he will be long gone. He won't be there when the corporation loses the $5 million, only when the corporation makes the $2 million. If his salary did not vary on the basis of the corporation's profits, maybe he would be indifferent about the new packaging; but, if, as is common, he receives a bonus every year based on the corporation's profits, it would be rational to approve the new packaging even though the corporation's owners would not want him to.

This is a classic *agency cost*—in this example, the executive's unfaithfulness is going to cost the corporation $3 million. Because of agency costs like this, some conservatives say that class actions do not deter corporate misconduct.[43]

But this is true only if corporations do not try very hard to align the interests of corporate officers and the corporation. All that is required is a little imagination. Take, for example, our corporate executive here. How might the corporation solve the problem that he might make bad decisions because his time horizon is much shorter than the time horizon of the corporation's owners? Write into his contract that his bonus will be paid on the basis of not *this* year's profits but *future* profits; that is, he will have to wait and see how much his bonus will be, and, if he makes bad decisions today that cost the company money tomorrow, that bonus will be smaller.[44] Easy, right? So easy that many corporations figured this out long ago.[45] Many agency problems can be solved with well-designed contracts.[46]

In short, this criticism of the theory of deterrence is pretty weak. Indeed, one sign that it is weak is what its implications are beyond class action lawsuits. The exact same principal-agent problems that some conservative critics say make corporate executives unresponsive to class action lawsuits would make them unresponsive to every other type of lawsuit as well. Are conservative critics saying that the *entire* theory of general deterrence is wrong? That would be quite ironic given that conservatives created it. Indeed, not only does this criticism suggest that the theory of deterrence is wrong; it also suggests that the theory of market feedback loops that we love so much is wrong as well. If we cannot make corporate executives respond to the threat of lawsuits, then why would we think that we can make them respond to the threat of consumer, employee, or shareholder boycotts?[47] I don't have an answer to that question. And neither do the conservative critics of class actions. The truth is this: if class action lawsuits can't deter corporate misconduct because of agency costs, then nothing else that costs the corporation money can either. If we contend that the class action lawsuits are failures, then we have to admit that other lawsuits and the market feedback loops are, too. But no conservative I know wants to admit all that.

This brings me to the second reason some conservatives say class actions don't generate deterrence: corporations cannot avoid the misconduct that leads to class actions because they cannot predict which of their activities will lead to class actions.[48] Class actions, they say, target behavior at random; no corporate executive can guess why he will be sued. If you can't predict beforehand why you will be sued, then you can't change your behavior to avoid the lawsuit. On this view, running a corporation is something like playing Russian roulette: you just go to work day in and day out never knowing which day a class action might be fired at you.

There is no doubt that there is uncertainty in our system of justice. Lawyers and judges may or may not come up with new legal doctrines. Witnesses may or may not break down on the stand. Juries may or may not see things your way. You may recall from a previous chapter that some of this uncertainty is a good thing: we don't want rigid rules in place that box companies in and prevent them from innovating; we'd rather let companies do what they want to do and make them pay the costs later if they harm people. Uncertainty means flexibility.

But it also means that it is sometimes hard to predict what will happen when a company does something new. But hard to predict does not mean impossible. If there is a fifty-fifty chance a company might lose a lawsuit, then the corporate executives do not just throw up their hands and say, "We don't know what will happen, so let's not worry about it." They do what any other rational person would do: they discount the amount of money they would pay out if they lose the lawsuit by the 50 percent chance they might *not* lose the lawsuit. Thus, harking back to the example I gave above, if putting a falsehood on a product's package will lead to a 50 percent chance the company will lose a $10 million lawsuit, the company knows this business decision is expected to cost it $5 million.

But this assumes that the company knows it might be sued for the falsehood to begin with. What if it is impossible for the company to know which of its business decisions might get it into trouble? Is it supposed to assume that every decision might lead to a 50 percent chance it will lose a lawsuit? How does it figure out what the damages would be in the lawsuit if it can't even figure out what it might be sued for to begin with?

These are all hard questions, but corporations long ago found a solution to them: they hire lawyers! Yes, they hire dozens or even hundreds of them, pay them big salaries, and ask them to do something called *risk assessment*. That's right: they sit around all day and assess the risk that the corporation might be sued for something it does and how much it might pay out if it is sued. I am most familiar with risk-assessment departments in the automotive industry because one of my colleagues, Kip Viscusi, has chronicled them in great detail,[49] but every other industry does the same sort of thing in one way or another with their in-house legal departments.[50]

Admittedly, sometimes it is too difficult even for in-house legal departments to figure all this lawsuit stuff out, but the corporations have devised a solution in these circumstances, too: they hire more lawyers! Not in-house lawyers, but outside lawyers, who work at law firms and sometimes charge $1,000 per hour or more.[51] They ask them to write opinion letters assessing whether what the corporation wants to do is legal, the chance the corporation might be sued, and what might happen if the corporation is sued[52]—in other words, all the information the corporation needs to know in order to be discouraged from misconduct by the threat of a lawsuit. I know all this because for several years I was one of the lawyers who wrote these letters. Indeed, sometimes my firm did not even wait for the corporations to ask for help; sometimes we sent unsolicited letters—for free!—on how to avoid potential lawsuits, letters just like this one: "Mitigating Consumer Fraud Class Action Litigation Risk: Top Ten Methods for 2015."[53]

I will admit that sometimes even all these lawyers are completely hopeless at seeing what the future might hold. In some physical injury cases where the harm caused by a company's products does not manifest itself for decades after the company sold the product, I admit that it may be impossible for a company to anticipate that it might be sued.[54] Who knows what law—let alone science—will look like twenty years from now? But the good news is that there are almost no class action cases of this sort; it is almost impossible to bring a class action for physical injuries.[55] More to the point: for the types of market rules that we conservatives support— breach of contract, fraud, and horizontal price-fixing—we rarely if ever have to wait twenty years to find out that we've been wronged.

This is why corporations are spending the gobs and gobs of money I mentioned assessing their risks of facing class actions and other lawsuits.

Only fools would spend gobs and gobs of money for nothing. Corporate executives may be many things, but they are not fools. They spend this money because it works: it helps them predict when they will be sued and what will happen if they are.

But you do not have to take my word for it. We can ask the corporate executives themselves. A legal scholar at Suffolk Law School, Linda Simard, did just that.[56] She sent a questionnaire to the top lawyer—the general counsel—at every company in the Fortune 500.[57] She asked these individuals about the class action lawsuits they had faced and whether they had any ability to predict the lawsuits at the time their corporations made the business decisions giving rise to the class actions.[58] Dozens of them wrote back to her. What did they say? They said that their ability to predict the class actions they had faced varied depending on what kind of lawsuits they were. For some class actions, over 90 percent of the time they said they had "moderate" or "high" ability to predict that they would be sued.[59] But even for the wiliest class actions of all—those resting on a completely novel legal theory—still 25 percent of the corporate lawyers said they had a "moderate" or "high" ability to predict they were coming.[60] Our system is hardly random if even the *new* legal theories can be anticipated 25 percent of the time. Although surveys are not necessarily the most reliable way to study the question (I get to more reliable ways in the next section),[61] it should be noted that Simard is not the only person corporate lawyers have told such things to.[62]

I should pause here to note something: even though these corporate lawyers knew they might be sued in a class action lawsuit, their companies did not always decide to refrain from the behavior; they sometimes went ahead and harmed people anyway. You might be asking yourself, How are class actions deterring anything if corporations are committing misconduct even when they know they might be sued? One answer is that even if the deterrence is imperfect—maybe damages are set too low by our laws?—it is better than nothing. But another answer goes back to the cost-benefit analysis I described earlier: we do not always want to stop corporations from harming people because sometimes the benefits to society outweigh the harms. What we do want, however, is for corporations to know they will pay for the harms before they decide to act so they act only when the benefits outweigh the harms. Class actions help them know that. (What we also want is for the people who are harmed to be made whole, and, as I explained in the previous chapter, class actions help with that, too.)

The good news in all this is that we law professors have not been misleading our students for the past fifty years: the conservative theory of general deterrence is still sound. We still have every reason to think that lawsuits—including class action lawsuits—deter corporate misconduct.

The Data on General Deterrence

Everything I have said thus far about general deterrence is a theory. It is a strong theory, as even many class action critics admit[63]—this is why every law school teaches it to every incoming class of students every single year—but it is still a theory. Naturally, the critics of class actions have picked up on this fact. Thus, the last argument that some conservatives make about class actions and deterrence is this one: the theory may be good, but you have no evidence that it actually works in practice.[64] Until we have some evidence, they suggest, we cannot assume that class actions generate any deterrence. As Linda Mullenix at the University of Texas puts it: "The deterrence theory suffers from a lack of empirical evidence and is based on conjectured hypotheses about corporate behavior. . . . [S]ocial scientists have not been able to empirically measure . . . the deterrent effect of class litigation. . . . Thus, judicial and scholarly arguments relating to the deterrent effect of class litigation are largely theoretical, conclusory pronouncements."[65]

I do not like this argument very much. We have a strong theory that class action lawsuits generate deterrence. The critics do not have a strong theory that they do not. If anyone should have the burden of coming up with some evidence, it should be the people without a theory, not the people with a theory.

But the good news is that there is indeed evidence. It is not reams and reams of evidence, but there now are several studies, they span different time periods, they involve different types of class actions, and, with one exception, they all say the same thing: class actions deter misconduct.

And these are just the class action studies. There *are* reams and reams of studies showing that other types of lawsuits deter misconduct. These other studies are not as uncontroverted as the class action studies, but there are many, many more studies finding that lawsuits generate deterrence than studies finding that they don't. These other studies are important because, as I noted above, some of the arguments critics raise about the theory of deterrence are not specific to class action lawsuits: if the evidence shows that corporate executives respond to the threat of individual lawsuits, then there is reason to think that they respond to the threat of class action lawsuits, too.

One note about these studies: many of them do not measure misconduct directly. That is because it is often impossible to measure misconduct directly. For example, it is impossible to observe whether companies are secretly conspiring with one another to fix prices—they do it in secret! Thus, most of the studies discussed below measure deterrence by looking at proxies for misconduct rather than misconduct itself—for example, for price fixing, the studies look at whether prices go up or down. It's not perfect, but it is the best science can do right now. But the best science can do suggests that lawsuits deter misconduct.

Let's start with the class action studies.

In 1981, several economists set out to examine whether increasing the threat of an antitrust enforcement action by the federal government deterred companies from price fixing.[66] They examined the white bread industry. (This was back before nutrition was popular.) They looked at the markup (the price above the price of the ingredients) on a loaf of white bread in various places in the United States between 1965 and 1976; the markup was their proxy for potential price fixing.[67] They compared these markups to the enforcement budget of the US Department of Justice's Antitrust Division over time. They hypothesized that, the more money the federal government devoted to enforcement, the greater the threat of an enforcement action against price fixers would become; thus, if federal enforcement deterred price fixing, the markups would be smaller when the federal government's enforcement budget was bigger.[68]

But that's not what they found. The federal government's enforcement budget had no effect on price markups until 1972; only then did a bigger budget lead to lower prices.[69] Why? The economists concluded that only after 1972 did companies face the threat of private antitrust class action lawsuits (recall that only in 1966 was the modern money damages class action created) and that *it was the private lawsuits that the companies were afraid of.*[70] They found that "settlements in class actions for price fixing in the bread industry were almost 10 times greater than government-imposed fines" and that "the deterrent effect of [Department of Justice] enforcement efforts came not from the threat of publicly imposed fines or imprisonment, but from the increased likelihood of an award of private treble damages."[71] In other words: "Class actions represent the effective penalty in price-fixing cases."[72]

There have been several more recent studies, all of them concerning securities fraud class actions, and, with one exception, all of them likewise find that, the greater the threat of a lawsuit, the less corporate misconduct.

Two of these studies examined what happened when a US Supreme Court decision in 2010 insulated some foreign companies from American securities fraud class action lawsuits. The securities fraud laws make it illegal for companies to misrepresent or hide relevant information from shareholders. When the threat of class action lawsuits went away, did the companies disclose less information to their shareholders than they had before? Both studies found that the answer was a resounding yes: the threat of a class action lawsuit had induced the companies to be more forthcoming with their shareholders.[73]

A third study examined disclosures to shareholders over a larger set of companies and over a longer time period, 1996–2010.[74] The authors attempted to compare disclosure made by companies at a higher risk of facing securities fraud class actions to disclosure made by those at a lower risk; they identified which companies faced higher risks with a model that depended on the size of the company, the company's industry (e.g., whether a software company or a biotechnology company), and a host of other variables.[75] What did they find? They found that companies at higher risk of being sued disclosed more information to shareholders, updated their disclosures more often, and rendered those disclosures in more readable language than did companies at lower risk.[76] To top it all off, they also examined whether this disclosure gap narrowed after 2005 when the Securities and Exchange Commission started requiring all companies—whether they were at high or low risk of being sued—to disclose all the same information on the forms they file every year with the federal government.[77] They found that the gap did indeed narrow when the companies no longer had any choice but to make the disclosures.[78] This means that, when the companies did have a choice, it was the threat of a securities fraud class action that made them do it.

A fourth study looked at what influenced corporate decisions to misrepresent earnings to shareholders in the years 1997–2008. Did the fact that a company got sued in a securities fraud class action for earnings manipulation discourage *other companies* in that same industry or geographic region from manipulating their own earnings? Here again, after controlling for numerous other variables, the authors concluded that the answer was yes: class actions deter misbehavior.[79]

Against these five class action studies, I found only one study that points in the opposite direction. Three scholars examined whether American corporations disclose more information to shareholders than Canadian corporations do.[80] Because American securities fraud laws are more robust, that is what the deterrence theory would suggest. But they found precisely the opposite: more disclosure in Canada.[81] As I noted in a previous chapter, it is hard to do cross-country empirical studies because it is impossible to control for all the ways in which different countries differ from one another. And this study is directly contradicted by the several American-only studies, discussed above, showing that more liability leads to more disclosure. As a result, I do not put much stock in the Canadian study. And, as I said, it is the *only* contrary study I have found.

What about studies of other lawsuits? These studies are even *more numerous*. For decades and decades, scholars have studied the data on deterrence, and, for decades and decades, the studies have generally corroborated what the class action studies show: the threat of a lawsuit deters misconduct.

The studies outside the class action realm are too numerous to discuss comprehensively here. And not all of them deal with misconduct by corporations. But I will summarize them to give you a taste of what they say:

- *Tort liability and safety research.* Scholars have found that the industries that face more tort liability spend more money researching safety measures for their products.[82]
- *Workers' compensation and workplace injuries.* Scholars have found that, when the benefits employers would have to pay out for workplace injuries increased, fewer workplace deaths followed.[83]
- *Bartender liability and alcohol-related traffic deaths.* Scholars have found that, when liability was imposed on bartenders for inebriated driving by their patrons, fewer alcohol-related traffic deaths followed.[84]
- *Medical malpractice liability and negligence, deaths, and defensive medicine.* Scholars have found that, when liability for medical malpractice decreases, doctors and hospitals spend less time and money on patients,[85] and more medical negligence and deaths follow.[86]
- *Tort reform and traffic accidents*: Scholars have found that, when liability for traffic accidents decreases, more traffic accidents follow.[87]

As I said, these studies are not uncontroverted, and I have cited opposing studies in the notes.[88] But the important point is that the lion's share of studies *support* the theory of general deterrence. Indeed, as two of the famous conservative Chicago school economists conclude: "What empirical evidence there is indicates that tort law deters."[89]

None of this should be surprising to conservatives. We invented the theory of deterrence. We've been teaching it to our students for fifty years. We should be happy to learn that we've been right all this time!

CHAPTER NINE

The Conservative Class Action

Throughout this book, I have attempted to respond to the criticisms that we hear about the class action. Sometimes I have said that those criticisms are unfounded, and I tried to point to data showing as much. Other times I have said those criticisms are inconsistent with fundamental conservative principles, such as preferring private sector solutions to social problems. But sometimes I have said that the criticisms have validity; my answer to these criticisms was, not to throw the class action out in its entirety, but to tweak it so we could keep the good and get rid of the bad. In this chapter, I explain how conservative principles can reform the class action. As I say throughout this book, we can mend it; we don't have to end it.

Limit Class Actions to the Enforcement of Laws We Actually Like

Let me begin with the most serious beef that conservatives have with the class action and the reason why I say I believe that conservatives turned their backs on private enforcement to begin with: class actions are used to enforce laws that we do not like. As I explained in a previous chapter, I believe that the reason why conservatives abandoned private enforcement during the Reagan administration is that they came to the realization that it was not politically possible to roll back all the unnecessary rules and regulations that had been imposed on businesses; the second-best solution to free business from these undue burdens was to undermine the enforcement of the law. I agree with conservatives that we regulate businesses way too much. I also agree that it is a shame that we have been unable to persuade our fellow citizens of that. My own preference would be to fight all this out in the democratic process, but I understand why impatient conservatives have tried to do the next best thing and roll back enforcement instead, including rolling back class action lawsuits. Even still, there is no reason to roll back *all* class action enforcement; we should roll back only those class actions that enforce the laws we don't like.

Which laws would those be? As I said in a previous chapter, almost all conservatives believe that we need laws against breach of contract, fraud, and price fixing. We should at least keep class actions for those laws. Some conservatives may quibble with some of the laws we label *fraud* and some breach-of-contract doctrines. Fair enough. If we don't like certain aspects of fraud and contract laws, then we can say that class actions can't be used to enforce those aspects. But, in the main, we should keep the class action for breach of contract, fraud, and price fixing.

I think that a principled conservative could stop there, but many of us won't stop there. After securities class actions, the next biggest category of class actions is employment and labor cases.[1] Although many conservative scholars do not believe that we should saddle businesses with minimum wage, overtime, employment discrimination, and employment benefit laws,[2] many conservative policymakers do not share these views anymore. So conservatives may disagree among themselves about which laws we want vigorously enforced and which laws we don't. But my point is that we can pick and choose; we can have as many class actions as we want or as few as we want. It does not have to be all or nothing.

It is true that this would be something of a change for our procedural rules in court. Our system of rules is what we academics call *transsubstantive*: the exact same procedural rules apply no matter what type of lawsuit you bring, whether for fraud or something else.[3] The idea is that our system is easier to navigate if lawyers must learn only one set of procedures for every case than if every case has a different set of procedures.[4] Fair enough. But I am not talking about changing every procedure; I am talking about changing one procedure. It would not overly complicate our system to make class actions available in some cases and not others. Indeed, we already have that system, but by judicial interpretation rather than rule: it is almost impossible to certify class actions for physical injuries as opposed to those for economic injuries. Yet we've managed just fine.

Limit Class Actions to Remedies That Do Not Overdeter

There is one big category of class action cases, however, that I think all conservatives should want to rein in: those known as statutory damages class actions. I mentioned these class actions in a previous chapter. *Statutory damages* are monetary remedies that are fixed by statute for certain violations of the law; plaintiffs can recover these damages regardless of how much or how little they were injured by the defendant. Congress and state legislatures intentionally set these damages much higher than plaintiffs are usually injured.[5] A prominent example is the federal Telephone Consumer Protection Act; the law says that every single one of us is entitled to $500 (or even $1,500 in some circumstances) every time a merchant uses a robo dialer to call our cell phones without our permission.[6] Annoying as it is when companies do this to us, I think that most of us would be hard-pressed to say that we are injured $500 every time this happens to us. So why did Congress give us more? To induce us to sue. Congress thought that no one would sue if they could get only their actual damages; companies would therefore be able to use robo dialers with impunity. In order to deter this misconduct, Congress gives us a bonus if we are one of the courageous ones who comes forward.[7] It was hoped that enough people would come forward to make companies think twice about doing this.

All this makes perfect sense in a world without class actions. If few people will sue when they are injured, give the ones who do a bonus, and hope that the bonuses add up to cover all the harm of the people who don't sue; that way companies know that, if they robo dial people without their permission, they will have to pay the total amount of harm they cause. This gives companies the right incentives: they will robo dial only if the benefits to consumers outweigh the harm. This is the conservative theory of deterrence through lawsuits that I mentioned in a previous chapter. But, in a world with class actions, there is no reason to give people bonuses anymore. We don't need to induce people to come forward because, by definition, the class action includes everyone who has been robo dialed by the defendant. If we give *everyone* a bonus—not just the select few who sued—the company will end up paying much, much more than it caused in actual harm. That's great if you want to put companies out of business indiscriminately; it's not so great if you want to induce companies to avoid harming people unless the benefit outweighs the harm.

When I say *put companies out of business indiscriminately*, I am not exaggerating. I have seen robo-dial cases where all the phone calls would add up to over $1 trillion.[8] No company—not even Apple!—can pay that. It would not be socially desirable to put Apple out of business over some cell phone calls. We call this *overdeterrence*. As I noted in a previous chapter, companies complain that class actions lead to overdeterrence like this all the time.

In order to avoid overdeterrence, I think that what we lawyers call *extracompensatory damages* should not be recoverable in class action lawsuits. If you want to bring a robo-dial class action, you should not be able to recover any more than the class's actual harm; if you don't like that, then go ahead and sue individual by individual for $500 a call.[9] The same goes for so-called treble damages—that is, *tripling* of actual damages—awarded under the antitrust and racketeering laws. It also goes for punitive damages generally. None of these things should be recoverable in class actions because they threaten, not just deterrence, but overdeterrence. Other conservative scholars agree.[10]

Delay Discovery in Meritless Cases and Make It Even Easier to Dismiss Them

As I explained in a previous chapter, many corporations complain that class action cases are meritless but that they are forced to settle them nonetheless owing to the expense and risk of defending class actions. I agree that class actions can be expensive and risky to defend—and I offer some proposals to mitigate these things below. But I do not agree that the cases companies are settling are meritless. As I noted, corporations have an inexpensive device to get rid of meritless cases: the motion to dismiss. If companies settle class action cases, it is usually because they have some merit. This doesn't mean that companies don't overpay to settle these meritorious cases because of litigation expenses and risk—that's what I take up below—but it does mean that the notion that our system is overrun with meritless cases is not true.

There are only two circumstances in which a company might pay to settle a meritless case despite the availability of the motion to dismiss. One is where the judge does not delay *discovery*—the stage of the case at which the parties gather and exchange evidence—while the company's motion to dismiss is pending. It defeats the entire purpose of the motion to dismiss to make companies pay to continue litigating the case while the motion is pending; if the judge ends up dismissing the case, all that money is wasted. I can understand why companies would settle meritless cases to avoid wasting that money. Most judges delay discovery while the motion to dismiss is pending, but some do not.[11] In my view, we should change the rules to make discovery delays mandatory. We've already done this for securities fraud class actions;[12] we ought to do it for other class actions, too.

The other circumstance occurs when the judge makes a mistake and denies a motion to dismiss when he or she shouldn't, thereby saddling companies with the choice of paying a lot of money to lawyers to defend the case or settling instead. Judges, like the rest of us, are not perfect; they make mistakes, too. We correct those mistakes by letting litigants appeal mistaken decisions to higher courts, but litigants can usually do that only after the case is over.[13] That means that a corporation would have to pay to go through all the other stages of a case—discovery, summary judgment, and trial—in order to appeal a mistaken opinion at the beginning. That's expensive. Indeed, the fact that a judge might make a mistaken decision on the motion to dismiss is exacerbated by the ability of class action lawyers to do what we lawyers call *forum shop*: like all lawyers, class action lawyers choose to file their cases in courts where they think the judges will treat them most favorably. That is, they may seek out courts with lenient attitudes toward motions to dismiss, thereby increasing the chance that a meritless case will slip through.

Although I am not sure how big a problem this really is—as I noted in a previous chapter, it is hard to find examples of ridiculous cases that survive a motion to dismiss—we can do something about it if we think it is a problem. We can let corporations appeal judges' decisions denying their motions to dismiss right away. As I noted, we usually make litigants wait until the end to appeal, but sometimes we let parties appeal in the middle. We call this an *interlocutory appeal*: the case isn't over yet, but we pause it for a while to let the appeals court take a look at what the lower court did.

We have long been more willing to let parties take interlocutory appeals in class action cases.[14] Why? Because the expense and risk of a class action are so great that companies almost always settle these cases in the end, thereby denying an appellate court the opportunity to review what the lower court did.[15]

Allowing defendants to take an interlocutory appeal of denial of their motions to dismiss will obviously delay class action cases; that is the downside to interlocutory appeals: piecemeal appeals make our system less efficient.[16] Nonetheless, class action cases are not such a big portion of our court system that permitting more interlocutory appeals would muck things up much.[17] At the same time, these cases are more important than the typical case, which justifies more judicial scrutiny.[18] But, if all of that isn't enough to convince you, consider this: the current rule against interlocutory appeals gives plaintiffs something of an advantage. Why? Because, if the court *grants* the defendant's motion to dismiss, plaintiffs *do* have the ability to take an immediate appeal (because the case is over when it is dismissed). If plaintiffs can appeal the decisions they don't like on the motion to dismiss, it's hard to see why defendants shouldn't be able to do so, too.

I am not the only scholar who believes that we should make it easier to dismiss meritless class action cases. Although their proposals are different from mine, even scholars who aren't particularly conservative share this view.[19]

Make Class Actions Less Risky

As I noted above and at various points throughout this book, there may be some validity to the concern of corporations that they pay more than they should to settle class action cases because defending class actions are so risky: because one jury decides much or all of the class action trial, corporations risk a single jury messing up, not one person's claim, but thousands or even millions of people's claims. Thus, an outlier jury could sock the company with millions or billions of dollars in damages in these circumstances—even if the average jury would award nothing at all or only a small amount. Companies say that this forces them to settle cases rather than go to trial. If class action lawyers know that corporations have no choice but to settle, then they can extract a premium from them during settlement negotiations: corporations will be willing to settle for, not what they believe the average jury outcome will be, but also some amount above that to avoid the unlikely possibility of the extreme jury outcome.[20] This is known in scholarly circles as *risk aversion*.[21]

The problem with risk premiums is that they can lead to the same sort of overdeterrence that I described above when I discussed extracompensatory damages: if corporations systematically pay more than the harm they cause, then we will end up chilling socially useful corporate activity—that is, activity for which the benefits to society outweigh the harms. We want corporations to pay for the harm they cause, not less than that, and not more than that either. Risk aversion can force companies to pay too much.

Some scholars doubt that corporations are ever really willing to pay risk premiums.[22] They note that corporations usually have liability insurance to pay any class action judgments against them, and, by definition, insurers are not risk averse: they are in the business of diversifying their risk exposure.[23] On the other hand, corporations are run by people, and the people may worry about their job security if the company has to pay a big judgment on their watch. Thus, corporate officials might be willing to pay risk premiums even though corporate shareholders may not want them to.[24] This is another example of what I have called *agency costs*: costs companies bear because their agents do things that are in the agents' best interest rather than the company's best interest. Although, as I noted in the previous chapter, agency costs can be mitigated with well-designed employment contracts, I am not sure that the willingness to pay risk premiums can be mitigated quite as easily as other agency costs can be. So there may be some validity to the complaint that the riskiness of class actions leads companies to overpay to settle cases.

At the end of the day, I am not sure how big of a problem corporate risk aversion really is. Even if corporations do exhibit risk aversion, class action lawyers can also be risk averse. Class action lawyers don't have as much insurance as corporations do, and they put their livelihoods at risk when they take cases on contingency in a way that not even corporate officials do when they defend these cases. All this makes class action lawyers willing to *accept too little* to settle cases.[25] Thus, risk aversion may cancel itself out in the end.

Nonetheless, there is an easy way to make class action trials less risky, and I see little reason not to do it, for the good of both sides. How? By doing what statisticians call *sampling*: instead of letting one jury decide all the class's claims, we could randomly pick a small number of class members—maybe ten or twenty—and try their claims individually before different juries and then average the results over the rest of the class.[26] Companies would not be so afraid of trial if they had ten or twenty chances; if one jury did something really extreme, it would get averaged out by the other juries.[27]

Scholars have advocated sampling for many years,[28] and some courts have tried it,[29] but the Supreme Court put a damper on the idea a few years ago in a case called *Wal-Mart v. Dukes*.[30] The Court decried "Trial by Formula" and suggested that using sampling could violate the due process rights of defendants.[31] But the sampling at issue in *Wal-Mart*—and the sampling that other courts have tried—is different than what I am proposing here. The courts that used sampling in the past did so to get around individual defenses that defendants wanted to raise to particular class members' claims; these defenses would have made the class action unwieldy, so courts blew past them by using sampling: they examined individual defenses in a few cases and then applied the results to other class members.[32] I am not proposing using sampling to facilitate class action treatment for cases that would otherwise be inappropriate for class action treatment; I am proposing using sampling for cases that are otherwise appropriate for class treatment. Nothing changes under my proposal except for the fact that, rather than one jury deciding the class's claims, multiple juries would do so. But, if we are really worried that this might interfere with the due process rights of defendants, we could make my proposal available at the option of defendants: if they consent—and they should want to—then there can be no violation of their due process rights.[33]

You may be worried that my proposal will greatly increase the expense of class action litigation because now the parties must prepare for ten or twenty trials rather than just one. But I doubt that many more cases will go to trial under my proposal. Parties will still settle their cases—it is too rational not to do so because parties who settle can avoid litigation expenses[34]—but now they will settle against a backdrop of a trial format that is not so risky. If the trial format is less risky, then defendants will have less reason to pay a risk premium.

Share Discovery Expenses with Plaintiffs

As I also noted throughout this book, there may be some validity to the concern of corporations that they pay more than they should to settle class action cases because defending class actions is too expensive.[35] Research by economists shows that parties may settle litigation for more than what they expect a jury might award in order to avoid paying the litigation expenses that would be needed to get the case all the way through a jury trial.[36] For example, let us say that a corporation believes that the average jury would award $1 million to the class if a class action case went to trial. But it would cost the corporation another $1 million to litigate the case. A rational company would be willing to settle this case for up to $2 million even though, if the average jury award is an accurate reflection of the harm that the corporation caused, the company caused only $1 million in harm.[37] If companies systematically pay more than the harm they cause because of litigation expenses, then, again, we could end up with socially undesirable overdeterrence.

The same dynamic occurs on the plaintiff side: plaintiffs are willing to settle cases for less than the expected jury award to avoid their own litigation expenses. Thus, we might think that litigation expenses cancel each other out and result in settlements at the right price. But many scholars think that is not correct: it is thought that defendants have much greater litigation expenses than do class action plaintiffs and that, for this reason, the settlement range is skewed against them.[38]

The main reason why defendants are thought to pay so much more in litigation expenses than are class action plaintiffs in the same cases is because of a phase of litigation I mentioned above called *discovery*. In discovery, each side is given the opportunity to ask the other side for information. You can ask the other side to answer your questions. You can take testimony from the other side's witnesses under oath. And you can ask the other side to turn over relevant documents to you.

It's that last thing that drives up corporate discovery costs. Corporations have lots and lots and lots of computer files and other data they have to look through to find all the documents class action lawyers request. This creates perverse incentives: class action lawyers can ask for more and more and more, forcing defendants to pay more and more and more in litigation expenses, slowly driving up the settlement value of their cases.[39] Can't corporations do the same thing to the class action lawyers? Ask them for more and more and more documents from class members? No. Class action plaintiffs rarely have any documents at all to turn over. If you or I filed a class action against a company for fraud because something we bought was mislabeled, how many documents in our files at home or on our computer could we possibly need to find for the lawsuit? Maybe our store receipt showing we bought the product? The company we sued would have to look through billions upon billions of documents to find all the emails and other documents its employees circulated about that label we are suing about.

In other words, discovery expenses can lead companies systematically to oversettle cases, fostering more overdeterrence. Thus, they are a valid corporate concern. The solution, however, is not to throw out the class action altogether. The solution is to do something about discovery expenses.

Indeed, scholars and policymakers have been trying to do something about discovery expenses for a long time,[40] and the current reform is to ask judges to curtail the plaintiff's discovery requests if they seem unreasonable and to ask plaintiffs to pay for some of those costs even if the requests are reasonable.[41] I do not like the current reform because it will create a lot of additional litigation over what should be discovered and who should pay how much for it.[42] I prefer something simpler and more effective: to require plaintiffs to pay the same amount of money that they force companies to pay when the companies respond to their discovery requests. I call this idea the *discovery tax*.[43] Plaintiffs would pay this tax automatically and without any need to ask the court to get involved. The tax would both *discipline plaintiffs* not to be so cavalier with their requests for information—it is easy to request information when it is free; it is harder when you have to pay for it—and *maintain discipline on corporations* to be efficient in their production of information.[44] As we academics put it, my tax idea would force both sides to a lawsuit to fully internalize the costs of discovery, thereby getting everyone's incentives right.

If this idea seems too radical, we could start with a smaller tax—for example, make plaintiffs pay 5 percent of what they force defendants to pay—and see how that goes. But the important point is this: some form of discovery-cost sharing is needed to mitigate the overdeterrence that can result from litigation expenses—and doing it automatically rather than by asking courts to get involved on every discovery request like we do now would be even more effective. Again, I am not the only conservative scholar who believes things like this.[45]

Some people worry that class action lawyers will not have access to the necessary resources to pay even a portion of the defendants' discovery costs. It is true that class action lawyers do not have bank accounts as big as the corporations they sue. But they have plenty of access to capital these days, whether from other lawyers, from banks, or from the burgeoning industry known as *third-party litigation finance*.[46] What is third-party finance? Hedge funds and other investors are buying shares of lawsuits or extending nonrecourse loans to class action lawyers and others.[47] In other words, if your lawsuit is profitable, someone these days will give you money to file and prosecute it. Litigants in other countries have relied on third-party financing for a long time to deal with fee and cost sharing in litigation.[48] There's no reason why litigants in our country can't do so as well.

Better Align Lawyers' Profit Motives with Good Results

Throughout this book I address conservative concerns that the profit motive will inevitably lead class action lawyers to overenforce the law and file abusive class action lawsuits. I have generally parried these concerns by explaining that, as with any other profit motive, we can put rules in place to channel it toward good, socially useful behavior and away from bad, socially destructive behavior. We do this with corporate profit motives all the time.

Some of the other reforms I advocate in this chapter—especially sharing discovery expenses—will help channel the profit motive of class action lawyers toward good behavior. But more can be done. Indeed, I spoke at length in chapter 7 about the reforms we should adopt when it comes to calculating the attorneys' fees that class action lawyers earn when they settle or win a class action case. For the most part, thanks to conservative law and economics theory, courts are doing a pretty good job aligning the incentives of lawyers with the results they obtain for class members. But I summarize here my proposed changes:

- Unless we have no other choice—because a fee-shifting statute demands it or a settlement consists only of injunctive relief and no cash—courts should award lawyers a percentage of what they recover rather than pay them by the hour, just like all other contingency fee lawyers in America. Lawyers who are paid by the hour have the incentive to drag cases along; lawyers who are paid a percentage have the incentive to recover the most they can as quickly as possible. Some courts try to sneak the hourly method—known as the *lodestar method*—in the back door by crosschecking the percentage award with class counsel's hours. This has the effect of capping class counsel's percentage at a multiple of class counsel's hours. It gives class counsel all the same bad incentives as the lodestar method itself. Courts should stop crosschecking and pay class action lawyers for their results and their results alone. If anything, they should pay class action lawyers a percentage *plus* their lodestar.
- Courts should award lawyers a percentage of everything they recover that contributes to compensation and deterrence—including payments to charities, monies spent on notice and processing class member claims, and future savings reaped from behavior-modification provisions—not just the cash that immediately ends up in class members' hands. For example, sometimes the money the lawyers recover cannot be distributed to class members because it is too

difficult or expensive to find them. If the money goes to a charity instead, the lawyers should still be awarded a percentage of that money. Why? Because, even though class members are not being compensated, the corporation is being deterred from misconduct when it has to pay money to someone; it does not matter for the purpose of deterrence whom it pays. Class members and all the rest of us benefit from deterrence because corporations are less likely to cheat us in the first place if they know they will have to pay for all the harm they cause, even when it is difficult to return the money to the victims.

- Courts should award lawyers a percentage of everything they recover only if they actually recover it, not if they only potentially recover it. Under current US Supreme Court precedent, courts are permitted to award lawyers a percentage of the face value of class action settlements even if some of the money ends up going back to the defendant. Money that goes back to the defendant does not further compensation or deterrence, and lawyers should not be rewarded for it.
- Courts should not cut the percentages they award lawyers when the lawyers recover more money. This ends up giving class action lawyers the incentive to settle big cases for less rather than more so they can free up time to work on smaller cases where the percentage awarded will be higher. If anything, courts should *increase* fee percentages as recoveries increase.

Amend the Federal Arbitration Act

None of the reforms I offer in this chapter will make any difference if something is not done about arbitration clauses with class action waivers. As I explained in the first chapter, 5–4 majorities of the US Supreme Court have said that corporations can ask all of us to waive our rights to join class actions so long as they do so in arbitration agreements. The Supreme Court said so even if state contract law would hold the class action waivers unenforceable; the Court said that a federal law, the Federal Arbitration Act of 1925, overrides state laws. As I explained, if these decisions are allowed to stand, it is only a matter of time until few, if any, class actions will be filed against big corporations. Thus, for any of this chapter to matter, Congress must amend the Federal Arbitration Act to make it clear that class action waivers are not enforceable over contrary state contract law.

But is amending the Federal Arbitration Act the conservative thing to do? Aren't arbitration clauses freely agreed to by consenting adults?

Didn't I explain in chapter 2 that we conservatives like to enforce contracts? Why *shouldn't* we override state law if it is interfering with freely agreed to class action waivers?

These are good questions, but there are answers to them.

To begin with, many people think that arbitration clauses are not freely agreed to.[49] When is the last time you noticed the arbitration clause in a contract you signed or on the packaging of a product you bought? I suspect you have never noticed one. Few of us have. And, even if we had noticed it, would we be able to tell the company to take it out? No. Most contracts these days are take it or leave it; negotiation is not allowed. For this reason, many people believe that there is no real meeting of the minds when it comes to arbitration clauses; no one really consents to these things.[50] And one of the primary reasons that libertarian conservatives like to enforce contracts is because they are voluntary, consensual transactions. On the other hand, as I explained in a previous chapter, contract law long ago left behind the meeting of minds as one of its touchstones; we traded the liberty of subjective consent for the utilitarian speed and efficiency of objective consent.[51] If we say that arbitration clauses are invalid for lack of real consent, we would have to say that pretty much all contract law these days is invalid for the same reason. Few conservatives want to say that, including me. So this is not reason enough to amend the Federal Arbitration Act.

Other people think that, even if arbitration clauses could be freely agreed to, people are not capable of assessing them rationally. This is the finding of behavioral economics that I mentioned in the previous chapter.[52] Behavioral economists say that we systematically underappreciate provisions in contracts like arbitration clauses because they involve distant events that are unlikely to occur—that is, a dispute with a merchant or an employer.[53] Some of them go so far as to say that courts should not enforce provisions that people cannot evaluate rationally.[54] As I explained in the last chapter, not many conservatives like the policy prescriptions of behavioral economics because they are so paternalistic: we don't like someone else us telling us when we are and when we aren't rational enough to enter into a contract.[55]

But conservatives sometimes *do* think that we should override contracts for other reasons. I mentioned two examples in chapter 2: contracts procured by fraud and contracts to engage in price fixing. As I explained, fraud is much like theft, and it is easy to see why conservatives are against that. But price fixing is a little different. Why shouldn't two merchants be able to agree among themselves on prices? The answer that conservatives give is this one: because that would be bad for competition in the marketplace. Although it would be good for the parties to the contract, it would be bad for everyone else. We call that a *negative externality*, and it is one of the most fundamental reasons conservatives and libertarians believe that it is permissible for government to interfere with markets.[56]

I think that class action waivers pose a similar negative externality. When you agree to waive your right to be part of a class action, it hurts, not just you, but other people. How? Because, as I explained in the last chapter, one of the principal benefits of the class action is that it deters misconduct. Even if a class action is never filed, the mere threat of one stops companies from doing bad things. But, as the law and economics scholar Keith Hylton has shown, if enough people sign a class action waiver, then the company knows that it will not face a class action and, therefore, will not be deterred from committing small misdeeds.[57] This means that even someone who *didn't* sign the waiver will suffer.[58] That's an externality, and it's a bad one: if companies do not face serious threats that the law will be enforced, then they won't follow the law, including the laws that conservatives believe are necessary for the market to work in the first place. If we conservatives want companies to follow any rules at all in the marketplace—and, as I explained in chapter 2, we do—then we can't let people opt out of enforcement of those rules.[59] In other words, deterrence is a positive externality that the law should not let us contract away.

But, if that is not enough to persuade you that amending the Federal Arbitration Act is the conservative thing to do, here is an easier reason: states' rights. The truth of the matter is that contract law is none of the federal government's business. It has been the traditional domain of the states since the founding of the country.[60] The Federal Arbitration Act was intended to respect that: it says that it does not override any "grounds as exist" in state law "for the revocation of any contract." As I explained in chapter 1, in a feat of jurisprudential jujitsu,[61] the conservatives on the Supreme Court read those words to exclude normal state law doctrines for the revocation of any contract that have existed for decades. That wasn't very good textual analysis, and, when it overrides a traditional do-main of the states, it isn't very conservative, either.

Is Any of This Possible?

I suspect that many of my conservative friends will have the following re-action to this list of ideas: Some of these are great thoughts, but are they possible? Many of these changes will require cooperation from liberals—liberals in Congress or liberals on the committees that propose changes in the rules of procedure. If it were so easy to get liberals to agree to things like this, conservatives wouldn't have had to get behind the scorched-earth, end-all-class-actions position that we've gotten behind. We fell into this position because that was the only one available to us: we needed only the five conservatives on US Supreme Court to reinterpret the Federal Arbitration Act to deliver it.

I sympathize with this reaction: over the past thirty years, it has been difficult to get liberals in Congress or on the committees to go along with reform because reform would take work away from class action lawyers and class action lawyers are now a major financial constituency of the Democratic Party. Occasionally they did so: hence the Private Securities Litigation Reform Act of 1995 and the Class Action Fairness Act of 2005. But, as I explained in chapter 1, these laws made relatively minor adjustments to class action litigation; I am advocating something more serious here. I understand why Republicans decided that more meaningful reform was impossible in Congress and the rules committees and that the next best thing was just to ask the Supreme Court to get rid of the class action altogether.

But I don't think this logic holds any longer. Liberals are now *very eager* to compromise on class actions because of those same Supreme Court decisions on the Federal Arbitration Act. The status quo is no longer lots and lots of class actions like it was before 2011. The status quo is now few and maybe no class actions. If liberals want to save class actions, they have to come to the bargaining table. The truth of the matter is this: conservatives hold all the cards now; we no longer have to throw the baby out with the bathwater.

I suspect that my liberal friends will say the following in response to this: Why would the Chamber of Commerce go along with any of this? If the status quo is few and maybe no class actions, why would the Chamber go along with reforms that would bring class actions back? And, if the Chamber doesn't go along with it, then what chance is there that Republican politicians would?

I don't expect the Chamber to want to bring class actions back, even with these reforms. For the Chamber, the optimal number of class actions is zero. But, as I noted in the introduction, what the Chamber wants and what conservative principles demand are two different things. As Milton Friedman told us, it is up to the rest of us—not the Chamber—to save the free enterprise system. Although some Republican politicians will never cross the Chamber, there are plenty of others who will when they believe that conservative principles demand it. There are plenty who vote for states' rights over Chamber demands for watered-down regulation from Washington or vote against the crony capitalism of government subsidies for some corporations but not others.[62] There are even some Republican politicians who have already bucked the Chamber on class action lawsuits. When the Chamber recently sought to drive another stake through the heart of class actions in the US Congress, not only did the Democrats oppose the move, but so did a group of Republicans who call themselves the House Liberty Caucus.[63]

I hope that this book will convince other conservatives that the optimal number of class action lawsuits is not zero. We really can mend the class action. We really don't have to end it.

Notes

Introduction

1. Milton Friedman, "The Source of Strength" (speech delivered to the Presidents' Club of Michigan General Corp., April 2, 1977), 3–4. It should be noted that Friedman worried only about the corrupting influence on government of *big* businesses. As he says: "The one group in this country that over and over again is on the right side, in my opinion, has been the group of small businessmen." Ibid. This rivalry between big and small business continues to this day; "many economists say" we are now experiencing a "decline in the creation of new businesses" because "the rising power of the biggest corporations . . . is stifling entrepreneurship by making it easier for incumbent businesses to swat away challengers." Ben Casselman, "The Start-Up Slump Is a Drag on the Economy; Maybe Big Business Is to Blame," *New York Times*, September 21, 2017.

2. Milton Friedman, *Bright Promises, Dismal Performance: An Economist's Protest* (Wilmington, MA: Mariner, 1983), 131. See also Luigi Zingales bemoaning "the intellectual confusion between a promarket system and a probusiness one." *A Capitalism for the People: Recapturing the Lost Genius of American Prosperity* (New York: Basic, 2012), 254.

3. See, e.g., Ken Connor, "Federal Preemption: Crony Capitalism at Its Worst," Renew America, November 15, 2008, http://www.renewamerica.com/columns/connor/081115.

4. See sec.5 of the Fairness in Class Action Litigation and Furthering Asbestos Claim Transparency Act of 2017, HR 985: "In coordinated or consolidated pretrial proceedings for personal injury claims conducted by judges assigned by the judicial panel on multidistrict litigation, plaintiffs must . . . receive not less than 80% of any monetary recovery obtained for those claims."

5. See Brian T. Fitzpatrick, "An Empirical Study of Class Action Settlements and Their Fee Awards," *Journal of Empirical Legal Studies* 7, no. 4 (2010): 811–46, 825, table 4.

6. Bill Rubenstein traces to the 1940s the use of the precise term *private attorney general* as a "label to describe private attorneys whose work for private clients contributes to the public interest by supplementing the government's enforcement of laws and public policies." William B. Rubenstein, "On What a 'Private Attorney General' Is—and Why It Matters," *Vanderbilt Law Review* 57, no. 6 (2004): 2129–73, 2146. But Judge Jed Rakoff traces the idea back even further:

> Litigation originated by lawyers . . . [is] justified by the concept of the "private attorney general." At least since the time of the Civil War, various federal laws had provided "bounties," i.e., financial incentives, for private parties to bring actions that would supplement federal enforcement. Thus, the False Claims Act, enacted in 1863, provided that a private party could bring a lawsuit for a fraud committed against the federal government that the government itself had not yet detected. . . . The Sherman Antitrust Act, enacted in 1890, guaranteed that victims of antitrust violations who successfully sued the violators would receive mandatory treble damages, plus their attorneys' fees—the theory being that these rewards would both motivate antitrust victims to expose violations of which the government was not yet aware and enhance deterrence of violations even in the those instances where the government had already discovered the misconduct.
>
> Based on such precedents, proponents of private class actions argued that while the cases might be originated by lawyers, those lawyers . . . were serving the "established" role of private attorneys general.

"The Cure for Corporate Wrongdoing: Class Actions vs. Individual Prosecutions," *New York Review of Books*, November 11, 2015.

7. See Harry Kalven Jr. and Maurice Rosenfield, "The Contemporary Function of the Class Suit," *University of Chicago Law Review* 8, no. 4 (1941): 684–721, 686. To justify his veto, Roosevelt said: "The bill that is now before me is one of the repeated efforts . . . to have all processes of Government conducted through lawsuits [rather than] regulation." Franklin D. Roosevelt, "Veto of a Bill Regulating Administrative Agencies," December 8, 1940, The American Presidency Project, http://www.presidency.ucsb.edu/ws/index.php?pid=15914.

8. See Stephen B. Burbank and Sean Farhang, *Rights and Retrenchment: The Counterrevolution against Federal Litigation* (New York: Cambridge University Press, 2017), 12.

9. Much of this history is chronicled by Burbank and Farhang. Consider, e.g., their description of the debate over the Civil Rights Act of 1964: "Wielding the powers of a pivotal voting bloc, conservative Republicans stripped the EEOC of the strong administrative powers in the bill initially proposed by civil rights

liberals, and they provided instead for enforcement by private lawsuits. . . . [T]o conservative Republicans and their business constituents, private litigation was preferable to public bureaucracy. Thus, conservative Republican support for Title VII was conditioned on a legislative deal that traded public for private enforcement." *Rights and Retrenchment*, 9.

10. Richard A. Epstein, e.g., argues for "direct government regulation" over class action lawsuits because of "the real and persistent danger of distortion through aggregation." "Class Actions: Aggregation, Amplification, and Distortion," *University of Chicago Legal Forum* 2003, no. 1 (2003): 475–518, 516–18. Zachary D. Clopton writes: "Many critics of private enforcement expressly endorse public enforcement." "Class Actions and Executive Power," *New York University Law Review* 92, no. 4 (2017): 878–94, 891.

11. See, e.g., Brief of the Chamber of Commerce of the United States of America as Amicus Curiae in Support of Petitioner, AT&T Mobility LLC v. Concepcion, 563 U.S. 333 (2011), https://www.americanbar.org/content/dam/aba/publishing/preview/publiced_preview_briefs_pdfs_09_10_09_893_PetitionerAmCuCoC.authcheckdam.pdf.

12. Henry G. Manne, ed., "Constitutional Protections of Economic Activity: How They Promote Individual Freedom," special issue, *George Mason University Law Review*, vol. 11, no. 2 (1988).

13. Friedrich A. Hayek, *The Constitution of Liberty* (Chicago: University of Chicago Press, 1960), 397–411 ("Why I Am Not a Conservative").

14. James M. Buchanan, *Why I, Too, Am Not a Conservative: The Normative Vision of Classical Liberalism* (Northampton, MA: Edward Elgar, 2005).

15. Charles Murray, *What It Means to Be a Libertarian: A Personal Interpretation* (New York: Broadway, 1997).

16. Veronique de Rugy, "Mainstreaming Liberty," *Reason*, October 2015, http://reason.com/archives/2015/10/01/mainstreaming-liberty (invoking Milton Friedman, Friedrich Hayek, James Buchanan, Gordon Tullock, and Ronald Coase).

17. Roger Clegg, Michael E. DeBow, and John McGinnis, *Conservative and Libertarian Legal Scholarship: Annotated Bibliography*, Federalist Society for Law and Public Policy Studies, 2011, https://fedsoc.org/commentary/publications/conservative-libertarian-legal-scholarship-annotated-bibliography.

Chapter One

1. The Federal Rules of Civil Procedure require that courts certify that the representative party in a class action—i.e., the person who filed the lawsuit—"will fairly and adequately protect the interests of the class." Fed. R. Civ. P. 23(a)(4).

2. Fed. R. Civ. P. 23(c)(2)(B)(v) (allowing class members to opt out of money damages class actions).

3. Most class actions allege violations of laws that specifically govern the behavior of businesses, such as securities fraud laws, labor and employment laws, consumer protection laws, and antitrust laws. See Fitzpatrick, "An Empirical Study of Class Action Settlements and Their Fee Awards," 818, table 1.

4. The available data indicate that corporations pay billions of dollars annually to settle class action suits. See Fitzpatrick, "An Empirical Study of Class Action Settlements and Their Fee Awards," 829.

5. In my "The Ironic History of Rule 23," Legal Studies Research Paper no. 17-41 (Nashville: Vanderbilt University Law School, 2017), https://papers.ssrn.com/sol3/papers.cfm?abstract_id=3020306, I describe the pre-1966 practice as follows:

> Under the original Federal Rules of Civil Procedure promulgated in 1938 and the practices that preceded them, class actions were largely confined to small-knit classes of litigants who had some sort of preexisting, voluntary association with one another—such as co-owners of a corporation or fellow congregants of a church. Today's class actions, where large numbers of consumers, employees, and shareholders who have never met one another before are combined into a class were largely foreign to this world.
>
> The one exception was the so-called "spurious" class action. A creation of the 1938 Rules, the spurious class action was permitted whenever class members shared a "question of law or fact" in "common" and sought "common" relief. Spurious class actions were where strangers could be aggregated like they can today. But the spurious class action bound only class members who affirmatively opted in to the class. They called this an "invitation" for class members to intervene; today, we would call it an "opt in" class action. As you can imagine, the opt-in feature limited the use of the spurious class action, and many commentators thought the feature defeated the entire purpose of a class action.
>
> When the Advisory Committee on the Civil Rules was reconstituted in 1960, one of the matters it tackled was Rule 23, and one of its primary orders of business there was to end the opt-in feature of the spurious class action. Its handwork became law in 1966 as Rule 23(b)(3). Now, class members with even one issue of law or fact in common are automatically included in any (b)(3) judgment (so long as the class meets the other prerequisites of Rule 23) unless they opt out.

Linda S. Mullenix also acknowledges the central role of the 1966 revisions in creating the modern class action, writing: "The damage class action was the invention of the 1966 rulemakers; there were virtually no damage class actions prior to the 1966 revision of the Rule, which added the (b)(3) provision." "Ending Class

Actions as We Know Them: Rethinking the American Class Action," *Emory Law Journal* 64, no. 2 (2014): 399–449, 439.

6. The only public gesture from the corporate world that could plausibly be construed as opposition to the 1966 amendments was a letter opposing the proposed revisions to the rule from the American College of Trial Lawyers, a group dominated by corporate defense lawyers. However, that letter was focused on the impact of these amendments on the autonomy rights of plaintiffs, not on how the proposal would affect defendants. See Fitzpatrick, "The Ironic History of Rule 23."

7. See Fitzpatrick, "The Ironic History of Rule 23."

8. The Rules Enabling Act (REA) permits the Supreme Court to create procedural rules governing the federal courts. See 28 U.S.C. § 2071–77. At the time of the REA's enactment, there was no expectation that the Court itself would draft these rules, and the Court has never done so, instead relying on groups of experts to do the work of drafting. See Brooke D. Coleman, "Recovering Access: Rethinking the Structure of Federal Civil Rulemaking," *New Mexico Law Review* 39 (2009): 261–97, 274. Since 1958, that responsibility has rested with the Judicial Conference of the United States, which has itself relied on a set of advisory committees to draft revisions to the procedural rules governing the federal courts. See Stephen B. Burbank and Sean Farhang, "Federal Court Rulemaking and Litigation Reform: An Institutional Approach," *Nevada Law Journal* 15 (2015): 1559–96, 1564. While today the membership of the Advisory Committee on the Civil Rules largely consists of judges, in 1966 most of the members of the committee were practitioners or academics. Ibid., 1568, table 1.

9. For a description of the pre-1966 practice, see n. 5 above.

10. Fed. R. Civ. P. 23(c)(2)(b).

11. As I note in "The Ironic History of Rule 23," much of the opposition to the 1966 revisions was "because people thought class members would lose too much autonomy if they could become bound to a class action judgment without their affirmative consent through something like the opt-in procedure." See also Burbank and Farhang, *Rights and Retrenchment*, 74 n. 19.

12. Burbank and Farhang outline the limited steps the committee took to publicize the proposed revisions. See *Rights and Retrenchment*, 76.

13. Burbank and Farhang write that there is "no evidence that the proposals that became the 1966 amendments were published." *Rights and Retrenchment*, 76 n. 22.

14. I explore the scope of written opposition to the proposed 1966 revisions in "The Ironic History of Rule 23": "Although opposition to (b)(3) from outside the committee was limited by the closed nature of the rulemaking process back then, the committee nonetheless received a number of letters against its proposal. Indeed, both the leading mouthpiece for the corporate defense bar at the time—the American College of Trial Lawyers—and the leading mouthpiece of the plaintiffs' bar (still today)—the American Association of Trial Lawyers—opposed (b)(3).

So did the bar associations of Philadelphia, New York, and California, as well as the Judicial Conference of the Ninth Circuit."

15. Fitzpatrick, "The Ironic History of Rule 23."

16. Arthur R. Miller writes: "The Committee obviously could not predict the great growth in complicated federal and state substantive law that would take place in such fields as race, gender, disability, and age discrimination; consumer protection; fraud; products liability; environmental safety; and pension litigation, let alone the exponential increase in class action and multiparty/multi-claim practice that would flow from the expansion of those legal subjects." "The Preservation and Rejuvenation of Aggregate Litigation: A Systemic Imperative," *Emory Law Journal* 64, no. 2 (2014): 293–327, 295. He put this argument as such in an earlier article: "The class action onslaught caught everyone, including the draftsmen, by surprise. With hindsight, the causes of the proliferation now seem clear: the nature of federal litigation changed in ways unforeseen and unforeseeable during the reformulation of rule 23. In almost every substantive area presently identified with class actions, there occurred major substantive changes unrelated to the rule's revision." Arthur R. Miller, "Of Frankenstein Monsters and Shining Knights: Myth, Reality, and the 'Class Action Problem,'" *Harvard Law Review* 92 (1979): 670 (see generally 664–94). Other scholars have made this argument as well. See David Marcus, "The History of the Modern Class Action, Part I: Sturm Und Drang, 1953–1980," *Washington University Law Review* 90, no. 3 (2013): 587–652, 606–7; Mary J. Davis, "Toward the Proper Role for Mass Tort Class Actions," *Oregon Law Review* 77, no. 1 (1998): 157–233, 174–77; Georgene Vairo, "What Goes Around, Comes Around: From the Rector of Barkway to Knowles," *Review of Litigation* 32, no. 4 (2013): 721–804, 743–44; and Patricia A. Seith, "Civil Rights, Labor, and the Politics of Class Action Jurisdiction," *Stanford Journal of Civil Rights and Civil Liberties* 7, no. 1 (2011): 83–128, 90.

17. See the sources cited in the previous note.

18. The most prominent example of corporate America's involvement in other debates on changes to procedural rules was its active opposition to the Multidistrict Litigation Act, a different method of aggregating litigation. Fitzpatrick, "The Ironic History of Rule 23." As Andrew D. Bradt notes, passing the Multidistrict Litigation Act required "overcoming resistance from corporate defense lawyers who sought to kill the proposal." "A Radical Proposal: The Multidistrict Litigation Act of 1968," *University of Pennsylvania Law Review* 165, no. 4 (2017): 831–916, 834.

19. Indeed, members of the advisory committee specifically referenced antitrust and fraudulent misrepresentation cases as being possible candidates for class treatment under the proposed revisions. Fitzpatrick, "The Ironic History of Rule 23"; Benjamin Kaplan, "Continuing the Work of the Civil Committee: 1966 Amendments of the Federal Rules of Civil Procedure (I)," *Harvard Law Review* 81 (1967): 356–416, 393.

20. Fitzpatrick, "The Ironic History of Rule 23."

21. Fitzpatrick, "The Ironic History of Rule 23."

22. The Federal Rules of Civil Procedure state that "the claims, issues, or defenses of a certified class may be settled, voluntarily dismissed, or compromised only with the court's approval." Fed. R. Civ. P. 23(e). The rules also state that, "in a certified class action, the court may award reasonable attorney's fees and nontaxable costs that are authorized by law or by the parties' agreement." Fed. R. Civ. P. 23(h).

23. As I wrote recently ("The Ironic History of Rule 23"): "Although courts would have to scrutinize any settlement or enter any declaration, commentators worried [that the class action mechanism would unfairly benefit corporate defendants because] . . . corporate litigants would induce or file these suits before friendly judges as well. Many commentators cited a notorious state court class action where that is precisely what appeared to have happened."

24. Fitzpatrick, "The Ironic History of Rule 23." The most prominent example of such an effort by a corporation was Pennsylvania R.R v. United States 111 F.Supp. 80 (D.N.J. 1953). This case was referenced in the advisory committee's debate on the proposed revisions.

25. For an approachable discussion of this problem in the modern era from a federal court, see Reynolds v. Beneficial Nat. Bank, 288 F.3d 277 (7th Cir. 2002) (Posner, J.).

26. Fitzpatrick, "The Ironic History of Rule 23."

27. Fitzpatrick, "The Ironic History of Rule 23"; American College of Trial Lawyers, *Report and Recommendations of the Special Committee on Rule 23 of the FRCP* (Newport Beach, CA: American College of Trial Lawyers, 1972), pt. 3, pp. 4–15.

28. Fitzpatrick, "The Ironic History of Rule 23"; American College of Trial Lawyers, *Report and Recommendations*.

29. Burbank and Farhang, "Federal Court Rulemaking and Litigation Reform," 1580–85; Burbank and Farhang, *Rights and Retrenchment*, 100–101; David Marcus, "The History of the Modern Class Action, Part II: Litigation and Legitimacy, 1981–1994," *Fordham Law Review* 86, no. 4 (2018): 1785–1845.

30. See the sources cited in Fitzpatrick, "The Ironic History of Rule 23." Mullenix notes: "Suggestions to amend class action procedure to revert to an opt-in principle have been repeatedly advanced and rejected." "Ending Class Actions as We Know Them," 165n. See generally Scott Dodson, "An Opt-In Option for Class Actions," *Michigan Law Review* 115 (2016): 171–214; and Marcus "The History of the Modern Class Action, Part II."

31. Burbank and Farhang write: "The committee concluded that consequential change to Rule 23 was so freighted with controversy among interest groups, and hence so likely to engender political controversy, that it should not be attempted . . . by rulemaking." *Rights and Retrenchment*, 25.

32. For an example of such an effort, see Lawyers for Civil Justice, Federation of Defense and Corporate Counsel, DRI—the Voice of the Defense Bar, and

the International Association of Defense Counsel. "To Restore a Relationship between Classes and Their Actions: A Call for Meaningful Reform of Rule 23." Comment to the Civil Rules Advisory Committee and its Rule 23 Subcommittee. August 9, 2013. http://www.uscourts.gov/sites/default/files/fr_import/13-CV -G-suggestion.pdf.

33. See, e.g., Fed. R. Civ. P. 23(f)(1998). Rule 23(f) permits appeals of class certification decisions before the end of a case. Although Rule 23(f) can be used by both plaintiffs and defendants, in practice it has been of greater benefit to defendants. Robert H. Klonoff, "The Decline of Class Actions," *Washington University Law Review* 90, no. 3 (2013): 729–838, 739–42; Burbank and Farhang, *Rights and Retrenchment*, 141.

34. As Burbank and Farhang write, in response to efforts to roll back the opt-out class action, "the changes [the Advisory Committee on the Civil Rules] recommended . . . were far more restrained than champions of retrenchment advocated, and they avoided the core elements of the rule." *Rights and Retrenchment*, 118–19. See also their comment that advocates for the elimination of class actions, and for the reduction of litigation as a regulatory tool more generally, have been "only modestly successful in the domain of court rulemaking." Stephen B. Burbank and Sean Farhang, "The Subterranean Counterrevolution: The Supreme Court, the Media, and Litigation Retrenchment," *DePaul Law Review* 65, no. 2 (2016): 293–322, 296.

35. Myriam Gilles provides an outline of these anti–class action efforts. See "The Day Doctrine Died: Private Arbitration and the End of Law," *University of Illinois Law Review* 2016, no. 2 (2016): 371–424, 377–90.

36. Burbank and Farhang write: "The legislative project of private enforcement retrenchment mounted by the Republican Party was largely a failure." *Rights and Retrenchment*, 46. Elsewhere, Burbank and Farhang note that efforts to end class actions—or block the use of litigation as a regulatory tool more generally—were "largely a failure in the elected branches." "The Subterranean Counterrevolution," 296. John C. Coffee Jr. reaches a similar conclusion in *Entrepreneurial Litigation: Its Rise, Fall, and Future* (Cambridge, MA: Harvard University Press, 2015), 125–27. David Marcus writes: "Little of concrete, lasting import had happened to Rule 23 or class action doctrine by the end of 1994." "The History of the Modern Class Action, Part II," 1842.

37. See Private Securities Litigation Reform Act of 1995, Pub. L. No. 104-67, 109 Stat. 737 (1995).

38. See Class Action Fairness Act of 2005, Pub. L. No. 109-2, 119 Stat. 4 (2005).

39. Burbank and Farhang systematically went through federal legislative efforts to reduce the use of litigation as a tool for the private enforcement of federal law, finding: "The ninety-seventh Congress (1981–82) is the first one in our data set in which Republican support for anti-litigation measures exceeds Democratic support. From rough parity when Reagan took office, there emerged a partisan gap

which grew until it peaked in the 105th Congress (1995–96), with Republicans supporting anti-litigation proposals at a level about 563% above Democrats." *Rights and Retrenchment*, 54n.

40. Burbank and Farhang note that, of the eight bills to limit the use of class actions in this period, "seven were introduced by Democrats, and of 31 total sponsors, 27 were Democrats." *Rights and Retrenchment*, 45.

41. "The proposed legislation would have repealed Rule 23(b)(3) . . . and replaced the small-claims class action with a public action (brought by or on behalf of the United States)." Burbank and Farhang, *Rights and Retrenchment*, 43–45. David Freeman Engstrom provides the most thorough overview of this bill's creation, controversy, and eventual abandonment. See "Jacobins at Justice: The (Failed) Class Action Revolution of 1978 and the Puzzle of American Procedural Political Economy," *University of Pennsylvania Law Review* 165 (2017): 1531–63. For a description of the bill given by an attorney for the Department of Justice, see US Congress, Senate, Committee on the Judiciary, Subcommittee on Judicial Machinery, *Reform of Class Action Litigation Procedures: Hearings before the Subcommittee on Judicial Machinery*, 95th Cong., 2nd sess., 1978, 4–5.

42. Burbank and Farhang, *Rights and Retrenchment*, 43–45 (cosponsored by Democratic senator DeConcini).

43. "[The] proposed legislation [was] developed by the Office for Improvements in the Administration of Justice in the Carter Administration's DOJ." Burbank and Farhang, *Rights and Retrenchment*, 43–44. See generally Engstrom, "Jacobins at Justice."

44. Much of this history is chronicled in Stephen Burbank and Sean Farhang's *Rights and Retrenchment*. Consider, e.g., their description of the debate over the Civil Rights Act of 1964: "Wielding the powers of a pivotal voting bloc, conservative Republicans stripped the EEOC of the strong administrative powers in the bill initially proposed by civil rights liberals, and they provided instead for enforcement by private lawsuits. . . . To conservative Republicans and their business constituents, private litigation was preferable to public bureaucracy. Thus, conservative Republican support for Title VII was conditioned on a legislative deal that traded public for private enforcement." *Rights and Retrenchment*, 9.

45. Burbank and Farhang write: "Until Reagan took office, Democrats provided more support for proposals [to weaken private enforcement] than Republicans." *Rights and Retrenchment*, 39 (see generally 39–46). With respect to the Civil Rights Act: "Civil right groups regarded the substitution of private lawsuits . . . for strong administrative powers as a bitterly disappointing evisceration of Title VII's enforcement regime." Ibid., 10.

46. See US Congress, Senate, Committee on the Judiciary, Subcommittee on Judicial Machinery, *Reform of Class Action Litigation Procedures: Hearings before the Subcommittee on Judicial Machinery*, 95th Cong., 2nd sess., 1978, 4–5; and Engstrom, "Jacobins at Justice," 1538–46. Carter's bill was opposed by many in

the big-business community. See David Ignatius and Stan Crock, "U.S. Plan to Revamp Class-Action Rules Could Be Costly for Corporate Violators," *Wall St. Journal*, August 23, 1978; and George B. Mickum and Carol A. Rhees, "Federal Class Action Reform: A Response to the Proposed Legislation," *Kentucky Law Journal* 69 (1980): 799–826, 825 n. 110 (noting that the bill was opposed by the Business Roundtable and the National Association of Manufacturers).

47. Burbank and Farhang write: "The campaign to retrench private enforcement crystallized early in the Reagan administration. Recognizing the political impossibility of repealing the substantive rights that underpinned the growing American regulatory state, the architects of the movement's strategy instead sought to constrict opportunities and incentives for their enforcement." "The Subterranean Counterrevolution," 295. They make a similar point in *Rights and Retrenchment*, 26–29.

48. The initial efforts focused on private lawsuits against the government but by the 1990s had expanded to all private lawsuits, including class actions. See Gilles, "The Day Doctrine Died," 378–84. For example, an early Reagan administration effort to cap legal fees for plaintiffs' attorneys applied only to lawsuits against the government. Burbank and Farhang, "The Subterranean Counterrevolution," 295, 14n. Burbank and Farhang write: "The initial private enforcement retrenchment in the Reagan administration did not attempt to restrict fees in suits against the private (business) sector." *Rights and Retrenchment*, 29–32. Similarly, David Marcus notes the "class action's low political salience in the 1980s." "The History of the Modern Class Action, Part II," 1796.

49. Thomas F. Burke explains that the American Trial Lawyers Association (ATLA) formed close relationships with Democratic legislators in response to these antilitigation efforts, writing: "ATLA chose an insider approach to influencing Congress. By cultivating relationships with legislators, especially Democratic legislators on relevant committees, the organization could usually stop tort reforms from reaching the floor. . . . State-level plaintiff lawyers have adopted variations on this approach." *Lawyers, Lawsuits, and Legal Rights: The Battle over Litigation in American Society* (Berkeley and Los Angeles: University of California Press, 2004), 47–48. Robert A. Kagan notes that, from 1989 to 1994, ATLA donated more to Democratic politicians than did the top five contributing labor unions combined. *Adversarial Legalism: The American Way of Law* (Cambridge, MA: Harvard University Press, 2001), 148–50.

50. Linda Mullenix observes: "An alignment of interest groups and organizations frequently appear as amici curiae in major class litigation, supporting defense positions in these cases. These repeat-player litigants include the Business Roundtable, the Cato Institute, the Chamber of Commerce of the United States, the DRI—the Voice of the Defense Bar, the International Association of Defense Counsel, the National Association of Manufacturers, the Pharmaceutical Research and Manufacturers of America, the Products Liability Advisory Council, the Securities Industry and Financial Markets Association, and the Washington

Legal Foundation. In most recent class litigation before the Supreme Court, combinations of these interest groups have filed amici briefs on behalf of the corporate defendants." "Ending Class Actions as We Know Them," 413 n. 57.

51. David Marcus says that the Supreme Court's decisions from 1981 to 1994 regarding class actions "mostly involved peripheral issues that did not significantly affect what sorts of classes got certified, incentives to litigate class actions, or the design of settlements." "The History of the Modern Class Action, Part II," 1793. This period coincided with an increasing embrace of the class action as a method for resolving disputes by the lower courts. See Klonoff, "The Decline of Class Actions," 736–39.

52. AT&T Mobility LLC v. Concepcion, 563 U.S. 333 (2011).

53. 9 U.S.C. § 2 (2012).

54. Roger S. Haydock and Jennifer D. Henderson note that, before 1925, use of arbitration tended to be limited to merchants. "Arbitration and Judicial Civil Justice: An American Historical Review and a Proposal for a Private/Arbitral and Public/Judicial Partnership," *Pepperdine Dispute Resolution Law Journal* 2, no. 2 (2002): 141–98, 144. I should note that, when I say that arbitration was not popular in the 1920s, I am using *arbitration* to refer to a specific type of informal dispute resolution, not all forms of informal dispute resolution. As Carrie Menkel-Meadow describes: "There is a long history of informal justice in the U.S., with religious, local community and business groups negotiating, mediating or arbitrating their own disputes since the early colonial period and continuing to the present." "Regulation of Dispute Resolution in the United States of America: From the Formal to the Informal to the 'Semi-Formal,'" in *Regulating Dispute Resolution: ADR and Access to Justice at the Crossroads*, ed. Felix Steffek, Hannes Unberath, Hazel Genn, Reinhard Greger, and Carrie Menkel-Meadow (Oxford: Hart, 2013), 419–54, 430.

55. See the previous note.

56. Margret L. Moses explains that, under the law before the Federal Arbitration Act and its state equivalents, litigants seeking to get out of an arbitration agreement could simply refuse to arbitrate "at any time prior to the award" and courts would not enforce the agreement. "Statutory Misconstruction: How the Supreme Court Created a Federal Arbitration Law Never Enacted by Congress," *Florida State University Law Review* 34, no. 1 (2006): 99–160, 101.

57. See 9 U.S.C. § 2 (2012).

58. See, e.g., Christopher R. Leslie's statement that "courts initially limited arbitration to use for resolving commercial disputes between merchants." "The Arbitration Bootstrap," *Texas Law Review* 94, no. 2 (2015): 265–330, 271. See also Andrea Doneff, "Is *Green Tree v. Randolph* Still Good Law? How the Supreme Court's Emphasis on Contract Language in Arbitration Clauses Will Impact the Use of Public Policy to Allow Parties to Vindicate Their Rights," *Ohio Northern University Law Review* 39, no. 1 (Winter 2012): 63–112, 69. Imre Stephen Szalai

writes: "The FAA was designed for simple contract disputes between merchants, not complex statutory claims of a public nature between parties of unequal bargaining power." "More Than Class Action Killers: The Impact of *Concepcion* and *American Express* on Employment Arbitration," *Berkeley Journal of Employment and Labor Law* 35, no. 1 (2014): 31–59, 57 n. 178. Szalai also explains that, "based on the examples given by commercial interests during the 1924 Hearings, it appears the FAA was intended to cover disputes arising in the 'daily business transactions' of 'merchants' who were citizens of different states." "The Federal Arbitration Act and the Jurisdiction of the Federal Courts," *Harvard Negotiation Law Review* 12 (2007): 319–75, 319.

59. Leslie makes a persuasive case on this point, writing: "Congress did not intend the FAA to facilitate firms imposing arbitration clauses on consumers through contracts of adhesion. . . . For example, in colloquy, when senators raised the issue of contracts of adhesion, the bill's supporters testified that the FAA would not apply to such situations." "The Arbitration Bootstrap," 309. He goes on to note: "During the earliest hearings for the FAA, concerns were expressed that the Act could cover employment. . . . The Act's text was amended [to exclude] 'contracts of employment of . . . any . . . class of workers engaged in foreign or interstate commerce.' . . . [T]he amendment appeased labor interests, who removed their opposition to the bill." Ibid., 310–11. Moses summarizes the evidence when she writes: "No one in 1925—not the drafters, the Secretary of Commerce, organized labor, nor members of Congress—believed that the [Federal Arbitration Act] applied to employment contracts." "Statutory Misconstruction," 147.

60. The Federal Arbitration Act says that courts can reject arbitration agreements "upon such grounds as exist at law or in equity for the revocation of any contract." 9 U.S.C. § 2 (2012).

61. See AT&T Mobility LLC v. Concepcion, 563 U.S. 333, 337–38.

62. The contract specifically stated that any claims brought in arbitration had to be brought in the customer's "individual capacity, and not as a plaintiff or class member in any purported class or representative proceeding." AT&T Mobility LLC v. Concepcion, 563 U.S. 333, 336.

63. See Laster v. AT&T Mobility LLC, 584 F.3d 849, 853 (9th Cir. 2009), rev'd sub nom. AT&T Mobility LLC v. Concepcion, 563 U.S. 333 (2011).

64. See American Law Institute, *Second Restatement of Contracts*, §208. The Ninth Circuit explained California's unconscionability doctrine as follows: "To be unenforceable under California law, a contract provision must be both procedurally and substantively unconscionable. Procedural unconscionability generally takes the form of a contract of adhesion, that is, a contract drafted by the party of superior bargaining strength and imposed on the other, without the opportunity to negotiate the terms. Substantive unconscionability focuses on overly harsh or one-sided contract terms. Both elements of unconscionability need not be present to the same degree; California courts use a sliding-scale: the more substantively

unconscionable the contract term, the less procedurally unconscionable it need be to be unenforceable and vice versa." Laster v. AT&T Mobility LLC, 584 F.3d 849, 853 (9th Cir. 2009), rev'd sub nom. AT&T Mobility LLC v. Concepcion, 563 U.S. 333 (2011) (internal citations omitted).

65. The California Supreme Court previously held: "When [a class action] waiver is found in a consumer contract of adhesion in a setting in which disputes between the contracting parties predictably involve small amounts of damages, and when it is alleged that the party with the superior bargaining power has carried out a scheme to deliberately cheat large numbers of consumers out of individually small sums of money, then, at least to the extent the obligation at issue is governed by California law, the waiver becomes in practice the exemption of the party from responsibility for its own fraud, or willful injury to the person or property of another. Under these circumstances, such waivers are unconscionable under California law and should not be enforced." Discover Bank v. Superior Court, 36 Cal. 4th 148, 163, (2005) abrogated by AT&T Mobility LLC v. Concepcion, 563 U.S. 333 (internal citations and quotations omitted).

66. As the Court's opinion put it: "Our cases place it beyond dispute that the [Federal Arbitration Act] was designed to promote arbitration. They have repeatedly described the Act as 'embod[ying] [a] national policy favoring arbitration,' and 'a liberal federal policy favoring arbitration agreements, notwithstanding any state substantive or procedural policies to the contrary[.]' Thus, in Preston v. Ferrer, holding preempted a state-law rule requiring exhaustion of administrative remedies before arbitration, we said: 'A prime objective of an agreement to arbitrate is to achieve "streamlined proceedings and expeditious results,"' which objective would be 'frustrated' by requiring a dispute to be heard by an agency first. That rule, we said, would 'at the least, hinder speedy resolution of the controversy.'" AT&T Mobility LLC v. Concepcion, 563 U.S. 333, 345–46 (2011) (internal citations omitted).

67. Joanna C. Schwartz argues that the Supreme Court justified its decisions restricting class actions under the Federal Arbitration Act and in other cases "as a means of protecting business defendants." "The Cost of Suing Business," *DePaul Law Review* 65, no. 2 (2016): 655–86, 659.

68. The Court notes that, because "class arbitration greatly increases risks to defendants," it is "hard to believe that defendants would bet the company with no effective means of review." AT&T Mobility LLC v. Concepcion, 563 U.S. 333, 351 (2011). It went still further in a note, writing: "It is not reasonably deniable that requiring consumer disputes to be arbitrated on a classwide basis will have a substantial deterrent effect on [defendants'] incentives to arbitrate." Ibid., 351 n. 8.

69. See AT&T Mobility LLC v. Concepcion, 563 U.S. 333, 347–48 (2011).

70. In particular, I have argued that *Concepcion* is a weak decision on textualist grounds. See Brian T. Fitzpatrick, "Justice Scalia and Class Actions: A Loving Critique," *Notre Dame Law Review* 92, no. 5 (2017): 1977–95, 1984–87.

71. My old boss Justice Scalia expresses the conservative position eloquently when he explains that federalism is one of "the Constitution's structural protections of liberty": "'Just as the separation and independence of the coordinate branches of the Federal Government serve to prevent the accumulation of excessive power in any one branch, a healthy balance of power between the States and the Federal Government will reduce the risk of tyranny and abuse from either front.'" Printz v. United States, 521 U.S. 898, 921 (1997) (quoting Gregory v. Ashcroft, 501 U.S. 452, 458 (1991).

72. Gilles describes how "huge swaths of modern commerce" are governed by standard form contracts drafted by large corporations and outlines the available empirical literature supporting that premise. See "The Day Doctrine Died," 407. See also the analysis in Brian T. Fitzpatrick, "The End of Class Actions?," *Arizona Law Review* 57, no. 1 (2015): 176–81.

73. As I have explained elsewhere: "With respect to consumers, in light of advances both in technology and in legal notions of contract formation, producers of almost any product can now bind purchasers to contractual language. Even if the purchase is unlike the cell phone purchase in *Concepcion* that required consumers to sign a document, businesses can bind consumers to contractual language by placing the language on the product's packaging. Indeed, even if the consumer could not read the language until after he or she purchased the product, many courts have found the language to be binding. This means that even consumers who buy through intermediaries can be asked to consent to pre-dispute contractual provisions." "The End of Class Actions?," 176–77.

74. Indeed, the Consumer Financial Protection Bureau rule has been eliminated. See Renae Merle and Tory Newmyer, "Congressional Republicans Use Special Maneuver to Kill 'Arbitration Rule,'" *Washington Post*, October 25, 2017.

75. This move has been delayed by the Securities and Exchange Commission's aggressive position that companies cannot place arbitration waivers of shareholder claims in corporate charters. But this position does not appear to be consistent with federal securities law. See Fitzpatrick, "The End of Class Actions?," 181–83. And the commission has now begun reconsidering it. See "U.S. SEC's Piwowar Urges Companies to Pursue Mandatory Arbitration Clauses," Reuters, July 18, 2017.

Chapter Two

1. In this book, I use the words *regulation* and *legal rules* interchangeably. Some conservatives do not like that. See, e.g., Thomas Lambert: "A workable definition of regulation would be any threat-backed governmental directive aimed at fixing a defect in 'private ordering'—the world that would exist if people did their own thing without government intervention *beyond enforcing common law rights to person, property, and contract*." *How to Regulate: A Guide for Policymakers*

(Cambridge, MA: Cambridge University Press, 2017), 4 (emphasis added). But I find it rhetorically cumbersome to assign different meanings to those words.

2. See Robert E. Litan, Peter Swire, and Clifford Winston's comment: "One method for spreading losses is to have government-administered (and taxpayer-financed) programs for compensating injured parties." "The U.S. Liability System: Background and Trends," in *Liability: Perspectives and Policy*, ed. Robert E. Litan and Clifford Winston (Washington, DC: Brookings Institution Press, 1988), 1–15, 4.

3. For example, before you can sell an automobile in the United States, the Environmental Protection Agency must certify that it meets emissions laws. Yet, as I note later in this chapter, Volkswagen evaded those laws for years until a private organization discovered the wrongdoing. Jack Ewing, *Faster, Higher, Farther: The Volkswagen Scandal* (New York: Norton, 2017), 164–74.

4. See Liz Alderman, "Equal Pay. Now Prove It," *New York Times*, March 29, 2017; and Egill Bjarnason and Christine Hauser, "Equal Pay Law Taking Effect in Iceland," *New York Times*, January 4, 2018.

5. See Andrew Higgins, "Russia Wants Innovation, but It's Arresting Its Innovators," *New York Times*, August 9, 2017.

6. Kagan, *Adversarial Legalism*, 16. See also Samuel Issacharoff: "What is distinctive about the United States is the extent to which we regulate not entry but consequences." "Regulating After the Fact," *DePaul Law Review* 56, no. 2 (2007): 375–88, 377; and Burke, *Lawyers, Lawsuits, and Legal Rights*, xxiv.

7. Coffee, *Entrepreneurial Litigation*, 30. See also Burke, *Lawyers, Lawsuits, and Legal Rights*, xxiv.

8. Hayek, *The Road to Serfdom* (London: Routledge, 1944), 36.

9. Hayek, *The Road to Serfdom*, 36.

10. Hayek, *The Constitution of Liberty*, 222.

11. Milton Friedman and Rose Friedman, *Free to Choose: A Personal Statement* (San Diego, CA: Harcourt Brace Jovanovich, 1990), 30.

12. Milton Friedman, *Capitalism and Freedom* (Chicago: University of Chicago Press, 1962), 34.

13. See, e.g., Gregory Mitchell's statement that "a fundamental tenet of libertarianism is that each individual determines how he or she choose to live and others must respect those choices so long as they do not infringe on others." "Libertarian Nudges," *Missouri Law Review* 82, no. 3 (2017): 695–708, 703.

14. Hayek writes: "The rules of property . . . are required to delimit the individual's private sphere wherever the resources or services needed for the pursuit of his aims are scarce and must, in consequence, be under the control of some man or another." *The Constitution of Liberty*, 141.

15. Hayek, *The Constitution of Liberty*, 140–41. "It is one of the accomplishments of modern society that freedom may be enjoyed by a person with practically no property of his own . . . and that we can leave the care of the property

that serves our needs largely to others. . . . [T]hat other people's property can be serviceable in the achievement of our aims is due mainly to the enforceability of contracts." Ibid., 140. "The rules of property and contract are required to delimit the individual's private sphere wherever the resources or services needed for the pursuit of his aims are scarce and must, in consequence, be under the control of some man or another." Ibid., 141. "Humans . . . must have a *law of contract*." Richard A. Epstein, "The Libertarian Quartet," *Reason*, January 1999, 1–66, 62–63. "These first four rules, autonomy, property, contract, and tort . . . remain a part and parcel of every sensible system of legal rules." Richard A. Epstein, "The Uneasy Marriage of Utilitarian and Libertarian Thought," *Quinnipiac Law Review* 19, no. 4 (2000): 783–803, 786. "[Government must] enforce contractual promises." Richard A. Epstein, *The Classical Liberal Constitution: The Uncertain Quest for Limited Government* (Cambridge, MA: Harvard University Press, 2014), 20. "The second legitimate use of the police power is to enable people to enter into enforceable voluntary agreements—contracts. . . . [T]he right of contract means that a third party—ultimately the government—will guarantee that each party is held to account." Murray, *What It Means to Be a Libertarian*, 9.

16. Hayek notes that "the most essential prerequisite" of "an effective competitive system" is "the prevention of fraud and deception." *The Road to Serfdom*, 39. "The state [can] deal with the problems that call for government intervention even under the classical liberal view: . . . fraud in all its manifold forms; . . . the regulation of monopoly." Epstein, *The Classical Liberal Constitution*, 15–16. "Classical liberal theory . . . limit[s] government intervention to cases of force, fraud, and monopoly." Ibid., 303. "In commercial contexts fraud can take a variety of forms, including false statements designed to induce individuals to buy worthless shares of stock at high prices or to sell valuable assets at low prices." Ibid., 407. "Fraud in commerce poses a grave threat to the operation of voluntary markets. . . . When the incorrect estimations of value derive solely from the misleading acts of one party to the agreement, the willingness in common law to allow damages or rescission makes sense." Ibid., 407. "The exchange need only be monitored for the process whereby it takes place, that is to ensure that force and fraud and incompetence are not involved." Richard A. Epstein, *Forbidden Grounds: The Case against Employment Discrimination Laws* (Cambridge, MA: Harvard University Press, 1992), 25. "Without question the first order of public business is the control of fraud." Richard A. Epstein, "The Neoclassical Economics of Consumer Contracts," *Minnesota Law Review* 92, no. 3 (2008): 803–35, 807. "I am quite happy to recognize—indeed, to insist upon—limitations of freedom of contract [for] . . . fraud . . . [and that] restrain trade." Epstein, "Uneasy Marriage," 795. "The case against fraudulent misrepresentation is easy to make out. . . . [N]o social good can derive from the systematic production of misinformation." Richard A. Epstein, "Unconscionability: A Critical Reappraisal," *Journal of Law and Economics*, 18, no. 2 (1975): 239–315, 298. "The equivalence of force and fraud is both long-asserted and well-accepted

by classical liberals." Randy E. Barnett, *The Structure of Liberty*, 2nd ed. (Oxford: Oxford University Press, 2014), 103. Murray endorses laws "against fraud and deceptive practice." *What It Means to Be a Libertarian*, 60. See also Jan Narveson, *The Libertarian Idea* (Philadelphia: Temple University Press, 1988), chap. 15 passim; and Robert Nozick, *Anarchy, State, and Utopia* (New York: Basic, 1974), 26; 63–65, 152, and passim.

17. David Friedman advocates for a society in which private actors take over the most fundamental government functions—police, courts, and national defense—and describes a future society in which there are no government police but instead private protection agencies that sell the service of protecting their clients against crime. "The Machinery of Freedom: Guide to a Radical Capitalism," in *Anarchy and the Law: The Political Economy of Choice*, ed. Edward P. Stringham (New Brunswick, NJ: Transaction, 2011), 40–56, 40–42.

18. Friedman argues there is no need for the government to enforce private arbitration decisions because private parties will refuse to contract with firms that do not honor the results of agreed-on arbitration proceedings. Ibid., "The Machinery of Freedom," 42. James W. Child argues against fraud laws. "Can Libertarianism Sustain a Fraud Standard?," *Ethics* 104, no. 4 (July 1994): 722–38.

19. As Child reports, e.g., "I have read or talked to many libertarians on this point and have not found one who is willing to countenance fraud." "Can Libertarianism Sustain a Fraud Standard?," 723 n. 4.

20. Nathan B. Oman notes that, although "rudimentary markets can exist without law . . . because other social mechanisms—such as self-help, reputation, or ostracism—can be used to deal with the problems addressed by legal institutions," this "does not mean that large-scale, well-functioning markets can develop without the assistance of legal institutions." *The Dignity of Commerce* (Chicago: University of Chicago Press, 2016), 34–35. Some early readers of this book have asked why I do not include private adjudication—such as through arbitration—as another way in which market participants can protect themselves from theft, breach of contract, and fraud without government. But arbitration is not governmentless. The only way to enforce an arbitration decree if one party does not comply with it is to file a lawsuit in court. This has been true from the very beginning of arbitration, as Christian Burset chronicles in "The Rise of Modern Commercial Arbitration and the Limits of Private Ordering" (paper in progress, 2017), https://papers.ssrn.com/sol3/papers.cfm?abstract_id=3009713: "the arbitration bond" always "created the possibility of judicial enforcement."

21. Francisco Toro, "Uganda's Bad Seeds," *Reason*, March 2017, 26–27, https://reason.com/archives/2017/02/12/ugandas-bad-seeds.

22. "95 percent of Ugandan farmers . . . [save] part of [their] harvest each season to plant the following season." Toro, "Uganda's Bad Seeds," 27.

23. "To farmers here, high-yield seed looks less like an investment and more like a dangerous bet." Toro, "Uganda's Bad Seeds," 29.

24. "The legal system offers little recourse—the fees to bring a suit could easily amount to [a] life-time [of] earnings." Toro, "Uganda's Bad Seeds," 27.

25. Toro, "Uganda's Bad Seeds," 30.

26. Toro, "Uganda's Bad Seeds," 30.

27. Oman notes, e.g., that "contract law strengthens and extends markets" by creating "security of exchange": "In a world where the law provides no recourse in the face of breach, . . . many trades will not occur. Rather than expose themselves to opportunism by counterparties, people will simply avoid exchanges . . . [or] divert resources away from trade and into mechanisms for managing the risk of opportunism." *The Dignity of Commerce*, 36.

28. "The answer to the question of whether securities [fraud] laws matter is a definite yes. Financial markets do not prosper when left to market forces alone." Rafael La Porta, Florencio Lopez-de-Silanes, and Andrei Shleifer, "What Works in Securities Laws?," *Journal of Finance* 61, no. 1 (February 2006): 1–32, 27.

29. Zingales, *A Capitalism for the People*, 254.

30. Frank H. Easterbrook writes: "Enforcement of the rule against naked horizontal restraints appears to be beneficial." "Limits of Antitrust," *Texas Law Review* 63, no. 1 (1984): 1–40, 3. Michael E. DeBow notes: "Even scholars identified with the 'Chicago school' (particularly Robert H. Bork, Richard A. Posner, and Frank Easterbrook) . . . have defended the prohibition of horizontal price-fixing agreements. . . . In fact, the prohibition on horizontal price-fixing has enjoyed consistent support from lawyers and economists across the American political spectrum. . . . [T]he overwhelming majority of both conservative and liberal students of antitrust law would agree with Bork that the 'contributions to consumer welfare over the decades' from the law's prohibition of price fixing 'have been enormous.'" "What's Wrong with Price Fixing: Responding to the New Critics of Antitrust," *Regulation* 12, no. 2 (1988): 44–50, 44. Brandon Kressin writes: "The majority of libertarians subscribe to the 'consequentialist' or 'utilitarian school.' . . . A consequentialist . . . would support policies prohibiting horizontal restraints." "The Debate within Libertarianism on Antitrust Law," *NYU Journal of Law and Liberty* (blog), November 8, 2011, http://lawandlibertyblog.com/nyujll/ujll.com/2011/11/debate-within-libertarianism-on.html. Lambert endorses antitrust laws. *How to Regulate*, 183–84.

31. Zingales notes that "antitrust law" is "promarket but sometimes antibusiness." *Capitalism for the People*, 5. He later writes: "The genius of capitalism is the continuous trial-and-error process it encourages. Without trial and error, it is exceedingly difficult to produce innovation and growth. Accordingly, the purpose of an antitrust law is to prevent excessive consolidation, which deprives consumers of the benefits of innovation and growth." Ibid., 37. He also says: "For markets to work . . . the playing field must be kept level and open to new entrants. When these conditions fail, free markets degenerate into inefficient monopolies—and when these monopolies extend their power to the political arena, we enter the realm of crony capitalism." Ibid., 47.

32. Richard A. Posner writes: "From a normative economic standpoint the goal of regulation, whether by courts or by agencies, is to solve economic problems that cannot be left to the market to solve—such as problems created by positive or negative large externalities that market forces cannot internalize because transaction costs are too great for the Coase theorem to apply." "Regulation (Agencies) versus Litigation (Courts): An Analytical Framework," in *Regulation versus Litigation: Perspectives from Economics and Law*, ed. Daniel P. Kessler (Chicago: University of Chicago Press, 2012), 11–26, 11–12. Clifford Winston writes: "The [tort] liability system administered by the courts also, in theory, seeks to reduce the cost of externalities by encouraging firms and consumers to behave in a more socially efficient manner." *Government Failure versus Market Failure: Microeconomics Policy Research and Government Performance* (Washington, DC: Brookings Institution Press, 2006), 27 n. 1. See also Richard A. Epstein, "Externalities Everywhere? Morals and the Police Power," *Harvard Journal of Law and Public Policy* 21, no. 1 (1997): 61–69, 62; Hayek, *The Road to Serfdom*, 87; Epstein, "Neoclassical Economics," 826; Jeff McMahon, "What Would Milton Friedman Do About Climate Change? Tax Carbon," *Forbes*, October 12, 2014, http://www.forbes.com /sites/jeffmcmahon/2014/10/12/what-would-milton-friedman-do-about-climate -change-tax-carbon; and Lambert, *How to Regulate*, 57–59 (writing about externalities), 217 (discussing mandatory disclosure for information asymmetries).

33. Zingales writes: "Individual market participants, especially powerful ones, can benefit from trying to restrict competition and hollow out liquidity. Here lies a fundamental challenge for libertarians. Unrestricted freedom of contract can lock in potential traders in a way that dries up liquidity and prevents market development. If companies could lock in workers at a young age, for instance, the labor market for managerial talent would be constricted. The more comprehensive contracts can be, the shallower the market. This is one of the reasons for prohibiting indentured servitude." Zingales, *A Capitalism for the People*, 232.

34. Fred L. Smith Jr. calls for the abolition of all antitrust price fixing laws. "Why Not Abolish Antitrust?," *Regulation* 7, no. 1 (1983): 23–33, 23. He calls for the abolishment of all antitrust laws or, in the alternative, significant deregulatory reforms. Fred L. Smith Jr., "The Case for Reforming the Antitrust Regulations (If Repeal Is Not an Option)," *Harvard Journal of Law and Public Policy* 23, no. 1 (1999): 23–58, 23–24, 53–57. Donald J. Boudreaux and Andrew N. Kleit argue that "markets themselves contain incentives and opportunities for firms to police against monopolization" and that "such opportunities would be greater were it not for existing antitrust laws" in *How the Market Self-Polices Against Predatory Pricing* (Washington, DC: Competitive Enterprise Institute, June 1996), http://www .cei.org/PDFs/predatorypricing.pdf. Donald J. Boudreaux writes: "On no topic in microeconomics does the Austrian approach differ so profoundly from that of mainstream neoclassical economics as it does on the topic of competition." "Antitrust and Competition from a Market-Process Perspective," in *Research*

Handbook on Austrian Law and Economics, ed. Todd J. Zywicki and Peter J. Boettke (Northampton, MA: Edward Elgar, 2017), 78–295, 278. Easterbrook notes: "Suits against mergers more often than not have attacked combinations that increased efficiency, and the dissolution of mergers has led to higher prices in the product market." "Limits of Antitrust," 3. DeBow notes a "small but tenacious group" "identified with the 'Austrian school' of economics" and "of libertarian origin" that argues "for the repeal of all antitrust statutes." "What's Wrong with Price Fixing," 45. Kressin writes: "The other, smaller (in my estimation) subset of libertarians might be alternately referred to as 'deontological' or 'natural rights' libertarians. These libertarians take their cues from moral and ethical philosophy rather than economics. . . . [U]nder the purely natural rights conception of libertarianism, courts would enforce collusive contracts just as they would any other agreement." "The Debate within Libertarianism." Dominick T. Armentano argues that "perfect competition theory is both illogical and irrelevant" and, therefore, that "the legitimacy of all antitrust policy must be open to the most serious question," including the notion that "horizontal price agreements [are] inherently inefficient and antisocial." *Antitrust and Monopoly: Anatomy of a Policy Failure* (New York: Wiley, 1982), 32.

Some libertarians support antitrust laws against horizontal price fixing and even laws against monopolies. Epstein calls for this numerous times. "The wisest course of action is to confine the operation of antitrust law to cartels and mergers that have the consequence of raising prices and restricting output." Richard A. Epstein, "Monopoly Dominance or Level Playing Field? The New Antitrust Paradox," *University of Chicago Law Review* 72, no. 1 (2005): 49–72, 49. "I am quite happy to recognize—indeed, to insist upon—limitations of freedom of contract [for] . . . fraud . . . [and that] restrain trade." Epstein, "Uneasy Marriage," 795. "Antitrust laws . . . were all to the good when they restricted various territorial and price-fixing arrangements." Epstein, *The Classical Liberal Constitution*, 37. "At its best antitrust law seeks to neutralize the risk by prohibiting or terminating trusts and monopolies that restrict output, raise prices, or divide territories." Epstein, "Neoclassical Economics," 805. "The state [can] deal with the problems that call for government intervention even under the classical liberal view: . . . fraud in all its manifold forms; . . . the regulation of monopoly." Epstein, *The Classical Liberal Constitution*, 15–16. "Classical liberal theory . . . limits government intervention . . . to cases of force, fraud, and monopoly." Ibid., 303. Hayek writes: "Property should be sufficiently dispersed so that the individual is not dependent on particular persons who alone can provide him with what he needs or who alone can employ him." *The Constitution of Liberty*, 141.

35. Winston contrasts conservative regulation "to enhance microeconomic efficiency" with liberal "government interventions whose explicit objective is to redistribute income" or to "ensur[e] fairness." *Government Failure versus Market Failure*, 10.

36. Joseph William Singer notes that "most regulations supported by liberals serve [one of] four purposes," including ensuring "equal opportunity." *No Freedom without Regulation: The Hidden Lesson of the Subprime Crisis* (New Haven, CT: Yale University Press, 2015), 162–63. "What causes liberals to worry about markets and private property is that they seem to protect the rights of those who have while leaving the have-nots out in the cold." Ibid., 172–73. Epstein notes that liberals regulate for "the equalization of wealth and the elimination of private forms of (invidious) discrimination." *The Classical Liberal Constitution*, 16. Winston notes liberal "government interventions whose explicit objective is to redistribute income." *Government Failure versus Market Failure*, 10.

37. Singer makes this point repeatedly: "We need laws preventing banks from selling mortgages to people who cannot afford them." *No Freedom without Regulation*, 85. He defends paternalistic laws. Ibid., 88–94. "They protect you from obligations you yourself would not take on if you had a perfect understanding of the relevant information. . . . Of course, we cannot be sure about this, but we have enough experience to believe that we are doing this . . . because it is what you yourself would want if you had perfect information." Ibid., 89–90. And he relies on behavioral economics literature to conclude: "One reason for . . . regulations is to protect us from mistakes we are likely to make and likely to regret." Ibid., 90–91.

38. Singer provides many examples: "Liberals are not against markets. . . . What they want are just markets." *No Freedom without Regulation*, 22. He advocates for bans on subprime mortgage practices because they are "unfair" and do not promote "justice" as well as because they are deceptive and because they "are beneath our dignity" and do not "treat . . . individuals with equal concern and respect" and do not ensure "that each of us is equally free to pursue opportunity and happiness." Ibid., 81, 23–24. "The question is, what legal framework for property and markets best enables us to exercise our liberties in a manner consistent with the values of a free and democratic society that treats each person with equal concern and respect and works to promote our legitimate interests?" Ibid., 4. "It is . . . impossible for either markets or property to exist without laws ensuring that we treat each other with dignity, as free and equal persons." Ibid., 13.

39. Michael Greve, e.g., argues that objectionable class actions "rest in large part on *statutory* laws . . . separate and apart from the common-law rules that traditionally governed relations." *Harm-Less Lawsuits? What's Wrong with Consumer Class Actions* (Washington, DC: American Enterprise Institute, 2005), 2. Robert A. Kagan notes that conservative tort reform efforts have been concerned with the substance of the law, not who the enforcer is. "American Adversarial Legalism in the Early 21st Century" (typescript, University of California, Berkeley, March 2015), 7. Alexandra Lahav notes: "The real concern of critics is not litigation per se, but the underlying rights people are seeking to enforce by bringing lawsuits." *In Praise of Litigation* (New York: Oxford University Press, 2017), 11. She continues later: "The battle over enforcement of the law through litigation is really a

disagreement over whether certain conduct should be regulated and how much regulation is appropriate, although the debate is often presented as being about lawyer overreach or frivolous lawsuits." Ibid., 33.

40. Lahav, *In Praise of Litigation*, 10.

41. Fitzpatrick, "An Empirical Study of Class Action Settlements and Their Fee Awards," 818.

42. Greve, e.g., remarks on the "breathtaking breadth" of California's Unfair Competition Law. *Harm-Less Lawsuits?*, 23. Anthony J. Anscombe and Stephanie A. Sheridan write: "California's Unfair Competition Law is, for defendants, the most dangerous state consumer protection statute in the country." "A Critical Look at the UCL's Role in Food and Beverage Class Actions," Bloomberg BNA Class Action Litigation Report, November 14, 2014, http://www.americanbar.org /content/dam/aba/administrative/litigation/materials/2015-joint-cle/written_ma terials/03_class_action_litigation_report.authcheckdam.pdf (link inactive). They also note attempts to use the law to punish promoting as "natural" products with genetically modified organisms or refined sugar or promoting as "footlong" sandwiches that are eleven inches.

43. Adam C. Pritchard testified: "No other nation has adopted the open-ended private liability for misrepresentations affecting the secondary market price of corporate securities that we have in the United States, and for good reason." "Evaluating S. 1551: The Liability for Aiding and Abetting Securities Violation Act of 2009," Statement to the Senate Committee on the Judiciary, Subcommittee on Crime and Drugs, September 17, 2009, https://www.judiciary.senate.gov/imo /media/doc/09-09-17%20Pritchard%20Testimony.pdf. For scholarship supporting federal securities laws, see Zingales: "When shareholders are not well protected, competition favors the most crooked managers. When investors are ignorant, competition favors the biggest swindlers, not the best money managers. When customers are poorly informed, competition induces firms to exploit this ignorance rather than to improve efficiency." *A Capitalism for the People*, xxxi. "Securities markets need to be regulated because in anonymous markets, reputation cannot restrain fraud and abusive practices." Ibid., 233.

44. Gary Becker and George Stigler, "Law Enforcement, Malfeasance, and Compensation of Enforcers," *Journal of Legal Studies* 3, no. 1 (January 1974): 1–18, 16.

45. Litan, Swire, and Winston note: "Injuries pose . . . different and potentially conflicting challenges for all societies. One is efficiently to deter behavior that causes injuries. [Another] challenge is to compensate victims for their injuries." "The U.S. Liability System," 3.

46. For a description of some of the virtues and vices of each of these boxes, see Daniel P. Kessler, introduction to *Regulation versus Litigation: Perspectives from Economics and Law*, ed. Daniel P. Kessler (Chicago: University of Chicago Press, 2011), 1–10.

47. Herbert J. Hovenkamp writes: "Libertarians and conservatives have been particularly critical of the progressive state . . . [in] contrast . . . [to] the common law." "Appraising the Progressive State," *Iowa Law Review* 102 (2017): 1063–1112, 1086–87.

48. See, e.g., the arguments for common law rules of contract and tort to replace New Deal legislation in Richard A. Epstein, "A Common Law for Labor Relations: A Critique of the New Deal Labor Legislation," *Yale Law Journal* 92, no. 8 (1983): 1357–1408, "Unconscionability," and "A Theory of Strict Liability," *Journal of Legal Studies* 2, no. 1 (1973): 151–204. Epstein summarizes his view when he says: "We would have more vibrant labor markets by scrapping the entire government apparatus in favor of the 19th-century common law regime." "The Libertarian Quartet," 63.

49. See Milton Friedman and Rose Friedman's endorsement of private tort lawsuits over the Food and Drug Administration to "[keep] dangerous drugs off the market." Friedman and Friedman, *Free to Choose*, 207. The liberal economist Paul Krugman accurately summarizes Friedman's views when he writes: "Milton Friedman famously called for the abolition of the Food and Drug Administration. . . . His answer was to rely on tort law. Corporations, he claimed, would have the incentive not to poison people because of the threat of lawsuits." "Phosphorus and Freedom," *New York Times*, August 11, 2014, A15. Liberal economists make the case for box 1 by arguing that judges have neither the incentives nor the expertise to fashion rules of liability for market behavior. See, e.g., Andrei Shleifer, "Efficient Regulation," in *Regulation versus Litigation: Perspectives from Economics and Law*, ed. Daniel P. Kessler (Chicago and London: University of Chicago Press, 2011), 27–44, 31–42. As I explain in the next chapter when comparing boxes 2 and 4, I am very skeptical that decentralized, independent, generalist judges are inferior to centralized, politically compromised, albeit specialized, government bureaucrats. The case is even more dubious for box 1. As Shleifer explains: "With respect to the creation of rules, there are even deeper concerns about regulators than about judges." "Efficient Regulation," 39. See also Steven Shavell, "A Fundamental Enforcement Cost Advantage of the Negligence Rule over Regulation," *Journal of Legal Studies* 42, no. (2013): 275–302, 275. Indeed, although comparative studies of this sort are difficult to do well, we now have empirical evidence that box 4 nations have better economies than box 1 nations. For example, Rafael La Porta, Florencio Lopez-de-Silanes, and Andrei Shleifer recount studies showing "the superior performance of . . . common law countries." "The Economic Consequences of Legal Origins," *Journal of Economic Literature* 46, no. 2 (2008): 285–332, 286.

50. See Ryan Lizza's quotation of Gary Johnson explaining why libertarians would oppose enforcement of environmental laws by the Environmental Protection Agency: "Libertarians would say, 'You and I have the ability to sue [an environmental polluter]. We can bring them to bear from a private standpoint.'" "The Libertarians' Secret Weapon," *New Yorker*, July 25, 2016, 33.

51. Andrew Thierer, *Permissionless Innovation: The Continuing Case for Comprehensive Technological Freedom* (Arlington, VA: Mercatus Center, 2014). See also Veronique de Rugy, "Beyond Permissionless Innovation," *Reason*, January 2016, 14, https://reason.com/archives/2015/12/22/beyond-permissionless-innovati.

52. Thierer, *Permissionless Innovation*, 75–77.

53. There are many examples of this phenomenon. J. R. Deshazo and Jody Freeman discuss how coal companies supported the Air Quality Act of 1967, a federal law regulating pollution. "Timing and Form of Federal Regulation: The Case of Climate Change," *University of Pennsylvania Law Review* 155 (2007): 1499–1561, 1508 n. 23. Robert Pear reports that both drug companies and physicians supported the National Childhood Vaccine Injury Act, a bill to expand federal regulation of vaccines. "Reagan Signs Bill on Drug Exports and Payment for Vaccine Injuries," *New York Times*, November 15, 1986. More recently, 462 private companies and trade associations signed a letter supporting federal regulation of the labeling of foods containing genetically modified organisms. Coalition for Safe and Affordable Food to the US House of Representatives, July 21, 2015, https://www.uschamber.com/sites/default/files/7.21.15-_coalition_letter_to_house_supporting_h.r._1599_the_safe_and_accurate_food_labeling_act.pdf. Similarly, a group of chemical manufacturers recently backed a bill significantly expanding federal authority to regulate toxic chemicals. Coalition for Safe and Affordable Food. "Business Alliance Comments on Bipartisan Chemical Safety Legislation in Senate." Press release, July 21, 2015. https://www.uschamber.com/sites/default/files/7.21.15-_coalition_letter_to_house_supporting_h.r._1599_the_safe_and_accurate_food_labeling_act.pdf. In the same vein, the American Car Rental Association backed a bill to expand federal regulation of the car rental industry. "ACRA Applauds Car Rental Recall Provisions in Highway Bill Conference Report" (press release, December 23, 2015), https://www.acraorg.com/2015/12/acra-applaus-car-rental-recall-provisions-in-highway-bill-conference-report. Around the same time, the Chamber of Commerce backed the "enactment of a truly uniform national data breach notification law." Chamber of Commerce to the Chairman and Ranking Member of the House Committee on Energy and Commerce, April 15, 2015, https://www.uschamber.com/sites/default/files/4.15.15-_hill_letter_supporting_the_data_security_and_breach_notification_act.pdf.

54. Indeed, the reason each of the industries described in the previous note backed the federal regulations in question was because each planned expansion of federal regulation would preempt state law. Deshazo and Freeman note that the reason coal companies supported the Air Quality Act of 1967 was because of its federal preemption provisions. "Timing and Form of Federal Regulation," 1508 n. 23. Pear notes that the National Childhood Vaccine Injury Act substantially limited vaccine manufacturers' liability for state law claims through preemption. "Reagan Signs Bill on Drug Exports and Payment for Vaccine Injuries." Industry groups supporting federal regulation of labeling of genetically modified organisms

cited the fact that it would "[put] a stop to the patchwork of state-based labeling requirements" as a reason to back the bill. Coalition for Safe and Affordable Food to the US House of Representatives. The chemical industry trade group discussed above backed an expansion of federal authority to regulate toxic chemicals in part because it would lead to federal preemption. American Alliance for Innovation, "Business Alliance Comments on Bipartisan Chemical Safety Legislation in Senate." The car rental industry backed a bill to expand federal regulation of the car rental industry because it would result in "one federal rental vehicle safety recall standard rather than a patchwork of potentially conflicting state laws." American Car Rental Association, "ACRA Applauds Car Rental Recall Provisions." And the Chamber of Commerce backed federal regulation of data breach notification law because it would "preempt state law regarding data security." Chamber of Commerce to the Chairman and Ranking Member of the House Committee on Energy and Commerce.

55. For example, Burke notes that, in backing the National Childhood Vaccine Injury Act, vaccine manufacturers supported a government-run social insurance scheme to supplant tort liability. *Lawyers, Lawsuits, and Legal Rights*, 121–50. Barry Brownstein describes how the nuclear power industry successfully lobbied to create a government insurance scheme to compensate victims of nuclear accidents. "The Price-Anderson Act: Is It Consistent with a Sound Energy Policy?," *Policy Analysis*, no. 36 (April 17, 1984), https://www.cato.org/publications/policy -analysis/priceanderson-act-is-it-consistent-sound-energy-policy. Business lobbying was a key factor in many states' decision to expand Medicaid eligibility following the passage of the Affordable Care Act. Alexander Hertel-Fernandez, Theda Skocpol, and David Lynch, "Business Associations, Conservative Networks, and the Ongoing Republican War over Medicaid Expansion," *Journal of Health Politics, Policy, and Law* 41, no. 2 (2016): 239–86. Raymond L. Mariani notes that a core purpose of the 9/11 Victims Compensation Fund was to protect the airline industry against lawsuits. "The September 11th Victim Compensation Fund of 2001 and the Protection of the Airline Industry: A Bill for the American People," *Journal of Air Law and Commerce* 67 (2002): 141–86, 172–74. J. D. Harrison reports: "80 percent of business owners said they oppose proposals to save federal money by curbing Social Security benefits, which have been floated in varying degrees by both parties in Washington. Nearly three in four said lawmakers shouldn't cut back on Medicare, and two in three said the same about proposed cuts to Medicaid." "Business Owners Urge Congress to Take Medicare, Social Security Cuts off the Table," *Washington Post*, February 20, 2013. Robert Pear has identified lobbying efforts by the food and beverage industries as a key part of the opposition to restrictions on the use of food stamps. "Soft Drink Industry Fights Proposed Food Stamp Ban," *New York Times*, April 29, 2011. This opposition is often public; a Walmart vice president said in a public statement: "Any reduction in SNAP benefits creates additional financial pressure on our customers who count on these

benefits. . . . [W]e encourage [Congress] to adopt reforms that do not impact those who need the program the most." Jack Sinclair, "Walmart Statement on SNAP Reductions," Corporate Walmart, December 6, 2013, https://corporate.walmart .com/_news_/news-archive/2013/11/01/walmart-statement-on-snap-reductions.

56. See the US Chamber Institute for Legal Reform report discussing a survey that found 65 percent of small business leaders are "very concerned" about the threat of litigation. *Creating Conditions for Economic Growth: The Role of the Legal Environment* (US Chamber Institute for Legal Reform, October 26, 2011), 7, http:// www.instituteforlegalreform.com/uploads/sites/1/Economic_Growth_Working _Paper_Oct2011_0.pdf. See also the argument that "direct administrative action trumps a [product liability] class action by leaps and bounds" and that "the simple remedy for misrepresentation of the status of ongoing merger talks is a [government] fine." Epstein, "Class Actions: Aggregation, Amplification, and Distortion," 516–18.

57. See generally Todd J. Zywicki, "Rent-Seeking, Crony Capitalism, and the Crony Constitution," *Supreme Court Economic Review* 23, no. 1 (2015): 77–103; and Paul H. Rubin, "Crony Capitalism," *Supreme Court Economic Review* 23, no. 1 (2015): 105–20.

58. Some people point to early New Deal legislation where the federal government delegated gatekeeping power to private trade associations as box 3 examples. See, e.g., A.L.A. Schechter Poultry Corp. v. United States, 295 U.S. 495 (1935). For similar schemes in Europe today, see, e.g., C. Boyden Gray, "Democracy at Home," *Texas Review of Law and Politics* 9, no. 2 (Spring 2005): 205–11, 209. But in these examples the government holds ultimate gatekeeping power and chooses to adopt what the private associations propose to it; these are not purely private schemes. Purely private ex ante schemes are very rare, with organizations that certify products as kosher and the like perhaps the best examples.

59. See Becker and Stigler, "Law Enforcement, Malfeasance, and Compensation of Enforcers"; and William M. Landes and Richard A. Posner, "The Private Enforcement of Law," *Journal of Legal Studies* 4, no. 1 (January 1975): 1–46.

60. See Becker and Stigler, "Law Enforcement, Malfeasance, and Compensation of Enforcers," 16–17.

61. See Landes and Posner, "The Private Enforcement of Law," 30.

62. See Landes and Posner's argument that there are "area[s] in which private enforcement is in fact clearly preferable to public enforcement" and that "perhaps the existing division of enforcement between the public and private sectors approximates the optimal division." "The Private Enforcement of Law," 3. Landes and Posner further explain that "society has left enforcement to the private sector in areas where private enforcement is clearly optimal." Ibid., 32.

63. For example, some of Hayek's endorsement of the common law has been interpreted to rest on the virtues of private enforcement and not just the virtues of judicial lawmaking. Peter J. Boettke and Rosolino Candela theorize: "If the law

itself can emerge endogenously, much like capital formation in a market economy through the mutual adjustment of diverse individual ends, then why cannot the mechanisms for its enforcement emerge endogenously as well? . . . If the market requires competition in order to utilize relevant information to correct errors in prices, then so does law as well." "Hayek, Leoni, and Law as a Fifth Factor of Production," *Atlantic Economic Journal* 42, no. 2 (2014): 123–31, 129. They go on to note: "Centralized law enforcement faces knowledge and accountability problems similar to those of central economic planners. Not only does the centralization of law lack the negative feedback loops of correcting errors made in legislation or interpreting legal precedents, but it is also susceptible to self-interested judges and legislators capturing the law to pursue their own ends in the name of the public interest. Consistent with Hayek's reconsideration of the merits of central banking . . . based on his own theory of spontaneous order, the decentralization of law into a plurality of competitive legal systems must also be considered on the same basis as well." Ibid., 130.

64. See Kagan's comment: "For example, conservative senators' reluctance to fund a federal enforcement bureaucracy led liberal sponsors of the 1968 Truth-in-Lending Act to enact an enforcement system that relied primarily on private lawsuits against lenders. Similarly, in 1991, as case backlogs swelled at the under-staffed Equal Employment Opportunity Commission, the response of Republican president George Bush (and the Democratic Congress) was not to bolster the EEOC but to encourage more private lawsuits to implement antidiscrimination laws." *Adversarial Legalism*, 50–51.

65. See Sean Farhang's discussion of the history of the Civil Rights Act of 1964, where he notes: "[Republican senator] Dirksen was adamant from the outset, and ultimately proved impossible to move, in his insistence that the central burden of enforcing the equal employment standards of Title VII lay with private plaintiffs. In the first circulated draft of Dirksen's proposed amendments to Title VII . . . [he] eliminat[ed] the EEOC's right to sue and reduc[ed] its role to nothing more than investigator and supervisor of voluntary conciliation efforts." *The Litigation State: Public Regulation and Private Lawsuits in the U.S.* (Princeton, NJ: Princeton University Press, 2010), 107–8. Farhang explains that a similar process played out with the Fair Housing Act of 1968: "As in 1964, Dirksen's enforcement formula [for the Fair Housing Act of 1968] attracted sufficient support from conservative Republicans to secure cloture. Private litigation was again offered by conservative Republicans as a substitute for bureaucratic state-building, and it again commanded broader consensus than the administrative power sought by liberal civil rights activists." Ibid., 120.

66. See Andrei Shleifer's explanation of the history: "Until the end of the nineteenth century, the U.S. . . . followed the laissez-faire ideal in which private litigation was the principal way of dealing with socially harmful acts. . . . Over thirty years, reformers eroded the nineteenth-century belief that private litigation was

the sole appropriate response to social wrongs. During the Progressive Era, regulatory agencies at both the state and the federal level took over the social control of competition, anti-trust policy, railroad pricing, food and drug safety, and many other areas." *The Failure of Judges and the Rise of Regulators* (Cambridge, MA: MIT University Press, 2012), 143, 148. Shleifer further notes: "Economists in the Coasian tradition typically focus on courts as enforcers of good conduct. . . . Economists on the left argue, in contrast, that government regulation is needed to prevent harmful conduct." Ibid., 147.

67. See Shleifer, *The Failure of Judges and the Rise of Regulators*. See also William B. Rubenstein's statement that "the private attorney general concept . . . was resisted by New Deal jurists who considered these so-called litigants mere rent-seekers challenging the new administrative state." "On What a Private Attorney General Is," 2135.

68. See Kalven and Rosenfield, "The Contemporary Function of the Class Suit," 686. For the text of the veto message, see Franklin D. Roosevelt, "Veto of a Bill Regulating Administrative Agencies." December 8, 1940. The American Presidency Project. http://www.presidency.ucsb.edu/ws/index.php?pid=15914.

69. See Burbank and Farhang, *Rights and Retrenchment*, 12.

70. See Burbank and Farhang, *Rights and Retrenchment*, 12.

71. For example, Lawyers for Civil Justice, an advocacy group for the corporate defense bar, submitted a public comment joined by several other corporate defense lobby groups arguing against private class action lawsuits because "this country has no shortage of actual, public attorneys general." Lawyers for Civil Justice et al., "To Restore a Relationship between Classes and Their Actions." Linda Mullenix argues: "The corporate behavior that gives rise to small claim harms ought to be dealt with through regulatory action, including penalties, fines, product recall or withdrawals, or criminal sanctions." "Ending Class Actions as We Know Them," 440.

Chapter Three

1. See John D. Donahue's explanation: "Privatization, as today's fiscally ambitious, ideologically charged phenomenon, began as a British import. English academics and Conservative party officials prepared a sweeping privatization agenda as Margaret Thatcher took office in 1979, and the British government shed major assets and responsibilities throughout the 1980s." *The Privatization Decision: Public Ends, Private Means* (New York: Basic, 1991), 4. For another discussion of the origins of the conservative privatization movement in the Thatcher government, see Stuart M. Butler, *Privatizing Federal Spending: A Strategy to Eliminate the Deficit* (New York: Universe, 1985), 34.

2. The Reason Foundation claims, without exaggeration, that "Reason works at the forefront of privatization policy." *Annual Privatization Report 2006: Trans-*

forming Government through Privatization (Los Angeles: Reason Foundation, 2006), 2, https://reason.org/wp-content/uploads/files/d767317fa4806296191436e9 5f68082a.pdf.

3. Alfred C. Aman Jr. notes that "Robert Poole, founder of the Reason Foundation (the leading think tank of the privatization movement), has been credited with inventing the term 'privatization' in the 1960s." "Privatization and Democracy: Resources in Administrative Law," in *Government by Contract: Outsourcing and American Democracy*, ed. Jody Freeman and Martha Minow (Cambridge, MA: Harvard University Press, 2009), 61–288, 262. See also the Reason Foundation's citation of Peter Drucker's *The Age of Discontinuity* (London: William Heinemann, 1969) and William Wooldridge's *Uncle Sam, the Monopoly Man* (New Rochelle, NY: Arlington House, 1970) for conceiving of privatization as an intellectual movement. *Transforming Government*, 21.

4. The Reason Foundation catalogs some of the connections between the conservative and libertarian movements and privatization. For example, it notes that the Annual Privatization Report "is the brainchild of Reason Foundation Trustee David Koch." *Transforming Government*, 2. It lists contributions to the report by Margaret Thatcher, Mitch Daniels, Mark Sanford, Stephen Goldsmith, Robert Poole, E. S. Savas, Ronald Utt, John Blundell, William Eggers, Roger Feldman, Lawrence Martin, and Grover Norquist. Ibid., 6. It recounts privatization efforts in the Reagan administration, including the 1985 White House seminar on privatization and the President's Commission on Privatization led by Elizabeth Dole, divesting two DC airports, selling Conrail, and proposals not adopted by Congress that included "privatization of federal lands, Coast Guard rescue responsibilities, adjudication of federal tax disputes, the US Postal Service, the Naval Petroleum Reserves, the US Helium Reserves, the uranium enrichment program, and many others." Ibid., 22–25. It traces this history into the George W. Bush administration, including a push for competitive sourcing of government functions. Ibid., 23–30. And it notes that, "in the mid-1980s . . . , the concept of turning over public services or infrastructure to the private sector was strongly associated with center-right parties and politicians like Ronald Reagan and Margaret Thatcher." Ibid., 36.

Donahue also acknowledges the deep connection between privatization and conservatism, noting that "conservative intellectuals in the United States set out to emulate the British example," and cites Savas, a senior Reagan appointee, Manuel Johnson, an influential governor of the Federal Reserve, and Stuart Butler, the director of the Heritage Foundation, as American conservative proponents of this viewpoint. *The Privatization Decision*, 4. Aman writes: "The 'Reagan Revolution' [was] a deliberate and sustained focus on economic reforms that included . . . 'privatization.' . . . A concerted attempt to move toward increased privatization of government was always central to the revolution's ideological goals." "Privatization and Democracy." 452 n. 1. Later, he cites Newt Gingrich as another conservative advocate for privatization. Ibid., 454 n. 6. Anthony B. L. Cheung writes that "privatization is advocated by the neo-classical economists as the medicine to cure the ailing Western interventionist state which was used to Keynesian demand-management and state welfare." "The Rise of Privatization Policies: Similar Faces, Diverse Motives," *International Journal of Public Administration* 20, no. 12 (1997): 2213–45, 2214. He further notes that "the main theoretical justifications for contemporary privatizations have come from 'New Right activists' and 'pro-market think-tanks.'" Ibid., 2221.

5. David Osborne and Ted Gaebler write that "conservatives have long argued that governments should turn over many of their functions to the private sector—by abandoning some, selling others, and contracting with private firms to handle others." *Reinventing Government: How the Entrepreneurial Spirit Is Transforming the Public Sector* (New York: Penguin, 1993), 45. Matt Zwolinski comments: "Libertarians have been some of the earliest and most vocal supporters of 'privatization.' And this should come as no surprise. For the basic idea of privatization involves transferring power out of the hands of the state and into the hands of the market. Whether it be selling off industries that were formerly owned and controlled by the state . . . or merely opening up state services to competitive bidding from the private sector . . . , privatization appears to move society in the direction of greater competition, greater efficiency, and smaller government. What's a libertarian not to love?" "A Libertarian Case for the Moral Limits of Markets," *Georgetown Journal of Law and Public Policy* 13, no. 2 (2015): 275–90, 283. Similarly, Richard C. Box surveys the history: "It was in the 1980s, amid the antigovernment ideology of the Reagan administration and a wave of public sentiment for shrinking the public sector, that market-like concepts broke through the weak wall of separation between the values of the market and the values of public management. Trickle-down, supply-side economics and public choice economics pointed the way to prosperity through smaller government, and it was thought that bureaucratic waste could be eliminated through contracting out and becoming entrepreneurial." "Running Government Like a Business: Implications for Public Administration Theory and Practice," *American Review of Public Administration* 29, no. 1 (1999): 19–43, 29.

6. See, e.g., Donahue's division of privatization schemes into categories depending on whether the services or goods are delivered by public or private entities and whether the payment is collective or individual. *The Privatization Decision*, 7. E. S. Savas lists this spectrum of activity from more privatized to less privatized: market, franchise, vouchers, grants, contract, government vending, intergovernment agreement, and government. *Privatization and Public-Private Partnerships* (New York: Chatham House, 2000), 88, table 4.6.

7. See Donahue's statement: "Two concepts share the same word—privatization. The first concept . . . involves removing certain responsibilities, activities, or assets from the collective realm. This is the chief meaning of privatization in countries retreating from postwar, postcolonial experiments with socialism, as they separate

factories, mines, airlines and railroads from public control. The United States, for most of its history, has so tenaciously resisted collectivism that there is not much of a socialized sector to dismantle, however favorable the political winds may be." *The Privatization Decision*, 215. Stan Soloway and Alan Chvotkin make a similar point: "In some countries, particularly Great Britain . . . , 'privatization' has been a steady trend for decades. . . . In the United States, . . . true privatization is actually significantly more limited and is generally driven by some combination of financial pressures (particularly the availability to the government of investment capital) and a desire to put into place a competitive alternative to activities that are believed to be poorly functioning." "Federal Contracting in Context: What Drives It, How to Improve It," in Freeman and Minow, eds., *Government by Contract*, 192–240, 196.

8. See Donahue's recognition that, "[in the United States, there is a] second meaning of privatization: retaining collective financing but delegating delivery to the private sector." *The Privatization Decision*, 215. The Reason Foundation makes a similar point: "In its purest form, the term [privatization] refers to the divesture of government-owned assets. . . . As the concept has evolved, privatization has grown to resemble more of an umbrella term to account for greater private sector participation in the delivery of services." *Transforming Government*, 3. Jon Michaels also makes much the same point, explaining: "In other contexts, privatization refers to different practices, including the sale of state assets. But the outsourcing of service responsibilities is the dominant meaning of privatization in the American context." "Running Government Like a Business . . . Then and Now," *Harvard Law Review* 128, no. 4 (2015): 1152–82, 1171 n. 84.

9. See, e.g., Gary S. Becker and Richard A. Posner, *Uncommon Sense: Economic Insights, from Marriage to Terrorism* (Chicago: University of Chicago Press, 2009), 91–94, 293–96; President's Commission on Privatization, *Privatization: Toward More Effective Government* (Washington, DC: President's Commission on Privatization, June 1988), xvii, http://pdf.usaid.gov/pdf_docs/PNABB472.pdf; Butler, *Privatizing Federal Spending*, 133; and Reason Foundation, *Transforming Government*, 22.

10. See, e.g., Robert W. Poole, *Cutting Back City Hall* (New York: Universe, 1980), 86; and Reason Foundation, *Transforming Government*, 26.

11. See, e.g., Becker and Posner, *Uncommon Sense*, 91–94, 293–96; Randal O'Toole, "Stopping the Runaway Train: The Case for Privatizing Amtrak," Policy Analysis no. 712 (Washington, DC: Cato Institute, 2012), https://www.cato.org/publications/policy-analysis/stopping-runaway-train-case-privatizing-amtrak; Ronald Utt, "Chairman Mica's New Amtrak Proposal Would Use the Private Sector to Reform Passenger Rail," *Web Memo* no. 3290 (June 13, 2011), http://thf_media.s3.amazonaws.com/2011/pdf/wm3290.pdf; President's Commission on Privatization, *Privatization: Toward More Effective Government*, xix; and Butler, *Privatizing Federal Spending*, 76–78.

12. See, e.g., James T. Bennett and Manuel H. Johnson, *Better Government at Half the Price: Private Production of Public Services* (Ottawa, IL: Jameson, 1982), 1.

13. See, e.g., President's Commission on Privatization, *Privatization: Toward More Effective Government*, xvii; Savas, *Privatization and Public-Private Partnerships*, 273; and Reason Foundation, *Transforming Government*, 131–42.

14. See, e.g., Bennett and Johnson, *Better Government at Half the Price*, 1.

15. See, e.g., Ronald Utt, *Privatize the General Services Administration through an Employee Buyout* (Washington, DC: Heritage Foundation, May 26, 1995), https://www.heritage.org/government-regulation/report/privatize-the-general-services-administration-through-employeebuyout.

16. See, e.g., Becker and Posner, *Uncommon Sense*, 91–94, 293–96; President's Commission on Privatization, *Privatization: Toward More Effective Government*, 193; and House Budget Committee, *The Path to Prosperity: A Blueprint for American Renewal* (112th Congress, 2012), 14, http://budget.house.gov/uploadedfiles/pathtoprosperity2013.pdf.; Katherine Mangu-Ward, "It's Time to Privatize the V.A.," *Reason*, November 2017, https://reason.com/archives/2017/10/30/its-time-to-privatize-the-va.

17. See, e.g., Becker and Posner, *Uncommon Sense*, 91–94, 293–96.

18. See, e.g., Becker and Posner, *Uncommon Sense*, 91–94, 293–96.

19. See, e.g., President's Commission on Privatization, *Privatization: Toward More Effective Government*, 209.

20. See, e.g., President's Commission on Privatization, *Privatization: Toward More Effective Government*, 7; and Butler, *Privatizing Federal Spending*, 66.

21. See, e.g., President's Commission on Privatization, *Privatization: Toward More Effective Government*, 218; Savas, *Privatization and Public-Private Partnerships*, 128; and Reason Foundation, *Transforming Government*, 89.

22. See, e.g., President's Commission on Privatization, *Privatization: Toward More Effective Government*, 218; House Budget Committee, *The Path to Prosperity*, 26; and Brian Riley and Brett Shaefer, *Time to Privatize OPIC* (Washington, DC: Heritage Foundation, May 19, 2014), https://www.heritage.org/global-politics/report/time-privatize-opic.

23. See, e.g., James P. Beckwith Jr., "Parks, Property Rights, and the Possibilities of Private Law," *Cato Journal* 1, no. 2 (1981): 473–99; Butler, *Privatizing Federal Spending*, 111; and Terry L. Anderson, Vernon L. Smith, and Emily Simmons, "How and Why to Privatize Federal Lands," *Policy Analysis*, no. 363 (November 9, 1999), https://www.perc.org/wp-content/uploads/old/pa1.pdf.

24. See, e.g., President's Commission on Privatization, *Privatization: Toward More Effective Government*, 176.

25. See, e.g., Becker and Posner, *Uncommon Sense*, 91–94, 293–96; President's Commission on Privatization, *Privatization: Toward More Effective Government*, 101; and Butler, *Privatizing Federal Spending*, 124.

26. See, e.g., Bennett and Johnson, *Better Government at Half the Price*, 1; and Savas, *Privatization and Public-Private Partnerships*, 117.

27. See, e.g., Alexander Volokh, "Prison Vouchers," *University of Pennsylvania Law Review* 160, no. 3 (2012): 779–863; Alexander Volokh, "The Constitutional Possibilities of Prison Vouchers," *Ohio State Law Journal* 72, no. 5 (2011): 983–1042; President's Commission on Privatization, *Privatization: Toward More Effective Government*, 146; and Reason Foundation, *Transforming Government*, 215.

28. See, e.g., Butler, *Privatizing Federal Spending*, 160; and Newt Gingrich, "Unleashing Growth and Innovation to Move Beyond the Welfare State" (press release, November 21, 2011), http://www.presidency.ucsb.edu/ws/index.php?pid =97588; and Reason Foundation, *Transforming Government*, 160.

29. See, e.g., Edward L. Hudgins, "Time to Privatize NASA," *Baltimore Sun*, January 26, 1998.

30. See, e.g., Bennett and Johnson, *Better Government at Half the Price*, 1; and Savas, *Privatization and Public-Private Partnerships*, 176.

31. See, e.g., Savas, *Privatization and Public-Private Partnerships*, 213; and Reason Foundation, *Transforming Government*, 3.

32. See, e.g., Savas's argument that "government is too big, too powerful, too intrusive in people's lives and therefore is a danger to democracy." *Privatization and Public-Private Partnerships*, 5. Savas continues, reviewing ideological arguments against government from political and economic philosophy in his argument for privatization. Ibid., 6–9. Later, he argues that "contracting limits the size of government." Ibid., 110. Butler makes a similar point, advocating privatization to "cut the public sector down to size" and "cutting the federal budget." *Privatizing Federal Spending*, 34; 57. Poole, in a section entitled "limiting the growth of government," states that "the total size of government . . . can held down or cut back by using contracting." *Cutting Back City Hall*, 29. Veronique de Rugy argues that funding infrastructure through user fees "lessens the need for massive federal expenditures." "Federal Infrastructure Spending Is a Bad Deal," *Reason*, March 2017, https://rea son.com/archives/2017/02/09/federal-infrastructure-spendin/print. And Jody Freeman and Martha Minow comment: "The impetus to outsource government work is driven to a significant extent by both pragmatism and ideology. . . . [Some] embrace outsourcing as a way to limit government." "Introduction: Reframing the Outsourcing Debates," in Freeman and Minow, eds., *Government by Contract*, 1–20, 8.

33. See, e.g., Michaels' observation that, "in the absence of opportunities to maximize pay, salaried careerists would . . . use their discretion to aggrandize their own administrative fiefdoms." "Running Government Like a Business," 1169. Michaels also notes that "privatization advocates insist that private actors have the financial incentives to outperform salaried government workers." Ibid., 1172.

34. See, e.g., [James Madison], "The Alleged Danger from the Powers of the Union to the State Governments Considered," Federalist Papers, no. 45, 1788, Avalon Project, Yale Law School, http://avalon.law.yale.edu/18th_century/fed45.asp.

35. See Murray Newton Rothbard, *For a New Liberty: The Libertarian Manifesto*, 2nd ed. (Auburn, AL: Ludwig von Mises Institute, 2007), 192.

36. See, e.g., the Reason Foundation's citation of "expanded choices, higher quality services, and lower costs" as a justification for privatization. *Transforming Government*, 3. Madsen Pirie argues that the private sector performs "more efficiently, more cheaply, and with greater satisfaction" than the public sector does. *Dismantling the State: The Theory and Practice of Privatization* (Dallas: National Center for Policy Analysis, 1985), 4. Maxwell L. Sterns and Todd J. Zywicki write that "studies of government-owned corporations indicate that as compared with otherwise similar private market actors, government employees tend to work less and at lower efficiency, while drawing higher salaries for any given level of professional responsibility." *Public Choice Concepts and Applications in Law* (Eagan, MN: West Academic, 2009), 349.

37. See, e.g., Butler's explanation: "The notion of ownership is central to the idea of privatizing federal assets. Ownership provides people with a stake in an asset and encourages them to manage and use it as efficiently as they can. When they have no such stake, they tend to behave differently towards the asset." *Privatizing Federal Spending*, 65.

38. Poole quotes a government contractor as saying: "We have the greatest incentive in the world to innovate, to pioneer, to analyze every little step." *Cutting Back City Hall*, 27–28.

39. See, e.g., Bennett and Johnson's statement: "Incentives usually consist of two parts: the 'carrot' of reward for good performance and the 'stick' of punishment for bad performance. Unfortunately, neither the carrot nor the stick is present in government bureaucracies." *Better Government at Half the Price*, 20. The same authors make a similar point when they write: "In contrast to the public sector, both the carrot of reward and the stick of punishment fully operate in private enterprise." Ibid., 31.

40. See, e.g., Savas's argument that "contracting is more efficient because . . . the costs and benefits of managerial decisions are felt more directly by the decision maker, whose own rewards are often directly at stake." *Privatization and Public-Private Partnerships*, 109. Savas expands on this point later in his book, summarizing academic literature comparing the "motivation and performance of public and private organizations" to say that "in the public sector there is little incentive to perform efficiently, and management lacks effective control over human and capital resources; in the private sector generally there are both carrots, in the form of raises and promotions, and sticks, in the form of demotions and firings" and that "whereas a private firm generally prospers by satisfying paying customers, a public agency can prosper (i.e., get a bigger budget) even if the customers remain unsatisfied": "In fact, paradoxically, sometimes the budget grows even as customer dissatisfaction grows." Ibid., 112.

41. Peter H. Schuck, *Why Government Fails So Often: And How It Can Do Better* (Princeton, NJ: Princeton University Press, 2014), 101, 205.

42. For example, the Environmental Protection Agency estimates that American sewers release raw sewage into the water supply twenty-three to seventy-five thousand times a year. "Sanitary Sewer Overflows (SSOs)," https://www.epa.gov /npdes/sanitary-sewer-overflows-ssos. The Federal Highway Administration estimates that 56,007 bridges in the United States are structurally deficient. Department of Transportation, "National Bridge Inventory: Deficient Bridges by Highway System 2016," https://www.fhwa.dot.gov/bridge/nbi/no10/defbr16.cfm. The American Society of Civil Engineers estimates that, over the next decade, America's failure to invest in infrastructure will cost $4 trillion in lost GDP. *Failure to Act: Closing the Infrastructure Investment Gap for America's Economic Future* (Reston, VA: American Society of Civil Engineers, May 23, 2016), 4, https://www.infrastructurereport card.org/wp-content/uploads/2016/05/ASCE-Failure-to-Act-Report-for-Web-5.23 .16.pdf.

43. The Department of the Treasury estimates that IRS enforcement spending has a six-to-one direct return on investment and an indirect return on investment as a result of deterrence three times the direct impact. *The Budget in Brief: Internal Revenue Service: FY 2015* (Washington, DC: Department of the Treasury, 2015), https:// www.irs.gov/pub/irs-news/IRS%20FY%202015%20Budget%20in%20Brief.pdf.

44. As Brandon DeBot, Emily Horton, and Chuck Marr note: "The IRS has been targeted for sharp funding cuts since 2010. Its current budget of $11.2 billion is 18 percent below the 2010 level, after adjusting for inflation." "Trump Budget Continues Multi-Year Assault on IRS Funding Despite Mnuchin's Call for More Resources," Center on Budget and Policy Priorities, March 16, 2017, https://www .cbpp.org/research/federal-budget/trump-budget-continues-multi-year-assault-on -irs-funding-despite-mnuchins.

45. See Schuck's summary: "Studies indicate that . . . services can usually be provided better and more cheaply by private groups due to . . . more access to capital . . . and other efficiencies." *Why Government Fails So Often*, 101. Likewise, Soloway and Chvotkin observe that, "in the United States, . . . privatization . . . is generally driven by . . . financial pressures . . . [such as] [un]availability to the government of investment capital." "Federal Contracting in Context," 196.

46. Savas explains the situation by suggesting: "A would-be contractor might offer . . . a campaign contribution . . . to a public official to influence the award in his favor, or the official might take the initiative and solicit a payment. . . . [Or] consider the situation where public-sector employee unions give endorsements, make campaign contributions, and supply campaign workers to favored candidates for office." *Privatization and Public-Private Partnerships*, 99. Bennett and Johnson write that "there is an even simpler way to avoid the political corruption that can accompany contracting out: eliminate the role of government altogether." *Better Government at Half the Price*, 80.

47. See Winston's detailed chart showing which interest groups rent seek in which policy areas. *Government Failure versus Market Failure*, 83–84.

48. See Zingales's explanation: "The reason that regulatory capture is a persuasive hypothesis is that economic incentives encourage even the best-intentioned regulators to cater to the interests of the businesses they regulate. To begin with, regulators depend upon the regulated for much of the information they need to do their jobs properly. This dependency creates an incentive to be friendly to the information providers. Also, regulators' human capital is highly industry-specific, and their best future jobs are likely to be with the regulated; hence, their desire to preserve future career options makes it difficult not to cater to those they regulate. Finally, the regulated are the only real audience of the regulators, since taxpayers seldom care about regulatory findings; hence the regulators will naturally define their on-the-job performance with the regulated in mind, a process that will again incentivize them to sympathize with the interests of the regulated." *A Capitalism for the People*, 95.

49. Schuck writes: "Officials pursue their self-interest. . . . The body of scholarship that advances and seeks empirical support for this rational-actor model is known as 'public choice' . . . theory. . . . It claims to show that these utility-maximizing policy-oriented actors . . . produce policies that tend to be inefficient and cost-ineffective, and to benefit discrete, well-organized interests at the expense of the diffuse general public." *Why Government Fails So Often*, 130. See also Patrick Dunleavy, "Explaining the Privatization Boom: Public Choice versus Radical Approaches," *Public Administration* 64, no. 1 (1986): 13–34, 16.

50. Schuck discusses "agency 'capture'" where "mutuality of influences and interests are fundamental aspects of regulatory politics that cause program performance to deviate, often greatly, from policy goals." *Why Government Fails So Often*, 215. Zingales also discusses "regulatory capture." *A Capitalism for the People*, 95.

51. See Michaels's observation that, "were government officials motivated by . . . monetary incentives, they would strive to maximize their pay—and thus be far less susceptible to special interests' pressures and enticements." "Running Government Like a Business," 1168.

52. See Lahav's reasoning: "When experts within an agency have close ties to the companies they regulate, when they stand to benefit from the success of those companies, or plan to work there in the future, their opinion about the safety of drugs is suspect. It is well known that experts and agency staff move from positions in government to private industry (and back again) and can capitalize on the knowledge developed in each position. This revolving door . . . is worrisome." *In Praise of Litigation*, 36. Zingales cites examples of this in the financial industry, including the decision by big banks to come under more regulation of the Federal Reserve after the financial crisis: "From the beginning . . . large banks made it clear that they wanted to be regulated. . . . The reason wasn't that the Fed had the best record in solving problems or that it was the most logical regulator. . . . Rather, it was that the Fed was already influenced by the large banks, which choose the board of the New York Fed and provide much of the information needed by the Fed to operate." *A Capitalism for the People*, xxi (see also xviii–xix, xxvii).

53. Winston writes that "government intervention may prove to be counterproductive . . . because policymakers . . . are subject to political forces that enable certain interest groups to benefit at the expense of the public." *Government Failure versus Market Failure*, 75.

54. See Schuck's summary that "studies indicate that . . . services can usually be provided better and more cheaply by private groups due to competition . . . and other efficiencies." *Why Government Fails So Often*, 101. Savas argues that "contracting is more efficient because [it] harnesses competitive forces." *Privatization and Public-Private Partnerships*, 109. Likewise, Donahue posits that "*public versus private* matters, but *competitive versus noncompetitive* usually matters more." *The Privatization Decision*, 78. Soloway and Chvotkin comment that, "in the United States, . . . [privatization] is generally driven by . . . a desire to put into place a competitive alternative to activities that are believed to be poorly functioning." "Federal Contracting in Context," 196.

55. Hayek, *The Constitution of Liberty*, 263. See also the recent book by the conservative federal judge Jeff Sutton, who makes the case for decentralization in the context of interpreting the Constitution. *51 Imperfect Solutions: States and the Making of American Constitutional Law* (Oxford University Press, 2018), 20.

56. See Aman's comment that "proponents present competition as a driver for efficiency, cost saving, and improved ratios of cost and quality, as well as a mechanism to enhance the performance of current government-run enterprises." "Privatization and Democracy," 269.

57. Pirie writes that "private programs are subject to economic disciplines, and respond to choices made by the beneficiaries of these programs." *Dismantling the State*, 3. He expands on this, writing that "the market measures, and responds to, the choices and preferences of people more accurately than the political process." Ibid., 4. Indeed, he explains that the market "can give consumers choice and input" and respond to "competition and cost controls." Ibid., 25.

58. Margaret H. Lemos, "Privatizing Public Litigation," *Georgetown Law Journal* 104, no. 3 (2016): 515–82, 538, 540.

59. Freeman and Minow survey a range of objections to privatization brought by liberal scholars. "Introduction: Reframing the Outsourcing Debates," 4–5, 9.

60. Farhang observes that "it privatizes a huge majority of the costs of enforcement." *The Litigation State*, 55. Similarly, Stephen Burbank, Sean Farhang, and Herbert Kritzer note: "Private enforcement regimes can . . . shift the costs of regulation off of government budgets and onto the private sector . . . [and] limit the need for direct and visible intervention by the bureaucracy in the economy and society." "Private Enforcement," *Lewis and Clark Law Review* 17, no. 3 (2013): 637–722, 662. They go on to posit: "[Private litigation] may be preferred to bureaucratic state-building by legislators with antistatist preferences, a significant strand of the American political tradition, particularly as applied to the central state in the United States' federalist system. Indeed, private enforcement regimes may be

embraced by such legislators as a way of thwarting the growth of bureaucracy." Ibid., 665.

61. Gold explains: "Use of the private right of action is thus appropriately open to the plaintiff's discretion. Within this rubric, there is a reason why corrective justice is not a state-compelled remedy. The rights at issue belong to the party who was wronged. She gets to decide whether to do something about being wronged, including whether to make use of her entitlement to enforce her rights. If the state intervened as a matter of course, the party who was wronged would have less control over the counterparty's duties than her moral enforcement rights provide for." Andrew S. Gold, "A Moral Rights Theory of Private Law." *William and Mary Law Review* 52, no. 6 (2011): 1873–1931, 1912.

62. See Walter Olson, *The Litigation Explosion: What Happened When America Unleashed the Lawsuit* (New York: Penguin, 1991), 46, 48. See also David L. Schwartz, "The Rise of Contingent Fee Representation in Patent Litigation," *Alabama Law Review* 64, no. 2 (2012): 335–88.

63. Steven Shavell explains: "Under contingency fee arrangements, the lawyer's incentives are different [than the incentives of an hourly rate attorney], leading the lawyer to press for settlement more often than when the settlement offer exceeds the expected judgment net of litigation costs, because the lawyer bears all the litigation costs but obtains only a percentage of the settlement." *Foundations of Economic Analysis of Law* (Cambridge, MA: Harvard University Press, 2009), 435.

64. David Freeman Engstrom cites scholars who argue that "profit-motivated private enforcers supply salutary forms of legal innovation." "Private Enforcement's Pathways: Lessons from Qui Tam Litigation," *Columbia Law Review* 114, no. 8 (2014): 1913–2006, 1918. He goes on to note that a "common claim is that entrepreneurial private enforcers serve as incubators, bringing fresh ideas to the regulatory marketplace." Ibid., 1931. And he writes that "champions assert that the profit-motivated nature of private enforcement renders it more cost-effective and nimbler than poorly incentivized or sclerotic public enforcement bureaucracies." Ibid., 1925. John C. Coffee Jr. theorizes that "the private attorney general is induced by the profit motive to seek out cases that otherwise might go undetected" or to "intensif[y] the penalty [in cases that are otherwise detected]." "Rescuing the Private Attorney General: Why the Model of the Lawyer as Bounty Hunter Is Not Working," *Maryland Law Review* 42, no. 2 (1983): 215–88, 220, 223. Elsewhere, he reasons that "the plaintiff's attorney in these actions behaves as a risk-taking entrepreneur." John C. Coffee Jr., "Understanding the Plaintiff's Attorney: The Implications of Economic Theory for Private Enforcement of Law through Class and Derivative Actions," *Columbia Law Review* 86, no. 4 (1986): 669–727, 677. Lemos posits that "government attorneys . . . have 'low powered' incentives compared to private employees" (quotation marks omitted). "Privatizing Public Litigation," 540. She expands on this elsewhere, commenting that "the percentage-fee arrangement under which most private class counsel work has the advantage of

linking the interests of attorney and clients: the attorney's fee increases as the clients' recovery grows." Margaret H. Lemos, "Aggregate Litigation Goes Public:
Representative Suits by State Attorneys General," *Harvard Law Review* 126, no. 2
(2012): 486–549, 515. Anthony Casey and Anthony Niblett present evidence "that
the court-centric private-plaintiff [qui tam] mechanism is superior to the agency-
centric mechanism when there is asymmetric information." "Noise Reduction:
The Screening Value of Qui Tam," *Washington University Law Review* 91, no. 5
(2014): 1169–1217, 1174–75. Lahav observes: "The interests of the lawyers bringing these cases are well-aligned with the merits of the legal action. Many private
lawyers are paid only if they win." *In Praise of Litigation*, 38–39. Martin Redish
observes: "The concept of the bounty hunter holds a venerable position in our
nation's history. . . . [T]he pursuit of private gain motivates private individuals to
expose legal activity, thereby supposedly furthering the broader public interest in
having the corporate world adhere to the broad behavioral proscriptions set by
governmental authorities." *Wholesale Justice: Constitutional Democracy and the
Problem of the Class Action Lawsuit* (Stanford, CA: Stanford University Press,
2009), 26. Later, he comments: "Private litigation may often do the government's
work for it, by deterring and punishing violations of law. By seeking to benefit
the individual litigants . . . adjudication [has] the incidental impact of advancing
the public interest." Ibid., 31. Lemos and Minzner note that some of the fire of the
profit motive can be introduced among government lawyers if the departments
they work for are permitted to keep the enforcement monies they recover instead
of remitting them to the general treasury. See their chronicling of "when enforcement agencies are permitted to retain all or some of the proceeds of enforcement"
and how they accordingly "are likely to behave more like private enforcers than
is commonly appreciated" even though "their employees are paid by salary" and
do not profit financially. Margaret H. Lemos and Max Minzner, "For-Profit Public
Enforcement," *Harvard Law Review* 127, no. 3 (2014): 853–913, 854.

65. Becker and Stigler write that "the essence of victim enforcement is compensation of enforcers on performance . . . instead of by a straight salary." "Law
Enforcement, Malfeasance, and Compensation of Enforcers," 14. They expand
on this point, theorizing: "The right of amount of self-protection by potential victims is encouraged, not the excessive (wasteful) self-protection that results when
victims are not completely compensated, or the inadequate self-protection that
results when they are automatically compensated. Further, the rewards of innovation will spur technical progress in private enforcement as in other economic
callings." Ibid., 15.

66. Olson, *The Litigation Explosion*, 42.

67. Sometimes this is because the profit motive creates incentives for too much
litigation, but sometimes it is because private actors are not profit motivated
enough. Conservatives sometimes complain about the latter with respect to so-
called citizen suits under our environmental laws, where ideological zealots can

bring lawsuits even when they are economically irrational. Conservatives generally oppose environmental citizen suits in favor of the government because they do not like this profit-unconstrained ideological zealotry. See, e.g., the comment that "environmental citizen suits" are brought by "public spirited activists and citizen groups concerned about local environmental problems" without " 'bounties' paid to the initiators of the suit," which leads them to sometimes sue "the least significant" violator. Jonathan H. Adler, "Stand or Deliver: Citizen Suits, Standing, and Environmental Protection," *Duke Environmental Law and Policy Forum* 12, no. 1 (2001): 39–83, 45, 51. Alternatively, as with many class action lawsuits, I suspect that they simply oppose the underlying environmental laws and wish them enforced as little as possible.

68. Schuck, *Why Government Fails So Often*, 223.

69. See Burbank, Farhang, and Kritzer's summary: "Regulation scholars have often observed that budgetary limitations are a core and recurring constraint on the administrative state's enforcement capacity." "Private Enforcement," 662. Kenneth W. Dam observes that "the public enforcement agency is subject to a budget constraint." "Class Actions: Efficiency, Compensation, Deterrence, and Conflict of Interest," *Journal of Legal Studies* 4, no. 1 (January 1975): 47–73, 67. Landes and Posner comment that "budgets of public enforcement agencies tend to be small in relation to the potential gains from enforcement as they would be appraised by a private, profit-maximizing enforcer." "The Private Enforcement of Law," 36. And Lahav explains that "the benefit of regulation through private litigation is that it does not depend on funding agencies or lawyers employed by the government." *In Praise of Litigation*, 38.

70. Coffee, *Entrepreneurial Litigation*, 117.

71. Joseph A. Grundfest, "Disimplying Private Rights of Action under the Federal Securities Laws: The Commission's Authority," *Harvard Law Review* 107, no. 5 (1994): 961–1024, 969 (internal quotation marks omitted).

72. Nishal Ray Ramphal, "The Role of Public and Private Litigation in the Enforcement of Securities Laws in the United States" (PhD diss., Rand Graduate School, 2007), 103.

73. Brandon L. Garrett quotes with approval a *New York Times* report making this point. *Too Big to Jail: How Prosecutors Compromise with Corporations* (Cambridge, MA: Harvard University Press, 2014), 267.

74. Coffee observes that "the private attorney general offers four key benefits [including] expanded resources that are independent of the budgetary process." *Entrepreneurial Litigation*, 232. Burbank, Farhang, and Kritzer posit that "private enforcement regimes can . . . multiply resources devoted to prosecuting enforcement actions . . . [and] take advantage of private information." "Private Enforcement," 662. Rubenstein suggests that "private attorneys may be better . . . because public attorneys may be fewer in number, underfunded, less skilled." "On What a Private Attorney General Is," 2149–50. Amanda M. Rose argues that a "factor

that might tip the scales in favor of private enforcement is simple resource advantage." "Reforming Securities Litigation Reform: Restructuring the Relationship between Public and Private Enforcement of Rule 10b-5," *Columbia Law Review* 108, no. 6 (2008): 1301–64, 1344. And Daniel A. Crane writes that "a system of private enforcement . . . supplies . . . enhanced enforcement resources." "Optimizing Private Antitrust Enforcement," *Vanderbilt Law Review* 63, no. 3 (2010): 675–723, 677.

75. See Brian T. Fitzpatrick, "Do Class Action Lawyers Make Too Little?," *University of Pennsylvania Law Review* 158, no. 7 (2010): 2062.

76. Landes and Posner, "The Private Enforcement of Law," 36.

77. Lemos, "Aggregate Litigation Goes Public," 524.

78. Zachary D. Clopton writes: "The most likely result is that public enforcers accept a reduction in overall levels of deterrence and enforcement." "Class Actions and Executive Power," 889.

79. Schuck notes that "there are many reasons for limited, weak enforcement, . . . [including that] the officials who run the regulatory agencies tend to be mindful of the need—both political and bureaucratic—to cultivate and sustain the regulated industry." *Why Government Fails So Often*, 221–22. He goes on to explain that the "enforcement . . . and administrative implementation of regulatory statutes is always shaped by a process in which industry lobbying plays an important role." Ibid., 223. Furthermore, he observes that "politicians sometimes seek to restrain enforcement against putative violators who are their constituents, allies, or favored interests." Ibid., 226. Coffee argues that "*elected* state officials are particularly likely to serve as unfaithful agents of class members' interests." *Entrepreneurial Litigation*, 192. Engstrom observes that "public prosecutors and agency administrators have their own mix of politically inflected and careerist incentives that can cause public enforcement to deviate from the ideal." "Private Enforcement's Pathways," 1930. He goes on to note that agencies are "imperfect guardians" because of "regulatory 'capture'" and "politically conscious agencies will allocate resources with an eye to collecting political rewards and ensuring the continued flow of resources to the agency." Ibid., 1930, 1939. Ramphal recalls that "for most of its history the [SEC] has been plagued by . . . the political whims of all varieties of politicians." "The Role of Public and Private Litigation," 103. However, Lahav notes that "private litigants are . . . not subject to regulatory capture, as government employees looking toward their next job in the private sector might be." *In Praise of Litigation*, 38. Clopton suggests that "public enforcers may be less likely to pursue cases against their political allies." "Class Actions and Executive Power," 893.

80. Hovenkamp, "Appraising the Progressive State," 1086.

81. See Shleifer's citation of "the Chicago School" for the proposition that "the political process of regulation is typically captured by the regulated industry itself." *The Failure of Judges and the Rise of Regulators*, 4.

82. See James M. Buchanan and Gordon Tullock, *The Calculus of Consent: Logical Foundations of Constitutional Democracy* (Ann Arbor: University of Michigan Press, 1962).

83. Anahad O'Connor, "Study Warns of Diet Supplement Dangers Kept Quiet by FDA," *New York Times*, April 7, 2015.

84. See Danielle Ivory, "Federal Auditor Finds Broad Failures at NHTSA," *New York Times*, June 19, 2015.

85. Rena Steinzor, "(Still) 'Unsafe at Any Speed': Why Not Jail for Auto Executives?," *Harvard Law and Policy Review* 9, no. 2 (2015): 443–69, 451.

86. See Eric Lipton's reporting that "attorneys general are now the object of aggressive pursuit by lobbyists and lawyers who use campaign contributions . . . and other means to push them to drop investigations, change policies, negotiate favorable settlements or pressure federal regulators," "there are few revolving-door restrictions or disclosure requirements governing state attorneys general," and the "cause and effect" from the lobbying is "laid bare" in emails. "Lobbyists, Bearing Gifts, Pursue Attorneys General," *New York Times*, October 28, 2014. Clopton suggests that, "the smaller, the more localized, and the more specialized the governmental unit, the more sway that concentrated interests might wield." "Class Actions and Executive Power," 893. The New York University law professor Richard Revesz disagrees. See "Federalism and Environmental Regulation: A Public Choice Analysis," *Harvard Law Review* 115, no. 2 (2001): 553–641.

87. See David Freeman Engstrom, "Harnessing the Private Attorney General: Evidence from Qui Tam Litigation," *Columbia Law Review* 112, no. 6 (2012): 1244–1325, 1314.

88. See Farhang's comment that "it . . . insulates enforcement powers from subversion by the president, future legislative majorities, and disobedient bureaucrats." *The Litigation State*, 55. Coffee notes that "the private attorney general offers four key benefits . . . [including] protection against political capture." *Entrepreneurial Litigation*, 232. Engstrom argues that "profit-seeking private enforcers will provide a politically insulated, 'failsafe' source of enforcement if public enforcement agencies . . . suffer from . . . 'capture' by regulated interests." "Private Enforcement's Pathways," 1925. Burbank, Farhang, and Kritzer explain that "private enforcement regimes can . . . emit a clear and consistent signal that violations will be prosecuted, providing insurance against the risk that a system of administrative implementation will be subverted." "Private Enforcement," 662. Coffee notes that "private enforcement also performs an important failsafe function by ensuring that legal norms are not wholly dependent on the current attitudes of public enforcers or . . . lobby[ing] against public enforcement efforts." "Rescuing the Private Attorney General," 217. Rubenstein suggests that "private attorneys may be better . . . because public attorneys may be . . . prone to political pressures." "On What a Private Attorney General Is," 2149–50.

89. See Zingales's observation: "Law enforcement seem[s] to work better in common-law countries, a well-established empirical fact. The decentralized nature

of common law makes it less subject to capture. To get your way in litigation in a civil-law country like Italy or Brazil, it is sufficient to influence legislators, since judges apply the law, no matter how unjust or corrupt it is. By contrast, in common-law countries, you would have to influence the judges, too, a process that is more difficult, time-consuming, and expensive." *A Capitalism for the People*, 191.

90. For example, although some scholars might believe that federal courts are not perfectly insulated from capture, they still do not believe that federal courts are as open to capture as other government officials. See, e.g., J. Jonas Anderson, "Court Capture," *Boston College Law Review* 59, no. 5 (2018): 1545–94, 1547.

91. See, e.g., Shleifer's argument that during the Gilded Age judges were captured by regulated industries by means ranging from "superior legal talent to political pressure to outright bribery." *The Failure of Judges and the Rise of Regulators*, 152.

92. See, e.g., Burbank, Farhang, and Kritzer's articulation that, "given that intense preferences for under-enforcement exist in the regulated population, while preferences for enforcement are far more diffuse, the regulated population has incentives and opportunities to use lobbying, campaign contributions, and other means to seek to influence or capture an agency so as to discourage enforcement." "Private Enforcement," 664–65.

93. See, e.g., Schuck's understanding: "As a mechanism for preventing loss, [the private cause of action] can be a decentralized, privately initiated, privately processed alternative to other tools." *Why Government Fails So Often*, 83. Crane notes that "a system of private enforcement allows for decentralized decisionmaking." "Optimizing Private Antitrust Enforcement," 677. Lahav observes: "American society values decentralization and individualized enforcement of the law as opposed to enforcement through a bureaucracy engaged in centralized decision-making. Private litigation reflects these values." *In Praise of Litigation*, 39.

94. Of course, plaintiffs' firms specialize, and some areas of the law may end up with only fifty or even ten private firms suing wrongdoers. The securities fraud bar is thought to be particularly concentrated. Some argue that a small number of experienced firms may be the optimal way to enforce the law. See e.g., Engstrom, "Harnessing the Private Attorney General," 1256–63. This may be true, but, as in all industries, we need to reassure ourselves of that by keeping barriers to entry low so that new firms can test incumbents. This is one of the greatest virtues of the rise of the third-party litigation funding that I mention below when I discuss the fall of champerty and maintenance: it democratizes the plaintiffs' bar.

95. Todd J. Zywicki, "Posner, Hayek and the Economic Analysis of Law," *Iowa Law Review* 93, no. 2 (2008): 559–603, 588. See also Todd J. Zywicki and Edward P. Stringham, "Austrian Law and Economics and Efficiency in the Common Law," in *Research Handbook on Austrian Law and Economics*, ed. Todd J. Zywicki and Peter J. Boettke (Northampton, MA: Edward Elgar, 2017), 192–208, 199–202. Zywicki and others have criticized Hayek's support for the common law as a bit

undertheorized. See ibid., 202–3; John Hasnas, "Hayek, Common Law, and Fluid Drive," *New York University Journal of Law and Liberty* 1 (2005): 79–110, 98–109; and Adrian Vermeule, "Many-Minds Arguments in Legal Theory," *Journal of Legal Analysis* 1, no. 1 (2009): 1–45, 13–16. But even these critics end up fairly positive on the common law method. For example, Hasnas says: "I frequently argue for the common law in preference to legislation myself." "Hayek, Common Law, and Fluid Drive," 105. And Zywicki and Stringham conclude: "Those who take Hayek's discussion of the importance of discovery through competition seriously, should question the idea that the state must provide law centrally." "Austrian Law and Economics," 205.

96. Barnett, *The Structure of Liberty*, 115–28.

97. Becker and Stigler, "Law Enforcement, Malfeasance, and Compensation of Enforcers," 13. As Zywicki and Stringham put it: "The common law . . . has been subject to much praise from economists in both the neoclassical and Austrian traditions." "Austrian Law and Economics," 192.

98. See Zywicki and Stringham, "Austrian Law and Economics," 192–94.

99. See, e.g., the research described in Zywicki and Stringham, "Austrian Law and Economics," 195–96; and Schleifer, "Efficient Regulation," 37.

100. See, e.g., Butterfield v. Forrester (1809) 103 Eng. Rep. 926 (KB).

101. As John C. Moorhouse, Andrew P. Morriss, and Robert Whaples put it: "One of the most sweeping changes in tort law during the twentieth century was the shift from contributory negligence to comparative negligence." "Law and Economics and Tort Law: A Survey of Scholarly Opinion," *Albany Law Review* 62, no. 2 (1998): 667–96, 673.

102. Moorhouse, Morriss, and Whaples, "Law and Economics and Tort Law," 674 (noting the "shift . . . in the consensus in law and economics scholarship" on comparative negligence from against it to in favor of it). But see Epstein's muted objection: "Where the nineteenth-century system could be criticized for allowing [the plaintiff's] misconduct to block all recovery, even in cases where the defendant was as much responsible as the plaintiff for a loss, the response to that criticism is a system of comparative negligence that divides the losses between the parties. Although this shift does not by itself mark a disintegration of the appropriate standards of plaintiff conduct; once again the erosion in standards is unmistakable." Richard A. Epstein, *Principles for a Free Society: Reconciling Individual Liberty with the Common Good* (Reading, MA: Perseus, 1998), 177.

103. One federal court explained the traditional history by noting: "A significant doctrinal struggle in the development of contract law revolved around whether it was a party's actual or apparent assent that was necessary. This was a struggle between subjective and objective theorists. The subjectivists looked to actual assent. Both parties had to actually assent to an agreement for there to be a contract. External acts were merely necessary evidence to prove or disprove the requisite state of mind. The familiar cliche was that a contract required a 'meeting of the

minds' of the parties." Newman v. Schiff, 778 F.2d 460, 464 (8th Cir. 1985). Some scholarship has disputed this traditional account, suggesting that this subjective theory of assent was never actually the law. See Joseph M. Perillo, "The Origins of the Objective Theory of Contract Formation and Interpretation," *Fordham Law Review* 69, no. 2 (2000): 427–77, 428.

104. As Wayne Barnes puts it: "Objective theory has prevailed as the unifying principle governing the formation of contracts." "The Objective Theory of Contracts," *University of Cincinnati Law Review* 76 (2008): 1119–58, 1124.

105. This move has been most prominently supported by the conservative law and economics movement. Judge Easterbrook, one of the leading figures of this movement, authored perhaps the most famous case: Hill v. Gateway 2000, Inc., 105 F.3d 1147, 1148 (7th Cir. 1997). But conservative and libertarian scholars from outside the law and economics movement have also defended this change. See, e.g., Randy E. Barnett, "Consenting to Form Contracts," *Fordham Law Review* 71, no. 3 (2002): 627–45, 641.

106. *Black's Law Dictionary*, 8th ed., s.v. "Champerty"; *Black's Law Dictionary*, 8th ed., s.v. "Maintenance."

107. See Brian T. Fitzpatrick, "Can and Should the New Third-Party Litigation Financing Come to Class Actions?," *Theoretical Inquiries in Law* 19, no. 1 (2018): 109–23, 112.

108. As Richard Epstein puts it: "Rules of champerty are basically silly. Shareholding is a perfectly good way to diversify your risks. What's wrong with inciting litigation?" Leslie Spencer, "Some Call It Champerty," *Forbes*, April 30, 1990, 72. Indeed, I have written an entire article in support of this change. See Fitzpatrick, "Can and Should the New Third-Party Litigation Financing Come to Class Actions?" Nonetheless, as with the comparative negligence, opinion on the right is not unanimous. See, e.g., US Chamber Institute for Legal Reform, "Selling Lawsuits, Buying Trouble: The Emerging World of Third-Party Litigation Financing in the United States," US Chamber Institute for Legal Reform, 2009, https://www.instituteforlegalreform.com/research/selling-lawsuits-buying-trouble-the-emerging-world-of-third-party-litigation-financing-in-the-united-states; and Paul H. Rubin, "Third-Party Financing of Litigation," *Northern Kentucky Law Review* 38 (2011): 673–85.

109. For example, Burbank, Farhang, and Kritzer comment: "Private enforcement regimes can . . . encourage legal and policy innovation." "Private Enforcement," 662. They also note: "The decentralized nature of private enforcement litigation, as contrasted with centralized bureaucracy, can also encourage policy innovation for reasons similar to those associated with federalist governing arrangements. As distinguished from the imposition of a policy solution at the top of a centralized and hierarchical bureaucracy, litigation of an issue among many parties and interests, and across many judicial jurisdictions, can lead to experimentation with a multiplicity of policy responses to a problem, and successful policy

solutions will gain traction and spread." Ibid., 664. Engstrom posits that "sclerotic public bureaucracies may be less organizationally dexterous than their private counterparts and thus less efficient at mobilizing or demobilizing enforcement capacity." "Private Enforcement's Pathways," 1930. Dam writes that "a second . . . justification for private enforcement lies in its diversity." "Class Actions," 68. And Lemos notes that "one of the potential benefits of outsourcing is that private contractors can bring new perspectives to government work, spurring innovation that would not have occurred." "Privatizing Public Litigation," 554.

110. See, e.g., Crane's observation that "a system of private enforcement . . . supplies a set of 'on the street' enforcers closer to the relevant problems." "Optimizing Private Antitrust Enforcement," 677.

111. Myriam Gilles, "Reinventing Structural Reform Litigation: Deputizing Private Citizens in the Enforcement of Civil Rights," *Columbia Law Review* 100, no. 6 (2000): 1384–1453, 1413.

112. See Bill Vlasic and Aaron M. Kessler, "It Took E.P.A. Pressure to Get VW to Admit Fault," *New York Times*, September 21, 2015. Ewing recounts how the International Council on Clean Transportation initiated the study of Volkswagen's emissions by enlisting a lab at the University of West Virginia. *Faster, Higher, Farther*, 164–74.

113. See Bill Vlasic, "An Engineer's Eureka Moment with a G.M. Flaw," *New York Times*, March 28, 2014.

114. See Alexander Dyck, Adair Morse, and Luigi Zingales, "Who Blows the Whistle on Corporate Fraud?," *Journal of Finance* 65, no. 6 (2010): 2213–53, 2225, table II(A)(2). Short sellers, competitors/clients, equity holders, and law firms totaled to 25.7 percent. Analysts added another 13.8 percent, auditors 10.5 percent, employees 17.1 percent, and the media 13.2 percent. Other government agencies made up some portion of the 13.2 percent attributable to industry regulators, government agencies, and self-regulatory organizations.

115. See, e.g., David M. Uhlmann, "Justice Falls Short in GM Case," *New York Times*, September 19, 2015. Perhaps the most exhaustive study is Brandon Garrett's, which documents "outrage that corporations are getting leniency" yet "no employees are being held accountable" either. *Too Big to Jail*, 95.

116. Sharon Dolovich provides a detailed discussion of how the sets of metrics used to evaluate private prisons are often misaligned with society's broader obligations to incarcerated people. "How Privatization Thinks: The Case of Prisons," in Freeman and Minow, eds., *Government by Contract*, 128–47.

117. As Zywicki and Stringham put it: "A constantly-changing legal system— even in the name of modernization or updating—adds uncertainty." "Austrian Law and Economics," 198.

118. As La Porta, Lopez-de-Silanes, and Shleifer summarize the findings: "Common law is associated with (a) better investor protection, which in turn is associated with improved financial development, better access to finance, and higher ownership dispersion, (b) lighter government ownership and regulation, which

are in turn associated with less corruption, better functioning labor markets, and smaller unofficial economies, and (c) less formalized and more independent judicial systems, which are in turn associated with more secure property rights and better contract enforcement." "The Economic Consequences of Legal Origins," 298.

119. See Coffee, *Entrepreneurial Litigation*, 174–75, table 9.1. See also the insight: "Private securities class actions currently represent the principal means by which financial penalties are imposed in cases of securities fraud and manipulation. In the aggregate, they impose penalties that overshadow those imposed by federal and state authorities and by self-regulatory organizations." John C. Coffee Jr., "Reforming the Securities Class Action: An Essay on Deterrence and Its Implementation," *Columbia Law Review* 106, no. 7 (2006): 1534–86, 1536.

120. See Ramphal's finding that "settling [private] actions against public companies outnumbered successful [government] enforcement actions by a factor of six" in all such actions between 1998 and 2004. "The Role of Public and Private Litigation," 182.

121. See Coffee's observation that "there is a cutoff level in terms of market capitalization below which private enforcement appears not to work." "Reforming the Securities Class Action," 1544.

122. See Coffee, "Reforming the Securities Class Action," 1542–43, tables 2–3.

123. See Ramphal's finding that "class actions are more effective in obtaining investor restitution recovering on average almost four times more than the corresponding enforcement action." "The Role of Public and Private Litigation," 4. This holds even in joint class action and enforcement action scenarios based on a data set of all such actions between 1998 and 2004. Ibid., 22, table 1; 53, table 17.

124. See Joshua P. Davis and Robert H. Lande's findings that Department of Justice (DOJ) recoveries between 1990 and 2007 were $8.18 billion, while the private bar produced recoveries of somewhere between $34 and $36 billion during the same period. "Toward an Empirical and Theoretical Assessment of Private Antitrust Enforcement," *Seattle Law Review* 36, no. 3 (2013): 1269–1335, 1276–78. Davis and Lande also found that the private impact was still over three times the DOJ impact even if the DOJ is credited for $6 million in deterrence for each year each antitrust defendant served in prison and $3 million for each year of house arrest.

125. See Michael Block, Frederick Nold, and Joseph Sidak's finding that "settlements in class actions for price fixing in the bread industry were almost 10 times greater than government-imposed fines." "The Deterrent Effect of Antitrust Enforcement," *Journal of Political Economy* 89, no. 3 (1981): 429–45, 441 n. 35.

126. Urska Velikonja, "Public Compensation for Private Harm: Evidence from the SEC's Fair Fund Distributions," *Stanford Law Review* 67, no. 2 (2015): 331–95, 341, 63n (citing 15 USC 78u(d)(3)(C)(i)).

127. See the Federal Trade Commission's statement that, "generally, the FTC gets claims from 5 to 20 percent of potential claimants." *Office of Claims and Refunds Annual Report 2017* (Washington, DC: Federal Trade Commission, 2017), 2, https://www.ftc.gov/system/files/documents/reports/bureau-consumer-protection

-office-claims-refunds-annual-report-2017-consumer-refunds-effected-july/re
dressreportformattedforweb122117.pdf.

128. Velikonja, "Public Compensation for Private Harm," 334.

129. Velikonja, "Public Compensation for Private Harm," 334 n. 12.

130. See Adam S. Zimmerman's comment that "administrative agencies may fail to hear victims' claims, identify potential conflicts between parties, or afford anything more than cursory judicial review over the settlement and distribution of awards." "Distributing Justice," *New York University Law Review* 86, no. 2 (2011): 500–572, 505.

131. See Gretchen Morgensen's reporting that "the SEC struck a settlement with Citigroup . . . over 16 months ago" and "the wronged investors are not only still awaiting their money, but they have yet to see any plan outlining how the $180 million will be distributed." "SEC Inertia on Paybacks Adds to Investor Harm," *New York Times*, January 13, 2017. Michael Patrick Wilt notes that most compensation schemes arising out of the government's litigation against banks for mortgage misconduct are *not* "directed to identifiable victims" and that instead "banks get to choose which consumers receive relief, what type, how much, and when" and that some people "have raised cronyism concerns regarding the government's favorable treatment of certain banks." "Evaluating 'Consumer Relief' Payments in Recent Bank Settlement Agreements," *Journal of Business and Securities Law* 17, no. 2 (2017): 253–303, 275, 276. Kevin McCoy reports that, "nearly 8.5 years after Madoff's arrest," victims of his "huge Ponzi scheme have so far received no repayments" because the Department of Justice "is still working to finalize reviews and recommendations for 63,580 claims." "Madoff Fund Hasn't Paid Victims A Dime," *USA Today*, May 24, 2017.

132. See Ramphal's finding that "jointly enforced suits are also fairly rare, constituting just 4.1% of all SEC enforcement actions and 8.25% of all class actions" in a study of all such actions between 1998 and 2004. "The Role of Public and Private Litigation," 4. See also the Consumer Financial Protection Bureau's (CFPB) observation that a "study of securities class actions from 1990 to 2003 found that 19% of the private class action securities cases settled during that period had a parallel SEC enforcement action challenging the same conduct underlying the private suit, but did not attempt to determine whether private or public proceedings tended to start first." *Arbitration Study: Report to Congress, pursuant to Dodd–Frank Wall Street Reform and Consumer Protection Act § 1028(a)*, March 2015, §9.2, http://files.con sumerfinance.gov/f/201503_cfpb_arbitration-study-report-to-congress-2015.pdf.

133. See the CFPB's note that "one study of antitrust cases from 1977 to 1983 showed that about 25% of private antitrust claims were 'follow-on' cases to government enforcement actions." *Arbitration Study*, § 9.2. Davis and Lande find that 67 percent of their antitrust cases were "not preceded by government action" and that "this percentage is similar to . . . the classic study by Kauper and Snyder who found that no more than 20% of all private antitrust cases followed DOJ cases." "Private Antitrust Enforcement," 1292, 1299. Thomas E. Kauper and Edward A. Snyder examine private antitrust cases filed in five district courts from 1973 to 1983 and find

that "independently initiated cases dominate the full sample of non-MDL cases, accounting for 91% of the total 1938 cases in the five-district sample," and that, of the 9 percent of follow-on cases, "151 follow DOJ cases and 22 cases follow FTC actions." "An Inquiry into the Efficiency of Private Antitrust Enforcement: Follow-on and Independently Initiated Cases Compared," *Georgetown Law Journal* 74, no. 4 (1986): 1163–1230, 1175. However, they note that that "MDLs are more likely to be follow-ons," finding 403 cases in follow-on MDLs and 82 cases in independent MDLs. Ibid., 1219. They find the total percentage of follow-ons—including MDL and non-MDL—to be 24 percent. Ibid., 1219–20. Overall, they find 416 independently initiated horizontal price-fixing cases and only 107 follow-on cases. Ibid., 1180.

134. See the CFPB's finding that overlapping government enforcement actions existed in only 32 percent of private consumer financial class actions. *Arbitration Study*, § 9.4.

135. See the CFPB's chart showing that, when there was overlap, government actions followed private actions more often than not. *Arbitration Study*, § 9.4, 14, table 1. Jessica Erickson finds that the typical SEC investigation follows the filing of a securities fraud class action in the seven hundred derivative lawsuits she studied filed in 2005 and 2006. "Overlitigating Corporate Fraud: An Empirical Analysis," *Iowa Law Review* 97, no. 1 (2011): 49–100, 73. Davis and Lande note that "private enforcement sometimes preceded . . . DOJ enforcement." "Private Antitrust Enforcement," 1299.

136. La Porta, Lopez-de-Silanes, and Shleifer, "What Works in Securities Laws?," 1.

137. Howell E. Jackson and J. Mark Roe sought to improve the La Porta, Lopez-de-Silanes, and Shleifer study by refining the proxies for public enforcement used; they showed that doing so eliminated the findings in favor of private enforcement and against public enforcement. See "Public and Private Enforcement of Securities Laws: Resource-Based Evidence," *Journal of Financial Economics* 93, no. 2 (2009): 207–38, 207. But, curiously, they did not try to simultaneously refine the proxies for private enforcement that La Porta and his coauthors used.

138. The best summary of these studies is in Rafael La Porta, Florencio Lopez-de-Silanes, and Andrei Shleifer, "Law and Finance After a Decade of Research," in *Handbook of the Economics of Finance*, ed. George M. Constantinides, Milton Harris, and Rene M. Stulz (Amsterdam: Elsevier, 2013), 425–83.

Chapter Four

1. Olson, *The Litigation Explosion*, 45.

2. See, e.g., Stefaan Voet, "Consumer Collective Redress in Belgium: Class Actions to the Rescue?," *European Business Organization Law Review*, 16, no. 1 (2015): 121–43, 128.

3. See, e.g., Coffee's observation: "In truth, the plaintiff's attorney does not simply supplement public enforcement but extends and drives the law's development,

sometimes pushing it in directions that public enforcers would not have gone. . . . [I]t is seldom constrained by the same principles of prosecutorial discretion that guide public enforcers." *Entrepreneurial Litigation*, 17.

4. See 15 U.S.C. § 1681c(g) and 15 U.S.C. § 1681n.

5. See, e.g., Engstrom's explanation that "profit-seeking private enforcers . . . will also relentlessly push into legal interstices, exploiting statutory and regulatory ambiguities in suits against much or all of an industry rather than targeting the patently illegal conduct of a few malefactors." "Private Enforcement's Pathways," 1921–22. Engstrom further finds that "qui tam litigation has steadily expanded in its scale and regulatory scope, moving away over time from targeting uncontroversial frauds . . . and instead moving towards exploiting regulatory ambiguities." Ibid., 1923. He predicts that "private enforcers will, as a litigation regime matures, shift from targeting relatively clear to relatively ambiguous segments of the statutory and regulatory code as a growing corps of private attorneys general makes sanction for breach of the former a virtual certainty." Ibid., 1934–35. This is a source for concern because, as Lemos notes, "government attorneys cannot (and should not) go after every apparent violation of the law." "Privatizing Public Litigation," 546. She explains: "Many laws are written in broad and general terms that, if taken literally, could embrace a range of benign activities. . . . Unlike private litigants and lawyers, who can be expected to pursue any litigation that serves their self-interest, governmental entities and their attorneys are supposed to prioritize initiatives that best serve the public interest." Ibid., 547. See also Landes and Posner's discussion of how "enforcer nullification would not be a feature of private enforcement: all laws would be enforced that yield a positive expected net return": "Both economic theory and simple observation suggest that rules of law are almost always overinclusive. . . . If enforced to the letter, an overinclusive rule could impose very heavy social costs." "The Private Enforcement of Law," 38.

6. See, e.g., Coffee's note: "This is the standard criticism made by the defense bar. In their view, plaintiff's attorneys lack discretion and judgment and will sue whenever the damages are high enough so that the case has a settlement value that covers their fees." *Entrepreneurial Litigation*, 220. Coffee acknowledges that "the incentive to overreach and litigate every profitable opportunity, regardless of merit, does demonstrably exist." Ibid., 221.

7. See Richard A. Nagareda, "Class Actions in the Administrative State: Kalven and Rosenfield Revisited," *University of Chicago Law Review* 75, no. 2 (2008): 603–48, 615–18. But see Engstrom's counterpoint that "one might expect a similar trend in regimes delegating enforcement authority solely to prosecutors and agencies." "Private Enforcement's Pathways," 1936.

8. See Stephen Choi and Adam Pritchard, "SEC Investigations and Securities Class Actions: An Empirical Comparison," *Journal of Empirical Legal Studies* 13, no. 1 (2016): 27–49, 27.

9. Choi and Pritchard find: "These market measures of disclosure credibility suggest that private class action attorneys target disclosure violations more precisely than the SEC. We also find evidence that the SEC Only category has a significantly lower incidence of top officer resignations relative to the Class Action Only category. . . . [T]his result also undermines the frequently invoked argument that SEC enforcement targets disclosure violations more accurately than plaintiffs' lawyers." "SEC Investigations and Securities Class Actions," 46.

10. "SEC Investigations and Securities Class Actions," 47.

11. See, e.g., Olson's comment that "the question is always whether the effort is aimed in the right direction." *The Litigation Explosion*, 42.

12. See, e.g., Coffee's observation that, "if anything is evident from the politics surrounding contemporary class action litigation, it is that persistent overzealousness can be curbed by a variety of legislative and judicial controls." *Entrepreneurial Litigation*, 221. Compare this view with A. Mitchell Polinsky's stance, which, although critical of private enforcement, concedes that "regulating private enforcers by paying them something different than the fine for each violation detected can achieve the socially most preferred outcome in the competitive case." "Private versus Public Enforcement of Fines," *Journal of Legal Studies* 9, no. 1 (1980): 105–27, 108.

13. See, e.g., Steven Shavell's observation: "With regard . . . to the issue of incentives, it seems that the motive of private parties to find liable parties could either fall short of or exceed the socially correct motive to invest resources in that task, depending on circumstance." "The Optimal Structure of Law Enforcement," *Journal of Law and Economics* 36, no. 1 (1993): 255–87, 269. Shavell remarks: "One problem is that, if the reward is available to anyone, rather than to a single enforcing party, there might be a wasteful effort devoted to finding the party, akin to the waste involved in patent races or fishing in a common fishing area. Another problem is that the best technologies for finding liable parties often require coordination of many individuals. . . . Additionally, it is efficient for various information systems . . . to be developed, even though the benefits of these systems would be hard for the private sector fully to capture." Ibid., 270. He continues "All of this suggests that use of financial rewards paid to those who identify liable parties might not lead to as well-functioning a system as that established by a single public entity." Ibid., 270. Similarly, Engstrom expresses the concern that "private enforcement [may] defy meaningful political, democratically accountable control." "Private Enforcement's Pathways," 1936. He notes: "[Although] courts, agencies, and even the legislature itself stand ready to check or override private litigation efforts that stray beyond statutory purposes, . . . theory and evidence suggest that drift . . . can be substantial. Part of the reason is the fragmented supermajoritarian structure of the American state and the limited institutional will and capacity of courts, legislatures, and agencies." Ibid, 1936–37. He observes that "judges possess neither policy-specific expertise nor a synoptic view of the enforcement landscape,

sharply limiting their ability to gauge how a given legal innovation urged upon them maps onto legislative policy aims." Ibid., 1938. Likewise, he suggests that "legislators too, may prove unreliable [because] the American separation-of-powers system, with its multiple veto gates, makes legislative inertia a distinct possibility [and because] [r]ational legislators may . . . lack any preferences apart from staying above the fray." Ibid. Indeed, he worries: "Privately driven legal innovation will often be incremental in ways that can frustrate and even defeat political-control efforts. As a result, political override of privately driven legal innovations will rarely be rapid. . . . Worse, the need for override may not be apparent until litigation outcomes are irreversible." Ibid., 1940. This concern is amplified, he points out, by the fact that "large paydays provide the plaintiffs' bar with a war chest with which to protect its hard-fought litigation gains through the legislative and administrative process." Ibid., 1941.

14. See, e.g., Engstrom's response to the question, "How might a regulatory designer optimize private enforcement efforts?" "One approach involves curtailing remedies or erecting procedural barriers in ways that directly shape litigation incentives and thus achieve a desired level of enforcement activity." "Harnessing the Private Attorney General," 1254. Elsewhere, Engstrom posits that "a trio of institutional actors—courts with adjudicatory authority, agencies with rulemaking or other oversight powers, and the legislature itself—stand ready to check or override private litigation." "Private Enforcement's Pathways," 1933. He cites empirical research on "the ability of . . . legislators . . . to manipulate the quantity of lawsuits in [private enforcement] regimes." Ibid., 1918. He also describes the "optimistic" view as one where there is "public control over litigation flows" because "a legislature . . . need only dial up or down payouts . . . or attorneys' fees." Ibid., 1926. Landes and Posner observe: "An alternative to discretionary nonenforcement is to permit unlimited private enforcement but rewrite the substantive law to eliminate overinclusion. . . . The legislature may not have to rewrite the law. The courts may refuse to enforce foolish or perverse applications of a statute. . . . Alternatively, an administrative agency with broad interpretive powers could be interposed between the legislature and the private enforcer." "The Private Enforcement of Law," 40. R. Preston McAfee, Hugo M. Mialon, and Sue H. Mialon write that "private enforcement can . . . achieve the social optimum with private damages that are efficiently multiplied and decoupled." "Public v. Private Antitrust Enforcement: A Strategic Analysis," *Journal of Public Economics* 92, nos. 10–11 (2008): 1863–75, 1863.

15. See, e.g., Coffee's observation that "there is a cutoff level in terms of market capitalization below which private [securities fraud] enforcement appears not to work." "Reforming the Securities Class Action," 1544.

16. For example, there is evidence that, when the SEC sues corporate wrongdoers, it pursues corporate governance reforms more often than the private bar does. See Ramphal's finding that SEC enforcement actions led to settlements with

corporate governance reforms 3.3 percent of the time vs. 2.1 percent of the time in private class actions. "The Role of Public and Private Litigation," 118–20. Ramphal writes further that "there are reasons to believe that the SEC will actually tend to require more penetrative corporate reforms than private class action securities suits." Ibid., 130. However, his statistical work found that, in most regards, there are not statistically significant differences between the SEC's and the private bar's approaches to corporate reforms. Ibid., 131. Indeed, the private bar is statistically more likely to pursue multigovernance reforms than is the SEC. Ibid., 133.

17. See, e.g., Jessica Erickson's insight: "Government enforcement actions are more promising from the standpoint of individual deterrence. The government often targets individuals, and these individuals are far more likely than their corporate counterparts to pay financial penalties or face other meaningful sanctions. For example, approximately 75% of the SEC suits against individuals in the study ended with one or more individuals paying money out of their own pockets to settle the claims against them. Slightly more than 50% of these suits ended with an individual defendant agreeing to a ban on serving as a director or officer of a public company for a specified period of time." "Overlitigating Corporate Fraud," 78. Erickson further notes that "the [settlements in the] securities class actions in the study . . . typically stated that the company would pay the full settlement amount. [I]ndividual defendants rarely had to contribute a penny to settle the claims." Ibid., 77.

18. See Burbank, Farhang, and Kritzer's observation that "private enforcement litigation can actually enhance the efficient use of scarce bureaucratic resources by allowing administrators to focus enforcement efforts on violations that do not provide adequate incentives for private enforcement, while resting assured that those that do will be prosecuted by private litigants." "Private Enforcement," 663.

19. Rose, "Reforming Securities Litigation Reform," 1354–58; Grundfest, "Disimplying Private Rights of Action," 976–1006. Liberal scholars also advocate this, which is not surprising given their greater affinity for the government sector. See, e.g., David Freeman Engstrom, "Agencies as Litigation Gatekeepers," *Yale Law Journal* 123, no. 3 (2013): 530–861, 620 nn. 5–6; and Matthew C. Stephenson, "Public Regulation of Private Enforcement: The Case for Expanding the Role of Administrative Agencies," *Virginia Law Review* 91, no. 1 (2005): 93–173, 95.

20. As Coffee explains: "Even if public/private partnerships are needed, one potential reform seems clearly misconceived: giving veto power to the public agency. Conferring such a veto power to administrative agencies over private suits may screen out frivolous or predatory actions, but it risks undercutting the independence of the private attorney general. To the extent that greater oversight is needed the better means to this end would be for the court to ask for the administrative agency's views . . . at the settlement stage. If too many frivolous actions are being brought, the better alternative . . . is probably a modest version of the 'loser pays' rule." *Entrepreneurial Litigation*, 233.

21. See Catherine Sharkey, "CAFA Settlement Notice Provision: Optimal Regulatory Policy?," *University of Pennsylvania Law Review* 156 (2008): 1971–99, 1971.

22. Sharkey, "CAFA Settlement Notice Provision."

23. The Trump Administration's Department of Justice has begun objecting to class action settlements pursuant to the invitation in the Class Action Fairness Act and intends to continue doing so. See Perry Cooper, "DOJ Urges Court to Block Wine Pricing Class Settlement," *Bloomberg Law*, February 20, 2018, https://www .bna.com/doj-urges-court-n57982089084; and Cogan Schneier, "Rachel Brand Says DOJ Looking to Get Involved in More Class Actions," *National Law Journal*, February 15, 2018, https://www.law.com/nationallawjournal/sites/national lawjournal/2018/02/15/doj-wants-more-regular-voice-in-reviewing-class-action -fairness-rachel-brand-says/?slreturn=20180118130409.

24. Zachary Clopton writes: "While legal scholars have been slow to appreciate the benefits of redundancy, other disciplines have taken the lead. Engineers have explored how redundant components can increase systemic reliability when components are independent. Political scientists have applied these lessons to public administration." "Redundant Public-Private Enforcement," *Vanderbilt Law Review* 69, no. 2 (2016): 285–332, 307. He also notes that, while "redundancy creates direct costs and risks over-enforcement" and "many critics stop here," it "may be a response to under-enforcement resulting from errors, resource constraints, information problems, and agency costs if agents are sufficiently differentiated." Ibid., 313. He continues, arguing: "By failing to move beyond the first principle, critics of redundancy miss the potential of multiple diverse agents to improve law enforcement." Ibid. Indeed, he posits: "Redundant authority may improve case selection by reducing errors, aggregating resources and information, and improving monitoring. This logic supports redundant authority but not redundant litigation. Preclusion should bar duplicative suits." Ibid., 317.

25. See, e.g., Coffee's observation that "the newest critique of the private attorney general has been that private enforcement is unaccountable, undemocratic, and chaotically uncoordinated." *Entrepreneurial Litigation*, 225. Rose notes that "private enforcers are not subject to electoral discipline." "Reforming Securities Litigation Reform," 1343. Erin L. Sheley and Theodore H. Frank include in the "disadvantages to court-driven regulation" the "lack of accountability." "Prospective Injunctive Relief and Class Settlements," *Harvard Journal of Law and Public Policy* 39, no. 3 (April 2012): 769–832, 792.

26. See, e.g., Farhang's insight that "the flip side of the insulation phenomenon is that private litigants, lawyers, and lifetime tenured judges are less susceptible to ongoing supervision even by the enacting Congress than are bureaucrats, who can be called into hearings and have their budgets slashed, and thus the use of private enforcement regimes may entail a greater loss of control over policy by the enacting Congress." *The Litigation State*, 55. Farhang continues: "Some regulation scholars have suggested that . . . private enforcement regimes . . . are

antidemocratic because they allow minorities to extort policy concessions and monetary side-payments that they could not secure through ordinary legislative politics." Ibid., 56. Michaels notes: "Many privatization scholars emphasize, with good reason, the accountability problems associated with potentially poorly supervised, runaway contractors." "Running Government Like a Business," 1173 n. 94. Engstrom cites scholars who argue that "private enforcement and the legal innovations it generates are dangerously immune from democratically accountable control." "Private Enforcement's Pathways," 1918–19. He specifically identifies "a trio of institutional actors—courts with adjudicatory authority, agencies with rule-making or other oversight powers, and the legislature itself—[that] stand ready to check or override private litigation." Ibid., 1933. Burbank, Farhang, and Kritzer comment that "private enforcement regimes . . . empower judges, who lack policy expertise, to make policy [and] lack legitimacy and accountability." "Private Enforcement," 667. Lemos points out that "government litigators are subject to various democratic controls that are foreign to private litigation." "Privatizing Public Litigation," 527. She builds on this, observing: "[Outsourcing] allows private actors to influence the conduct and direction of government litigation, thereby subverting public control over important aspects of sovereign authority. In that sense, the privatization of public litigation triggers concerns about democratic governance that are familiar to the broader debates over privatization." Ibid., 569. And Lahav writes that "private attorneys, driven by a profit motive, may also bring suits that try to expand the law in directions not intended by the legislature." *In Praise of Litigation*, 40.

27. See Engstrom's citation of empirical research on "the ability of . . . legislators . . . to manipulate the quantity of lawsuits in [private enforcement] regimes." "Private Enforcement's Pathways," 1918. Engstrom also describes the "optimistic" view as one in which there is "public control over litigation flows" because "a legislature . . . need only dial up or down payouts . . . or attorneys' fees." Ibid., 1926. However, he also offers a more critical view of this question, noting that "courts, legislators, and agencies can only imperfectly police private enforcement efforts." Ibid., 1922. There is a risk, he writes, that "private enforcement [may] defy meaningful political, democratically accountable control." Ibid., 1936. Building on this, he notes: "[Although] courts, agencies, and even the legislature itself stand ready to check or override private litigation efforts that stray beyond statutory purposes, . . . theory and evidence suggest that drift . . . can be substantial. Part of the reason is the fragmented supermajoritarian structure of the American state and the limited institutional will and capacity of courts, legislatures, and agencies." Ibid., 1936–37. He continues, commenting: "Judges . . . possess neither policy-specific expertise nor a synoptic view of the enforcement landscape, sharply limiting their ability to gauge how a given legal innovation urged upon them maps onto legislative policy aims." Ibid., 1938. Similarly: "Legislators, too, may prove unreliable [because] the American separation-of-powers system, with its multiple veto gates, makes

legislative inertia a distinct possibility [and because] [r]ational legislators may . . . lack any preferences apart from staying above the fray." Ibid. Indeed, he summarizes: "Privately driven legal innovation will often be incremental in ways that can frustrate and even defeat political-control efforts. As a result, political override of privately driven legal innovations will rarely be rapid. . . . Worse, the need for override may not be apparent until litigation outcomes are irreversible." Ibid., 1940.

28. See Engstrom's statement that "large paydays provide the plaintiffs' bar with a war chest with which to protect its hard-fought litigation gains through the legislative and administrative process." "Private Enforcement's Pathways," 1941.

29. Coffee, *Entrepreneurial Litigation*, 226.

30. See, e.g., Sheley and Frank's inclusion in "the disadvantages to court-driven regulation" the lack of "uniformity" and "predictability." "Prospective Injunctive Relief and Class Settlements," 779–80.

31. See Shleifer, *The Failure of Judges and the Rise of Regulators*, 53.

32. Burbank, Farhang, and Kritzer write that "private enforcement regimes . . . tend to produce inconsistent and contradictory doctrine from courts [and] weaken the administrative state's capacity to articulate a coherent regulatory scheme by preempting administrative rulemaking." "Private Enforcement," 667. Writing alone, Farhang notes: "Some regulation scholars have suggested that . . . private enforcement regimes produce policy inconsistency and uncertainty because policy emanates from a multitude of litigants and judges." *The Litigation State*, 56. Shleifer suggests that "perhaps the most fundamental feature of regulation is that it tends to homogenize the requirements for appropriate conduct." *The Failure of Judges and the Rise of Regulators*, 16. Lemos argues that "centralization helps ensure that public litigation adheres to a coherent set of guiding principles." "Privatizing Public Litigation," 527. And Gilles reasons: "A regime in which private litigants have standing on their own to seek forward-looking reformist remedies would [be] highly inefficient. Such a regime necessarily fosters a patchwork of uncoordinated litigation efforts. . . . Nor would a helter-skelter rash of private litigation do much to promote the evolution of national standards." "Reinventing Structural Reform Litigation," 1424.

33. Donahue, *The Privatization Decision*, 216.

34. Lemos, "Privatizing Public Litigation," 540.

35. Lemos, "Privatizing Public Litigation," 540.

36. See Nicholas Parrillo's argument: "Americans are an entrepreneurial people, but they are also a people whose other values—such as anti-monopolism, interest-group pluralism, and voluntarism—counsel the separation of the profit motive from the state under modern conditions." *Against the Profit Motive: The Salary Revolution in American Government, 1780–1940* (New Haven, CT: Yale University Press, 2013), 361.

37. See Parrillo's explanation: "But the very intensity . . . was the bounty's undoing: it led to such disappointing and perverse results that lawmakers soured on

bounties and rejected them altogether. Yes, such payments instigated the aggressive exercise of coercive power. But the construction of a workable state . . . could not rest upon coercion alone, for it was impossible to deploy enough enforcers to achieve the requisite deterrence. The effective implementation of legislative will depended . . . on a large degree of mass voluntary cooperation by the affected individuals, and bounties turned out to undermine such cooperation. The officer's monetary incentive to impose sanctions on laypersons placed him in such an adversarial posture toward them as to vitiate their trust in government and elicit from them a mirror-image adversarial response. In addition, officers' profit motive discouraged them from making the kind of subjective and discretionary decisions that were necessary to sand off the hard edges of modern state power so it can win acceptance by the population." *Against the Profit Motive*, 4. Parrillo goes on, writing that "salaries, at least in the American story, are actually a concession to the inadequacy of rules to constrain self-interested human behavior." Ibid., 17. Before salarization, "conviction fees [for federal prosecutors] pushed prosecutors to focus too much on piling up convictions for extremely minor and technical offenses": "The defendants were guilty, yes, but usually of violations so picayune that punishing them only increased local contempt for federal law." Ibid., 43. Parrillo summarizes: "Bounty-seeking [for tax collectors] was unproductive. It meant that state agents benefited when citizens violated the law en masse and were then forced to comply. This placed state and citizen in an adversarial relation and alienated them from each other, thus undermining the intrinsic desire of citizens to comply with the law for its own sake and poisoning their trust in the state." Ibid., 186.

38. See Michaels's explanation: "Parrillo contends that this decision to embrace salarization was . . . necessary in order to legitimate and render far more trustworthy an expanding administrative state." "Running Government Like a Business," 1154.

39. See Kagan's analysis: "To the New Dealers, 'a system of centralized and unified powers, bypassing the states and the judiciary, seemed indispensable to allow for dramatic and frequent governmental regulation.' The Roosevelt administration strengthened the central government and extended its administrative reach, substituting national, bureaucratically administered programs for markets and state law." *Adversarial Legalism*, 43. He continues: "The New Deal tried to consolidate and extend the powers of the central government and its new bureaucracies, displacing state governments and the courts." Ibid., 46.

40. See Michaels' comment that "the administrative state . . . terminat[ed] what in essence was America's *last* sustained romance with business-like government—a romance that united government service with the pursuit of profit." "Running Government Like a Business," 1153. Michaels continues, noting: "In light of contemporary American government's wholesale reliance on private, for-profit contractors to carry out public responsibilities . . . we have seemingly come full circle." Ibid., 1153. He concludes that "contemporary privatization is in part a neoliberal reversion to the pre-salarization era." Ibid., 1171. See also Jessica

Silver-Greenberg and Stacy Cowley, "I.R.S. Hires Debt Collectors, Raising Fears of Scams and Abuse," *New York Times*, April 21, 2017.

41. Parrillo observes: "Laypeople accept law in part because they come to view the officialdom as a legitimate and reasonable body deserving at least a modicum of trust, not as an opponent to be outsmarted. In building that trust, the incentives furnished to government enforcers have an expressive or symbolic effect distinct from their effect on the enforcers' behavior and its effect on laypersons' fear of being caught and punished." *Against the Profit Motive*, 4.

42. See Duff McDonald, *The Golden Passport: Harvard Business School, the Limits of Capitalism, and the Moral Failure of the MBA Elite* (New York: Harper-Collins, 2017).

43. Lemos offers a different view: "Skepticism about private litigation allows defendants to shrug off private suits as the products of profit-seeking plaintiffs and attorneys. Public actions are harder to dismiss. . . . In short, putting the government's name on a case changes the way it is perceived by the public, by courts, and maybe even by opponents." "Privatizing Public Litigation," 575.

44. See J. Randy Beck, "The False Claims Act and the English Education of *Qui Tam* Legislation," *North Carolina Law Review* 78 (2000): 565–607.

45. Coffee has observed: "During the Civil War . . . Congress passed the False Claims Act, which resurrected the medieval 'qui tam' action that authorized private persons who had suffered no injury themselves, to prosecute suits against those who had cheated the federal government and retain a share of any recovery as their reward. This was the original 'private attorney general' statute in U.S. law . . . because it both liberalized standing and explicitly used private attorneys to supplement public enforcement." *Entrepreneurial Litigation*, 14.

46. The government does have the power to dismiss qui tam lawsuits, but it uses that power "sparingly." Michael D. Granston, "Factors for Evaluating Dismissal Pursuant to 31 U.S.C. § 3730(c)(2)(A)," memorandum to Department of Justice Attorneys, January 10, 2018, 1, https://assets.documentcloud.org/documents/4358602/Memo-for-Evaluating-Dismissal-Pursuant-to-31-U-S.pdf. See also 31 U.S.C. § 3730(c)(2)(A). That is, in the vast majority of instances where the government does not join the suit, the suit proceeds with the private plaintiff.

47. See Gilles's statement: "Congress amended the statute in 1943 to limit the circumstances under which a private individual could bring suit. Underlying the 1943 amendment was the government's belief that it could discover and prosecute fraud on its own. . . . As it turns out, the government was wrong on this score. . . . Congress amended the FCA in 1986 in order to generate a greater number of private suits." "Reinventing Structural Reform Litigation," 1421. Beck discusses the 1986 law at length. "The False Claims Act," 561–65.

48. See Lemos's example: "The Federal Deposit Insurance Corporation regularly contracts with private attorneys to handle the agency's litigation work with respect to failing banks. Similarly, the DOJ contracts with private attorneys to

litigate claims regarding nontax debts owed to the United States. . . . In other instances, government agencies reach out to private counsel to help with a specific case, as when DOJ's antitrust division hired David Boies to litigate the blockbuster antitrust case against Microsoft." "Privatizing Public Litigation," 531. Lemos also notes that, "increasingly, the states are represented by private law firms working for contingent fees" and that "several Louisiana cities hired contingent-fee private counsel to help them pursue claims against BP." Ibid., 533.

Chapter Five

1. The Federal Rules of Civil Procedure require that the courts ensure that the representative party "will fairly and adequately protect the interests of the class." Fed. R. Civ. P. 23(a)(4).

2. The Federal Rules of Civil Procedure state that, "unless a statute provides otherwise, a court that certifies a class must appoint class counsel." Fed. R. Civ. P. 23(g)(1). When deciding whom to appoint as class counsel, the court must consider a number of factors, including "(i) the work counsel has done in identifying or investigating potential claims in the action; (ii) counsel's experience in handling class actions, other complex litigation, and the types of claims asserted in the action; (iii) counsel's knowledge of the applicable law; and (iv) the resources that counsel will commit to representing the class." Fed. R. Civ. P. 23(g)(1)(a).

3. The Federal Rules of Civil Procedure outline the relevant notice requirements in detail: "The court must direct to class members the best notice that is practicable under the circumstances, including individual notice to all members who can be identified through reasonable effort. The notice must clearly and concisely state in plain, easily understood language: (i) the nature of the action; (ii) the definition of the class certified; (iii) the class claims, issues, or defenses; (iv) that a class member may enter an appearance through an attorney if the member so desires; (v) that the court will exclude from the class any member who requests exclusion; (vi) the time and manner for requesting exclusion; and (vii) the binding effect of a class judgment on members under Rule 23(c)(3)." Fed. R. Civ. P. 23(c)(2)(b).

4. Kagan writes that "the class action is a distinctively American legal invention, eschewed by other political systems but quite congruent with American political propensities." *Adversarial Legalism*, 118. This may be changing. See Voet, "Consumer Collective Redress in Belgium," 130–33; and Stefaan Voet, "Belgian Court Recognizes U.S. Opt-Out Class Action Settlement," Conflict of Laws, April 9, 2017, http://con flictoflaws.net/2017/belgian-court-recognizes-us-opt-out-class-action-settlement.

5. As the trial court put it: "The Complaints further allege that Defendant Banks deploy advanced software to automate their overdraft systems to maximize the number of overdrafts and, thus, the amount of overdraft fees charged per customer." *In re* Checking Account Overdraft Litig., 694 F. Supp. 2d 1302, 1309 (S.D. Fla. 2010).

6. The trial court summarized the plaintiffs' theory as follows: "Plaintiffs further state the most common way in which the Banks manipulate and alter customer accounts is by reordering debit transactions on a single day, or over multiple days, from largest to smallest amount, regardless of the actual chronological sequence in which the customer engaged in these transactions. Almost without exception, reordering debit transactions from highest to lowest results in more overdrafts than if the transactions were processed chronologically. For example, if a customer, whose account has a $50 balance at the time a bank processed several transactions, made four transactions of $10 and one subsequent transaction of $100 on the same day, the bank would reorder the debits from largest to smallest, imposing four overdraft fees on the customer. Conversely, if the $100 transaction were debited last—consistent with the chronological order of the transactions, and with consumers' reasonable expectations—only one overdraft fee would be assessed. By holding charges rather than posting them immediately to an account, the Banks are able to amass a number of charges on the account. Subsequently, the Banks post all of the amassed charges on a single date, in order of largest to smallest, rather than in the order in which they were received or charged. This delayed posting results in multiple overdraft fees that would not otherwise be imposed." *In re* Checking Account Overdraft Litig., 694 F. Supp. 2d 1302, 1309 (S.D. Fla. 2010).

7. Bank of America argued that its contracts with its customers permitted it to reorder debit card transactions however it pleased. See Omnibus Motion to Dismiss and/or for Judgment on the Pleadings and Incorporated Memorandum of Law at 40–49, *In re* Checking Account Overdraft Litig., 830 F.Supp.2d 1330 (S.D. Fla. June 10, 2009) (No. 1:09-md-02036). It is worth noting that many banks still use high-to-low transaction ordering when customers write checks. See Ann Carrns, "Customers Can Lose When Banks Shuffle Payments," *New York Times*, April 11, 2014.

8. According to the trial judge, Bank of America may have skimmed as much as $4.5 billion from consumer accounts in this manner. See *In re* Checking Account Overdraft Litig., 830 F. Supp. 2d 1330, 1345 (S.D. Fla. 2011).

9. *In re* Checking Account Overdraft Litig., 830 F. Supp. 2d 1330, 1368.

10. *In re* Checking Account Overdraft Litig., 830 F. Supp. 2d 1330, 1358.

11. Richard Epstein, "Class Actions: The Need for a Hard Second Look," *Civil Justice Report* 4 (2002): 1–17, 5.

12. Peter Rutledge, e.g., argues that arbitration serves as an "essential release valve for the country's overburdened civil justice system," providing "a cheaper, faster, more effective forum for a variety of disputes" than class action litigation can. *Arbitration—a Good Deal for Consumers: A Response to Public Citizen* (Washington, DC: US Chamber Institute for Legal Reform, April 2008), 6, http://stmedia.startribune.com/documents/docload.pdf. Other scholars have defended arbitration against criticism on similar grounds. See, e.g., Jason Scott Johnston and Todd J. Zywicki, "The Consumer Financial Protection Bureau's Arbitration

Study: A Summary and Critique," Public Law and Legal Theory Research Paper no. 51 (Charlottesville: University of Virginia School of Law, 2015), 9–14.

13. The agreement at issue in *AT&T v. Concepcion* is one such example of a generous arbitration agreement. The Supreme Court summarized AT&T's arbitration agreement as follows: "The revised agreement provides that customers may initiate dispute proceedings by completing a one-page Notice of Dispute form available on AT&T's Web site. AT&T may then offer to settle the claim; if it does not, or if the dispute is not resolved within 30 days, the customer may invoke arbitration by filing a separate Demand for Arbitration, also available on AT&T's Web site. In the event the parties proceed to arbitration, the agreement specifies that AT&T must pay all costs for nonfrivolous claims; that arbitration must take place in the county in which the customer is billed; that, for claims of $10,000 or less, the customer may choose whether the arbitration proceeds in person, by telephone, or based only on submissions; that either party may bring a claim in small claims court in lieu of arbitration; and that the arbitrator may award any form of individual relief, including injunctions and presumably punitive damages. The agreement, moreover, denies AT&T any ability to seek reimbursement of its attorney's fees, and, in the event that a customer receives an arbitration award greater than AT&T's last written settlement offer, requires AT&T to pay a $7,500 minimum recovery and twice the amount of the claimant's attorney's fees." AT&T Mobility LLC v. Concepcion, 563 U.S. 333, 336 (2011). Sarah Cole notes that this agreement was "unusually generous": "Most arbitration agreements do not offer the small claims court alternative or the minimum recovery guarantee." "On Babies and Bathwater: The Arbitration Fairness Act and the Supreme Court's Recent Arbitration Jurisprudence," *Houston Law Review* 48 (2011): 457–506, 490 n. 150.

14. As David Migoya reports, the litigation in the bank overdraft cases consisted of "nearly 60 different lawsuits from federal courts in 23 states against 33 banks" all of which were "amalgamated into a single class-action case in Miami." "Customers Challenge the Way Banks Reorder Debits in Order to Rack up Overdraft Fees," *Denver Post*, August 20, 2010.

15. CFPB, *Arbitration Study*.

16. CFPB, *Arbitration Study*, 8–40.

17. CFPB, *Arbitration Study*, 5–20, table 1. This is consistent with Judith Resnik's study of arbitration against AT&T: "We identified 134 individual consumers—or about 27 per year—who filed claims . . . against AT&T. Given the estimate that the number of AT&T subscribers rose over the course of this . . . period from 46 to 120 million customers each year, the available data reveal that virtually none use arbitrations." "Diffusing Disputes: The Public in the Private of Arbitration, the Private in Courts, and the Erasure of Rights," *Yale Law Journal* 124, no. 8 (2015): 2804–2939, 2894.

18. Zingales, *A Capitalism for the People*, 199.

19. Thierer, *Permissionless Innovation*, 75–77.

20. Martin Redish, "Rethinking the Theory of the Class Action: The Risks and Rewards of Capitalistic Socialism in the Litigation Process," *Emory Law Journal* 64, no. 2 (2014): 451–76, 457.

21. Epstein, "Class Actions: Aggregation, Amplification, and Distortion," 514–16.

22. As I have noted elsewhere: "The average award [of fees in class actions examined in my study] was 25.4 percent and the median was 25 percent." Fitzpatrick, "An Empirical Study of Class Action Settlements and Their Fee Awards," 833.

23. For a discussion of some of the ways in which the plaintiffs' bar finances class action lawsuits and some recent controversies surrounding them, see Brian T. Fitzpatrick, "Can and Should the New Third-Party Litigation Financing Come to Class Actions?," 111–12, 116–17.

24. Eric Helland and Jonathan Klick, "Regulation and Litigation: Complements or Substitutes," in *The American Illness: Essays on the Rule of Law*, ed. F.H. Buckley (New Haven, CT: Yale University Press, 2013), 118–36, 120.

25. See Mark Moller's analysis of the subject: "Modern class actions are a form of centralized judicial power. In the ordinary run of things, many different courts would consider the claims of many different plaintiffs alleging injury by one defendant. But a class action simply combines all of those claims into one single megaproceeding. Judge Easterbrook has rightly called this a form of judicial 'central planning' and warns that it is just as dangerous as centralizing power in one branch of government." "Controlling Unconstitutional Class Actions: A Blueprint for Future Lawsuit Reform," *Policy Analysis* 546 (June 2005): 1–22, 7–8. The quote Moller refers to from Easterbrook is an important reminder that the insights conservative economists have had about the dangers of state central planning apply to central planning by the judiciary as well. As Easterbrook writes: "The central planning model—one case, one court, one set of rules, one settlement price for all involved—suppresses information that is vital to accurate resolution. . . . One suit is an all-or-none affair, with high risk even if the parties supply all the information at their disposal. Getting things right the first time would be an accident. Similar, Gosplan or another central planner may hit on the price of wheat, but that would be serendipity. Markets instead use diversified decisionmaking to supply and evaluate information. Thousands of traders affect prices by their purchases and sales over the course of a crop year. This method looks 'inefficient' from the planner's perspective, but it produces more information, more accurate prices, and a vibrant, growing economy. When courts think of efficiency, they should think of market models rather than central-planning models." *In re* Bridgestone/Firestone, Inc., Tire Prods. Liab. Litig., 288 F.3d 1012, 1020 (7th Cir. 2002). See also Jeffrey S. Parker, "Civil Procedure Reconsidered," in *Research Handbook on Austrian Law and Economics*, ed. Todd J. Zywicki and Peter J. Boettke (Northampton, MA: Edward Elgar, 2017), 296–324, 321.

26. David Rosenberg, e.g., argues that "courts should automatically and immediately aggregate all potential and actual claims arising from mass tort events into a single mandatory-litigation class action, allowing no class member to exit." "Mandatory-Litigation Class Action: The Only Option for Mass Tort Cases," *Harvard Law Review* 115, no. 3 (2002): 831–97, 834.

27. Rosenberg provides a helpful analysis here: "Defendants face none of the organization costs and free-rider obstacles to classwide aggregation that confront individual plaintiffs. Because a defendant naturally aggregates all classable claims, it has optimal investment incentives, giving it an automatic advantage over plaintiffs. Litigating in the separate action process, plaintiffs' attorneys generally can aggregate only a fraction of claims on a voluntary basis, and then only at substantial cost in overcoming impediments to collective action. As the single entity to whom the total potential benefit gained by avoiding damages on all claims accrues, the defendant can spread the costs of its investment on the common questions over the claims of all plaintiffs." "Mandatory-Litigation Class Action," 852–53.

28. See *In re* Nat'l Football League Players Concussion Injury Litig., 821 F.3d 410, 420 (3d Cir.), as amended (May 2, 2016).

29. Dozens of former NFL players have been diagnosed with chronic traumatic encephalopathy (CTE), a serious neurological condition, after their deaths. See John Branch, "The N.F.L.'s Tragic C.T.E. Roll Call," *New York Times*, February 3, 2016.

30. Most players are entitled to substantially more than $100,000. See, e.g., the long form of the notice of settlement given to the class. *NFL Concussion Settlement Benefits and Legal Rights* (2014), 17, https://www.nflconcussionsettlement .com/documents/long-form_notice.pdf.

31. The trial court notes that NFL players would have "serious hurdles establishing causation" if their case went to trial, both because "investigation into repetitive mild TBI [traumatic brain injury], typical of Retired Players, is relatively new" and because the "overwhelming majority of Retired Players likely experienced similar hits [as they experienced in the NFL] in high school or college football before reaching the NFL." It also notes that players "would have to conclusively establish what and when the NFL Parties knew about the risks of head injuries" to prevail. *In re* Nat. Football League Players' Concussion Injury Litig., 307 F.R.D. 351, 388, 391, 393 (E.D. Pa. 2015), amended sub nom. *In re* Nat'l Football League Players' Concussion Injury Litig., No. 2:12-MD-02323-AB, 2015 WL 12827803 (E.D. Pa. May 8, 2015).

32. Rosenberg, whose scholarship I discussed earlier, is one such prominent advocate of this position. See "Mandatory-Litigation Class Action," 834. However, there are many other scholars who take this position. See, e.g., Mary Davis's view that "mass tort class actions . . . are not only appropriate, but desirable, when evaluated against the backdrop of substantive tort law policies." "Toward the Proper Role for Mass Tort Class Actions," 158. Similarly, Christine Bartholomew

notes that aggregating individual lawsuits into class actions, in both the small and the large suit context, allows plaintiffs to "shar[e] costs, counsel, and information about the defendants' alleged wrongdoing." "The Failed Superiority Experiment," *Vanderbilt Law Review* 65, no. 5 (2016): 1296–1348, 1333.

33. For example, consider the following from the libertarian legal scholar Mark Moller: "I would also tentatively favor . . . limiting Rule 23(b)(3) to negative-value claims." "Separation of Powers and the Class Action," *Nebraska Law Review* 95, no. 2 (2016): 366–431, 409.

34. See, e.g., Brief of the Chamber of Commerce of the United States of America as Amicus Curiae in Support of Petitioner, AT&T Mobility LLC v. Concepcion, 563 U.S. 333 (2011), https://www.americanbar.org/content/dam/aba/publishing/preview/publiced_preview_briefs_pdfs_09_10_09_893_PetitionerAmCuCoC.authcheckdam.pdf; or the Chamber's critique of the Consumer Protection Financial Bureau, https://www.uschamber.com/sites/default/files/documents/files/cfpb_arbitration_study_critique.pdf.

35. Walter Olson, e.g., argues: "Persons who press their legal rights to the limit should be discouraged from imagining that they are somehow performing a public service. We have all met the sorts of persons who invariably see trespass when a schoolchild cuts across their lawn, nuisance when the neighbors play their stereo too loud on Saturday night, fraud when the mail order purchase is not all they had hoped for. . . . [The law] should not let them set themselves up as general benefactors." *The Litigation Explosion*, 344–45. This view has attracted some sympathy from judges facing deeply overburdened dockets. As one court put it when dismissing a class action lawsuit against a junk mail sender: "The courts cannot solve every complaint or right every technical wrong, particularly one which causes no actual damage beyond the loss of the few seconds it takes to open an envelope and examine its contents. Our courts are too heavily overburdened to be used as a vehicle to punish by one whose only real damage is feeling foolish for having opened what obviously was junk mail." Harris v. Time, Inc., 237 Cal. Rptr. 584, 589–90 (Ct. App. 1987), as modified (May 21, 1987).

36. Carnegie v. Household Int'l, Inc., 376 F.3d 656, 661 (7th Cir. 2004).

37. Murray Rothbard sets forth "a set of libertarian principles by which to gauge and reconstruct the law," including opposition to class action suits, because "the only plaintiffs who should be affected by a suit are those who voluntarily join." *The Logic of Action II: Applications and Criticism from the Austrian School* (Cheltenham: Edward Elgar, 1997), 166.

38. Rothbard writes that "the libertarian creed rests upon one central axiom: that no man or group of men may aggress against the person or property of anyone else." *For a New Liberty*, 27.

39. Matthew Dimick states that "an allocation is Pareto efficient if no one can be made better off without also making someone else worse off." "Should the Law Do Anything about Economic Inequality?," *Cornell Journal of Law and Public Policy* 26, no. 1 (2016): 1–69, 14.

40. Jules L. Coleman notes that Pareto efficiency "is often thought of as normatively rooted in classical utilitarianism," though he argues that it is defensible on other grounds. "Efficiency, Utility, and Wealth Maximization," *Hofstra Law Review* 8, no. 3 (1980): 509–51, 515.

41. Lisa Grow Sun and Brigham Daniels write that "we could describe positive externalities as benefits that an actor's decisions confer on third parties—benefits that, again, the actor is unlikely to account for in his decision-making, as he does not capture those benefits for himself." "Mirrored Externalities," *Notre Dame Law Review* 90 (2014): 135–86, 137.

42. Compare this to Milton Friedman and Rose Friedman's discussion of how positive externalities can arise in contract: "Voluntary arrangements can allow for third-party effects to a much greater extent than may at first appear. To take a trivial example, tipping at restaurants is a social custom that leads you to assure better service for people you may not know or even meet and, in return, be assured better service by the actions of still another group of anonymous third parties." *Free to Choose*, 32.

43. Richard Epstein writes: "Moral-rights or natural law libertarians disavow the idea that the social consequences of any legal rule could justify its adoption or rejection, and thereby reject any abstract measure of social welfare. Taken to their logical extreme, these natural law theories have—or, at least, ought to have—as their central maxim, *fiat justitia ruat caelom* (let justice be done though the heavens may fall). If consequences never count in deciding the rights and wrongs of individual actions, then disastrous consequences cannot count either." *Principles for a Free Society*, 11–12.

44. Nozick, e.g., argues that the only morally tolerable government is the "minimal state," which "treats us as inviolate individuals, who may not be used in certain ways by others as means or tools," as, he contends, government action to promote the common good does. *Anarchy, State, and Utopia*, 333–34.

45. A small minority of libertarians argue that, even when people know about their opt-out rights, those rights are not sufficient to protect liberty. These arguments are usually made in defense of irrational individuals. What good are opt-out rights if you are too irrational to take advantage of them? See, e.g., Mitchell, "Libertarian Nudges," 704–5. But I think they are equally applicable to opt-out rights that are worthless to the rational individuals as well. As I note, small-stakes class action opt-out rights are worthless because individual suits are not viable for small sums of money.

46. It is worth additionally noting that the rules protect those who truly desire to preserve their individual right not to be a part of a money damages class action through the opt-out mechanism. Indeed, Ryan C. Williams argues that most opt outs are likely symbolic protests: "It is probably not unreasonable to view a class member's decision to opt out as merely a form of 'self-harming symbolic protest.'" "Due Process, Class Action Opt-Outs, and the Right Not to Sue," *Columbia Law Review* 115, no. 3 (2015): 599–659, 637.

47. Epstein, "Class Actions: The Need for a Hard Second Look," 6.

48. Owen M. Fiss states the problem plainly when he writes: "The truly disquieting fact about the class action is that it creates a situation in which I may be represented in proceedings I know nothing about and by someone I do not know and had no role whatsoever in choosing. The social purposes served by the class action may well justify this odd form of representation, but it would be a mistake to ignore or deny its very oddity and the fact it runs counter to the individualistic values that so permeate our legal system." "The Political Theory of the Class Action," *Washington and Lee Law Review* 53, no. 1 (1996): 21–32, 31. Martin Redish makes much the same argument: "Of particular significance in the class action debate is the emphasis that liberalism places on an individual's right to personal autonomy. . . . I conclude that the subordination of the individual to external considerations conflicts with the importance placed on process-based individual autonomy by liberal theory." *Wholesale Justice*, 88–89. Judith Resnik, Dennis E. Curtis, and Deborah R. Hensler offer a broader critique of, not just class actions, but other forms of aggregating litigation as well, declaring: "Aggregation has too often operated to submerge the interests and needs of participants and to undermine the rationales for court decisionmaking. Some attention needs to be paid to the diverse clients; some form of what Deborah Rhode has termed a 'pluralistic approach' should inform the processing and outcomes of mass torts. Group litigation has basically belonged to judges, special masters, and lawyers talking only with each other and making decisions about categories of claims. We think it time to change." "Individuals within the Aggregate: Relationships, Representation, and Fees," *New York University Law Review* 71 (1996): 296–401, 399.

49. See Moller, "Controlling Unconstitutional Class Actions," 1–4. See also Greve's comment that "contemporary class actions often dispense with . . . a 'reliance' element that connects the plaintiffs' alleged losses to the defendants' alleged misdeeds." *Harm-Less Lawsuits*, 1.

50. Epstein, "Class Actions: Aggregation, Amplification, Distortion," 502–14.

51. Epstein, "Class Actions: Aggregation, Amplification, Distortion," 509.

52. Federal law requires federal courts to interpret the Rules of Civil Procedure so that they do not "abridge, enlarge or modify any substantive right." 28 U.S.C. § 2072.

53. As Justice Scalia, writing for the Court, put it in a recent decision: "A class cannot be certified on the premise that [the defendant] will not be entitled to litigate its statutory defenses to individual claims." Wal-Mart Stores, Inc. v. Dukes, 564 U.S. 338, 367 (2011). Strictly speaking, Dukes was decided under Rule 23, not the Constitution's Due Process Clause. However, Dukes's reasoning makes it clear that the states are not free to do this either. The Court has previously held that "due process requires that there be an opportunity to present every available defense." Lindsey v. Normet, 405 U.S. 56, 66 (1972). As Theodore J. Boutrous Jr. and Bradley J. Hamburger argue: "Given its prior precedents recognizing that due process includes the right to present every available defense, and the Court's

clear determination that 'Trial by Formula' did in fact preclude the presentation of individualized defenses, there is little doubt that the Court would have found a due process violation if it had been necessary for it to reach the issue." "Three Myths About *Wal-Mart Stores, Inc. v. Dukes*," *George Washington Law Review Arguendo* 82 (2014): 45–58, 54–55.

54. Epstein, e.g., concedes that we should keep at least some class actions around: "The class action is here to stay . . . [a]s it should be." "Class Actions: Aggregation, Amplification, and Distortion," 514.

55. See, e.g., Coffee's comment that "the most persuasive account of why class actions frequently produce unsatisfactory results is the hypothesis that such actions are uniquely vulnerable to collusive settlements." John C. Coffee Jr., "Understanding the Plaintiff's Attorney: The Implications of Economic Theory for Private Enforcement of Law through Class and Derivative Actions," *Columbia Law Review* 86, no. 4 (1986): 669–727, 677.

56. One mechanism through which such a result can be obtained is something like a race to the bottom: "The defendant in a series of class actions picks the most ineffectual class lawyers to negotiate a settlement with in the hope that the district court will approve a weak settlement that will preclude other claims against the defendant. The ineffectual lawyers are happy to sell out a class they anyway can't do much for in exchange for generous attorneys' fees, and the defendants are happy to pay generous attorneys' fees since all they care about is the bottom line—the sum of the settlement and the attorneys' fees—and not the allocation of money between the two categories of expense." Reynolds v. Beneficial Nat. Bank, 288 F.3d 277, 282 (7th Cir. 2002). The possibility of such a race has been diminished in recent years with the growth of litigation under the Multidistrict Litigation Act. Under this act, all related cases in federal court are consolidated for pretrial proceedings before one judge who appoints one group of lawyers to represent any class. Nonetheless, the race to the bottom is not the only way in which unscrupulous lawyers can collude with defendants. As Coffee writes: "Collusion within the class action context essentially requires an agreement—actual or implicit—by which the defendants receive a 'cheaper' than arm's length settlement and the plaintiffs' attorneys receive in some form an above-market attorneys' fee. The mechanics of such an agreement varies with the litigation context." John C. Coffee Jr., "Class Wars: The Dilemma of the Mass Tort Class Action," *Columbia Law Review* 95, no. 6 (1995): 1343–1465, 1367.

57. Service payments are not an uncommon practice. In an empirical study of the practice, Theodore Eisenberg and Geoffrey Miller conclude that "incentive awards are given in a nontrivial fraction, but still a minority (27.8 percent), of class action settlements." "Incentive Awards to Class Action Plaintiffs: An Empirical Study," *UCLA Law Review* 56 (2006): 1303–51, 1348.

58. To quote the Federal Rules of Civil Procedure: "The claims, issues, or defenses of a certified class may be settled, voluntarily dismissed, or compromised

only with the court's approval. . . . If the [settlement] proposal would bind class members, the court may approve it only after a hearing and on finding that it is fair, reasonable, and adequate." Fed. R. Civ. P. 23(e).

59. See, e.g., Jonathan R. Macey and Geoffrey P. Miller's discussion of settlement hearings, a type of court proceeding that evaluates whether a proposed settlement is appropriate: "Settlement hearings are typically pep rallies jointly orchestrated by plaintiffs' counsel and defense counsel. Because both parties desire that the settlement be approved, they have every incentive to present it as entirely fair. . . . Trial courts happily play along with the camaraderie. In approving settlement, courts often engage in paeans of praise for counsel or lambaste anyone rash enough to object to the settlement. Not surprisingly, it is uncommon to find cases where trial courts reject settlements that are presented to them by defense counsel and plaintiffs' attorneys." "The Plaintiffs' Attorney's Role in Class Action and Derivative Litigation: Economic Analysis and Recommendations for Reform," *University of Chicago Law Review* 58, no. 1 (1991): 1–118, 46–48.

60. See William B. Rubenstein, "The Fairness Hearing: Adversarial and Regulatory Approaches," 53 *UCLA Law Review* 53 (2006): 1435–82, 1453–55.

61. Indeed, concerns about collusive class action settlements substantially predate the invention of the money damages class action. See Pergament v. Frazer, 93 F. Supp. 13, 20 (E.D. Mich. 1950), aff'd sub nom; Masterson v. Pergament, 203 F.2d 315 (6th Cir. 1953); and Webster Eisenlohr, Inc. v. Kalodner, 145 F.2d 316, 320 (3d Cir. 1944).

62. A news article from the time profiled Daniel Edelman, one of the "scores of lawyers nationwide who have entered into 'coupon settlements,' an increasingly popular device used by class action lawyers to resolve complaints." Joe Stephens, "Coupons Create Cash for Lawyers," *Washington Post*, November 19, 1999, A01.

63. Jennifer Gibson notes that, before the law was changed to prohibit this practice, "many courts calculate[d] attorneys' fees using the value of all the coupons a defendant offer[ed], even if the class [was] unlikely to use them." "New Rules for Class Action Settlements: The Consumer Class Action Bill of Rights," *Loyola of Los Angeles Law Review* 39, no. 3 (2006): 1103–34, 1105.

64. As Stephens reports: "The record in one case, against ITT Financial Corp., showed that consumers redeemed only two of 96,754 coupons issued, a redemption rate of 0.002 percent." "Coupons Create Cash for Lawyers."

65. For example, one court at the time approved a coupon settlement despite the fact that it acknowledged it could not "estimate how many class members will redeem their coupons for discounts nor for which or how many products class members will seek their discounts." Hanrahan v. Britt, 174 F.R.D. 356, 368 (E.D. Pa. 1997).

66. For the original text of the law in question, see An Act to Amend the Procedures That Apply to Consideration of Interstate Class Actions to Assure Fairer Outcomes for Class Members and Defendants, and for Other Purposes, Pub. L. No. 109-2, *U.S. Statutes at Large* 119 (2005): 2.

67. To quote the law: "If a proposed settlement in a class action provides for a recovery of coupons to a class member, the portion of any attorney's fee award to class counsel that is attributable to the award of the coupons shall be based on the value to class members of the coupons that are redeemed." 28 U.S.C. § 1712(a).

68. *Black's Law Dictionary*, 8th ed., s.v. "Cy Pres." Sometimes the law requires leftover money to be given to state governments instead of charities.

69. The *Manual for Complex Litigation*, a handbook prepared by judges to help other judges handle procedurally difficult cases, states: "Fee awards should be based only on the benefits actually delivered. It is common to delay a final assessment of the fee award and to withhold all or a substantial part of the fee until the distribution process is complete." *Manual for Complex Litigation*, 4th ed., § 21.71.

Chapter Six

1. See, e.g., Joanna Schwartz's statement that "the Chamber of Commerce has [argued] that class action claims are often meritless." "The Cost of Suing Business," 673.

2. See, e.g., Ted Frank again: "Bank of America gets sued because it's big, rather than because it did something wrong." "Responding to Professor Fitzpatrick on Class Action Fees," Point of Law, November 29, 2011, http://www.pointo flaw.com/archives/2011/11/responding-to-professor-fitzpatrick-on-class-actio.php.

3. Coffee, "Understanding the Plaintiff's Attorney," 676–77.

4. See, e.g., John Schwartz, "If Tech Execs Act Like Spoiled Brats, Should We Spank Them?," *New York Times*, July 14, 2017.

5. The US Supreme Court has—to much criticism by liberal scholars—made it easier and easier for judges to dismiss meritless cases on a motion to dismiss. See Ashcroft v. Iqbal, 556 U.S. 662 (2009); Bell Atl. Corp. v. Twombly, 550 U.S. 544 (2007). I am one of the few scholars to defend the Court's decisions on this issue. See Brian T. Fitzpatrick, "*Twombly* and *Iqbal* Reconsidered," *Notre Dame Law Review* 87, no. 4 (2012): 1621–46.

6. Thomas E. Willging, Laural L. Hooper, and Robert J. Niemic find that motions to dismiss are filed in between 31 and 63 percent of cases, depending on the district. "Empirical Study of Class Actions in Four Federal District Courts: Final Report to the Advisory Committee on Civil Rules" (Washington, DC: Federal Judicial Center, 1996), 171, table 24, https://www.uscourts.gov/sites/default /files/rule23_1.pdf. The same study finds that between 17 and 20 percent of cases terminate on the motion to dismiss. Ibid., 172, table 27. A later study by Emery G. Lee III and Thomas E. Willging finds that motions to dismiss are filed in a high percentage of cases, though it is unclear exactly how high because the motions tallied may have overlapped with each other. "Impact of the Class Action Fairness Act on the Federal Courts: Preliminary Findings from Phase Two's Pre-CAFA

Sample of Diversity Class Actions" (Federal Judicial Center, November 2008), 5, table 4, https://www.uscourts.gov/sites/default/files/preliminary_findings_from _phase_two_class_action_fairness_study_2008_1.pdf. This study finds that 12 percent of cases are terminated on the motion to dismiss. Ibid., 6, table 6. It also reports a high rate at which plaintiffs voluntarily dismissed their own cases (38 percent). Ibid., 2. It is not clear if these were meritless cases that plaintiffs knew they would lose after they saw the defendants' motions to dismiss, if they had merit and the defendants entered into a settlement with the plaintiffs to prevent them from seeking to certify the cases as class actions, or if they had merit and plaintiffs dismissed them in one venue to file them elsewhere. As Lee and Willging write: "Voluntary dismissals may represent a financial or equitable-relief settlement of the individual claims of the named plaintiffs or a dismissal of such claims without a settlement. . . . Dismissal without a settlement can also be divided into two types of cases: those dismissed for all time because of lack of merit or a solvent defendant, and those dismissed with an eye toward litigating the same case in another court. Docket records almost never indicate which of those scenarios is applicable to a given case. In the voluntary dismissals, plaintiffs and defendants may have agreed to file a proposed class settlement in another forum. Or . . . plaintiffs may have plans to pursue the dismissed claims in another, presumably more favorable, federal venue." Ibid., 10. However, the study does cast doubt on the possibility that voluntary dismissal was primarily driven by plaintiffs realizing that their cases were meritless as "defendants . . . were less likely to file dispositive motions in these cases than in other types of cases." Ibid. Another possibility is that the superior litigation resources of the defendants wore down the lawyers who brought these cases. See Deborah R. Hensler's comment that these dismissals may have also been for "lack of resources": the lawyers may have had "less financial wherewithal to persevere against deep pocket corporate defendants." "Can Private Class Actions Enforce Regulations? Do They? Should They?," in *Comparative Law and Regulation* (Cheltanham: Edward Elgar, 2016), 238–74, 258.

7. Choi, Nelson, and Pritchard find that, before 1995, securities class actions were dismissed 21.4 percent of the time but that, after 1995, such suits were dismissed 30.4 percent of the time. Stephen J. Choi, Karen K. Nelson, and Adam Pritchard, "The Screening Effect of the Private Securities Litigation Reform Act," *Journal of Empirical Legal Studies* 6, no. 1 (2009): 35–68, 36, table 1D. See also Cox, Thomas, and Bai, who find 28.6 percent of securities fraud class actions were dismissed between 1993 and 2006. James D. Cox, Randall S. Thomas, and Lynn Bai, "Do Differences in Pleading Standards Cause Forum Shopping in Securities Class Actions? Doctrinal and Empirical Analyses," *Wisconsin Law Review* 324 (2009): 421–53. Choi and Pritchard find 35.9 percent of securities fraud class actions were dismissed with prejudice between 2003 and mid-2007. Stephen J. Choi and Adam Pritchard, "Supreme Court's Impact on Securities Class Actions: An Empirical Assessment of *Tellabs*," *Journal of Law, Economics, & Organization*

28, no. 4 (2012): 850–81, 859. Stefan Boettrich and Svetlana Starykh find that 27.5 percent of all securities fraud class actions between 2000 and 2017 were dismissed with prejudice. *Recent Trends in Securities Class Action Litigation: 2017 Full-Year Review* (White Plains, NY: NERA Economic Consulting, January 29, 2018), 19. Although some of these studies and those in the previous note predate the Supreme Court's 2007 adoption of the requirement that lawsuits be at least plausible to survive a motion to dismiss, scholars have found that district courts dismissed lawsuits because they doubted their merits long before the Supreme Court gave them the green light to do so. Fitzpatrick, "*Twombly* and *Iqbal* Reconsidered," 1631–32.

8. As Choi, Nelson, and Prichard note, there is no general agreement on how to define a meritless case: "The difficulty of assessing merit . . . makes it impossible to measure precisely the proportion of nuisance settlements to settlements based on the strength of the claims." "The Screening Effect of the Private Securities Litigation Reform Act," 36.

9. As Choi, Nelson, and Pritchard note: "Defendants, anxious to avoid the distraction of litigation, high defense attorney fees, negative publicity surrounding a securities lawsuit, and the specter of potentially bankrupting damages, may be willing to pay a 'nuisance' settlement to make the case go away, even when they perceive the likelihood of the plaintiff succeeding at trial as rather low." "The Screening Effect of the Private Securities Litigation Reform Act," 36.

10. Shavell describes how it is rational for a defendant to settle a claim for any amount less than or equal to the anticipated defense costs of trial and the expected value of the plaintiff's claim. *Foundations of Economic Analysis of Law*, 401–2. He goes on to say that, "the larger are the legal expenses of either party, the greater are the chances of settlement, clearly, since the sum of legal costs will rise, and thus the greater will be the likelihood that the sum of legal costs will exceed any excess of the plaintiff's expectation over the defendant's expectation." Ibid., 406.

11. This concern reflects the fact that defendants can be risk averse. Shavell explains: "When we introduce risk aversion into the basic model [of settlement], we see that [risk aversion] leads to a greater likelihood of settlement. The reason is simply that a trial is a risky venture because its outcome is unknown. To a risk-averse party, settlement is more attractive than it is to a risk-neutral party. Further, as the degree of risk aversion of either party increases, or as the amount at stake increases—the size of the judgment or the size of legal fees—settlement becomes more likely, other things being equal." *Foundations of Economic Analysis of Law*, 406–7.

12. Shavell's model of settlement indicates that the anticipated cost of trial is, for rational actors, a part of every decision to settle. *Foundations of Economic Analysis of Law*, 401–2. Shavell further explains that settlement for a greater amount than the expected value of the plaintiff's claims is rational because, "if the plaintiff's minimum acceptable amount [for a settlement] is less than the defendant's maximum acceptable amount, a mutually beneficial settlement is possible—a

settlement equal to any amount in between these two figures would be preferable to a trial for each party." Ibid., 402.

13. For a discussion of how risk aversion can increase settlement, see n. 11 above.

14. Dain C. Donelson, Justin J. Hopkins, and Christopher G. Yust rely on several studies for this range, noting that "small settlements are unlikely to be related to the actual loss by shareholders and suggest that the defendants settled the suit solely to avoid continued litigation expenses." "The Role of Directors' and Officers' Insurance in Securities Fraud Class Action Settlements," *Journal of Law and Economics* 58, no. 4 (2015): 747–78, 751.

15. Stephen J. Choi writes that, "although settlements under $2 million may include both nuisance and nonnuisance suits, settlements over $2 million are likely meritorious." "Do the Merits Matter *Less* After the Private Securities Litigation Reform Act?," *Journal of Law, Economics, & Organization* 23, no. 3 (2007): 598–626, 613.

16. Fitzpatrick, "An Empirical Study of Class Action Settlements and Their Fee Awards," 828, table 5.

17. Willging, Hooper, and Niemic find that between 63 and 83 percent of settled cases had survived a ruling on a motion to dismiss or a motion for summary judgment. "Empirical Study of Class Actions in Four Federal District Courts," 411, table 58. Lee and Willging state that, based on their own findings, "in the typical class settlement case, the plaintiffs generally have to overcome at least one challenge directed at the merits of the case—a motion to dismiss or for summary judgment." "Impact of the Class Action Fairness Act on the Federal Courts," 10.

18. Davis and Lande, "Private Antitrust Enforcement," 1280–81.

19. Davis and Lande, "Private Antitrust Enforcement," 1284.

20. As I have noted elsewhere: "Of the 444 fee awards using the percentage-of-the-settlement approach [the most common method of determining legal fees in class action cases], 52 percent were approved by Republican appointees, 45 percent were approved by Democratic appointees, and 4 percent were approved by non-Article III judges (usually magistrate judges). The mean fee percentage approved by Republican appointees (25.6 percent) was slightly greater than the mean approved by Democratic appointees (24.9 percent). The medians (25 percent) were the same." "An Empirical Study of Class Action Settlements and Their Fee Awards," 833.

21. Deborah Hensler estimates that sixty-five hundred class actions are filed in the United States every year. See Hensler, "Can Private Class Actions Enforce Regulations?," 252, table 9.2. That number strikes me as quite high because it implies that only roughly one of ten class actions ends in a class action settlement, and studies suggest that proportion is too low. See, e.g., ibid., 257, table 9.4.

22. As Alexander summarizes her findings, for the class actions she studied the "link between settlement and the merits appears to have broken." Janet Alexan-

der, "Do the Merits Matter? A Study of Settlements in Securities Class Actions," *Stanford Law Review* 43, no. 3 (1991): 497–598, 505.

23. See, e.g., Leonard B. Simpson and William S. Dato's response that Alexander's study is "fundamentally flawed" and that "her conclusions are inconsistent with both a replication of her study done with the most obvious flaws corrected, and a broader, more reliable study." "Legislating on a False Foundation: The Erroneous Academic Underpinnings of the Private Securities Litigation Reform Act of 1995," *San Diego Law Review* 33, no. 3 (1996): 959–84, 962. See also Joel Seligman's critique of Alexander's data and methodology. "The Merits Do Matter: A Comment on Professor Grundfest's 'Disimplying Private Rights of Action under the Federal Securities Laws: The Commissioner's Authority,'" *Harvard Law Review* 108 (1994): 438–57, 453. James Bohn and Stephen Choi also critique Alexander's data and describe her results as "unconvincing." "Fraud in the New-Issues Market: Empirical Evidence on Securities Class Actions," *University of Pennsylvania Law Review* 144 (1996): 903–82, 923.

24. See, e.g., James D. Cox and Randall S. Thomas's finding that "we therefore see that merits do appear to matter in the settlements reached in class actions." "Mapping the American Shareholder Litigation Experience: A Survey of Empirical Studies of the Enforcement of the U.S. Securities Law," *European Company and Financial Law Review* 6, nos. 2–3 (2009): 164–203, 195. See also Donelson, Hopkins, and Yust's conclusion: "Our findings suggest that most securities fraud class action settlements are meritorious." "The Role of Directors' and Officers' Insurance in Securities Fraud Class Action Settlements," 747. Choi writes that "evidence suggests a closer relation between factors related to fraud and securities class actions after the passage of the PSLRA." "Do the Merits Matter *Less* After the Private Securities Litigation Reform Act?," 630. Similarly, Quinn Curtis and Minor Myers find that "incidence of lawsuits . . . was linked to merits-related measures of backdating activity" and that "the size of settlement is related to the merits of cases." "Do the Merits Matter? Empirical Evidence on Shareholder Suits from Options Backdating Litigation," *University of Pennsylvania Law Review* 164, no. 2 (2016): 291–347, 295. However, see Bohn and Choi's contrary result in the context of IPO litigation, where they write that, "although the results of these five tests are mixed, on the whole they do provide strong evidence that at least a significant fraction of IPO suits are frivolous." "Fraud in the New-Issues Market," 950. As I note in a later chapter, one area of class actions that may be rife with frivolous cases is merger litigation. See Minor Myers and Charles R. Korsmo's finding that the field seems "driven largely by factors unrelated to legal merit." "The Structure of Stockholder Litigation: When Do the Merits Matter?," *Ohio State Law Journal* 75, no. 5 (2014): 829–901, 829.

25. "ILR Releases Top Ten Most Ridiculous Lawsuits of 2016," US Chamber Institute for Legal Reform, http://www.instituteforlegalreform.com/resource/ilr-releases-top-ten-most-ridiculous-lawsuits-of-2016; "The Top Ten Most Ridiculous Lawsuits of 2015," Faces of Lawsuit Abuse, http://www.facesoflawsuitabuse

.org/2015/12/the-top-ten-most-ridiculous-lawsuits-of-2015; "U.S. Chamber Releases Most Ridiculous Lawsuits of 2014," US Chamber Institute for Legal Reform, http://www.instituteforlegalreform.com/resource/us-chamber-releases-most-ridiculous-lawsuits-of-2014; "U.S. Chamber Releases Most Ridiculous Lawsuits of 2013," US Chamber Institute for Legal Reform, http://www.instituteforlegalreform.com/resource/us-chamber-releases-most-ridiculous-lawsuits-of-2013-.

26. See the sources cited in the previous note.

27. See "Subway Sued Over 'Footlong' Subs," Faces of Lawsuit Abuse, http://www.facesoflawsuitabuse.org/2013/01/subway-sued-over-footlong-subs. See also Schwartz, "The Cost of Suing Business," 674. Ted Frank comments that this case represents "a pretty clear-cut example of lawyers abusing the system." See also Robert Loerzel, "Foot Fight: Subway Sandwich Suit Raises Class Action Questions," *ABA Journal*, February 2017, 17, http://www.abajournal.com/magazine/article/subway_sandwich_class_ac.

28. See *In re* Subway Footlong Sandwich Mktg. & Sales Practices Litig., 316 F.R.D. 240 (E.D. Wis. 2016). This settlement was rejected on appeal by the Seventh Circuit, and the Court of Appeals viewed the claims as meritless. See *In re* Subway Footlong Sandwich Mktg. & Sales Practices Litig., 869 F.3d 551, 557 (7th Cir. 2017).

29. See "Jimmy John's Lawsuit 'Sprouts' Hefty Payday for Lawyers—Vouchers for Victims," Faces of Lawsuit Abuse, http://www.facesoflawsuitabuse.org/2014/10/jimmy-johns-lawsuit-sprouts-hefty-payday-for-lawyers-vouchers-for-victims.

30. See Notice of Proposed Class Action Settlement in Heather Starks v. Jimmy John's, LLC, et al., Case No. BC501113 (Cal. Sup. Ct.).

31. See "Starbucks Feels the Heat from Two Abusive Lawsuits," Faces of Lawsuit Abuse, http://www.facesoflawsuitabuse.org/2016/07/too-much-ice-in-iced-coffees-too-much-steamed-milk-in-lattes-starbucks-feeling-the-heat-of-lawsuit-abuse.

32. See Pincus v. Starbucks Corporation, No. 16-cv-04705 (N.D. Ill. Oct. 14, 2016); and Strumlauf v. Starbucks Corp., No. 16-CV-01306-YGR, 2018 WL 306715, at *9 (N.D. Cal. Jan. 5, 2018).

33. See US Chamber Institute for Legal Reform, "Court Tosses Lawsuit over Lip Balm Left in Tube," Faces of Lawsuit Abuse, http://www.facesoflawsuitabuse.org/2016/04/court-tosses-lawsuit-over-lip-balm-left-in-tube; Ebner v. Fresh, Inc., 838 F.3d 958 (9th Cir. 2016).

34. See "Mom and Son Sue over Typo That Gave Test Takers Extra Time," Faces of Lawsuit Abuse, http://www.facesoflawsuitabuse.org/2016/04/mom-and-son-sue-over-sat-typo-that-gave-students-extra-test-time.

35. See Ellinghaus v. Educational Testing Service et al., No. 2:15-cv-03442 (E.D.N.Y., Sep. 30, 2016).

36. See "Mastercard Blasts 'Baseless' Lawsuit over Its 'Stand Up to Cancer' Fundraising Promotion," Faces of Lawsuit Abuse, http://www.facesoflawsuitabuse.org/2016/01/mastercard-blasts-baseless-lawsuit-over-its-stand-up-to-cancer-fundraising-promotion.

37. See Doyle v. Mastercard International Inc., No. 16-04270 (2d Cir. Jul. 6, 2017).

38. "Deceived by Jelly Beans, Woman Files Lawsuit against Jelly Belly," Faces of Lawsuit abuse, http://www.facesoflawsuitabuse.org/2017/08/deceived-by -jelly-beans-woman-files-lawsuit-against-jelly-belly.

39. See Gomez v. Jelly Belly Candy Co., No. ED-CV-1700575-CJCFFMX, 2017 WL 2598551, at *1 (C.D. Cal. June 8, 2017).

40. US Chamber Institute for Legal Reform, "Time Clock Lawsuit Filed Against Starbucks," Faces of Lawsuit Abuse, http://www.facesoflawsuitabuse.org /2017/07/time-clock-lawsuit-filed-against-starbucks.

41. See Troester v. Starbucks Corp., 680 F. App'x 511, 515 (9th Cir. 2016).

42. US Chamber Institute for Legal Reform, "Massachusetts Man Files Class Action Lawsuits over Fake Butter," Faces of Lawsuit Abuse, http://www.facesoflawsuit abuse.org/2017/04/massachusetts-man-files-class-action-lawsuit-over-fake-butter.

43. Daniel Victor, "Butter or Margarine? In Dunkin' Donuts Lawsuit, Man Accepts No Substitute," *New York Times*, April 4, 2017.

44. To quote the Seventh Circuit: "All of Subway's raw dough sticks weigh exactly the same, so the rare sandwich roll that fails to bake to a full 12 inches actually contains no less bread than any other." *In re* Subway Footlong Sandwich Mktg. & Sales Practices Litig., 869 F.3d 551, 554 (7th Cir. 2017).

45. See Ebner v. Fresh, Inc., 838 F.3d 958, 965 (9th Cir. 2016).

46. See Doyle v. Mastercard International Inc., No. 16-04270 (2d Cir. Jul. 6, 2017).

47. See generally *In re* Checking Account Overdraft Litigation, No. 1:09-md-02036 (S.D. Fla. 2011).

48. See generally Tennille v. W. Union Co., 785 F.3d 422, 426 (10th Cir. 2015).

49. See generally *In re* TFT-LCD (Flat Panel) Antitrust Litigation, Docket No. 3:07-md-01827 (N.D. Cal.).

50. See generally *In re* Fannie Mae Sec Litig., Docket No. 1:04-cv-01639 (D.D.C.).

51. Laura Femino describes the practice as follows: "A [leveraged buyout] is the acquisition of a target company financed by debt that is secured by the assets of the target company and paid with the target's future cash flows. Put more simply: The acquiring company borrows money from the lending bank to purchase the target company. That loan is secured by the target's assets and future cash flows. The acquirer might also use some of its own capital for the purchase along with the borrowed funds. The acquirer then uses these funds to buy the target from the target's current shareholders, often at a large premium, and the acquirer becomes the new owner." "Ex Ante Review of Leveraged Buyouts," *Yale Law Journal* 123, no. 6 (2014): 1830–73, 1834.

52. See generally Kirk Dahl et al. v. Bain Capital Partners LLC et al., No. 1:07-cv-12388 (D. Mass.).

53. Rabbi Maurice Lamm provides a description of the principle in *The Jewish Way in Death and Mourning* (Middle Village, NY: Jonathan David, 2000), 64–69. Portions of the book have been republished online and can be accessed at http://

www.chabad.org/library/article_cdo/aid/281579/jewish/The-Grave.htm. It is worth noting that this prohibition is not absolute and that there are some limited circumstances in which those who have been buried can be exhumed under Jewish law. Ibid. Needless to say, those circumstances were not present in this case.

54. See generally Robert Scott, et al. v. Service Corporation International, et al., No. BC421528 (Cal. Sup. Ct. L.A.).

55. See generally *In re* Oil Spill by the Oil Rig "Deepwater Horizon" in the Gulf of Mexico, No. 2:10-md-02179 (E.D. La.).

56. See generally Barfield et al. v. Sho-Me Power Electric Cooperative et al., No. 2:11-CV-04321 (E.D. Mo.).

57. See generally Ramah Navajo Chapter v. Jewell, No. 1:90-CV-957 (D.N.M.).

58. See generally *In re* High-Tech Employee Antitrust Litig., No. 5:11-CV-02509 (N.D. Cal.).

59. See generally *In re* Volkswagen "Clean Diesel" Mktg., Sales Practices, & Prod. Liab. Litig. No. 3:15-MD-02672 (N.D. Cal.).

60. See generally *In re* Nat'l Football League Players' Concussion Injury Litig., No. 2:12-MD-02323-AB, (E.D. Pa.).

61. See generally Gokare P.C. v. Federal Express Corp., Case No. 11-CV-02131 (W.D. Tenn.).

62. The IRS says that, in 2013, roughly 5.9 million active corporations filed taxes. *SOI Tax Stats—Corporation Complete Report Section 1* (Washington, DC: Internal Revenue Service, 2013), 1. However, it is likely that not all these corporations actually function as separate entities as many companies are organized in networks of subsidiaries.

63. See Hensler, "Can Private Class Actions Enforce Regulations?," 252, table 9.2.

64. See Alexander Dyck, Adair Morse, and Luigi Zingales, "How Pervasive Is Corporate Fraud?," Working Paper no. 2222608 (Toronto: Rotman School of Management, August 2014), http://faculty.chicagobooth.edu/luigi.zingales/papers/research/pervasive.pdf.

Chapter Seven

1. See, e.g., Zygimantas Juska's contention that "it appears undeniable that the remuneration scheme is created to overpay attorneys . . . because . . . class members are highly undercompensated." "The Effectiveness of Private Enforcement and Class Actions to Secure Antitrust Enforcement," *Antitrust Bulletin* 62 (2017): 603–37, 623. See also Scott Dodson's observation of the "concern that some class actions were being used to enrich plaintiff's lawyers rather than to compensate claimants." "A Negative Retrospective of Rule 23," *New York University Law Review* 92, no. 4 (2017): 917–36, 922. Joanna Schwartz traces much of this sentiment to big business: "The Chamber of Commerce has [argued] that plaintiffs' class

action attorneys bring these . . . claims not to benefit class members but to line their own pockets." She expands on this, writing: "According to the Chamber of Commerce and other business amici, plaintiffs' class action attorneys seek to re-cover astronomical attorneys' fees on cases . . . for which the class members receive little or no benefit." "The Cost of Suing Business," 673, 676. For a recent example of such advocacy, the American Bankers Association, along with two other trade groups, recently claimed in a letter to the Consumer Financial Protection Bureau: "Class actions benefit consumers' lawyers but not the consumers themselves. . . . [T]he vast majority of customers receive no benefit whatsoever from being a class member [and] any economic benefit to individual class members in a class settlement is insignificant." Letter to Consumer Financial Protection Bureau (July 13, 2015), https://www.cfpbmonitor.com/wp-content/uploads/sites/5/2015/07/March-10 -2015-Consumer-Arbitration-Study-Comment-Letter.pdf. Similarly, a recent study by a major law firm commissioned by the Chamber of Commerce claims that "counsel for plaintiffs . . . are frequently the only real beneficiaries of the class ac-tion." Mayer Brown, LLP, "Do Class Actions Benefit Consumers," Mayer Brown, LLP, 2013, 18, https://www.mayerbrown.com/files/uploads/Documents/PDFs/2013 /December/DoClassActionsBenefitClassMembers.pdf.

2. Fitzpatrick, "An Empirical Study of Class Action Settlements and Their Fee Awards," 813.

3. Fitzpatrick, "An Empirical Study of Class Action Settlements and Their Fee Awards," 814.

4. Fitzpatrick, "An Empirical Study of Class Action Settlements and Their Fee Awards," 813.

5. Fitzpatrick, "An Empirical Study of Class Action Settlements and Their Fee Awards," 814.

6. Fitzpatrick, "An Empirical Study of Class Action Settlements and Their Fee Awards," 833.

7. Fitzpatrick, "An Empirical Study of Class Action Settlements and Their Fee Awards," 814.

8. Fitzpatrick, "An Empirical Study of Class Action Settlements and Their Fee Awards," 843.

9. I know this because the vast majority of class action settlement money comes from securities fraud settlements. See Fitzpatrick, "An Empirical Study of Class Action Settlements and Their Fee Awards," 825, table 4. Also, securities fraud settlements are always distributed pro rata. See 15 U.S.C.A. § 78u-4(a)(4).

10. Howard Erichson summarizes the current state of the law when he says: "Reversionary settlements seem to have become uncommon in the face of judicial disfavor." "Aggregation as Disempowerment: Red Flags in Class Action Settle-ments," *Notre Dame Law Review* 92, no. 2 (2016): 859–911, 892.

11. Bill Rubenstein notes that "most courts and commentators" strongly dis-favor the use of reversionary settlements. William Rubinstein, Alba Conte, and

Herbert B. Newberg, *Newberg on Class Actions*, 5th ed. (Eagan, MN: Thompson Reuters, 2011–18), s.v. "§ 12:29. Reversion to defendant(s)."

12. *Black's Law Dictionary*, 8th ed., s.v. "Cy Pres." Sometimes the law requires leftover money to be given to state governments instead of charities.

13. Samuel Issacharoff, e.g., was quoted by the *New York Times* as saying that the cy pres process "is an invitation to wild corruption of the judicial process." Adam Liptak, "Doling Out Other People's Money," *New York Times*, November 26, 2007.

14. It is fairly clear that, in some cases, cy pres settlements have been donated to charities with little to no connection to the class. For example, in Fears v. Wilhelmina Model Agency, Inc., No. 02-4911, 2005 WL 1041134, at *10–16 (S.D.N.Y. May 5, 2005), the proceeds from an antitrust class action against modeling agencies were donated to a charity combating eating disorders. In *In re* San Juan Dupont Plaza Hotel Fire Litig., No. MDL-0721, 2010 WL 60955, at *2 (D.P.R. Jan. 7, 2010), the proceeds from a mass tort class action were donated to an animal rights group. Similarly, in *In re* Compact Disc Minimum Advertised Price Antitrust Litig., No. MDL 1361, 2005 WL 1923446, at *2–3 (D. Me. Aug. 9, 2005), the proceeds from an antitrust class action against compact disc makers were donated to a charity for the arts.

15. Not granting attorneys' fees at the time a case settles has been the practice in a number of recent major lawsuits. See, e.g., *In re* Volkswagen "Clean Diesel" Mktg., Sales Practices, & Prod. Liab. Litig., 229 F. Supp. 3d 1052, 1072 (N.D. Cal. 2017), enforcement granted, No. 2672 CRB (JSC), 2017 WL 914066 (N.D. Cal. Mar. 6, 2017); *In re* Oil Spill by Oil Rig Deepwater Horizon in Gulf of Mexico, 910 F. Supp. 2d 891, 909 (E.D. La. 2012), aff'd sub nom; *In re* Deepwater Horizon, 739 F.3d 790 (5th Cir. 2014). This is not just the practice in major class actions. For example, the *Manual for Complex Litigation*, a handbook prepared by judges to help other judges handle procedurally difficult cases, states: "Fee awards should be based only on the benefits actually delivered. It is common to delay a final assessment of the fee award and to withhold all or a substantial part of the fee until the distribution process is complete." *Manual for Complex Litigation*, 4th ed., § 21.71. This approach is also recommended by the influential American Law Institute. See American Law Institute, *Principles of the Law of Aggregate Litigation*, §308(a).

16. In 2015, Robert Gilbert and I summarized studies on factors affecting claims rates in class actions and conducted our own study. We found that, consistent with previous studies, claims rates were much higher when class members were directly sent payment rather than being forced to fill out claims forms. See Brian T. Fitzpatrick and Robert Gilbert, "An Empirical Look at Compensation in Consumer Class Actions," *New York University Journal of Law and Business* 11, no. 4 (2015): 767–92, 778, 782.

17. Gilbert and I found that "the size of class members' payouts influenced negotiation [cashing of settlement checks] rates: class members were more likely to negotiate larger denomination checks than smaller denomination ones."

Fitzpatrick and Gilbert, "An Empirical Look at Compensation in Consumer Class Actions," 784.

18. As Gilbert and I write: "We suspect that some class members were skeptical of checks they received in the mail through no effort of their own, and did not negotiate them for fear of becoming part of a scam." Fitzpatrick and Gilbert, "An Empirical Look at Compensation in Consumer Class Actions," 783–84.

19. In the two class actions using claim forms identified in my study with Gilbert, only 1 percent of class members collected money in one of the settlements, and only 7 percent collected in the other. Fitzpatrick and Gilbert, "An Empirical Look at Compensation in Consumer Class Actions," 787, table 3.

20. See *In re* Checking Account Overdraft Litig., 694 F. Supp. 2d 1302, 1309 (S.D. Fla. 2010).

21. As Gilbert and I explain at length: "We also believe that there are realistic opportunities to distribute settlements automatically. Many times defendants will have sufficient information about some or all of their customers to make automatic distributions feasible. These will include defendants who sell directly to customers, especially those who sell online, where the trail is more often preserved. Courts and counsel interested in the compensatory side should be attentive to these opportunities and insist that defendants preserve such information at the outset of a case. The ALI and other commentators have already encouraged this, but we think the opportunities for automatic distributions go beyond even what these commentators may have envisioned: if the files of defendants are bare, we think courts and counsel should turn to third-parties. For example, when defendants sell their wares through retailers, the retailers that sell online (e.g., Amazon) will have this information; and even those that sell offline keep purchase information on those of their customers who hold so-called loyalty cards. These third-party retailers can be subpoenaed for information, as they were in a recent class action for which one of us served as an expert." Fitzpatrick and Gilbert, "An Empirical Look at Compensation in Consumer Class Actions," 787–88.

22. As Robert Gilbert and I explain: "Although the opportunities to do so may be limited today, we believe they will only grow in the future as new forms of electronic banking are developed and as the so called 'big data' revolution continues to unfold. If we are correct about this, it suggests that the compensatory value of consumer class actions will be brighter in the future than in the past." Fitzpatrick and Gilbert, "An Empirical Look at Compensation in Consumer Class Actions," 771.

23. See, e.g., Linda Mullenix's statement that "there is scant evidence upon which to conclude that class action litigation and settlement actually accomplishes the stated goal of compensating victims of wrongdoing." "Ending Class Actions as We Know Them," 419. See also Crane's statement that "compensation fails because the true economic victims of most antitrust violations are usually downstream consumers who are too numerous and remote from the violation to locate and compensate." "Optimizing Private Antitrust Enforcement," 677.

24. See, e.g., Dam's comment: "The absence of actual compensation . . . is not dispositive. Here the concept of deterrence has its true role. Deterrence substitutes as a justification for compensation where compensation is not feasible. The principle of deterrence requires that the wrongdoer pay, but says nothing about who shall receive the payment. Hence the argument for nevertheless favoring the class action even though compensation can never be paid is that if class treatment is not accorded, the deterrent effect of the substantive rule will be forfeited." "Class Actions," 60–61.

25. See, e.g., *In re* Volkswagen "Clean Diesel" Mktg., Sales Practices, & Prod. Liab. Litig., No. 2672 CRB (JSC), 2017 WL 1352859, at *2 (N.D. Cal. Apr. 12, 2017); McDaniel v. Cty. of Schenectady, No. 04CV0757GLSRFT, 2007 WL 3274798, at *4 (N.D.N.Y. Nov. 5, 2007), aff'd, 595 F.3d 411 (2d Cir. 2010); and Mills v. Capital One, N.A., No. 14 CIV. 1937 HBP, 2015 WL 5730008, at *10 (S.D.N.Y. Sept. 30, 2015). For more examples, see also the cases in the following note.

26. See, e.g., *In re* Washington Pub. Power Supply Sys. Sec. Litig., 19 F.3d 1291, 1297 (9th Cir. 1994); Spark v. MBNA Corp., 157 F. Supp. 2d 330, 345 (D. Del. 2001), aff'd, 48 F. App'x 385 (3d Cir. 2002); Wallace on Behalf of Ne. Utilities v. Fox, 7 F. Supp. 2d 132, 135 (D. Conn. 1998); and *In re* PaineWebber Ltd. Partnerships Litig., 999 F. Supp. 719, 723 (S.D.N.Y. 1998).

27. *In re* Checking Account Overdraft Litig., 830 F. Supp. 2d 1330, 1359 (S.D. Fla. 2011).

28. The judge explains: "Class Counsel achieved an extraordinary result and overcame numerous procedural and substantive hurdles to obtain the Settlement for the Class. As Plaintiffs' several experts have noted, Class Counsel took on a great deal of risk in bringing this case, and turned a potentially empty well into a significant judgment. That kind of initiative and skill must be adequately compensated to insure that counsel of this caliber is available to undertake these kinds of risky but important cases in the future." *In re* Checking Account Overdraft Litig., 830 F. Supp. 2d 1330, 1359 (S.D. Fla. 2011).

29. See Gutierrez v. Wells Fargo Bank, N.A., 730 F. Supp. 2d 1080, 1140 (N.D. Cal. 2010), aff'd in part, rev'd in part and remanded sub nom. Gutierrez v. Wells Fargo Bank, NA, 704 F.3d 712 (9th Cir. 2012).

30. Gutierrez v. Wells Fargo Bank, N.A., No. C 07-05923 WHA, 2015 WL 2438274, at *8 (N.D. Cal. May 21, 2015).

31. Gutierrez v. Wells Fargo Bank, N.A., No. C 07-05923 WHA, 2015 WL 2438274, at *4 (N.D. Cal. May 21, 2015).

32. Gutierrez v. Wells Fargo Bank, N.A., No. C 07-05923 WHA, 2015 WL 2438274, at *8 (N.D. Cal. May 21, 2015).

33. Gutierrez v. Wells Fargo Bank, N.A., No. C 07-05923 WHA, 2015 WL 2438274, at *4 (N.D. Cal. May 21, 2015).

34. See, e.g., Jeffrey J. Rachlinski's comment that "the hindsight bias clearly has implications for the legal system." "A Positive Psychological Theory of Judging

in Hindsight," *University of Chicago Law Review* 65 (1998): 571–625, 572. Confirming this theory's relevance to judicial decisionmaking, Chris Guthrie, Jeffrey J. Rachlinski, and Andrew J. Wistrich conducted a psychological study using a group of judges and found that judges are susceptible to hindsight bias in decisionmaking, though the bias is less when the area where decisions were being made was more rule bound. "Blinking on the Bench: How Judges Decide Cases," *Cornell Law Review* 93, no. 1 (2007): 1–43, 26. Judicial decisions on attorneys' fees tend to be less rule bound than in most other areas of law, exacerbating the problem of hindsight bias.

35. The influence of law and economics on class action fee practices is particularly visible when one looks at the language courts used when discussing fees. For example, in an early landmark Third Circuit case that was widely cited as outlining the appropriate use of the lodestar method, the court focused on a discussion of the abstracted "value" of the attorney's services. See Lindy Bros. Builders of Phila. v. Am. Radiator & Standard Sanitary Corp., 487 F.2d 161, 168 (3d Cir. 1973). In contrast, when the Third Circuit revisited the wisdom of the Lindy standard in a report prepared by a judicial task force, it focused primarily on the incentives created by fee structures—a hallmark of the law and economics movement. Court Awarded Attorney Fees, 108 F.R.D. 237, 247 (1985).

36. As Easterbrook explains in *In re* Synthroid Marketing Litigation, 325 F.3d 974, 979 (7th Cir. 2003): "Contingent-fee arrangements are used when it is difficult to monitor counsel closely; otherwise some different arrangement, such as hourly rates, is superior." Or consider Richard Epstein: "One possible fee arrangement is for the informed client who is capable of monitoring his lawyer to pay an hourly fee. [B]ut whatever is good sense in ordinary litigation, it is stillborn in class action litigation for the simple reason that diffuse class members have no real way to monitor the behavior of their lawyers. [I] think that we can be confident that it is suicidal to allow the lawyers to collect fees on an hourly wage. [M]y own preference therefore is to stay away from this cost-plus formula with its intrinsic risk of padding the accounts, and to veer to the same kind of arrangement that ordinary lawyers use in tort actions: the contingent fee." "Class Actions: The Need for a Hard Second Look," 9–10.

37. Lodestar's decline was such that, by 1991, Monique Lapointe could survey the history of class action fee methods and conclude that "lodestar, a method of calculating attorney's fees based on time expended, is fast becoming a relic of common fund litigation" despite the fact that, "from the mid-1970s to the mid-1980s, lodestar was the fee-setting standard of choice in common fund cases in the federal court system." "Attorney's Fees in Common Fund Actions," *Fordham Law Review* 59, no. 5 (1991): 843–76, 843, 847.

38. As I have noted elsewhere: "My 2006–2007 data set shows that the percentage-of-the-settlement approach has become much more common than the lodestar approach. In 69% of the settlements reported in Table 7, district court judges

employed the percentage-of-the-settlement method with or without the lodestar crosscheck. They employed the lodestar method in only 12% of settlements." "An Empirical Study of Class Action Settlements and Their Fee Awards," 832.

39. As Epstein observes: "It is well known that in some cases the ordinary contingent fee lawyer will settle a case sooner than might be in the interest of his client." "Class Actions: The Need for a Hard Second Look," 9. Shavell explains why: "Under contingency fee arrangements, . . . the lawyer . . . press[es] for settlement more often than when the settlement offer exceeds the expected judgment net of litigation costs . . . because the lawyer bears all the litigation costs but obtains only a percentage of the settlement." *Foundations of Economic Analysis of Law*, 435.

40. See Kevin M. Clermont and John D. Currivan, "Improving on the Contingent Fee," *Cornell Law Review* 63, no. 4 (1978): 529–639, 546–50. This formula is not perfect if lawyers are paid only when they win. For a variation that perfects the formula, see A. Mitchell Polinsky and Daniel Rubinfeld, "Aligning the Interests of Lawyers and Clients," *American Law and Economics Review* 5, no. 1 (2003): 165–88, 166–69.

41. See Fitzpatrick, "An Empirical Study of Class Action Settlements and Their Fee Awards," 832.

42. As Easterbrook explains in Williams v. Rohm & Haas Pension Plan, 658 F.3d 629, 636 (7th Cir. 2011): "The . . . argument . . . that any percentage fee award exceeding a certain lodestar multiplier is excessive . . . echoes [practices] we rejected [as unlikely to be adopted by rational actors in a free market]."

43. This is true in cases where fees are shifted to the defendant by statute. To give one example, the Supreme Court explains that, "unlike the calculation of attorney's fees under the 'common fund doctrine,' where a reasonable fee is based on a percentage of the fund bestowed on the class, a reasonable fee under [a fee-shifting statute for federal civil rights claims] reflects the amount of attorney time reasonably expended on the litigation." Blum v. Stenson, 465 U.S. 886, 900 (1984).

44. See Fitzpatrick, "An Empirical Study of Class Action Settlements and Their Fee Awards," 838. I quote much of the relevant portion in n. 46 below.

45. *In re* Synthroid Mktg. Litig., 264 F.3d 712, 718 (7th Cir. 2001).

46. As I have explained elsewhere: "In Table 10, I . . . [set] forth the mean and median fee percentages, as well as the standard deviation, for each decile of the 2006–2007 settlements in which courts used the percentage-of-the-settlement method to award fees. The mean percentages ranged from over 28 percent in the first decile to less than 19 percent in the last decile. It should be noted that the last decile in Table 10 covers an especially wide range of settlements, those from $72.5 million to the Enron settlement of $6.6 billion. To give more meaningful data to courts that must award fees in the largest settlements, Table 11 shows the last decile broken into additional cut points. When both Tables 10 and 11 are examined together, it appears that fee percentages tended to drift lower at a fairly slow pace until a settlement size of $100 million was reached, at which point the fee percentages plunged well below 20 percent, and by the time $500 million was reached, they

plunged well below 15 percent, with most awards at that level under even 10 percent." Fitzpatrick "An Empirical Study of Class Action Settlements and Their Fee Awards," 838.

47. Easterbrook, writing for the Seventh Circuit, noted: "Many costs of litigation do not depend on the outcome; it is almost as expensive to conduct discovery in a $100 million case as in a $200 million case. Much of the expense must be devoted to determining liability, which does not depend on the amount of damages; in securities litigation damages often can be calculated mechanically from movements in stock prices. There may be some marginal costs of bumping the recovery from $100 million to $200 million, but as a percentage of the incremental recovery these costs are bound to be low. It is accordingly hard to justify awarding counsel as much of the second hundred million as of the first. The justification for diminishing marginal rates applies to $50 million and $500 million cases too, not just to $200 million cases. Awarding counsel a decreasing percentage of the higher tiers of recovery enables them to recover the principal costs of litigation from the first bands of the award, while allowing the clients to reap more of the benefit at the margin (yet still preserving some incentive for lawyers to strive for these higher awards)." Silverman v. Motorola Sols., Inc., 739 F.3d 956, 959 (7th Cir. 2013). In a different recent case, Easterbrook provides a summary of class actions in which this marginal declining fee structure was successfully used. See *In re* Synthroid Mktg. Litig., 264 F.3d 712, 721 (7th Cir. 2001).

48. As Easterbrook explains in *In re Synthroid I*: "Declining marginal percentages . . . create declining marginal returns to legal work. . . . This feature exacerbates the agency costs inherent in any percentage-of-recovery system." 264 F.3d 712, 721.

49. See the previous note.

50. See Easterbrook's discussion of how negotiated attorney's fee agreements in the securities context tend to use a marginal declining fee structure. *In re* Synthroid I, 264 F.3d 712, 719.

51. Epstein, "Class Actions: The Need for a Hard Second Look," 11.

52. Jill E. Fisch agrees that the "last dollars of recovery are generally the most costly to produce." "Lawyers on the Auction Block: Evaluating the Selection of Class Counsel by Auction," *Columbia Law Review* 102 (2002): 650–728, 678.

53. As David L. Schwartz finds in corporate patent litigation: "There are two main ways of setting the fees for the contingent fee lawyer: a[n increasing] graduated rate and a flat rate." "The Rise of Contingent Fee Representation in Patent Litigation," 360.

54. See Schwartz's statement: "The graduated rates typically . . . tied rates to recovery dates. As the case continued, the lawyer's percentage increased." "The Rise of Contingent Fee Representation in Patent Litigation," 360.

55. See, e.g., the court's description of the fee agreement between class counsel and the lead plaintiff, New Hampshire Retirement Systems: "The formula provided attorneys' fees would equal 15% of any settlement amount up to $25 million,

20% of any settlement amount between $25 million and $50 million, and 25% of any settlement amount over $50 million." *In re* AT&T Corp., 455 F.3d 160, 163 (3d Cir. 2006).

56. As Amanda Rose put it: "Despite the virtues of rising marginal contingency fees, courts do not award them"; thus, "the use of increasing marginal contingency fees should be encouraged." "Cutting Class Action Agency Costs: Lessons from the Public Company" (manuscript in progress, Nashville: Vanderbilt University School of Law, n.d.). See also Coffee's position: "The most logical answer to this problem of premature settlement would be to base fees on a graduated, increasing percentage of the recovery formula—one that operates, much like the Internal Revenue Code, to award the plaintiff's attorney a marginally greater percentage of each defined increment of the recovery." "Understanding the Plaintiff's Attorney," 697.

57. A recent series of cases from the Seventh Circuit reflect this approach to calculating the value of a settlement: Eubank v. Pella Corp., 753 F.3d 718 (7th Cir. 2014); Redman v. RadioShack Corp., 768 F.3d 622 (7th Cir. 2014); and Pearson v. NBTY, Inc., 772 F.3d 778 (7th Cir. 2014). In each of these cases, the Seventh Circuit either said that administrative costs should not be counted toward the class's recovery, that cy pres relief should not be treated as a true recovery for the class, or criticized the district court's valuation of injunctive relief. The American Law Institute opens the door to this undercounting of cy pres by stating that, "because cy pres payments . . . only indirectly benefit the class, the court need not give such payments the same full value for purposes of setting attorneys' fees as would be given to direct recoveries by the class." *Principles of the Law of Aggregate Litigation*, §3.13(a), cmt. a.

58. For example, see Epstein: "The defendant . . . cares not one whit who gets his money, but only about the likelihood and magnitude of payment. If deterrence of wrongdoing is the dominant goal, then what matters is who pays and how much: never who collects, or why." "Class Actions: Aggregation, Amplification, Distortion," 461. This is why it pains me that one of the proponents of this practice is the grandfather of the Chicago school law and economics movement: Richard Posner. Each of the cases cited in the previous note was authored by Judge Posner. I do not understand how his position is consistent with his own economic theories, and he did not explain how they were in these cases. I can only wonder whether he wanted to punish the lawyers for other reasons—namely, some shady practices. Each of the cases in the previous note involved deeply questionable behavior by class counsel: in *Pella*, class counsel had finagled it so that the class representative in that case was a family member (see 753 F.3d at 722); in *Redman*, class counsel had managed to get an employee of their law firm appointed class representative (see 768 F.3d at 638); and, in *Pearson*, the terms of the injunctive relief in the settlement could plausibly have left consumers worse off than they were before (see 772 F.3d at 780).

59. The Third Circuit explains this line of reasoning, writing: "Direct distributions to the class are preferred over cy pres distributions. The private causes of

action aggregated in this class action—as in many others—were created by Congress to allow plaintiffs to recover compensatory damages for their injuries. Cy pres distributions imperfectly serve that purpose by substituting for that direct compensation an indirect benefit that is at best attenuated and at worse illusory." *In re* Baby Prod. Antitrust Litig., 708 F.3d 163, 173 (3d Cir. 2013).

60. The American Law Institute states the typical legal standard when it writes: "The court, when feasible, should [in a cy pres settlement] require the parties to identify a recipient whose interests reasonably approximate those being pursued by the class. If, and only if, no recipient whose interests reasonably approximate those being pursued by the class can be identified after thorough investigation and analysis, a court may approve a recipient that does not reasonably approximate the interests being pursued by the class." *Principles of the Law of Aggregate Litigation*, § 3.07.

61. See, e.g., Schulte v. Fifth Third Bank, in which excess funds were donated to credit counseling organizations in the states where the defendant operated. 805 F. Supp. 2d 560, 568 (N.D. Ill. 2011).

62. See Boeing Co. v. Van Gemert, 444 U.S. 472, 481 (1980).

63. See Boeing Co. v. Van Gemert, 444 U.S. 472, 480 (1980).

64. See the Competitive Enterprise Institute's statement in an amicus brief that "the class is unambiguously worse off when any reduction in a fee award reverts to the defendant instead of the class." Brief of the Competitive Enterprise Institute as *Amicus Curiae*, Foster v. L-3 Communications EOTech, 6:15-cv-03519-BCW (May 25, 2017). The American Law Institute also disapproves of this practice. See the ALI's statement that "the actual value of the judgment or settlement to the class" should be the primary basis for attorneys' fees. *Principles of the Law of Aggregate Litigation* § 3.13(a).

65. As Epstein notes: "The ideal way to think about the matter is to ask what fee would have been negotiated if the class contained a single member who was able to negotiate a fee with his lawyer. [B]ut the blunt truth is that there is simply no way to recreate the ex ante environment in which ordinary contingent fee arrangements are negotiated." "Class Actions: The Need for a Hard Second Look," 10–11.

66. See Macey and Miller, "The Plaintiffs' Attorney's Role in Class Action and Derivative Litigation," 1. This idea has also been endorsed in Epstein, "Class Actions: The Need for a Hard Second Look," 7.

67. See, e.g., *In re* Oracle Sec. Litig., 131 F.R.D. 688, 697 (N.D. Cal.), modified, 132 F.R.D. 538 (N.D. Cal. 1990); and *In re* Amino Acid Lysine Antitrust Litig., 918 F. Supp. 1190, 1202 (N.D. Ill. 1996).

68. For example, in *In re* Oracle Sec. Litig., 132 F.R.D. 538, 547 (N.D. Cal. 1990), although multiple firms bid for the position, the district court ultimately found that only one firm had submitted a bid consistent with market rates.

69. See Easterbrook's observation: "Auctions do not work well unless a standard unit of quality can be defined and its delivery verified. There is no 'standard

quantity' of legal services, and verification is difficult if not impossible." Silverman v. Motorola Sols., Inc., 739 F.3d 956, 957–58 (7th Cir. 2013). As Epstein also notes: "The low bidder might put in less work than the high bidder. . . . [I]t is one thing to ask people to bid on assets that they will own outright once the sale is done. [B]ut when [ownership is less than 100 percent] we cannot be so confident that the shareholders get the right behavior from the class representatives solely because of the low bids." "Class Actions: The Need for a Hard Second Look," 7.

70. Becker and Stigler, "Law Enforcement, Malfeasance, and Compensation of Enforcers," 16.

Chapter Eight

1. See, e.g., Sean Farhang's definition of *specific deterrence*: "Specific deterrence refers to the effects of enforcement against a particular violator on *that* violator's future conduct." *The Litigation State*, 9.

2. See, e.g., Farhang's definition of *general deterrence*: "General deterrence refers to effects of visible enforcement efforts in the legal environment on other would-be violators who have yet to actually be the targets of enforcement and hope never to be." *The Litigation State*, 9.

3. See Fitzpatrick, "An Empirical Study of Class Action Settlements and Their Fee Awards."

4. See, e.g., Fernandez v. Merrill Lynch, Pierce, Fenner & Smith, No. 15-22782 (S.D. Fla., Nov. 28, 2017), where my expert declaration (found in exhibit 2 of the Motion for Attorneys' Fees) notes that the settlement did not include "an injunction obligating the defendant to secure mutual fund fee waivers in the future for class members' accounts . . . only because the defendant already transitioned those accounts to a platform that ensures they will not be charged the improper mutual fund fees in the future." Or see the overdraft fee class actions I discussed above: although many banks agreed to stop reordering transactions in order to increase the number of overdraft fees they charged as part of the class action settlements, many others did so before it came to that. CFPB, *Arbitration Study*, 121–22.

5. See, e.g., Sheley and Frank's complaint that many injunctions "amount to no more than a rearranging of the deck chairs to create the illusion of value to justify attorney's fees." "Prospective Injunctive Relief and Class Settlements," 779–870.

6. Frank, Twitter post, December 17, 2013, 1:29 p.m., https://twitter.com/tedfrank/status/413058425770487808.

7. Fitzpatrick, "An Empirical Study of Class Action Settlements and Their Fee Awards," 824, table 3.

8. See, e.g., Macey and Miller's discussion of class action settlement hearings: "Settlement hearings are typically pep rallies jointly orchestrated by plaintiffs' counsel and defense counsel. Because both parties desire that the settlement be

approved, they have every incentive to present it as entirely fair. . . . Trial courts happily play along with the camaraderie. In approving settlement, courts often engage in paeans of praise for counsel or lambaste anyone rash enough to object to the settlement. Not surprisingly, it is uncommon to find cases where trial courts reject settlements that are presented to them by defense counsel and plaintiffs' attorneys." "The Plaintiffs' Attorney's Role in Class Action and Derivative Litigation," 46–48.

9. Indeed, I have said as much in my prior scholarship, writing that "it is especially important that class members be given the opportunity to object to settlements; without objectors there would be no adversarial testing of class action settlements at all." Fitzpatrick, "The End of Objector Blackmail?," *Vanderbilt Law Review* 62 (2009): 1623–66, 1630. As I noted in a previous chapter, the concern with the one-sided presentations at settlement approval have led scholars to advocate for the appointment of a "devil's advocate." Rubenstein, "The Fairness Hearing," 1453–55.

10. Sheley and Frank, "Prospective Injunctive Relief and Class Settlements." Although Sheley and Frank do not contend that behavior-modification provisions are toothless, there are other lists that criticize these provisions as insufficiently efficacious. See, e.g., Michael Selmi, "The Price of Discrimination: The Nature of Class Action Employment Discrimination Litigation and Its Effects," *Texas Law Review* 81, no. 5 (2003): 1249–1335, 1249 (criticizing three employment discrimination settlements).

11. Jill E. Fisch, Sean J. Griffith, and Steven Davidoff Solomon, "Confronting the Peppercorn Settlement in Merger Litigation: An Empirical Analysis and a Proposal for Reform," *Texas Law Review* 93 (2015): 557–624, 557–58.

12. Sheley and Frank, "Prospective Injunctive Relief and Class Settlements," 779–80.

13. See Sean J. Griffith, "Private Ordering Post-*Trulia*: Why No Pay Provisions Can Fix the Deal Tax and Forum Selection Provisions Can't," in *The Corporate Contract in Changing Times: Is the Law Keeping Up?* ed. Steven Davidoff Solomon and Randall Thomas (Chicago: University of Chicago Press, forthcoming).

14. See Sean Griffith and Anthony Rickey, "Who Collects the Deal Tax, Where, and What Delaware Can Do about It," in *Research Handbook on Shareholder Litigation*, ed. Sean Griffith, Jessica Erickson, David H. Webber, and Verity Winship (Cheltenham: Edward Elgar, 2018), 140–55, (noting that these lawsuits now challenge over 90 percent of public mergers above $100 million).

15. I say this principally because the lawyers who file merger lawsuits hold special leverage over the defendants: not only can they impose litigation costs and litigation risk like other class action lawyers, but the mere filing of the lawsuit can also hold up the merger. It is not hard to see why companies would feel special pressure to pay off the lawyers in those cases.

16. Sheley and Frank, "Prospective Injunctive Relief and Class Settlements," 783–84.

17. For example, in a recent settlement resolving a class action alleging false advertising of a meatless protein, the settlement agreement both forbade the food company from using the specific language the plaintiffs alleged was misleading and prohibited the company from using that language's "functional equivalent" on "any future label" or "promotional material." "Class Action Settlement Agreement and Release," § III.B.3, Exhibit A to Memorandum of Points and Authorities in Support of Plaintiff's Unopposed Motion for Preliminary Approval of Class Action Settlement, Kimberly Birbrower v. Quorn Foods, Inc., No. 2:16-cv-01346 at 16–18 (C.D. Cal. February 26, 2017).

18. See "Campbell v. Facebook, Inc.," Competitive Enterprise Institute, July 6, 2017, https://cei.org/litigation/campbell-v-facebook-inc.

19. Sheley and Frank, "Prospective Injunctive Relief and Class Settlements," 800–802. See also "Allen v. Similasan Corp.," Competitive Enterprise Institute, July 6, 2017, https://cei.org/litigation/allen-v-similasan-corp.

20. See Pearson v. NBTY, Inc., 772 F.3d 778, 785 (7th Cir. 2014); and Allen v. Similasan Corp., No. 12-CV-00376-BAS-JLB, 2017 WL 1346404, at 4 (S.D. Cal. April 12, 2017).

21. For a time line of the relevant litigation prepared by a nonprofit that objected to the settlement, see Truth in Advertising, "Walgreen Glucosamine Supplements," https://www.truthinadvertising.org/walgreen-glucosamine-supplements.

22. Sheley and Frank, "Prospective Injunctive Relief and Class Settlements," 780 n. 41.

23. *In re* Johnson & Johnson Derivative Litig., 900 F. Supp. 2d 467, 494 (D.N.J. 2012).

24. Sheley and Frank, "Prospective Injunctive Relief and Class Settlements," 780 n. 42.

25. Staton v. Boeing Co., 327 F.3d 938, 961 (9th Cir. 2003).

26. Staton v. Boeing Co., 327 F.3d 938, 961 (9th Cir. 2003).

27. In several settlements in class action lawsuits against banks for reordering their customers' debit card transactions from chronological order to an order that maximized the number of overdraft fees the bank could charge them, the settlements included provisions forbidding the banks from reordering their customers' transactions in the future. See Harris v. Associated Bank, N.A., Docket No. 10-cv-22948-JLK (S.D. Fla., Aug., 2, 2013); Wolfgeher v. Commerce Bank, N.A., Docket No. 10-cv-22017-JLK (S.D. Fla., Aug. 2, 2013); McKinley v. Great Western Bank, Docket No. 10-cv-22770-JLK (S.D. Fla., Aug. 2, 2013); Eno v. M & I Marshall & Illsley Bank, Docket No. 10-cv-22730-JLK (S.D. Fla., Aug. 2, 2013); Blahut v. Harris Bank, N.A., Docket No. 10-cv-21821-JLK (S.D. Fla., Aug. 5, 2013); Casayuran, et al. v. PNC Bank, N.A., Docket No. 10-cv-20496-JLK (S.D. Fla., Aug. 5, 2013). In a settlement against Western Union for failing to notify its customers until years later when their transactions failed, the settlement agreement required Western Union to notify customers within ninety days going forward. Tennille v.

W. Union Co., No. 09-CV-00938-MSK-KMT, 2013 WL 6920449, at *2 (D. Colo. Dec. 31, 2013). See also the settlement against the company that sells meatless protein described in n. 17 above.

28. As Douglas Kysar notes: "Over the past half-century, . . . scholars influenced by legal economic theory have come to view tort law as implicitly serving a prospective, risk regulation function. Their project has been so successful that most observers now view tort law's deterrent *effect* as its primary *purpose*." And this is true, not only for tort lawsuits, but also for all private lawsuits. "The Public Life of Private Law: Tort Law as a Risk Regulation Mechanism," Public Law Research Paper no. 607 (New Haven, CT: Yale Law School, July 20, 2017), 2–3. As Coffee writes: "The conventional theory of the private attorney general stresses that the role of private litigation is not simply to secure compensation for victims, but is at least equally to generate deterrence, principally by multiplying the total resources committed to the detection and prosecution of the prohibiting behavior." "Rescuing the Private Attorney General," 218.

29. A description of the Chicago school's economic theory of deterrence can be found in Landes and Posner's landmark "The Private Enforcement of Law." For a discussion of how the theory of general deterrence became a central part of modern law, one need turn only to a commonly assigned first-year torts textbook. See John C. P. Goldberg, Anthony J. Sebok, and Benjamin C. Zipursky, *Tort Law: Responsibilities and Redress* (New York: Wolters Kluwer, 2016), 211.

30. Gary S. Becker first set forth a criminal law version of the theory in "Crime and Punishment: An Economic Approach," *Journal of Political Economy* 76, no. 2 (March–April 1968): 169–217. But it has been applied many times over to civil liability, such as by William M. Landes in "Optimal Sanctions for Antitrust Violations," *University of Chicago Law Review* 50 (1995): 652–78, 657.

31. See, e.g., Richard A. Posner, "A Theory of Negligence," *Journal of Legal Studies* 1, no. 1 (January 1972): 29–96.

32. See, e.g., Claire Finkelstein, "Legal Theory and the Rational Actor," in *The Oxford Handbook of Rationality*, ed. Alfred R. Mele and Piers Rawling (Oxford: Oxford University Press, 2004), 399–416, 399.

33. See, e.g., Logan Sawyer, "Book Review: Why the Right Embraced Rights: *The Other Rights Revolution*," *Harvard Journal of Law and Public Policy* 40 (2016): 729–57, 731.

34. In their seminal 1974 article, Becker and Stigler advocate for "reliance on victim enforcement," including "class action suits," to "enforce public statutes." Becker and Stigler, "Law Enforcement, Malfeasance, and Compensation of Enforcers," 16. Some trace the litigation theory of deterrence—and the role of class actions therein—all the way back to a famous 1941 article, Kalven and Rosenfield's "The Contemporary Function of the Class Suit." See Coffee's analysis: "As [Kalven and Rosenfield] saw it, the class representatives and their attorneys could ferret out wrongdoing and compel the return of ill-gotten gains that overworked

(or conflicted) regulators might miss. They were the first to recognize that the class action could be the procedural mechanism by which to arm and finance the private attorney general." *Entrepreneurial Litigation*, 53–54.

35. As Russell M. Gold explains, "litigation can and frequently does inflict non-legal harms on defendants such as harm to their reputation" because the "legal process draws attention to and is seen to substantiate allegations." "Compensation's Role in Deterrence," *Notre Dame Law Review* 91, no. 5 (1997): 1997–2048, 2007–23. Indeed, a number of empirical studies have found that this risk of reputational harm from litigation is a more effective deterrent than the monetary penalties companies face from losing lawsuits. See Brent Fisse and John Braithwaite's case studies of major corporate scandals in the 1960s and 1970s. *The Impact of Publicity on Corporate Offenders* (Albany, NY: State University of New York Press, 1983). 243. See also Jonathan M. Karpoff and John R. Lott Jr.'s research indicating that, from 1978 to 1987, 93.5 percent of companies' stock price declines after initial press reports of alleged corporate fraud was attributable to reputational loss and only 6.5 percent was attributable to formal legal penalties. "The Reputational Penalty Firms Bear from Committing Criminal Fraud," *Journal of Law and Economics* 36, no. 2 (October 1993): 757–802, 784. Similarly, John D. Graham writes that "the indirect effect of liability on consumer demand—operating through adverse publicity . . . is often the most significant contribution of liability to safety." "Product Liability and Motor Vehicle Safety," in *The Liability Maze: The Impact of Liability Law on Safety and Innovation*, ed. Peter W. Huber and Robert E. Litan (Washington, DC: Brookings Institution, 1991), 120–90, 181–82. Joni Hersch's research finds that the average drop in the equity value of a firm the day an employment discrimination class action is announced is triple the direct costs of settling the case. "Equal Employment Opportunity Law and Firm Profitability," *Journal of Human Resources* 26, no. 1 (1991): 139–53, 152. See also Jonathan M. Karpoff, D. Scott Lee, and Gerald S. Martin's research indicating securities enforcement proceedings generate reputational losses seven and a half times larger than the legal penalties produced by the same proceedings. "The Cost to Firms of Cooking the Books," *Journal of Financial and Quantitative Analysis* 43 (September 2008): 581–612.

36. To see this critique in an academic setting, see, e.g., Henry E. Smith's argument that contemporary law and economics, and systems of property law influenced by it, fail to encourage "human flourishing" because they are overly focused on the maximization of material prosperity. "Mind the Gap: The Indirect Relation between Ends and Means in American Property Law," *Cornell Law Review* 94, no. 4 (2009): 959–90. For a considerably broader but less academic variant of this critique, see Students for a Democratic Society, "The Port Huron Statement" (1962), https://history.hanover.edu/courses/excerpts/111huron.html.

37. As the Nobel Prize–winning economists Daniel Kahneman and Amos Tversky write: "In making predictions and judgments under uncertainty, people

do not appear to follow the calculus of chance or the statistical theory of prediction. Instead, they rely on a limited number of heuristics which sometimes yield reasonable judgments and sometimes lead to severe and systematic errors." "On the Psychology of Prediction," *Psychological Review* 8, no. 4 (1973): 237–51, 237. See also Daniel Kahneman and Amos Tversky, "Prospect Theory: An Analysis of Decision Under Risk," *Econometrica* 47, no. 2 (1979): 263–92.

38. For a sense of the scope of this field, in July 2017 Google Scholar counted approximately forty-five thousand academic citations to Kahneman and Tversky's "Prospect Theory" alone.

39. See Dan Ariely, *Predictably Irrational: The Hidden Forces That Shape Our Decisions* (New York: HarperCollins, 2008); Daniel Kahneman, *Thinking Fast and Slow* (New York: Farrar, Straus & Giroux, 2011); and Richard H. Thaler and Cass R. Sunstein, *Nudge: Improving Decisions about Health, Wealth, and Happiness* (New Haven, CT: Yale University Press, 2008).

40. See Justin Fox, "From 'Economic Man' to Behavioral Economics," *Harvard Business Review* 93, no. 5 (May 2015): 79–85.

41. Stefano DellaVigna explains why this is: "Unlike individual consumers, firms can specialize, hire consultants, and obtain feedback from large data sets and capital markets. Firms are also subject to competition. Compared to consumers, therefore, firms are less likely to be affected by biases, . . . and we expect them to be close to profit maximization." "Psychology and Economics: Evidence from the Field," *Journal of Economic Literature* 47, no. 2 (June 2009): 315–72, 361. It is true that there has been some research that indicates that firms are sometimes not perfectly rational actors. See Ulrike Malmendier and Geoffrey Tate, "CEO Overconfidence and Corporate Investment," *Journal of Finance* 60, no. 6 (2005): 2661–2700. However, there are three good reasons to think that firms behave more rationally than individuals. First, firm decisionmaking tends to be done by groups, and group decisionmaking tends to be more rational than individual decisionmaking. See Tamar Kugler, Edgar E. Kausel, and Martin G. Kocher, "Are Groups More Rational Than Individuals? A Review of Interactive Decision Making in Groups," *Wiley Interdisciplinary Review: Cognitive Science* 3, no. 4 (2012): 471–82, 425. Second, much of the literature identifying irrational corporate behavior does so by finding circumstances in which certain firms deviate from the rational behavior of other firms—suggesting that the default is rational behavior, punctuated by occasional failures. See Malmendier and Tate, "CEO Overconfidence and Corporate Investment." Third, and perhaps most importantly, research indicates that firms are consistent about pursuing their rational self-interest, unlike individuals, who are often more concerned with nonrational considerations. Phanish Puranam, Nils Stieglitz, Magda Osman, and Madan M. Pillutla, "Modelling Bounded Rationality in Organizations: Progress and Prospects," *Academy of Management Annals* 9, no. 2 (2015): 337–92, 392.

42. See Richard A. Posner, *Economic Analysis of Law* (New York: Wolters Kluwer Law and Business, 2014), 548–49.

43. This is an especially popular critique in the securities fraud literature. As Coffee explains: "The efficacy of deterrence . . . rests on the validity of enterprise liability: that is, on the claim that by imposing large penalties on the corporation, society induces increased monitoring of the corporate officials." "Reforming the Security Class Action," 1553. He argues, however: "Securities litigation is distinctive [because corporate managers have] stock options. [As such,] enterprise liability may work less well than a strategy that focuses directly on the managers themselves." Ibid., 1562–63. The critique of enterprise liability extends beyond scholarship on securities fraud. See Crane's analysis: "The average CEO holds her job for about six years. Mid-level executives, such as divisional managers, typically hold their jobs for an even shorter period, perhaps less than four years. Thus, most of the executives responsible for an antitrust violation will no longer be with the firm by the time a damages award is entered against the company." "Optimizing Private Antitrust Enforcement," 693–694.

44. Coffee's analysis is on point here as well: "Economic theory suggests that vicarious liability is efficient so long as the principal and agent can enter into contracts that reduce the probability of the wrong that is to be deterred. Even given the 'final period' problem, there are conceivable means by which the corporation could write such contacts with its managers, for example, by restricting stock options and other incentive compensation." "Reforming the Security Class Action," 1565.

45. As many as 90 percent of major publicly traded American companies have compensation recoupment policies—often termed *clawback* policies—that permit them to recover bonuses and other performance incentives under certain circumstances. PriceWaterhouseCoopers, "Executive Compensation: Clawbacks: 2014 Proxy Disclosure Study," January 2015. https://www.niri.org/NIRI/media/NIRI/Documents/pwc-executive-compensation-clawbacks-2014.pdf.

46. Richard A. Posner concludes: "A corporation has effective methods of preventing its employees from committing acts that impose huge liabilities on it." *Antitrust Law*, 2nd ed. (Chicago: University of Chicago Press, 2011), 271.

47. Robert H. Lande and Joshua P. Davis highlight this inconsistency well: "There is an odd—and usually unexplained—inconsistency when proponents of the free market claim that corporations should not be subject to civil liability . . . : [I]f the free market works in the sense that corporations respond in an efficient manner to market incentives, including by encouraging corporate representatives to act for the benefit of the corporation, why shouldn't the same be true of legal sanctions?" "Comparative Deterrence from Private Enforcement and Criminal Enforcement of the U.S. Antitrust Laws," *Brigham Young University Law Review* 2011, no. 2 (2011): 315–87, 316.

48. For example, Olson complains that litigation has become "essentially a random matter." *The Litigation Explosion*, 176–77. Similarly, the US Chamber of Commerce claims: "The class action . . . does not impose burdens only on businesses that engage in wrongful conduct. Instead, the burdens of class actions are

chiefly a function of who plaintiffs' lawyers choose to sue." Letter to Consumer Financial Protection Bureau 53 (December 11, 2013), http://blogs.reuters.com /alison-frankel/files/2013/12/mayerbrown-chamberletter.pdf. See also E. Donald Elliot's argument that tort law may not be predictable enough to shape how activities are undertaken, only how often they are undertaken. "Why Punitive Damages Don't Deter Corporate Misconduct Effectively," *Alabama Law Review* 40, no. 3 (1989): 1053–72, 1058.

49. Viscusi comprehensively outlines extensive and pervasive safety design risk analyses done at Ford, Chrysler, and GM. See W. Kip Viscusi, "Pricing Lives for Corporate Risk Decisions," *Vanderbilt Law Review* 68, no. 4 (2015): 1117–62. See also Graham's claim that, "according to one large vehicle manufacturer, in 1960 the typical in-house liability attorney spent 5 percent of his time working with design engineers. Today such an attorney spends 40 to 50 percent." "Product Liability and Motor Vehicle Safety," 126.

50. As Richard Marcus notes: "Articles about the importance corporations place on compliance are rife in the professional literature." "Revolution v. Evolution in Class Action Reform," *North Carolina Law Review* 96, no. 9 (2018): 903–44, 911–12.

51. See, e.g., Sara Randazzo and Jacqueline Palank, "Legal Fees Cross New Mark: $1,500 an Hour," *Wall Street Journal*, February 9, 2017.

52. Kelly A. Love notes the "widespread use" of opinion letters and discusses the history of the practice. "A Primer on Opinion Letters: Explanations and Analysis," *Transactions: The Tennessee Journal of Business Law* 9 (2007): 68–98, 68–72.

53. See Sidley Austin LLP, "Mitigating Consumer Fraud Class Action Litigation Risk: Top Ten Methods for 2015," email to clients, January 5, 2015. As the Consumer Protection Financial Bureau observes: "Companies monitor class litigation relevant to the products and services that they offer so that they can mitigate their liability by changing their conduct before being sued themselves. This effect is evident from the proliferation of public materials—such as compliance bulletins, law firm alerts, and conferences—where legal and compliance experts routinely and systematically advise companies about relevant developments in class action litigation." CFPB, *Arbitration Study*, 118–20 (listing examples).

54. Viscusi makes precisely this argument, positing that, in some cases, constant changes in the law and the lag between when a product is manufactured and when a company may face liability mean that "the tort liability system cannot create effective risk reduction incentives for producers." W. Kip Viscusi, *Reforming Products Liability* (Cambridge, MA: Harvard University Press, 1991), 158.

55. See, e.g., Robert H. Klonoff's findings: "A few courts have been willing to certify personal injury class actions for settlement purposes. Examples include the National Football League concussion litigation and the *Deepwater Horizon* case. For the most part, however, personal injury mass torts continue to be adjudicated outside of the class action arena." "Class Actions in the Year 2026: A Prognosis," *Emory Law Journal* 65, no. 6 (2016): 1569–1655, 1600.

56. See Linda Sandstrom Simard, "A View from within the Fortune 500: An Empirical Study of Negative Value Class Actions and Deterrence," *Indiana Law Review* 47, no. 3 (2014): 739–85, 739.

57. See Simard, "A View from within the Fortune 500," 750.

58. See Simard, "A View from within the Fortune 500," 757–61.

59. See Simard, "A View from within the Fortune 500," 760.

60. See Simard, "A View from within the Fortune 500," 757.

61. As Mitchell Polinsky and Steven Shavell note: "Surveys of this type are often of questionable reliability." "A Skeptical Attitude about Products Liability Is Justified: A Reply to Professors Goldberg and Zipursky," *Harvard Law Review* 123 (2010): 1949–68, 1961.

62. George C. Eads and Peter H. Reuter interviewed corporate product safety officials and found that, "of all the various external social pressures, products liability [lawsuits] ha[ve] the greatest influence on product design decisions." They also found that corporations deal with the uncertainty of liability by "monitoring the development of the law in many jurisdictions." *Designing Safer Products: Corporate Responses to Product Liability Law and Regulation* (Santa Monica, CA: Rand Corp., 1983), vii–ix. Similarly, when Andrew Popper conducted a survey of in-house counsel at Fortune 500 businesses, "73% [of respondents] agreed that a tort judgment against a company in the same line of commerce would prompt their company to 'examine methods of production . . . and, if needed, quietly take steps to make sure our products are in compliance.'" "In Defense of Deterrence," *Albany Law Review* 75, no. 1 (2012): 181–203, 197. E. Patrick McGuire's survey of five hundred CEOs found similar results; lawsuits caused 35 percent of the surveyed CEOs to improve safety, 47 percent to improve warnings, 36 percent to close companies or discontinue products, 15 percent to lay off workers, and 8 percent to close plants. *The Impact of Product Liability* (New York: Conference Board Research Reports, 1988). Small business owners also report that fear of litigation has caused them to change their business practices. Christopher Hodges's survey of small businesses found that 26 percent said fear of liability kept them from releasing new products or services. *Law and Corporate Behavior: Integrating Theories of Regulation, Enforcement, Compliance and Ethics* (Portland, OR: Hart, 2015), 79.

63. As Sheley and Frank concede: "It seems intuitive that the prospect of litigation might deter potential defendants from misconduct." "Prospective Injunctive Relief and Class Settlements," 827.

64. See, e.g., Greve's claim: "We have strikingly little evidence that torts acts as a deterrent." *Harm-Less Lawsuits?*, 16. Hodges expands on this line of argument: "There is almost no direct evidence on the actual effect of private enforcement of law, or on how litigation actually affects corporate decisions. The basic assumption is that since economic theory postulates that the imposition of a financial penalty will deter later wrongdoing, it must be so." *Law and Corporate Behavior*, 67. Popper notes this line of argument in his study as well, writing that "the deniers

believe there is insufficient empirical evidence to prove the power of deterrence." "In Defense of Deterrence," 195.

65. Mullenix, "Ending Class Actions as We Know Them," 420.

66. See Block, Nold, and Gregory Sidak, "The Deterrent Effect of Antitrust Enforcement," 429.

67. See Block, Nold, and Gregory Sidak, "The Deterrent Effect of Antitrust Enforcement," 437.

68. As Block, Nold, and Sidak write: "Our theoretical model suggests that increases in enforcement levels or penalties for price fixing generally reduce collusive markups." "The Deterrent Effect of Antitrust Enforcement," 434.

69. See Block, Nold, and Sidak, "The Deterrent Effect of Antitrust Enforcement," 443. It should be noted that another economist found that the Department of Justice's budget had a weaker deterrent effect when other variables were included in the analysis, but this study did not challenge the original findings regarding the class action effect. See Craig M. Newmark, "Is Antitrust Enforcement Effective?," *Journal of Political Economy* 96, no. 6 (1988): 1315–28, 1315.

70. Block, Nold, and Sidak write that "only in the latter period, when class actions represented a credible threat, did a significant deterrent effect result." "The Deterrent Effect of Antitrust Enforcement," 443.

71. Block, Nold, and Sidak, "The Deterrent Effect of Antitrust Enforcement," 440–41.

72. Block, Nold, and Sidak, "The Deterrent Effect of Antitrust Enforcement," 443.

73. See James P. Naughton, Tjomme O. Rusticus, Clare Wang, and Ira Yeung, "Private Litigation Costs and Voluntary Disclosure: Evidence from the *Morrison* Ruling," *Accounting Review* (in press). See also Anywhere Sikochi, "The Effect of Shareholder Litigation Risk on the Information Environment," Working Paper no. 17-048 (Cambridge, MA: Harvard Business School, September 4, 2016), http://www.hbs.edu/faculty/Publication%20Files/17-048_413e9658-649c-4904-8d49-6779f11910ac.pdf.

74. Karen K. Nelson and A. C. Pritchard, "Carrot or Stick? The Shift from Vocabulary to Mandatory Disclosure of Risk Factors," *Journal of Empirical Legal Studies* 13, no. 2 (2016): 266–97, 266.

75. See Nelson and Pritchard, "Carrot or Stick?," online appendices A–C, https://onlinelibrary.wiley.com/action/downloadSupplement?doi=10.1111%2Fjels.12115&file=jels12115-sup-0001-suppinfo.pdf.

76. See Nelson and Pritchard, "Carrot or Stick?," 295.

77. See Nelson and Pritchard, "Carrot or Stick?," 267.

78. See Nelson and Pritchard, "Carrot or Stick?," 295.

79. See Simi Kedia, Kevin Koh, and Shivaram Rajgopal, "Evidence on Contagion in Earnings Management," *Accounting Review* 90, no. 6 (2015): 2337–73, 2337, 2363–67.

80. Stephen Baginski, John M. Hassell, and Michael D. Kimbrough, "The Effect of Legal Environment on Voluntary Disclosure: Evidence from Management Earnings Forecasts Issued in U.S. and Canadian Markets," *Accounting Review* 77 (2002): 25–50, 25–50.

81. Baginski, Hassell, and Kimbrough, "The Effect of Legal Environment on Voluntary Disclosure," 43–47.

82. Viscusi and Moore find that industries with higher tort liability loss ratios spent more on product-related research and development and conclude that "tort liability does . . . have safety incentive effect." W. Kip Viscusi and Michael J. Moore, "An Industrial Profile of the Links between Product Liability and Innovation," in *The Liability Maze*, 81–119, 114. However, Viscusi and Moore establish in other scholarship that this effect may taper off or become negative if liability grows too large. W. Kip Viscusi and Michael J. Moore, "Product Liability, Research and Development, and Innovation," *Journal of Political Economy* 101, no. 1 (February 1993): 161–84. Furthermore, Viscusi's scholarship also casts doubt on the effectiveness of punitive damages, finding that they do not affect the incidence of chemical accidents, chemical releases, or accident fatalities or increase insurance premiums. W. Kip Viscusi, "The Social Costs of Punitive Damages against Corporations in Environmental and Safety Tort," *Georgetown Law Journal* 87, no. 2 (November 1998): 285–346, 296–98.

83. See Michael J. Moore and W. Kip Viscusi, *Compensation Mechanisms for Job Risks: Wages, Workers' Compensation, and Product Liability* (Princeton, NJ: Princeton University Press, 1990), 133; and James R. Chelius, "Liability for Industrial Accidents: A Comparison of Negligence and Strict Liability Systems," *Journal of Legal Studies* 5, no. 2 (June 1976): 293–309, 303–6.

84. See Frank A. Sloan, Emily M. Stout, Kathryn Whetten-Goldstein, and Lan Liang, *Drinkers, Drivers, and Bartenders: Balancing Private Choices and Public Accountability* (Chicago: University of Chicago Press, 2000).

85. A number of scholars have found similar results supporting this conclusion. Daniel P. Kessler and Mark McClellan's research finds that medical malpractice reforms reduce hospital expenditures. "Do Doctors Practice Defensive Medicine?," *Quarterly Journal of Economics* 111, no. 2 (May 1996): 353–90, 353. Patricia M. Danzon outlines the evidence indicating that liability induces physicians to spend more time per patient visit. "Liability for Medical Malpractice," *Journal of Economic Perspectives* 5, no. 3 (1991): 51–69, 62. Similarly, Donald N. Dewees, David Duff, and Michael Trebilcock outline the evidence showing that greater malpractice insurance premiums are associated with more diagnostic testing. *Exploring the Domain of Accident Law: Taking the Facts Seriously* (New York: Oxford University Press, 1996), 104–5. However, there is scholarship that points in the opposite direction. Danzon reviews the evidence that medical malpractice liability is negatively correlated with frequency of lab tests. "Liability for Medical Malpractice," 62. Michael Frakes recites conflicting studies on whether malpractice liability is

associated with more cesarean sections. "Defensive Medicine and Obstetric Practices," *Journal of Empirical Legal Studies* 9, no. 3 (2012): 457–81, 457–62.

86. Again, a number of scholars have found results that support this conclusion, though this view is not unanimous. Zenon Zabinski and Bernard S. Black find that medical malpractice tort reforms increase the incidence of adverse outcomes other than death. "The Deterrent Effect of Tort Law: Evidence from Medical Malpractice Reform," Law and Economics Working Paper no. 13-09 (Evanston, IL: Northwestern University, November 15, 2018), https://ssrn.com/abstract=2161362. Michelle Mello and Troyen Brennan present evidence that liability for medical malpractice reduced negligence rates. "Deterrence of Medical Errors: Theory and Evidence for Malpractice Reform," *Texas Law Review* 80 (2002): 1595–1637, 1598. Joanna M. Shepherd finds that medical malpractice tort reforms increased deaths. "Tort Reforms' Winners and Losers: The Competing Effect of Care and Activity Levels," *UCLA Law Review* 55 (2008): 905–77, 905. Paul C. Weiler et al. conclude that "the more malpractice suits that are brought . . . the fewer the number of negligent medical injuries," despite the fact that "this result did not reach the conventional level of statistical significance." *A Measure of Malpractice: Medical Injury, Malpractice Litigation, and Patient Compensation* (Cambridge, MA: Harvard University Press, 1993), 129. However, as with the studies presented in the previous note, there is scholarship that points in the other direction. Kessler and McClellan find that malpractice tort reforms did not reduce mortality or medical complications. "Do Doctors Practice Defensive Medicine?," 353. And Michael Frakes and Anupam B. Jena find that malpractice tort reforms do not affect birth outcomes. "Does Medical Malpractice Law Improve Health Care Quality," *Journal of Public Economics* 143 (2016): 142–58, 142–58.

87. Paul H. Rubin and Joanna M. Shepherd find that collateral source reforms increase vehicle accident deaths. "Tort Reform and Accidental Deaths," *Journal of Law and Economics* 50, no. 2 (2007): 221–38, 221. Michelle J. White finds that drivers take less care in comparative fault systems than in contributory negligence systems. "An Empirical Test of the Comparative and Contributory Negligence Rules in Accident Law," *Rand Journal of Economics* 20, no. 3 (1989): 308–30, 325–29. Michael L. Smith finds: "Tests in the early studies produced mixed results, but later studies typically find that adoption of no-fault rules to replace common law tort liability leads to an increase in automobile accident fatality rates." "Deterrence and Origin of Legal System: Evidence from 1950–1999," *American Law and Economic Review* 7, no. 2 (2005): 350–78, 352. But see Rubin and Shepherd's finding that other tort reforms than collateral source reforms decreased vehicle accident deaths. "Tort Reform and Accidental Deaths," 221. See also W. Jonathan Cardi, Randall D. Penfield, and Albert H. Yoon's outline of conflicting studies on whether no-fault automobile accident compensation systems reduce or increase fatalities. "Does Tort Law Deter Individuals? A Behavioral Science Study," *Journal of Empirical Legal Studies* 9, no. 3 (2012): 567–603, 573–74 n. 31.

88. See also Kagan's overview of the topic in *Adversarial Legalism*, 141–44. Some studies examine, not real-world data, but, rather, simulations, where survey takers are asked hypothetical questions about how they would respond to potential liability in certain situations. These studies have found mixed evidence of deterrence. See, e.g., Cardi, Penfield, and Yoon's finding that potential tort liability did not affect decisions to engage in potentially tortious behavior even though the threat of criminal sanctions did. "Does Tort Law Deter Individuals?," 567. Theodore Eisenberg and Christoph Engel find that damages liability deterred in public good experiments. "Assuring Civil Damages Adequately Deter: A Public Good Experiment," *Journal of Empirical Legal Studies* 11, no. 2 (April 2014): 301–49, 301.

89. William M. Landes and Richard A. Posner, *The Economic Structure of Tort Law* (Cambridge, MA: Harvard University Press, 1987), 10.

Chapter Nine

1. Fitzpatrick, "An Empirical Study of Class Action Settlements and Their Fee Awards," 818, table 1.

2. See Epstein's statement that "there is no adequate theoretical foundation or practical justification for the employment discrimination laws." *Forbidden Grounds*, xii. See also Richard A. Posner, "The Efficiency and Efficacy of Title VII," *University of Pennsylvania Law Review* 136 (1987): 513–22, 521.

3. For one take on this idea, see David Marcus, "The Past, Present, and Future of Trans-Substantivity in Federal Civil Procedure," *DePaul Law Review* 59, no. 2 (2010): 371–430.

4. See Marcus, "The Past, Present, and Future of Trans-Substantivity in Federal Civil Procedure," 372.

5. See Sheila B. Scheuerman's statement: "Statutory damages allow a plaintiff to recover a prescribed sum in lieu of—or sometimes in addition to—actual damages. . . . The Supreme Court has recognized the deterrent function of statutory damages, noting that statutory damages are designed 'to sanction and vindicate the statutory policy.' The very function of a minimum amount of damages is to add cost to the defendant's wrongful conduct." "Due Process Forgotten: The Problem of Statutory Damages and Class Actions," *Missouri Law Review* 74, no. 1 (2009): 103–52, 110–11.

6. Telephone Consumer Protection Act, 47 U.S.C. § 227(b)(3)(B).

7. Telephone Consumer Protection Act, 47 U.S.C. § 227(b)(3)(B).

8. Tom Harvey, "Jury Finds Utah Companies Made 100 Million Illegal Calls," *Salt Lake Tribune*, May 29, 2016, http://archive.sltrib.com/article.php?id=3940513 &itype=CMSID.

9. A variation on this idea is already found in some statutory damages laws: these laws allow individual recoveries or class action recoveries capped at a reasonable

number, such as 1 percent of a company's revenues or $500,000, whichever is lesser. See, e.g., Fair Debt Collection Practices Act, 47 U.S.C. § 1692k.

10. As Coffee notes: "A context where the extortion thesis may make greater sense involves a combination of class actions and treble damages or other penalties. The purpose of punitive damages (including trebled damages) is to punish, not to compensate. But how much punishment is too much? When Congress authorized treble damages in the Sherman Anti-Trust Act in 1890, the modern class action did not then exist. Arguably, Congress would not want to punish at the astronomic level that the class action makes possible. Still, this critique implies only a limited reform, namely, that treble damages or other penalties should not be available in class actions." *Entrepreneurial Litigation*, 135. See also Jason Scott Johnston, "High Cost, Little Compensation, No Harm to Deter: New Evidence On Class Actions Under Federal Consumer Protection Statutes," *Columbia Business Law Review* 2017 (2017): 1–91, 68–69.

11. As Edward Hartnett notes: "Even when defendants move to stay discovery pending a motion to dismiss, some . . . district courts deny the motion." "Taming *Twombly*: An Update After *Matrixx*," *Law and Contemporary Problems* 75, no. 1 (2012): 37–53, 49.

12. "In any private action arising under this subchapter, all discovery and other proceedings shall be stayed during the pendency of any motion to dismiss, unless the court finds, upon the motion of any party, that particularized discovery is necessary to preserve evidence or to prevent undue prejudice to that party." 15 U.S.C. § 77z-1(b).

13. See 28 U.S.C. § 1291, requiring a "final decision" from a district court.

14. The Federal Rules of Civil Procedure have been revised to permit appeals of class certification decisions. Fed. R. Civ. P. 23(f). However, some lower courts permitted such appeals even before Rule 23 was revised. See *In re* Rhone-Poulenc Rorer Inc., 51 F.3d 1293 (7th Cir. 1995).

15. As the Seventh Circuit notes, class certification forces "defendants to stake their companies on the outcome of a single jury trial, or be forced by fear of the risk of bankruptcy to settle even if they have no legal liability." *In re* Rhone-Poulenc Rorer Inc., 51 F.3d 1293, 1299 (7th Cir. 1995).

16. The Supreme Court explains that the "rule, that a party must ordinarily raise all claims of error in a single appeal following final judgment on the merits, serves a number of important purposes . . . [including] promoting efficient judicial administration." Firestone Tire & Rubber Co. v. Risjord, 449 U.S. 368, 374 (1981).

17. My study of the federal courts found fewer than four hundred settlements per year. See Fitzpatrick, "An Empirical Study of Class Action Settlements and Their Fee Awards," 812.

18. The median value of class action settlements was more than $5 million. See Fitzpatrick, "An Empirical Study of Class Action Settlements and Their Fee Awards," 828, table 5.

19. See, e.g., the proposal by Robert G. Bone and David S. Evans to assess whether a putative class action has merit before certifying it for class treatment. "Class Certification and the Substantive Merits," *Duke Law Journal* 51, no. 4 (2002): 1251–1332, 1251.

20. As Joanna Schwartz observes: "The Chamber of Commerce and fellow business amici have repeatedly claimed that businesses are regularly forced to accept blackmail settlements in meritless cases to avoid the debilitating costs of discovery and the possibility of gargantuan judgments." "The Cost of Suing Business," 655. See also Coffee, *Entrepreneurial Litigation*, 134; and Moller, "Controlling Unconstitutional Class Actions," 3.

21. As Charles Silver notes: "The overpayment argument asserts that defendants facing class actions are risk averse." " 'We're Scared to Death': Class Certification and Blackmail," *New York University Law Review* 78 (2003): 1357–1430, 1374.

22. See " 'We're Scared to Death,' " 1414.

23. See " 'We're Scared to Death,' " 1414.

24. See Posner, *Economic Analysis of Law*, 548–49.

25. Myriam Gilles and Gary B. Friedman note that "class action plaintiffs' lawyers are indeed independent entrepreneurs driven by the desire to maximize their gain, even at the expense of class members' compensation." "Exploding the Class Action Agency Costs Myth: The Social Utility of Entrepreneurial Lawyers," *University of Pennsylvania Law Review* 155, no. 1 (2006): 103–64, 104.

26. See, e.g., Hillel J. Bavli, "Sampling and Reliability in Class Action Litigation," *Cardozo Law Review De Novo* (2016): 207–19, 207–8.

27. Bavli explains that "repeated adjudication may improve reliability . . . by averaging over multiple adjudications rather than relying on a single adjudication—and thus minimize error caused by judgment variability." "Sampling and Reliability in Class Action Litigation," 218.

28. Jay Tidmarsh urges a limited return to trial by statistics. "Resurrecting Trial by Statistics," *Minnesota Law Review* 99 (2015): 1459–1506, 1478–79. Robert G. Bone goes further, arguing that "statistical adjudication through sampling can be a very useful procedural tool." "Tyson Foods and the Future of Statistical Adjudication," *North Carolina Law Review* 95, no. 3 (2017): 607–72, 671.

29. See generally Hilao v. Estate of Marcos, 103 F.3d 767, 782–84 (9th Cir. 1996).

30. Wal-Mart v. Dukes, 564 U.S. 338, 356–57 (2011).

31. Wal-Mart v. Dukes, 564 U.S. 338, 367 (2011).

32. "Trial by statistics, of course, dispenses with proof of a causal connection for all the aggregated claims except for the sampled victims: the non-liability of the defendant to some unsampled class members is accounted for by reducing the average award. While this approach may get the aggregate liability of the defendant right, it fails to allow the defendant to prove that its conduct caused no harm to a given plaintiff." Tidmarsh, "Resurrecting Trial by Statistics," 1476.

33. It should be noted that statistical sampling has long been used by administrative agencies to detect, e.g., fraudulent Medicare and Medicaid claims without running afoul of the Due Process Clause of the Constitution. See Michael Sant'Ambrogio and Adam S. Zimmerman, "Inside the Agency Class Action," *Yale Law Journal* 126, no. 6 (2017): 1634–1728, 1640 n. 14. Indeed, the more serious constitutional concern with my proposal may be that it violates the right to a jury trial: the class members who are not randomly selected for the sample trials arguably do not get their claims decided by a jury because they are decided by the average of *other people's* juries.

34. Shavell, *Foundations of Economic Analysis of Law*, 402–3.

35. Silver notes the view that "the burdens of litigation, especially those relating to discovery and hearings on damages, are unmanageably great": "A defendant's choice is therefore to settle or bear high litigation costs indefinitely." " 'We're Scared to Death,' " 1363. See also Moller, "Controlling Unconstitutional Class Actions," 3; Schwartz, "The Cost of Suing Business," 11; and Coffee, *Entrepreneurial Litigation*, 134.

36. Shavell, *Foundations of Economic Analysis of Law*, 402–3.

37. See Shavell, *Foundations of Economic Analysis of Law*, 402–3.

38. This is because discovery is the largest part of litigation expenses, and as Posner explains: "In most suits against corporations or other institutions, . . . the plaintiff wants or needs more discovery of the defendant than the defendant wants or needs of the plaintiff, because the plaintiff has to search the defendant's records (and, through depositions, the minds of the defendant's employees) to obtain evidence of wrongdoing." Swanson v. Citibank, N.A., 614 F.3d 400, 411 (7th Cir. 2010) (Posner, J., dissenting).

39. Frank H. Easterbrook observes: "Litigants with weak cases have little use for bringing the facts to light and every reason to heap costs on the adverse party—on this supposition, the one in the right." "Discovery as Abuse," *Boston University Law Review* 69 (1989): 635–48, 636.

40. John H. Beisner, "Discovering a Better Way: The Need for Effective Civil Litigation Reform," *Duke Law Journal* 60 (2010): 547–96, 561, 566.

41. Currently, the Federal Rules of Civil Procedure require that discovery be "proportional to the needs of the case, considering the importance of the issues at stake in the action, the amount in controversy, the parties' relative access to relevant information, the parties' resources, the importance of the discovery in resolving the issues, and whether the burden or expense of the proposed discovery outweighs its likely benefit." Fed. R. Civ. P. 26(b)(1). This requirement is complemented by a fairly limited fee-shifting provision stating that the "court may, for good cause, issue an order to protect a party or person from annoyance, embarrassment, oppression, or undue burden or expense, including . . . specifying terms, including time and place or the allocation of expenses, for the disclosure or discovery." Fed. R. Civ. P. 26(c)(1)(B).

42. Brian T. Fitzpatrick, "The Discovery Tax," Legal Studies Research Paper no. 18-39 (Nashville: Vanderbilt University Law School, 2018), https://papers.ssrn.com/sol3/papers.cfm?abstract_id=3238363.

43. See Fitzpatrick, "The Discovery Tax."

44. See Fitzpatrick, "The Discovery Tax."

45. Many of these scholars advocate fee shifting, where the loser of the lawsuit repays the winner's litigation expenses. For example, Becker and Stigler propose "full compensation of persons acquitted of charges paid by the enforcement firms bringing these charges." "Law Enforcement, Malfeasance, and Compensation of Enforcers," 15. See also Coffee, *Entrepreneurial Litigation*, 165–67; and Mullenix, "Ending Class Actions as We Know Them," 448–49. For reasons I explain in "The Discovery Tax," I think that full internalization on both sides through a tax is superior to shifting expenses to only one side.

46. See Fitzpatrick, "Can and Should the New Third-Party Litigation Financing Come to Class Actions?," 111–13.

47. See Fitzpatrick, "Can and Should the New Third-Party Litigation Financing Come to Class Actions?"

48. See Deborah R. Hensler, "The Future of Mass Litigation: Global Class Actions and Third-Party Litigation Funding," *George Washington Law Review* 79, no. 2 (2011): 306–23, 320–21.

49. As Oman notes: "The concerns with boilerplate center on the role of consent in contract law. To many, the consent of a consumer presented with a boilerplate agreement seems too attenuated to justify its enforcement." *The Dignity of Commerce*, 134.

50. Oman, *The Dignity of Commerce*.

51. See Oman again: "The market argument, however, reformulates the role of consent in contract theory. . . . In the market argument, consent does not justify the enforcement of contracts. Rather, we enforce contracts because doing so strengthens and extends markets." *The Dignity of Commerce*, 134.

52. See, e.g., Daniel B. Klaff, "Debiasing and Bidirectional Bias: Cognitive Failure in Mandatory Employment Arbitration," *Harvard Negotiation Law Review* 15 (2010): 1–29, 1; Matthew T. Bodie, "Questions about the Efficiency of Employment Arbitration Agreements," *Georgia Law Review* 39 (2004): 31–39; and Russell Korobkin, "Bounded Rationality, Standard Form Contracts and Unconscionability," *University of Chicago Law Review* 70, no. 4 (2003): 1203–95, 1203.

53. See Klaff, "Debiasing and Bidirectional Bias"; Bodie, "Questions about the Efficiency of Employment Arbitration Agreements"; and Korobkin, "Bounded Rationality, Standard Form Contracts and Unconscionability."

54. See, e.g., Joshua D. Wright, "Behavioral Law and Economics, Paternalism, and Consumer Contracts: An Empirical Perspective," *NYU Journal of Law and Liberty* 2, no. 3 (2007): 470–511, 470.

55. Wright, "Behavioral Law and Economics, Paternalism, and Consumer Contracts."

56. See, e.g., Posner, "Regulation (Agencies) versus Litigation (Courts)," 11–12.

57. Keith N. Hylton, "The Economics of Class Actions and Class Action Waivers," *Supreme Court Economic Review* 23 (2015): 305–36, 324–26.

58. Hylton, "The Economics of Class Actions and Class Action Waivers." See also Einer Elhauge, "How *Italian Colors* Guts Private Antitrust Enforcement by Replacing It with Ineffective Forms of Arbitration," *Fordham International Law Journal* 38, no. 3 (2015): 771–78, 775.

59. This is why, when conservative and libertarian scholars endorse liability waivers, it is typically not for breach of contract, fraud, or price fixing. See, e.g., Richard A. Epstein, "Contractual Principle versus Legislative Fixes: Coming to Closure on the Unending Travails of Medical Malpractice," *DePaul Law Review* 54 (2005): 503–26, 509 (endorsing waivers for first-party tort liability); Keith N. Hylton, "Agreements to Waive or Arbitrate Legal Claims: An Economic Analysis," *Supreme Court Economic Review* 8 (2000): 209–63, 218–19 (same); and Hylton, "The Economics of Class Actions," 324, 335 (casting doubt on waivers for fraud and price fixing).

60. Erin O'Hara O'Connor and Larry Ribstein describe the traditional areas of state law as "torts, property, contracts, corporate law, family law, insurance law, trusts and estates, and agency law." "Preemption and Choice-of-Law Coordination," *Michigan Law Review* 111, no. 5 (2013): 647–714, 655.

61. I borrowed this phrase from Justice Scalia. See Kansas v. Crane, 534 U.S. 407, 425 (2002) (Scalia, J., dissenting).

62. See, e.g., some of the debate over the Export-Import Bank: Christian Britschgi, "The Senate's Rejection of Export-Import Bank Critic Shows How Entrenched Crony Capitalism Is in Washington," *Hit and Run* (blog), *Reason*, December 20, 2017, https://reason.com/blog/2017/12/20/the-senates-rejection-of-export-import-b.

63. "House Liberty Caucus Statement on H.R. 985, Fairness in Class Action Litigation Act of 2017," March 8, 2017, https://twitter.com/libertycaucus/status/839967179495837696/photo/1.

Bibliography

Adler, Jonathan H. "Stand or Deliver: Citizen Suits, Standing, and Environmental Protection." *Duke Environmental Law and Policy Forum* 12, no. 1 (2001): 39–83.

Alderman, Liz. "Equal Pay. Now Prove It." *New York Times*, March 29, 2017.

Alexander, Janet. "Do the Merits Matter? A Study of Settlements in Securities Class Actions." *Stanford Law Review* 43, no. 3 (1991): 497–598.

Aman, Alfred C., Jr. "Privatization and Democracy: Resources in Administrative Law." In *Government by Contract: Outsourcing and American Democracy*, ed. Jody Freeman and Martha Minow, 61–288. Cambridge, MA: Harvard University Press, 2009.

Coalition for Safe and Affordable Food. "Business Alliance Comments on Bipartisan Chemical Safety Legislation in Senate." Press release, July 21, 2015. https://www.uschamber.com/sites/default/files/7.21.15-_coalition_letter_to_house_supporting_h.r._1599_the_safe_and_accurate_food_labeling_act.pdf.

American Bankers Association, Consumer Bankers Association, and The Financial Services Roundtable to the Bureau of Consumer Financial Protection. July 13, 2015. https://www.cfpbmonitor.com/wp-content/uploads/sites/5/2015/07/March-10-2015-Consumer-Arbitration-Study-Comment-Letter.pdf.

American Car Rental Association. "ACRA Applauds Car Rental Recall Provisions in Highway Bill Conference Report." Press release, December 23, 2015. https://www.acraorg.com/2015/12/acra-applaus-car-rental-recall-provisions-in-highway-bill-conference-report.

American College of Trial Lawyers. *Report and Recommendations of the Special Committee on Rule 23 of the FRCP*. Newport Beach, CA: American College of Trial Lawyers, 1972.

American Law Institute. *Principles of the Law: Aggregate Litigation*. Philadelphia: American Law Institute, 2010.

———. *Restatement, Second, of the Law of Contracts*. St. Paul, MN: American Law Institute, 1981.

American Society of Civil Engineers. *Failure to Act: Closing the Infrastructure Investment Gap for America's Economic Future; Update to Failure to Act: The Impact of Infrastructure Investment on America's Economic Future*. Reston, VA: American Society of Civil Engineers, May 23, 2016. https://www.infrastructure reportcard.org/wp-content/uploads/2016/05/ASCE-Failure-to-Act-Report-for -Web-5.23.16.pdf.

Anderson, J. Jonas. "Court Capture." *Boston College Law Review* 59, no. 5 (2018): 1545–94.

Anderson, Terry L., Vernon L. Smith, and Emily Simmons. "How and Why to Privatize Federal Lands." *Policy Analysis*, no. 363 (November 9, 1999). https:// www.perc.org/wp-content/uploads/old/pa1.pdf.

Anscombe, Anthony J., and Stephanie A. Sheridan. "A Critical Look at the UCL's Role in Food and Beverage Class Actions." Bloomberg BNA Class Action Litigation Report, November 14, 2014. http://www.americanbar.org/content/dam /aba/administrative/litigation/materials/2015-joint-cle/written_materials/03 _class_action_litigation_report.authcheckdam.pdf (link inactive).

Ariely, Dan. *Predictably Irrational: The Hidden Forces That Shape Our Decisions*. New York: HarperCollins, 2008.

Armentano, Dominick T. *Antitrust and Monopoly: Anatomy of a Policy Failure*. New York: Wiley, 1982.

Baginski, Stephen, John M. Hassell, and Michael D. Kimbrough. "The Effect of Legal Environment on Voluntary Disclosure: Evidence from Management Earnings Forecasts Issued in U.S. and Canadian Markets." *Accounting Review* 77, no. 1 (2002): 25–50.

Barnes, Wayne. "The Objective Theory of Contracts." *University of Cincinnati Law Review* 76 (2008): 1119–58.

Barnett, Randy E. "Consenting to Form Contracts." *Fordham Law Review* 71, no. 3 (2002): 627–45.

———. *The Structure of Liberty*. 2nd ed. Oxford: Oxford University Press, 2014.

Bartholomew, Christine. "The Failed Superiority Experiment." *Vanderbilt Law Review* 65, no. 5 (2016): 1296–1348.

Bavli, Hillel J. "Sampling and Reliability in Class Action Litigation." *Cardozo Law Review De Novo* (2016): 207–19.

Beck, J. Randy. "The False Claims Act and the English Education of *Qui Tam* Legislation." *North Carolina Law Review* 78 (2000): 565–607.

Becker, Gary S. "Crime and Punishment: An Economic Approach." *Journal of Political Economy* 76, no. 2 (March–April 1968): 169–217.

Becker, Gary S., and Richard A. Posner. *Uncommon Sense: Economic Insights, from Marriage to Terrorism*. Chicago: University of Chicago Press, 2009.

Becker, Gary S., and George Stigler. "Law Enforcement, Malfeasance, and Compensation of Enforcers." *Journal of Legal Studies* 3, no. 1 (January 1974): 1–18.

Beckwith, James P., Jr. "Parks, Property Rights, and the Possibilities of Private Law." *Cato Journal* 1, no. 2 (1981): 473–99.

Beisner, John H. "Discovering a Better Way: The Need for Effective Civil Litigation Reform." *Duke Law Journal* 60 (2010): 547–96.

Bennett, James T., and Manuel H. Johnson. *Better Government at Half the Price: Private Production of Public Services*. Ottawa, IL: Jameson, 1982.

Bjarnason, Egill, and Christine Hauser. "Equal Pay Law Taking Effect in Iceland." *New York Times*, January 4, 2018.

Block, Michael, Frederick Nold, and Joseph Sidak. "The Deterrent Effect of Antitrust Enforcement." *Journal of Political Economy* 89, no. 3 (1981): 429–45.

Bodie, Matthew T. "Questions about the Efficiency of Employment Arbitration Agreements." *Georgia Law Review* 39 (2004): 31–39.

Boettke, Peter J., and Rosilino Candela. "Hayek, Leoni, and Law as a Fifth Factor of Production." *Atlantic Economic Journal* 42, no. 2 (2014): 123–31.

Boettrich, Stefan, and Svetlana Starykh. *Recent Trends in Securities Class Action Litigation: 2017 Full-Year Review*. White Plains, NY: NERA Economic Consulting, January 29, 2018.

Bohn, James, and Stephen Choi. "Fraud in the New-Issues Market: Empirical Evidence on Securities Class Actions." *University of Pennsylvania Law Review* 144 (1996): 903–82.

Bone, Robert G. "Tyson Foods and the Future of Statistical Adjudication." *North Carolina Law Review* 95, no. 3 (2017): 607–72.

Bone, Robert G, and David S. Evans. "Class Certification and the Substantive Merits." *Duke Law Journal* 51, no. 4 (2002): 1251–1332.

Boudreaux, Donald J. "Antitrust and Competition from a Market-Process Perspective." In *Research Handbook on Austrian Law and Economics*, ed. Todd J. Zywicki and Peter J. Boettke, 78–295. Northampton, MA: Edward Elgar, 2017.

Boudreaux, Donald J., and Andrew N. Kleit. *How the Market Self-Polices against Predatory Pricing*. Washington, DC: Competitive Enterprise Institute, June 1996. http://www.cei.org/PDFs/predatorypricing.pdf.

Boutrous, Theodore J., Jr., and Bradley J. Hamburger. "Three Myths about *Wal-Mart Stores, Inc. v. Dukes*." *George Washington Law Review Arguendo* 82 (2014): 45–58.

Box, Richard C. "Running Government Like a Business: Implications for Public Administration Theory and Practice." *American Review of Public Administration* 29, no. 1 (1999): 19–43.

Bradt, Andrew D. "A Radical Proposal: The Multidistrict Litigation Act of 1968." *University of Pennsylvania Law Review* 165, no. 4 (2017): 831–916.

Branch, John. "The N.F.L.'s Tragic C.T.E. Roll Call." *New York Times*, February 3, 2016.

Brownstein, Barry. "The Price-Anderson Act: Is It Consistent with a Sound Energy Policy?" *Policy Analysis*, no. 36 (April 17, 1984). https://www.cato.org/publica tions/policy-analysis/priceanderson-act-is-it-consistent-sound-energy-policy.

Buchanan, James M. *Why I, Too, Am Not a Conservative: The Normative Vision of Classical Liberalism*. Northampton, MA: Edward Elgar, 2005.

Buchanan, James M., and Gordon Tullock. *The Calculus of Consent: Logical Foundations of Constitutional Democracy*. Ann Arbor: University of Michigan Press, 1962.

Burbank, Stephen B., and Sean Farhang. "Federal Court Rulemaking and Litigation Reform: An Institutional Approach." *Nevada Law Journal* 15, no. 3 (2015): 1559–96.

———. *Rights and Retrenchment: The Counterrevolution against Federal Litigation*. New York: Cambridge University Press, 2017.

———. "The Subterranean Counterrevolution: The Supreme Court, the Media, and Litigation Retrenchment." *DePaul Law Review* 65, no. 2 (2016): 293–322.

Burbank, Stephen B., Sean Farhang, and Herbert M. Kritzer. "Private Enforcement." *Lewis and Clark Law Review* 17, no. 3 (2013): 637–722.

Burke, Thomas F. *Lawyers, Lawsuits, and Legal Rights: The Battle over Litigation in American Society*. Berkeley and Los Angeles: University of California Press, 2004.

Burset, Christian. "The Rise of Modern Commercial Arbitration and the Limits of Private Ordering." Paper in progress, 2017. https://papers.ssrn.com/sol3/papers.cfm?abstract_id=3009713.

Butler, Stuart M. *Privatizing Federal Spending: A Strategy to Eliminate the Deficit*. New York: Universe, 1985.

Cardi, W. Jonathan, Randall D. Penfield, and Albert H. Yoon. "Does Tort Law Deter Individuals? A Behavioral Science Study." *Journal of Empirical Legal Studies* 9, no. 3 (2012): 567–603.

Carrns, Ann. "Customers Can Lose When Banks Shuffle Payments." *New York Times*, April 11, 2014.

Casey, Anthony, and Anthony Niblett. "Noise Reduction: The Screening Value of *Qui Tam*." *Washington University Law Review* 91, no. 5 (2014): 1169–1217.

Casselman, Ben. "The Start-Up Slump Is a Drag on the Economy; Maybe Big Business Is to Blame." *New York Times*, September 21, 2017.

Chelius, James R. "Liability for Industrial Accidents: A Comparison of Negligence and Strict Liability Systems." *Journal of Legal Studies* 5, no. 2 (June 1976): 293–309.

Cheung, Anthony B. L. "The Rise of Privatization Policies: Similar Faces, Diverse Motives." *International Journal of Public Administration* 20, no. 12 (1997): 2213–45.

Child, James W. "Can Libertarianism Sustain a Fraud Standard?" *Ethics* 104, no. 4 (July 1994): 722–38.

Choi, Stephen J. "Do the Merits Matter *Less* After the Private Securities Litigation Reform Act?" *Journal of Law, Economics, and Organization* 23, no. 3 (2007): 598–626.

Choi, Stephen J., Karen K. Nelson, and Adam Pritchard. "The Screening Effect of the Private Securities Litigation Reform Act." *Journal of Empirical Legal Studies* 6, no. 1 (2009): 35–68.

Choi, Stephen J., and Adam Pritchard. "SEC Investigations and Securities Class Actions: An Empirical Comparison." *Journal of Empirical Legal Studies* 13, no. 1 (2016): 27–49.

———. "Supreme Court's Impact on Securities Class Actions: An Empirical Assessment of *Tellabs*." *Journal of Law, Economics, and Organization* 28, no. 4 (2012): 850–81.

Clegg, Roger, Michael E. DeBow, and John McGinnis. *Conservative and Libertarian Legal Scholarship: Annotated Bibliography*. Federalist Society for Law and Public Policy Studies, 2011. https://fedsoc.org/commentary/publications/conservative-libertarian-legal-scholarship-annotated-bibliography.

Clermont, Kevin M., and John D. Currivan. "Improving on the Contingent Fee." *Cornell Law Review* 63, no. 4 (1978): 529–639.

Clopton, Zachary D. "Class Actions and Executive Power." *New York University Law Review* 92, no. 4 (2017): 878–94.

———. "Redundant Public-Private Enforcement." *Vanderbilt Law Review* 69, no. 2 (2016): 285–332.

Coalition for Safe and Affordable Food to the US House of Representatives. July 21, 2015. https://www.uschamber.com/sites/default/files/7.21.15-_coalition_letter_to_house_supporting_h.r._1599_the_safe_and_accurate_food_labeling_act.pdf.

Coffee, John C., Jr. "Class Wars: The Dilemma of the Mass Tort Class Action." *Columbia Law Review* 95, no. 6 (1995): 1343–1465.

———. *Entrepreneurial Litigation: Its Rise, Fall, and Future*. Cambridge, MA: Harvard University Press, 2015.

———. "Reforming the Securities Class Action: An Essay on Deterrence and Its Implementation." *Columbia Law Review* 106, no. 7 (2006): 1534–86.

———. "Rescuing the Private Attorney General: Why the Model of the Lawyer as Bounty Hunter Is Not Working." *Maryland Law Review* 42, no. 2 (1983): 215–88.

———. "Understanding the Plaintiff's Attorney: The Implications of Economic Theory for Private Enforcement of Law through Class and Derivative Actions." *Columbia Law Review* 86, no. 4 (1986): 669–727.

Cole, Sarah. "On Babies and Bathwater: The Arbitration Fairness Act and the Supreme Court's Recent Arbitration Jurisprudence." *Houston Law Review* 48, no. 3 (2011): 457–506.

Coleman, Brooke D. "Recovering Access: Rethinking the Structure of Federal Civil Rulemaking." *New Mexico Law Review* 39 (2009): 261–97.

Coleman, Jules L. "Efficiency, Utility, and Wealth Maximization." *Hofstra Law Review* 8, no. 3 (1980): 509–51.

Competitive Enterprise Institute. "Allen v. Similasan Corp." Washington, DC: Competitive Enterprise Institute, July 6, 2017. https://cei.org/litigation/allen-v-similasan-corp.

———. "Campbell v. Facebook, Inc." Washington, DC: Competitive Enterprise Institute, July 6, 2017. https://cei.org/litigation/campbell-v-facebook-inc.

Connor, Ken. "Federal Preemption: Crony Capitalism at Its Worst." Renew Amer-
    ica, November 15, 2008. http://www.renewamerica.com/columns/connor/081115.
Consumer Financial Protection Bureau (CFPB). *Arbitration Study: Report to Con-*
    gress, Pursuant to Dodd-Frank Wall Street Reform and Consumer Protection
    Act § 1028(a). March 2015. http://files.consumerfinance.gov/f/201503_cfpb_ar
    bitration-study-report-to-congress-2015.pdf.
Cooper, Perry. "DOJ Urges Court to Block Wine Pricing Class Settlement."
    Bloomberg Law, February 20, 2018. https://www.bna.com/doj-urges-court-n579
    82089084.
Cox, James D., and Randall S. Thomas. "Mapping the American Shareholder
    Litigation Experience: A Survey of Empirical Studies of the Enforcement of
    the U.S. Securities Law." *European Company and Financial Law Review* 6,
    nos. 2–3 (2009): 164–203.
Cox, James D., Randall S. Thomas, and Lynn Bai. "Do Differences in Pleading
    Standards Cause Forum Shopping in Securities Class Actions? Doctrinal and
    Empirical Analyses." *Wisconsin Law Review* 324 (2009): 421–53.
Crane, Daniel A. "Optimizing Private Antitrust Enforcement." *Vanderbilt Law*
    Review 63, no. 3 (2010): 675–723.
Curtis, Quinn, and Minor Myers. "Do the Merits Matter? Empirical Evidence on
    Shareholder Suits from Options Backdating Litigation." *University of Pennsyl-*
    vania Law Review 164, no. 2 (2016): 291–347.
Dam, Kenneth W. "Class Actions: Efficiency, Compensation, Deterrence, and
    Conflict of Interest." *Journal of Legal Studies* 4, no. 1 (January 1975): 47–73.
Danzon, Patricia M. "Liability for Medical Malpractice." *Journal of Economic*
    Perspectives 5, no. 3 (Summer 1991): 51–69.
Davis, Joshua P., and Robert H. Lande. "Toward an Empirical and Theoretical
    Assessment of Private Antitrust Enforcement." *Seattle Law Review* 36, no. 3
    (2013): 1269–1335.
Davis, Mary J. "Toward the Proper Role for Mass Tort Class Actions." *Oregon Law*
    Review 77, no. 1 (1998): 157–233.
DeBot, Brandon, Emily Horton, and Chuck Marr. "Trump Budget Continues
    Multi-Year Assault on IRS Funding despite Mnuchin's Call for More Re-
    sources." Center on Budget and Policy Priorities, March 16, 2017. https://www
    .cbpp.org/research/federal-budget/trump-budget-continues-multi-year-assault
    -on-irs-funding-despite-mnuchins.
DeBow, Michael E. "What's Wrong with Price Fixing: Responding to the New
    Critics of Antitrust." *Regulation* 12, no. 2 (1988): 44–50.
DellaVigna, Stefano. "Psychology and Economics: Evidence from the Field."
    Journal of Economic Literature 47, no. 2 (June 2009): 315–72.
Department of the Treasury. *The Budget in Brief: Internal Revenue Service: FY*
    2015. Washington, DC: Department of the Treasury, 2015. https://www.irs.gov
    /pub/irs-news/IRS%20FY%202015%20Budget%20in%20Brief.pdf.

Deshazo, J. R., and Jody Freeman. "Timing and Form of Federal Regulation: The Case of Climate Change." *University of Pennsylvania Law Review* 155 (2007): 1499–1561.

Dewees, Donald N., David Duff, and Michael Trebilcock. *Exploring the Domain of Accident Law: Taking the Facts Seriously.* New York: Oxford University Press, 1996.

Dimick, Matthew. "Should the Law Do Anything about Economic Inequality?" *Cornell Journal of Law and Public Policy* 26, no. 1 (2016): 1–69.

Dodson, Scott. "A Negative Retrospective of Rule 23." *New York University Law Review* 92, no. 4 (2017): 917–36.

———. "An Opt-In Option for Class Actions." *Michigan Law Review* 115, no. 2 (2016): 171–214.

Dolovich, Sharon. "How Privatization Thinks: The Case of Prisons." In *Government by Contract: Outsourcing and American Democracy*, ed. Jody Freeman and Martha Minow, 128–47. Cambridge, MA: Harvard University Press, 2009.

Donahue, John D. *The Privatization Decision: Public Ends, Private Means.* New York: Basic, 1991.

Doneff, Andrea. "Is *Green Tree v. Randolph* Still Good Law? How the Supreme Court's Emphasis on Contract Language in Arbitration Clauses Will Impact the Use of Public Policy to Allow Parties to Vindicate Their Rights." *Ohio Northern University Law Review* 39, no. 1 (Winter 2012): 63–112.

Donelson, Dain C., Justin J. Hopkins, and Christopher G. Yust. "The Role of Directors' and Officers' Insurance in Securities Fraud Class Action Settlements." *Journal of Law and Economics* 58, no. 4 (November 2015): 747–78.

Dunleavy, Patrick. "Explaining the Privatization Boom: Public Choice versus Radical Approaches." *Public Administration* 64, no. 1 (1986): 13–34.

Dyck, Alexander, Adair Morse, and Luigi Zingales. "How Pervasive Is Corporate Fraud?" Working Paper no. 2222608. Toronto: Rotman School of Management, August 2014. http://faculty.chicagobooth.edu/luigi.zingales/papers/research/pervasive.pdf.

———. "Who Blows the Whistle on Corporate Fraud?" *Journal of Finance* 65, no. 6 (2010): 2213–53.

Eads, George C., and Peter H. Reuter. *Designing Safer Products: Corporate Responses to Product Liability Law and Regulation.* Santa Monica, CA: Rand, 1983.

Easterbrook, Frank H. "Discovery as Abuse." *Boston University Law Review* 69 (1989): 635–48.

———. "Limits of Antitrust." *Texas Law Review* 63, no. 1 (1984): 1–40.

Eisenberg, Theodore, and Christoph Engel. "Assuring Civil Damages Adequately Deter: A Public Good Experiment." *Journal of Empirical Legal Studies* 11, no. 2 (April 2014): 301–49.

Eisenberg, Theodore, and Geoffrey Miller. "Incentive Awards to Class Action Plaintiffs: An Empirical Study." *UCLA Law Review* 56 (2006): 1303–51.

Elhauge, Einer. "How *Italian Colors* Guts Private Antitrust Enforcement by Replacing It with Ineffective Forms of Arbitration." *Fordham International Law Journal* 38, no. 3 (2015): 771–78.

Elliot, E. Donald. "Why Punitive Damages Don't Deter Corporate Misconduct Effectively." *Alabama Law Review* 40, no. 3 (1989): 1053–72.

Engstrom, David Freeman. "Agencies as Litigation Gatekeepers." *Yale Law Journal* 123, no. 3 (2013): 530–861.

———. "Harnessing the Private Attorney General: Evidence from Qui Tam Litigation." *Columbia Law Review* 112, no. 6 (2012): 1244–1325.

———. "Jacobins at Justice: The (Failed) Class Action Revolution of 1978 and the Puzzle of American Procedural Political Economy." *University of Pennsylvania Law Review* 165 (2017): 1531–63.

———. "Private Enforcement's Pathways: Lessons from Qui Tam Litigation." *Columbia Law Review* 114, no. 8 (2014): 1913–2006.

Environmental Protection Agency. "Sanitary Sewer Overflows (SSOs)." n.d. https://www.epa.gov/npdes/sanitary-sewer-overflows-ssos.

Epstein, Richard A. "Class Actions: Aggregation, Amplification, and Distortion." *University of Chicago Legal Forum* 2003, no. 1 (2003): 475–518.

———. "Class Actions: The Need for a Hard Second Look." *Civil Justice Report* 4 (2002): 1–17.

———. *The Classical Liberal Constitution: The Uncertain Quest for Limited Government.* Cambridge, MA: Harvard University Press, 2014.

———. "A Common Law for Labor Relations: A Critique of the New Deal Labor Legislation." *Yale Law Journal* 92, no. 8 (1983): 1357–1408.

———. "Contractual Principle versus Legislative Fixes: Coming to Closure on the Unending Travails of Medical Malpractice." *DePaul Law Review* 54 (2005): 503–26.

———. "Externalities Everywhere? Morals and the Police Power." *Harvard Journal of Law and Public Policy* 21, no. 1 (1997): 61–69.

———. *Forbidden Grounds: The Case against Employment Discrimination Laws.* Cambridge, MA: Harvard University Press, 1992.

———. "The Libertarian Quartet." *Reason*, January 1999, 1–66.

———. "Monopoly Dominance or Level Playing Field? The New Antitrust Paradox." *University of Chicago Law Review* 72, no. 1 (2005): 49–72.

———. "The Neoclassical Economics of Consumer Contracts." *Minnesota Law Review* 92, no. 3 (2008): 803–35.

———. *Principles for a Free Society: Reconciling Individual Liberty with the Common Good.* Reading, MA: Perseus, 1998.

———. "A Theory of Strict Liability." *Journal of Legal Studies* 2, no. 1 (1973): 151–204.

———. "Unconscionability: A Critical Reappraisal." *Journal of Law and Economics* 18, no. 2 (1975): 239–315.

———. "The Uneasy Marriage of Utilitarian and Libertarian Thought." *Quinnipiac Law Review* 19, no. 4 (2000): 783–803.

Erichson, Howard. "Aggregation as Disempowerment: Red Flags in Class Action Settlements." *Notre Dame Law Review* 92, no. 2 (2016): 859–911.

Erickson, Jessica. "Overlitigating Corporate Fraud: An Empirical Analysis." *Iowa Law Review* 97, no. 1 (2011): 49–100.

Ewing, Jack. *Faster, Higher, Farther: The Volkswagen Scandal*. New York: Norton, 2017.

Farhang, Sean. *The Litigation State: Public Regulation and Private Lawsuits in the U.S.* Princeton, NJ: Princeton University Press, 2010.

Federal Highway Administration. "National Bridge Inventory: Deficient Bridges by Highway System 2016." December 31, 2016. https://www.fhwa.dot.gov/bridge/nbi/no10/defbr16.cfm.

Federal Trade Commission. *Office of Claims and Refunds Annual Report 2017*. Washington, DC: Federal Trade Commission, 2017. https://www.ftc.gov/system/files/documents/reports/bureau-consumer-protection-office-claims-refunds-annual-report-2017-consumer-refunds-effected-july/redressreportformatted forweb122117.pdf.

Femino, Laura. "Ex Ante Review of Leveraged Buyouts." *Yale Law Journal* 123, no. 6 (2014): 1830–73.

Finkelstein, Claire. "Legal Theory and the Rational Actor." In *The Oxford Handbook of Rationality*, ed. Alfred R. Mele and Piers Rawling, 399–416. Oxford: Oxford University Press, 2004.

Fisch, Jill E. "Lawyers on the Auction Block: Evaluating the Selection of Class Counsel by Auction." *Columbia Law Review* 102, no. 3 (2002): 650–728.

Fisch, Jill E., Sean J. Griffith, and Steven Davidoff Solomon. "Confronting the Peppercorn Settlement in Merger Litigation: An Empirical Analysis and a Proposal for Reform." *Texas Law Review* 93 (2015): 557–624.

Fiss, Owen M. "The Political Theory of the Class Action." *Washington and Lee Law Review* 53, no. 1 (1996): 21–32.

Fisse, Brent, and John Braithwaite. *The Impact of Publicity on Corporate Offenders*. Albany: State University of New York Press, 1983.

Fitzpatrick, Brian T. "Can and Should the New Third-Party Litigation Financing Come to Class Actions?" *Theoretical Inquiries in Law* 19, no. 1 (2018): 109–23.

———. "The Discovery Tax." Legal Studies Research Paper no. 18-39. Nashville: Vanderbilt University Law School, 2018. https://papers.ssrn.com/sol3/papers.cfm?abstract_id=3238363.

———. "Do Class Action Lawyers Make Too Little?" *University of Pennsylvania Law Review* 158, no. 7 (2010): 2043–83.

———. "An Empirical Study of Class Action Settlements and Their Fee Awards." *Journal of Empirical Legal Studies* 7, no. 4 (2010): 811–46.

———. "The End of Class Actions?" *Arizona Law Review* 57, no. 1 (2015): 162–99.

———. "The End of Objector Blackmail?" *Vanderbilt Law Review* 62 (2009): 1623–66.

———. "The Ironic History of Rule 23." Legal Studies Research Paper no. 17-41. Nashville: Vanderbilt University Law School, 2017. https://papers.ssrn.com/sol3/papers.cfm?abstract_id=3020306.

———. "Justice Scalia and Class Actions: A Loving Critique." *Notre Dame Law Review* 92, no. 5 (2017): 1977–95.

———. "*Twombly* and *Iqbal* Reconsidered." *Notre Dame Law Review* 87, no. 4 (2012): 1621–46.

Fitzpatrick, Brian T., and Robert Gilbert. "An Empirical Look at Compensation in Consumer Class Actions." *New York University Journal of Law and Business* 11, no. 4 (2015): 767–92.

Fox, Justin. "From 'Economic Man' to Behavioral Economics." *Harvard Business Review* 93, no. 5 (May 2015): 79–85.

Frakes, Michael. "Defensive Medicine and Obstetric Practices." *Journal of Empirical Legal Studies* 9, no. 3 (2012): 457–81.

Frakes, Michael, and Anupam B. Jena. "Does Medical Malpractice Law Improve Health Care Quality?" *Journal of Public Economics* 143 (2016): 142–58.

Frank, Ted. "Responding to Professor Fitzpatrick on Class Action Fees." Point of Law, November 29, 2011. http://www.pointoflaw.com/archives/2011/11/responding-to-professor-fitzpatrick-on-class-actio.php.

Frank, Ted (@tedfrank). "I have yet to see one single case with valuable injunctive relief for the class." Twitter post, December 17, 2013, 1:29 PM. https://twitter.com/tedfrank/status/413058425770487808.

Freeman, Jody, and Martha Minow. "Introduction: Reframing the Outsourcing Debates." In *Government by Contract: Outsourcing and American Democracy*, ed. Jody Freeman and Martha Minow, 1–20. Cambridge, MA: Harvard University Press, 2009.

Friedman, David. "The Machinery of Freedom: Guide to a Radical Capitalism." In *Anarchy and the Law: The Political Economy of Choice*, ed. Edward P. Stringham, 40–56. New Brunswick, NJ: Transaction, 2011.

Friedman, Milton. *Bright Promises, Dismal Performance: An Economist's Protest.* Wilmington, MA: Mariner, 1983.

———. *Capitalism and Freedom.* Chicago: University of Chicago Press, 1962.

———. "The Source of Strength." Speech delivered to the Presidents' Club of Michigan General Corp., April 2, 1977.

Friedman, Milton, and Rose Friedman. *Free to Choose: A Personal Statement.* San Diego, CA: Harcourt Brace Jovanovich, 1990.

Garrett, Brandon L. *Too Big to Jail: How Prosecutors Compromise with Corporations.* Cambridge, MA: Harvard University Press, 2014.

Gibson, Jennifer. "New Rules for Class Action Settlements: The Consumer Class Action Bill of Rights." *Loyola of Los Angeles Law Review* 39, no. 3 (2006): 1103–34.

Gilles, Myriam. "The Day Doctrine Died: Private Arbitration and the End of Law." *University of Illinois Law Review* 2016, no. 2 (2016): 371–424.

————. "Reinventing Structural Reform Litigation: Deputizing Private Citizens in the Enforcement of Civil Rights." *Columbia Law Review* 100, no. 6 (2000): 1384–1453.

Gilles, Myriam, and Gary B. Friedman. "Exploding the Class Action Agency Costs Myth: The Social Utility of Entrepreneurial Lawyers." *University of Pennsylvania Law Review* 155, no. 1 (2006): 103–64.

Gingrich, Newt. "Unleashing Growth and Innovation to Move beyond the Welfare State." Press release, November 21, 2011. http://www.presidency.ucsb.edu/ws/index.php?pid=97588.

Gold, Andrew S. "A Moral Rights Theory of Private Law." *William and Mary Law Review* 52, no. 6 (2011): 1873–1931.

Gold, Russell M. "Compensation's Role in Deterrence." *Notre Dame Law Review* 91, no. 5 (1997): 1997–2048.

Goldberg, John C. P., Anthony J. Sebok, and Benjamin C. Zipursky. *Tort Law: Responsibilities and Redress.* New York: Wolters Kluwer, 2016.

Graham, John D. "Product Liability and Motor Vehicle Safety." In *The Liability Maze: The Impact of Liability Law on Safety and Innovation*, ed. Peter W. Huber and Robert E. Litan, 120–90. Washington, DC: Brookings Institution, 1991.

Granston, Michael D. "Factors for Evaluating Dismissal Pursuant to 31 U.S.C. § 3730(c)(2)(A)." Memorandum to Department of Justice Attorneys, January 10, 2018. https://assets.documentcloud.org/documents/4358602/Memo-for-Evaluating-Dismissal-Pursuant-to-31-U-S.pdf. See also 31 U.S.C. § 3730(c)(2)(A).

Gray, C. Boyden. "Democracy at Home." *Texas Review of Law and Politics* 9, no. 2 (Spring 2005): 205–11.

Greve, Michael. *Harm-Less Lawsuits? What's Wrong with Consumer Class Actions.* Washington, DC: American Enterprise Institute, 2005.

Griffith, Sean J. "Private Ordering Post-*Trulia*: Why No Pay Provisions Can Fix the Deal Tax and Forum Selection Provisions Can't." In *The Corporate Contract in Changing Times: Is the Law Keeping Up?* ed. Steven Davidoff Solomon and Randall Thomas. Chicago: University of Chicago Press (forthcoming).

Griffith, Sean J., and Anthony Rickey. "Who Collects the Deal Tax, Where, and What Delaware Can Do about It." In *Research Handbook on Shareholder Litigation*, ed. Sean Griffith, Jessica Erickson, David H. Webber, and Verity Winship. 140–55. Cheltenham: Edward Elgar, 2018.

Grundfest, Joseph A. "Disimplying Private Rights of Action under the Federal Securities Laws: The Commission's Authority." *Harvard Law Review* 107, no. 5 (1994): 961–1024.

Guthrie, Chris, Jeffrey J. Rachlinski, and Andrew J. Wistrich. "Blinking on the Bench: How Judges Decide Cases." *Cornell Law Review* 93, no. 1 (2007): 1–43.

Harrison, J. D. "Business Owners Urge Congress to Take Medicare, Social Security Cuts off the Table." *Washington Post*, February 20, 2013.

Hartnett, Edward. "Taming *Twombly*: An Update After *Matrixx*." *Law and Contemporary Problems* 75, no. 1 (2012): 37–53.

Harvey, Tom. "Jury Finds Utah Companies Made 100 Million Illegal Calls." *Salt Lake Tribune*, May 29, 2016. http://archive.sltrib.com/article.php?id=3940513 &itype=CMSID.

Hasnas, John. "Hayek, Common Law, and Fluid Drive." *New York University Journal of Law and Liberty* 1 (2005): 79–110.

Haydock, Roger S., and Jennifer D. Henderson. "Arbitration and Judicial Civil Justice: An American Historical Review and a Proposal for a Private/Arbitral and Public/Judicial Partnership." *Pepperdine Dispute Resolution Law Journal* 2, no. 2 (2002): 141–98.

Hayek, Friedrich A. *The Constitution of Liberty*. Chicago: University of Chicago Press, 1960.

———. *The Road to Serfdom*. London: Routledge, 1944.

Helland, Eric, and Jonathan Klick. "Regulation and Litigation: Complements or Substitutes?" In *The American Illness: Essays on the Rule of Law*, ed. F. H. Buckley, 118–36. New Haven, CT: Yale University Press, 2013.

Hensler, Deborah R. "Can Private Class Actions Enforce Regulations? Do They? Should They?" In *Comparative Law and Regulation: Understanding the Global Regulatory Process*, ed. Francesca Bignami and David Zaring, 238–74. Cheltenham: Edward Elgar, 2016.

———. "The Future of Mass Litigation: Global Class Actions and Third-Party Litigation Funding." *George Washington Law Review* 79, no. 2 (2011): 306–23.

Hersch, Joni. "Equal Employment Opportunity Law and Firm Profitability." *Journal of Human Resources* 26, no. 1 (1991): 139–53.

Hertel-Fernandez, Alexander, Theda Skocpol, and David Lynch. "Business Associations, Conservative Networks, and the Ongoing Republican War over Medicaid Expansion." *Journal of Health Politics, Policy, and Law* 41, no. 2 (2016): 239–86.

Higgins, Andrew. "Russia Wants Innovation, but It's Arresting Its Innovators." *New York Times*, August 9, 2017.

Hodges, Christopher. *Law and Corporate Behavior: Integrating Theories of Regulation, Enforcement, Compliance and Ethics*. Portland, OR: Hart, 2015.

House Budget Committee. *The Path to Prosperity: A Blueprint for American Renewal*. 112th Congress, 2012. http://budget.house.gov/uploadedfiles/pathtoprosperity2013.pdf.

House Liberty Caucus (@libertycaucus). "House Liberty Caucus Statement on H.R. 985, Fairness in Class Action Litigation Act of 2017." Twitter post, March 8, 2017, 2:32 PM. https://twitter.com/libertycaucus/status/839967179495837696 /photo/1.

Hovenkamp, Herbert J. "Appraising the Progressive State." *Iowa Law Review* 102 (2017): 1063–1112.

Hudgins, Edward L. "Time to Privatize NASA." *Baltimore Sun*, January 26, 1998.

Hylton, Keith N. "Agreements to Waive or Arbitrate Legal Claims: An Economic Analysis." *Supreme Court Economic Review* 8 (2000): 209–63.

———. "The Economics of Class Actions and Class Action Waivers." *Supreme Court Economic Review* 23 (2015): 305–36.

Ignatius, David, and Stan Crock. "U.S. Plan to Revamp Class-Action Rules Could Be Costly for Corporate Violators." *Wall St. Journal*, August 23, 1978.

Internal Revenue Service. *SOI Tax Stats—Corporation Complete Report Section 1*. Washington, DC: Internal Revenue Service, 2013.

Issacharoff, Samuel. "Regulating After the Fact." *DePaul Law Review* 56, no. 2 (2007): 375–88.

Ivory, Danielle. "Federal Auditor Finds Broad Failures at NHTSA." *New York Times*, June 19, 2015.

Jackson, Howell E., and Mark J. Roe. "Public and Private Enforcement of Securities Laws: Resource-Based Evidence." *Journal of Financial Economics* 93, no. 2 (2009): 207–38.

Johnston, Jason Scott. "High Cost, Little Compensation, No Harm to Deter: New Evidence on Class Actions under Federal Consumer Protection Statutes." *Columbia Business Law Review* 2017 (2017): 1–91.

Johnston, Jason Scott, and Todd J. Zywicki. "The Consumer Financial Protection Bureau's Arbitration Study: A Summary and Critique." Public Law and Legal Theory Research Paper no. 51. Charlottesville: University of Virginia School of Law, 2015.

Juska, Zygimantas. "The Effectiveness of Private Enforcement and Class Actions to Secure Antitrust Enforcement." *Antitrust Bulletin* 62, no. 3 (2017): 603–37.

Kagan, Robert A. *Adversarial Legalism: The American Way of Law*. Cambridge, MA: Harvard University Press, 2001.

———. "American Adversarial Legalism in the Early 21st Century." Typescript, University of California, Berkeley, March 2015.

Kahneman, Daniel. *Thinking Fast and Slow*. New York: Farrar, Straus & Giroux, 2011.

Kahneman, Daniel, and Amos Tversky. "On the Psychology of Prediction." *Psychological Review* 8, no. 4 (1973): 237–51.

———. "Prospect Theory: An Analysis of Decision under Risk." *Econometrica* 47, no. 2 (1979): 263–92.

Kalven, Harry, Jr., and Maurice Rosenfield. "The Contemporary Function of the Class Suit." *University of Chicago Law Review* 8, no. 4 (1941): 684–721.

Kaplan, Benjamin. "Continuing the Work of the Civil Committee: 1966 Amendments of the Federal Rules of Civil Procedure (I)." *Harvard Law Review* 81 (1967): 356–416.

Karpoff, Jonathan M., D. Scott Lee, and Gerald S. Martin. "The Cost to Firms of Cooking the Books." *Journal of Financial and Quantitative Analysis* 43 (September 2008): 581–612.

Karpoff, Jonathan M., and John R. Lott. "The Reputational Penalty Firms Bear from Committing Criminal Fraud." *Journal of Law and Economics* 36, no. 2 (October 1993): 757–802.

Kauper, Thomas E., and Edward A. Snyder. "An Inquiry into the Efficiency of Private Antitrust Enforcement: Follow-on and Independently Initiated Cases Compared." *Georgetown Law Journal* 74, no. 4 (1986): 1163–1230.

Kedia, Simi, Kevin Koh, and Shivaram Rajgopal. "Evidence on Contagion in Earnings Management." *Accounting Review* 90, no. 6 (2015): 2337–73.

Kessler, Daniel P. Introduction to *Regulation versus Litigation: Perspectives from Economics and Law*, ed. Daniel P. Kessler, 1–10. Chicago: University of Chicago Press, 2011.

Kessler, Daniel P, and Mark McClellan. "Do Doctors Practice Defensive Medicine?" *Quarterly Journal of Economics* 111, no. 2 (May 1996): 353–90.

Klaff, Daniel B. "Debiasing and Bidirectional Bias: Cognitive Failure in Mandatory Employment Arbitration." *Harvard Negotiation Law Review* 15 (2010): 1–29.

Klonoff, Robert H. "Class Actions in the Year 2026: A Prognosis." *Emory Law Journal* 65, no. 6 (2016): 1569–1655.

———. "The Decline of Class Actions." *Washington University Law Review* 90, no. 3 (2013): 729–838.

Korobkin, Russell. "Bounded Rationality, Standard Form Contracts and Unconscionability." *University of Chicago Law Review* 70, no. 4 (2003): 1203–95.

Kressin, Brandon. "The Debate within Libertarianism on Antitrust Law." *NYU Journal of Law and Liberty* (blog), November 8, 2011, http://lawandlibertyblog .com/nyujll/ujll.com/2011/11/debate-within-libertarianism-on.html.

Krugman, Paul. "Phosphorus and Freedom." *New York Times*, August 11, 2014, A15.

Kugler, Tamar, Edgar E. Kausel, and Martin G. Kocher. "Are Groups More Rational Than Individuals? A Review of Interactive Decision Making in Groups." *Wiley Interdisciplinary Review: Cognitive Science* 3, no. 4 (2012): 471–82.

Kysar, Douglas. "The Public Life of Private Law: Tort Law as a Risk Regulation Mechanism." Public Law Research Paper no. 607. New Haven, CT: Yale Law School, July 20, 2017.

Lahav, Alexandra. *In Praise of Litigation*. New York: Oxford University Press, 2017.

Lambert, Thomas. *How to Regulate: A Guide for Policymakers*. Cambridge, MA: Cambridge University Press, 2017.

Lamm, Maurice. *The Jewish Way in Death and Mourning*. Middle Village, NY: Jonathan David, 2000.

Lande, Robert H., and Joshua P. Davis. "Comparative Deterrence from Private Enforcement and Criminal Enforcement of the U.S. Antitrust Laws." *Brigham Young University Law Review* 2011, no. 2 (2011): 315–87.

Landes, William M. "Optimal Sanctions for Antitrust Violations." *University of Chicago Law Review* 50 (1995): 652–78.

Landes, William M., and Richard A. Posner. *The Economic Structure of Tort Law*. Cambridge, MA: Harvard University Press, 1987.

———. "The Private Enforcement of Law." *Journal of Legal Studies* 4, no. 1 (January 1975): 1–46.

Lapointe, Monique. "Attorney's Fees in Common Fund Actions." *Fordham Law Review* 59, no. 5 (1991): 843–76.

La Porta, Rafael, Florencio Lopez-de-Silanes, and Andrei Shleifer. "The Economic Consequences of Legal Origins." *Journal of Economic Literature* 46, no. 2 (2008): 285–332.

———. "Law and Finance After a Decade of Research." In *Handbook of the Economics of Finance*, ed. George M. Constantinides, Milton Harris, and Rene M. Stulz, 425–83. Amsterdam: Elsevier, 2013.

———. "What Works in Securities Laws?" *Journal of Finance* 61, no. 1 (February 2006): 1–32.

Lawyers for Civil Justice, Federation of Defense and Corporate Counsel, DRI—the Voice of the Defense Bar, and the International Association of Defense Counsel. "To Restore a Relationship between Classes and Their Actions: A Call for Meaningful Reform of Rule 23." Comment to the Civil Rules Advisory Committee and its Rule 23 Subcommittee. August 9, 2013. http://www.uscourts.gov/sites/default/files/fr_import/13-CV-G-suggestion.pdf.

Lee, Emery G., III, and Thomas E. Willging. "Impact of the Class Action Fairness Act on the Federal Courts: Preliminary Findings from Phase Two's Pre-CAFA Sample of Diversity Class Actions." Washington, DC: Federal Judicial Center, November 2008. https://www.uscourts.gov/sites/default/files/preliminary_findings_from_phase_two_class_action_fairness_study_2008_1.pdf.

Lemos, Margaret H. "Aggregate Litigation Goes Public: Representative Suits by State Attorneys General." *Harvard Law Review* 126, no. 2 (2012): 486–549.

———. "Privatizing Public Litigation." *Georgetown Law Journal* 104, no. 3 (2016): 515–82.

Lemos, Margaret H., and Max Minzner. "For-Profit Public Enforcement." *Harvard Law Review* 127, no. 3 (2014): 853–913.

Leslie, Christopher R. "The Arbitration Bootstrap." *Texas Law Review* 94, no. 2 (2015): 265–330.

Liptak, Adam. "Doling Out Other People's Money." *New York Times*, November 26, 2007.

Lipton, Eric. "Lobbyists, Bearing Gifts, Pursue Attorneys General." *New York Times*, October 28, 2014.

Litan, Robert E., Peter Swire, and Clifford Winston. "The U.S. Liability System: Background and Trends." In *Liability: Perspectives and Policy*, ed. Robert E. Litan and Clifford Winston, 1–15. Washington, DC: Brookings Institution Press, 1988.

Lizza, Ryan. "The Libertarians' Secret Weapon." *New Yorker*, July 25, 2016.

Loerzel, Robert. "Foot Fight: Subway Sandwich Suit Raises Class Action Questions." *ABA Journal*, February 2017, http://www.abajournal.com/magazine/article/subway_sandwich_class_action.

Love, Kelly A. "A Primer on Opinion Letters: Explanations and Analysis." *Transactions: The Tennessee Journal of Business Law* 9 (2007): 68–98.

Macey, Jonathan R., and Geoffrey P. Miller. "The Plaintiffs' Attorney's Role in Class Action and Derivative Litigation: Economic Analysis and Recommendations for Reform." *University of Chicago Law Review* 58, no. 1 (1991): 1–118.

[Madison, James]. "The Alleged Danger from the Powers of the Union to the State Governments Considered." Federalist Papers, no. 45. 1788. Avalon Project Yale Law School. http://avalon.law.yale.edu/18th_century/fed45.asp.

Malmendier, Ulrike, and Geoffrey Tate. "CEO Overconfidence and Corporate Investment." *Journal of Finance* 60, no. 6 (2005): 2661–2700.

Mangu-Ward, Katherine. "It's Time to Privatize the V.A." *Reason*, November 2017. https://reason.com/archives/2017/10/30/its-time-to-privatize-the-va.

Manne, Henry G., ed. "Constitutional Protections of Economic Activity: How They Promote Individual Freedom." Special issue, *George Mason University Law Review*, vol. 11, no. 2 (1988).

Manual for Complex Litigation. 4th ed. Washington, DC: Federal Judicial Center, 2004. https://public.resource.org/scribd/8763868.pdf.

Marcus, David. "The History of the Modern Class Action, Part I: Sturm und Drang, 1953–1980." *Washington University Law Review* 90, no. 3 (2013): 587–652.

———. "The History of the Modern Class Action, Part II: Litigation and Legitimacy, 1981–1994." *Fordham Law Review* 86, no. 4 (2018): 1785–1845.

———. "The Past, Present, and Future of Trans-Substantivity in Federal Civil Procedure." *DePaul Law Review* 59, no. 2 (2010): 371–430.

Marcus, Richard. "Revolution v. Evolution in Class Action Reform." *North Carolina Law Review* 96, no. 9 (2018): 903–44.

Mariani, Raymond L. "The September 11th Victim Compensation Fund of 2001 and the Protection of the Airline Industry: A Bill for the American People." *Journal of Air Law and Commerce* 67 (2002): 141–86.

Mayer Brown, LLP. "Do Class Actions Benefit Consumers?" Mayer Brown, LLP, 2013. https://www.mayerbrown.com/files/uploads/Documents/PDFs/2013/December/DoClassActionsBenefitClassMembers.pdf.

McAfee, R. Preston, Hugo M. Mialon, and Sue H. Mialon. "Public v. Private Antitrust Enforcement: A Strategic Analysis." *Journal of Public Economics* 92, nos. 10–11 (2008): 1863–75.

McCoy, Kevin. "Madoff Fund Hasn't Paid Victims a Dime." *USA Today*, May 24, 2017.

McDonald, Duff. *The Golden Passport: Harvard Business School, the Limits of Capitalism, and the Moral Failure of the MBA Elite*. New York: HarperCollins, 2017.

McGuire, E. Patrick. *The Impact of Product Liability*. New York: Conference Board Research Reports, 1988.

McMahon, Jeff. "What Would Milton Friedman Do about Climate Change? Tax Carbon." *Forbes*, October 12, 2014. http://www.forbes.com/sites/jeffmc

mahon/2014/10/12/what-would-milton-friedman-do-about-climate-change-tax
-carbon.

Mello, Michelle, and Troyen Brennan. "Deterrence of Medical Errors: Theory and Evidence for Malpractice Reform." *Texas Law Review* 80 (2002): 1595–1637.

Menkel-Meadow, Carrie. "Regulation of Dispute Resolution in the United States of America: From the Formal to the Informal to the 'Semi-Formal.'" In *Regulating Dispute Resolution: ADR and Access to Justice at the Crossroads*, ed. Felix Steffek, Hannes Unberath, Hazel Genn, Reinhard Greger, and Carrie Menkel-Meadow, 419–54. Oxford: Hart, 2013.

Merle, Renae, and Tory Newmyer. "Congressional Republicans Use Special Maneuver to Kill 'Arbitration Rule.'" *Washington Post*, October 25, 2017.

Michaels, Jon. "Running Government Like a Business . . . Then and Now." *Harvard Law Review* 128, no. 4 (2015): 1152–82.

Mickum, George B., and Carol A. Rhees. "Federal Class Action Reform: A Response to the Proposed Legislation." *Kentucky Law Journal* 69 (1980): 799–826.

Migoya, David. "Customers Challenge the Way Banks Reorder Debits in Order to Rack Up Overdraft Fees." *Denver Post*, August 20, 2010.

Miller, Arthur R. "Of Frankenstein Monsters and Shining Knights: Myth, Reality, and the 'Class Action Problem.'" *Harvard Law Review* 92, no. 3 (1979): 664–94.

———. "The Preservation and Rejuvenation of Aggregate Litigation: A Systemic Imperative." *Emory Law Journal* 64, no. 2 (2014): 293–327.

Mitchell, Gregory. "Libertarian Nudges." *Missouri Law Review* 82, no. 3 (2017): 695–708.

Moller, Mark. "Controlling Unconstitutional Class Actions: A Blueprint for Future Lawsuit Reform." *Policy Analysis* 546 (June 2005): 1–22.

———. "Separation of Powers and the Class Action." *Nebraska Law Review* 95, no. 2 (2016): 366–431.

Moore, Michael J., and W. Kip Viscusi. *Compensation Mechanisms for Job Risks: Wages, Workers' Compensation, and Product Liability*. Princeton, NJ: Princeton University Press, 1990.

Moorhouse, John C., Andrew P. Morriss, and Robert Whaples. "Law and Economics and Tort Law: A Survey of Scholarly Opinion." *Albany Law Review* 62, no. 2 (1998): 667–96.

Morgensen, Gretchen. "SEC Inertia on Paybacks Adds to Investor Harm." *New York Times*, January 13, 2017.

Moses, Margaret. L. "Statutory Misconstruction: How the Supreme Court Created a Federal Arbitration Law Never Enacted by Congress." *Florida State University Law Review* 34, no. 1 (2006): 99–160.

Mullenix, Linda S. "Ending Class Actions as We Know Them: Rethinking the American Class Action." *Emory Law Journal* 64, no. 2 (2014): 399–449.

Murray, Charles. *What It Means to Be a Libertarian: A Personal Interpretation*. New York: Broadway, 1997.

Myers, Minor, and Charles R. Korsmo. "The Structure of Stockholder Litigation: When Do the Merits Matter?" *Ohio State Law Journal* 75, no. 5 (2014): 829–901.

Nagareda, Richard A. "Class Actions in the Administrative State: Kalven and Rosenfield Revisited." *University of Chicago Law Review* 75, no. 2 (2008): 603–48.

Narveson, Jan. *The Libertarian Idea.* Philadelphia: Temple University Press, 1988.

Naughton, James P., Tjomme O. Rusticus, Clare Wang, and Ira Yeung. "Private Litigation Costs and Voluntary Disclosure: Evidence from the *Morrison* Ruling." *Accounting Review* (in press).

Nelson, Karen K., and A. C. Pritchard. "Carrot or Stick? The Shift from Vocabulary to Mandatory Disclosure of Risk Factors." *Journal of Empirical Legal Studies* 13, no. 2 (2016): 266–97.

Newmark, Craig M. "Is Antitrust Enforcement Effective?" *Journal of Political Economy* 96, no. 6 (1988): 1315–28.

NFL Concussion Settlement Benefits and Legal Rights. 2014. https://www.nflconcus sionsettlement.com/documents/long-form_notice.pdf.

Nozick, Robert. *Anarchy, State, and Utopia.* New York: Basic, 1974.

O'Connor, Anahad. "Study Warns of Diet Supplement Dangers Kept Quiet by FDA." *New York Times*, April 7, 2015.

O'Connor, Erin O'Hara, and Larry Ribstein. "Preemption and Choice-of-Law Coordination." *Michigan Law Review* 111, no. 5 (2013): 647–714.

Olson, Walter. *The Litigation Explosion: What Happened When America Unleashed the Lawsuit.* New York: Penguin, 1991.

Oman, Nathan B. *The Dignity of Commerce.* Chicago: University of Chicago Press, 2016.

Osborne, David, and Ted Gaebler. *Reinventing Government: How the Entrepreneurial Spirit Is Transforming the Public Sector.* New York: Penguin, 1993.

O'Toole, Randal. "Stopping the Runaway Train: The Case for Privatizing Amtrak." Policy Analysis no. 712. Washington, DC: Cato Institute, 2012. https://www.cato.org/publications/policy-analysis/stopping-runaway-train-case-privatizing-amtrak.

Parrillo, Nicholas. *Against the Profit Motive: The Salary Revolution in American Government, 1780–1940.* New Haven, CT: Yale University Press, 2013.

Parker, Jeffrey S. "Civil Procedure Reconsidered." In *Research Handbook on Austrian Law and Economics*, ed. Todd J. Zywicki and Peter J. Boettke, 296–324. Northampton, MA: Edward Elgar, 2017.

Pear, Robert. "Reagan Signs Bill on Drug Exports and Payment for Vaccine Injuries." *New York Times*, November 15, 1986.

———. "Soft Drink Industry Fights Proposed Food Stamp Ban." *New York Times*, April 29, 2011.

Perillo, Joseph M. "The Origins of the Objective Theory of Contract Formation and Interpretation." *Fordham Law Review* 69, no. 2 (2000): 427–77.

Pirie, Madsen. *Dismantling the State: The Theory and Practice of Privatization.* Dallas: National Center for Policy Analysis, 1985.

Polinsky, A. Mitchell. "Private versus Public Enforcement of Fines." *Journal of Legal Studies* 9, no. 1 (1980): 105–27.

Polinsky, A. Mitchell, and Daniel Rubinfeld. "Aligning the Interests of Lawyers and Clients." *American Law and Economics Review* 5, no. 1 (2003): 165–88.

Polinsky, A. Mitchell, and Steven Shavell. "A Skeptical Attitude about Products Liability Is Justified: A Reply to Professors Goldberg and Zipursky." *Harvard Law Review* 123 (2010): 1949–68.

Poole, Robert W. *Cutting Back City Hall.* New York: Universe, 1980.

Popper, Andrew. "In Defense of Deterrence." *Albany Law Review* 75, no. 1 (2012): 181–203.

Posner, Richard A. *Antitrust Law.* 2nd ed. Chicago: University of Chicago Press, 2011.

———. *Economic Analysis of Law.* New York: Wolters Kluwer Law and Business, 2014.

———. "The Efficiency and Efficacy of Title VII." *University of Pennsylvania Law Review* 136 (1987): 513–22.

———. "Regulation (Agencies) versus Litigation (Courts): An Analytical Framework." In *Regulation versus Litigation: Perspectives from Economics and Law,* ed. Daniel P. Kessler, 11–26. Chicago: University of Chicago Press, 2012.

———. "A Theory of Negligence." *Journal of Legal Studies* 1, no. 1 (January 1972): 29–96.

President's Commission on Privatization. *Privatization: Toward More Effective Government.* Washington, DC: President's Commission on Privatization, June 1988. http://pdf.usaid.gov/pdf_docs/PNABB472.pdf.

PriceWaterhouseCoopers. "Executive Compensation: Clawbacks: 2014 Proxy Disclosure Study." PriceWaterhouseCoopers, January 2015. https://www.niri.org/NIRI/media/NIRI/Documents/pwc-executive-compensation-clawbacks-2014.pdf.

Pritchard, Adam C. "Evaluating S. 1551: The Liability for Aiding and Abetting Securities Violation Act of 2009." Statement to the Senate Committee on the Judiciary, Subcommittee on Crime and Drugs. September 17, 2009. https://www.judiciary.senate.gov/imo/media/doc/09-09-17%20Pritchard%20Testimony.pdf.

Puranam, Phanish, Nils Stieglitz, Magda Osman, and Madan M. Pillutla. "Modelling Bounded Rationality in Organizations: Progress and Prospects." *Academy of Management Annals* 9, no. 1 (2015): 337–92.

Rachlinski, Jeffrey J. "A Positive Psychological Theory of Judging in Hindsight." *University of Chicago Law Review* 65 (1998): 571–625.

Rakoff, Jed. "The Cure for Corporate Wrongdoing: Class Actions vs. Individual Prosecutions." *New York Review of Books,* November 11, 2015.

Ramphal, Nishal Ray. "The Role of Public and Private Litigation in the Enforcement of Securities Laws in the United States." PhD diss., Rand Graduate School, 2007.

Randazzo, Sara, and Jacqueline Palank. "Legal Fees Cross New Mark: $1,500 an Hour." *Wall Street Journal*, February 9, 2017.

Reason Foundation. *Annual Privatization Report 2006: Transforming Government through Privatization*. Los Angeles: Reason Foundation, 2006.

Redish, Martin. "Rethinking the Theory of the Class Action: The Risks and Rewards of Capitalistic Socialism in the Litigation Process." *Emory Law Journal* 64, no. 2 (2014): 451–76.

———. *Wholesale Justice: Constitutional Democracy and the Problem of the Class Action Lawsuit*. Stanford, CA: Stanford University Press, 2009.

Resnik, Judith. "Diffusing Disputes: The Public in the Private of Arbitration, the Private in Courts, and the Erasure of Rights." *Yale Law Journal* 124, no. 8 (2015): 2804–2939.

Resnik, Judith, Dennis E. Curtis, and Deborah R. Hensler. "Individuals within the Aggregate: Relationships, Representation, and Fees." *New York University Law Review* 71 (1996): 296–401.

Reuters. "U.S. SEC's Piwowar Urges Companies to Pursue Mandatory Arbitration Clauses." Reuters, July 18, 2017. https://www.reuters.com/article/us-usa-sec-arbitration-idUSKBN1A221Y.

Revesz, Richard. "Federalism and Environmental Regulation: A Public Choice Analysis." *Harvard Law Review* 115, no. 2 (2001): 553–641.

Riley, Brian, and Brett Shaefer. *Time to Privatize OPIC*. Washington, DC: Heritage Foundation, May 19, 2014. https://www.heritage.org/global-politics/report/time-privatize-opic.

Roosevelt, Franklin D. "Veto of a Bill Regulating Administrative Agencies." December 8, 1940. The American Presidency Project. http://www.presidency.ucsb.edu/ws/index.php?pid=15914.

Rose, Amanda M. "Cutting Class Action Agency Costs: Lessons from the Public Company." Manuscript in progress, Vanderbilt University School of Law, n.d.

———. "Reforming Securities Litigation Reform: Restructuring the Relationship between Public and Private Enforcement of Rule 10b-5." *Columbia Law Review* 108, no. 6 (2008): 1301–64.

Rosenberg, David. "Mandatory-Litigation Class Action: The Only Option for Mass Tort Cases." *Harvard Law Review* 115, no. 3 (2002): 831–97.

Rothbard, Murray Newton. *For a New Liberty: The Libertarian Manifesto*. 2nd ed. Auburn, AL: Ludwig von Mises Institute, 2007.

———. *The Logic of Action II: Applications and Criticism from the Austrian School*. Cheltenham: Edward Elgar, 1997.

Rubenstein, William B. "The Fairness Hearing: Adversarial and Regulatory Approaches." *UCLA Law Review* 53 (2006): 1435–82.

———. "On What a 'Private Attorney General' Is—and Why It Matters." *Vanderbilt Law Review* 57, no. 6 (2004): 2129–73.

Rubenstein, William, Alba Conte, and Herbert B. Newberg. *Newberg on Class Actions*. 5th ed. Eagan, MN: Thompson Reuters, 2011–18.

Rubin, Paul H. "Crony Capitalism." *Supreme Court Economic Review* 23, no. 1 (2015): 105–20.

———. "Third-Party Financing of Litigation." *Northern Kentucky Law Review* 38 (2011): 673–85.

Rubin, Paul H., and Joanna M. Shepherd. "Tort Reform and Accidental Deaths." *Journal of Law and Economics* 50, no. 2 (2007): 221–38.

Rugy, Veronique de. "Beyond Permissionless Innovation." *Reason*, January 2016. https://reason.com/archives/2015/12/22/beyond-permissionless-innovati.

———. "Federal Infrastructure Spending Is a Bad Deal." *Reason*, March 2017. https://reason.com/archives/2017/02/09/federal-infrastructure-spendin/print.

———. "Mainstreaming Liberty." *Reason*, October 2015. http://reason.com/archives/2015/10/01/mainstreaming-liberty.

Rutledge, Peter. *Arbitration—a Good Deal for Consumers: A Response to Public Citizen*. Washington, DC: US Chamber Institute for Legal Reform, April 2008. http://stmedia.startribune.com/documents/docload.pdf.

Sant'Ambrogio, Michael, and Adam S. Zimmerman. "Inside the Agency Class Action." *Yale Law Journal* 126, no. 6 (2017): 1634–1728.

Savas, Emanuel S. *Privatization and Public-Private Partnerships*. New York: Chatham House, 2000.

Sawyer, Logan E., III. "Book Review: Why the Right Embraced Rights; *The Other Rights Revolution*." *Harvard Journal of Law and Public Policy* 40 (2016): 729–57.

Scheuerman, Sheila B. "Due Process Forgotten: The Problem of Statutory Damages and Class Actions." *Missouri Law Review* 74, no. 1 (2009): 103–52.

Schneier, Cogan. "Rachel Brand Says DOJ Looking to Get Involved in More Class Actions." *National Law Journal*, February 15, 2018. https://www.law.com/nationallawjournal/sites/nationallawjournal/2018/02/15/doj-wants-more-regular-voice-in-reviewing-class-action-fairness-rachel-brand-says/?slreturn=20180118130409.

Schuck, Peter H. *Why Government Fails So Often: And How It Can Do Better*. Princeton, NJ: Princeton University Press, 2014.

Schwartz, David L. "The Rise of Contingent Fee Representation in Patent Litigation." *Alabama Law Review* 64, no. 2 (2012): 335–88.

Schwartz, Joanna C. "The Cost of Suing Business." *DePaul Law Review* 65, no. 2 (2016): 655–86.

Schwartz, John. "If Tech Execs Act Like Spoiled Brats, Should We Spank Them?" *New York Times*, July 14, 2017.

Seith, Patricia A. "Civil Rights, Labor, and the Politics of Class Action Jurisdiction." *Stanford Journal of Civil Rights and Civil Liberties* 7, no. 1 (2011): 83–128.

Seligman, Joel. "The Merits Do Matter: A Comment on Professor Grundfest's 'Disimplying Private Rights of Action under the Federal Securities Laws: The Commissioner's Authority.'" *Harvard Law Review* 108 (1994): 438–57.

Selmi, Michael. "The Price of Discrimination: The Nature of Class Action Employment Discrimination Litigation and Its Effects." *Texas Law Review* 81, no. 5 (2003): 1249–1335.

Sharkey, Catherine. "CAFA Settlement Notice Provision: Optimal Regulatory Policy?" *University of Pennsylvania Law Review* 156 (2008): 1971–99.

Shavell, Steven. *Foundations of Economic Analysis of Law*. Cambridge, MA: Harvard University Press, 2009.

———. "A Fundamental Enforcement Cost Advantage of the Negligence Rule over Regulation." *Journal of Legal Studies* 42, no. 2 (2013): 275–302.

———. "The Optimal Structure of Law Enforcement." *Journal of Law and Economics* 36, no. 1 (1993): 255–87.

Sheley, Erin L., and Theodore H. Frank. "Prospective Injunctive Relief and Class Settlements." *Harvard Journal of Law and Public Policy* 39, no. 3 (April 2012): 769–832.

Shepherd, Joanna M. "Tort Reforms' Winners and Losers: The Competing Effect of Care and Activity Levels." *UCLA Law Review* 55 (2008): 905–77.

Shleifer, Andrei. "Efficient Regulation." In *Regulation versus Litigation: Perspectives from Economics and Law*, ed. Daniel P. Kessler, 27–44. Chicago: University of Chicago Press, 2011.

———. *The Failure of Judges and the Rise of Regulators*. Cambridge, MA: MIT Press, 2012.

Sidley Austin LLP. "Mitigating Consumer Fraud Class Action Litigation Risk: Top Ten Methods for 2015." Email to clients, January 5, 2015. https://www.sidley.com/en/insights/newsupdates/2015/01/mitigating-consumer-fraud-class-action-litigation-risk-top-ten-methods-for-2015.

Sikochi, Anywhere. "The Effect of Shareholder Litigation Risk on the Information Environment." Working Paper no. 17-048. Cambridge, MA: Harvard Business School, September 4, 2016. http://www.hbs.edu/faculty/Publication%20Files/17-048_413e9658-649c-4904-8d49-6779f11910ac.pdf.

Silver, Charles. "'We're Scared to Death': Class Certification and Blackmail." *New York University Law Review* 78 (2003): 1357–1430.

Silver-Greenberg, Jessica, and Stacy Cowley. "I.R.S. Hires Debt Collectors, Raising Fears of Scams and Abuse." *New York Times*, April 21, 2017.

Simard, Linda Sandstrom. "A View from within the Fortune 500: An Empirical Study of Negative Value Class Actions and Deterrence." *Indiana Law Review* 47, no. 3 (2014): 739–85.

Simpson, Leonard B., and William S. Dato. "Legislating on a False Foundation: The Erroneous Academic Underpinnings of the Private Securities Litigation Reform Act of 1995." *San Diego Law Review* 33, no. 3 (1996): 959–84.

Sinclair, Jack. "Walmart Statement on SNAP Reductions." Corporate Walmart, December 6, 2013. https://corporate.walmart.com/_news_/news-archive/2013/11/01/walmart-statement-on-snap-reductions.

Singer, Joseph William. *No Freedom without Regulation: The Hidden Lesson of the Subprime Crisis.* New Haven, CT: Yale University Press, 2015.

Sloan, Frank A., Emily M. Stout, Kathryn Whetten-Goldstein, and Lan Liang. *Drinkers, Drivers, and Bartenders: Balancing Private Choices and Public Accountability.* Chicago: University of Chicago Press, 2000.

Smith, Fred L., Jr. "The Case for Reforming the Antitrust Regulations (If Repeal Is Not an Option)." *Harvard Journal of Law and Public Policy* 23, no. 1 (1999): 23–58.

———. "Why Not Abolish Antitrust?" *Regulation* 7, no. 1 (1983): 23–33.

Smith, Henry E. "Mind the Gap: The Indirect Relation between Ends and Means in American Property Law." *Cornell Law Review* 94, no. 4 (2009): 959–90.

Smith, Michael L. "Deterrence and Origin of Legal System: Evidence from 1950–1999." *American Law and Economics Review* 7, no. 2 (2005): 350–78.

Soloway, Stan, and Alan Chvotkin. "Federal Contracting in Context: What Drives It, How to Improve It." In *Government by Contract: Outsourcing and American Democracy*, ed. Jody Freeman and Martha Minow, 192–240. Cambridge, MA: Harvard University Press, 2009.

Spencer, Leslie. "Some Call It Champerty." *Forbes*, April 30, 1990.

Steinzor, Rena. "(Still) 'Unsafe at Any Speed': Why Not Jail for Auto Executives?" *Harvard Law and Policy Review* 9, no. 2 (2015): 443–69.

Stephens, Joe. "Coupons Create Cash for Lawyers." *Washington Post*, November 19, 1999, A01.

Stephenson, Matthew C. "Public Regulation of Private Enforcement: The Case for Expanding the Role of Administrative Agencies." *Virginia Law Review* 91, no. 1 (2005): 93–173.

Sterns, Maxwell L., and Todd J. Zywicki. *Public Choice Concepts and Applications in Law.* Eagan, MN: West Academic, 2009.

Students for a Democratic Society. "The Port Huron Statement." 1962. https://history.hanover.edu/courses/excerpts/111huron.html.

Sun, Lisa Grow, and Brigham Daniels. "Mirrored Externalities." *Notre Dame Law Review* 90, no. 1 (2014): 135–86.

Sutton, Jeff. *51 Imperfect Solutions: States and the Making of American Constitutional Law.* Oxford: Oxford University Press, 2018.

Szalai, Imre Stephen. "The Federal Arbitration Act and the Jurisdiction of the Federal Courts." *Harvard Negotiation Law Review* 12 (2007): 319–75.

———. "More Than Class Action Killers: The Impact of *Concepcion* and *American Express* on Employment Arbitration." *Berkeley Journal of Employment and Labor Law* 35, no. 1 (2014): 31–59.

Thaler, Richard H., and Cass R. Sunstein. *Nudge: Improving Decisions about Health, Wealth, and Happiness.* New Haven, CT: Yale University Press, 2008.

Thierer, Andrew. *Permissionless Innovation: The Continuing Case for Comprehensive Technological Freedom.* Arlington, VA: Mercatus Center, 2014.

Tidmarsh, Jay. "Resurrecting Trial by Statistics." *Minnesota Law Review* 99 (2015): 1459–1506.

Toro, Francisco. "Uganda's Bad Seeds." *Reason*, March 2017. https://reason.com /archives/2017/02/12/ugandas-bad-seeds.

Truth in Advertising. "Walgreen Glucosamine Supplements." https://www.truthin advertising.org/walgreen-glucosamine-supplements.

Uhlmann, David M. "Justice Falls Short in GM Case." *New York Times*, September 19, 2015.

US Chamber Institute for Legal Reform. "Court Tosses Lawsuit over Lip Balm Left in Tube." Faces of Lawsuit Abuse, April 25, 2016. http://www.facesoflaw suitabuse.org/2016/04/court-tosses-lawsuit-over-lip-balm-left-in-tube.

———. *Creating Conditions for Economic Growth: The Role of the Legal Environment.* US Chamber Institute for Legal Reform, October 26, 2011. http://www .instituteforlegalreform.com/uploads/sites/1/Economic_Growth_Working_Pa per_Oct2011_0.pdf.

———. "Deceived by Jelly Beans, Woman Files Lawsuit against Jelly Belly." Faces of Lawsuit Abuse, August 25, 2017. http://www.facesoflawsuitabuse.org/2017 /08/deceived-by-jelly-beans-woman-files-lawsuit-against-jelly-belly.

———. "ILR Releases Top Ten Most Ridiculous Lawsuits of 2016." US Chamber Institute for Legal Reform, December 19, 2016. http://www.instituteforlegalre form.com/resource/ilr-releases-top-ten-most-ridiculous-lawsuits-of-2016.

———. "Jimmy John's Lawsuit 'Sprouts' Hefty Payday for Lawyers—Vouchers for 'Victims.'" Faces of Lawsuit Abuse, October 16, 2014. http://www.faceso flawsuitabuse.org/2014/10/jimmy-johns-lawsuit-sprouts-hefty-payday-for-law yers-vouchers-for-victims.

———. "Massachusetts Man Files Class Action Lawsuits over Fake Butter." Faces of Lawsuit Abuse, April 5, 2017. http://www.facesoflawsuitabuse.org/2017/04 /massachusetts-man-files-class-action-lawsuit-over-fake-butter.

———. "Mastercard Blasts 'Baseless' Lawsuit over Its 'Stand Up to Cancer' Fundraising Promotion." Faces of Lawsuit Abuse, January 11, 2016. http://www .facesoflawsuitabuse.org/2016/01/mastercard-blasts-baseless-lawsuit-over-its -stand-up-to-cancer-fundraising-promotion.

———. "Mom and Son Sue over Typo That Gave Test Takers Extra Time." Faces of Lawsuit Abuse, April 25, 2016. http://www.facesoflawsuitabuse.org/2016/04 /mom-and-son-sue-over-sat-typo-that-gave-students-extra-test-time.

———. "Selling Lawsuits, Buying Trouble: The Emerging World of Third-Party Litigation Financing in the United States." US Chamber Institute for Legal Reform, 2009. https://www.instituteforlegalreform.com/research/selling-lawsuits -buying-trouble-the-emerging-world-of-third-party-litigation-financing-in-the -united-states.

———. "Starbucks Feels the Heat from Two Abusive Lawsuits." Faces of Lawsuit Abuse, July 27, 2016. http://www.facesoflawsuitabuse.org/2016/07/too-much-ice-in

-iced-coffees-too-much-steamed-milk-in-lattes-starbucks-feeling-the-heat-of-la
wsuit-abuse.

———. "Subway Sued over 'Footlong' Subs." Faces of Lawsuit Abuse, January 25, 2013. http://www.facesoflawsuitabuse.org/2013/01/subway-sued-over-foot
long-subs.

———. "Time Clock Lawsuit Filed against Starbucks." Faces of Lawsuit Abuse,
July 14, 2017. http://www.facesoflawsuitabuse.org/2017/07/time-clock-lawsuit-filed
-against-starbucks.

———. "The Top Ten Most Ridiculous Lawsuits of 2015." Faces of Lawsuit Abuse,
December 21, 2015. http://www.facesoflawsuitabuse.org/2015/12/the-top-ten
-most-ridiculous-lawsuits-of-2015.

———. "U.S. Chamber Releases Most Ridiculous Lawsuits of 2013." US Chamber Institute for Legal Reform, December 23, 2013. http://www.institute
forlegalreform.com/resource/us-chamber-releases-most-ridiculous-lawsuits
-of-2013-.

———. "U.S. Chamber Releases Most Ridiculous Lawsuits of 2014." US Chamber Institute for Legal Reform, December 22, 2014. http://www.institutefor
legalreform.com/resource/us-chamber-releases-most-ridiculous-lawsuits-of
-2014.

US Chamber of Commerce. "The CFPB's Flawed Arbitration 'Study.'" March 8,
2016. https://www.uschamber.com/issue-brief/the-cfpb-s-flawed-arbitration-study.

US Chamber of Commerce and US Chamber Institute for Legal Reform to Consumer Financial Protection Bureau. December 11, 2013. http://blogs.reuters
.com/alison-frankel/files/2013/12/mayerbrown-chamberletter.pdf.

US Chamber of Commerce to the Chairman and Ranking Member of the House
Committee on Energy and Commerce. April 15, 2015. https://www.uschamber
.com/sites/default/files/4.15.15-_hill_letter_supporting_the_data_security_and
_breach_notification_act.pdf.

US Senate Committee on the Judiciary. Subcommittee on Judicial Machinery. *Reform of Class Action Litigation Procedures: Hearings before the Subcommittee
on Judicial Machinery*. 95th Cong., 2nd sess., 1978.

Utt, Ronald. "Chairman Mica's New Amtrak Proposal Would Use the Private Sector to Reform Passenger Rail." *Web Memo* no. 3290 (June 13, 2011). http://
thf_media.s3.amazonaws.com/2011/pdf/wm3290.pdf.

———. *Privatize the General Services Administration through an Employee Buyout*.
Washington, DC: Heritage Foundation, May 26, 1995. https://www.heritage.org
/government-regulation/report/privatize-the-general-services-administration
-through-employeebuyout.

Vairo, Georgene. "What Goes Around, Comes Around: From the Rector of Barkway to Knowles." *Review of Litigation* 32, no. 4 (2013): 721–804.

Velikonja, Urska. "Public Compensation for Private Harm: Evidence from the
SEC's Fair Fund Distributions." *Stanford Law Review* 67, no. 2 (2015): 331–95.

Vermeule, Adrian. "Many-Minds Arguments in Legal Theory." *Journal of Legal Analysis* 1, no. 1 (2009): 1–45.

Victor, Daniel. "Butter or Margarine? In Dunkin' Donuts Lawsuit, Man Accepts No Substitute." *New York Times*, April 4, 2017.

Viscusi, W. Kip. "Pricing Lives for Corporate Risk Decisions." *Vanderbilt Law Review* 68, no. 4 (2015): 1117–62.

———. *Reforming Products Liability*. Cambridge, MA: Harvard University Press, 1991.

———. "The Social Costs of Punitive Damages against Corporations in Environmental and Safety Tort." *Georgetown Law Journal* 87, no. 2 (November 1998): 285–346.

Viscusi, W. Kip, and Michael J. Moore. "An Industrial Profile of the Links between Product Liability and Innovation." In *The Liability Maze: The Impact of Liability Law on Safety and Innovation*, ed. Peter W. Huber and Robert E. Litan, 81–119. Washington, DC: Brookings Institution, 1991.

———. "Product Liability, Research and Development, and Innovation." *Journal of Political Economy* 101, no. 1 (February 1993): 161–84.

Vlasic, Bill. "An Engineer's Eureka Moment with a G.M. Flaw." *New York Times*, March 28, 2014.

Vlasic, Bill, and Aaron M. Kessler. "It Took E.P.A. Pressure to Get VW to Admit Fault." *New York Times*, September 21, 2015.

Voet, Stefaan. "Belgian Court Recognizes US Opt-Out Class Action Settlement." Conflict of Laws, April 9, 2017. http://conflictoflaws.net/2017/belgian-court-re cognizes-us-opt-out-class-action-settlement.

———. "Consumer Collective Redress in Belgium: Class Actions to the Rescue?" *European Business Organization Law Review* 16, no. 1 (2015): 121–43.

Volokh, Alexander. "The Constitutional Possibilities of Prison Vouchers." *Ohio State Law Journal* 72, no. 5 (2011): 983–1042.

———. "Prison Vouchers." *University of Pennsylvania Law Review* 160, no. 3 (2012): 779–863.

Weiler, Paul C., Howard Hiatt, Joseph P. Newhouse, William G. Johnson, Troyen Brennan, and Lucian Leape. *A Measure of Malpractice: Medical Injury, Malpractice Litigation, and Patient Compensation*. Cambridge, MA: Harvard University Press, 1993.

White, Michelle J. "An Empirical Test of the Comparative and Contributory Negligence Rules in Accident Law." *Rand Journal of Economics* 20, no. 3 (1989): 308–30.

Willging, Thomas E., Laural L. Hooper, and Robert J. Niemic. "Empirical Study of Class Actions in Four Federal District Courts: Final Report to the Advisory Committee on Civil Rules." Washington, DC: Federal Judicial Center, 1996. https://www.uscourts.gov/sites/default/files/rule23_1.pdf.

Williams, Ryan C. "Due Process, Class Action Opt-Outs, and the Right Not to Sue." *Columbia Law Review* 115, no. 3 (2015): 599–659.

Wilt, Michael Patrick. "Evaluating 'Consumer Relief' Payments in Recent Bank Settlement Agreements." *Journal of Business and Securities Law* 17, no. 2 (2017): 253–303.

Winston, Clifford. *Government Failure versus Market Failure: Microeconomics Policy Research and Government Performance*. Washington, DC: Brookings Institution Press, 2006.

Wright, Joshua D. "Behavioral Law and Economics, Paternalism, and Consumer Contracts: An Empirical Perspective." *NYU Journal of Law and Liberty* 2, no. 3 (2007): 470–511.

Zabinski, Zenon, and Bernard S. Black. "The Deterrent Effect of Tort Law: Evidence from Medical Malpractice Reform." Law and Economics Working Paper no. 13-09. Evanston, IL: Northwestern University, November 15, 2018. https://ssrn.com/abstract=2161362.

Zimmerman, Adam S. "Distributing Justice." *New York University Law Review* 86, no. 2 (2011): 500–572.

Zingales, Luigi. *A Capitalism for the People: Recapturing the Lost Genius of American Prosperity*. New York: Basic, 2012.

Zwolinski, Matt. "A Libertarian Case for the Moral Limits of Markets." *Georgetown Journal of Law and Public Policy* 13, no. 2 (2015): 275–90.

Zywicki, Todd J. "Posner, Hayek and the Economic Analysis of Law." *Iowa Law Review* 93, no. 2 (2008): 559–603.

———. "Rent-Seeking, Crony Capitalism, and the Crony Constitution." *Supreme Court Economic Review* 23, no. 1 (2015): 77–103.

Zywicki, Todd J., and Edward P. Stringham. "Austrian Law and Economics and Efficiency in the Common Law." In *Research Handbook on Austrian Law and Economics*, ed. Todd J. Zywicki and Peter J. Boettke, 192–208. Northampton, MA: Edward Elgar, 2017.

Legal Sources

An Act to Amend the Procedures That Apply to Consideration of Interstate Class Actions to Assure Fairer Outcomes for Class Members and Defendants, and for Other Purposes, Pub. L. No. 109-2, 118 Stat. 119 (2005).

A.L.A. Schechter Poultry Corp. v. United States, 295 U.S. 495 (1935).

Allen v. Similasan Corp., No. 12-CV-00376-BAS-JLB, 2017 WL 1346404 (S.D. Cal. April 12, 2017).

Ashcroft v. Iqbal, 556 U.S. 662 (2009).

AT&T Mobility LLC v. Concepcion, 563 U.S. 333 (2011).

Barfield et al. v. Sho-Me Power Elec. Coop., No. 2:11-CV-04321 (E.D. Mo.).

Bell Atl. Corp. v. Twombly, 550 U.S. 544 (2007).

Blahut v. Harris Bank, N.A., No. 10-cv-21821-JLK (S.D. Fla. Aug. 5, 2013).

Blum v. Stenson, 465 U.S. 886, 900 (1984).

Boeing Co. v. Van Gemert, 444 U.S. 472, 481 (1980).

Brief of the Chamber of Commerce of the United States of America as *Amicus Curiae* in Support of Petitioner, *AT&T Mobility LLC v. Concepcion*, 563 U.S. 333 (2011), https://www.americanbar.org/content/dam/aba/publishing/preview /publiced_preview_briefs_pdfs_09_10_09_893_PetitionerAmCuCoC.authcheck dam.pdf.

Brief of the Competitive Enter. Instit., as *Amicus Curiae*, Foster v. L-3 Commc'ns EOTech, No. 6:15-cv-03519-BCW (May 25, 2017).

Butterfield v. Forrester (1809) 103 Eng. Rep. 926 (KB).

Carnegie v. Household Int'l, Inc., 376 F.3d 656, 661 (7th Cir. 2004).

Casayuran v. PNC Bank, N.A., No. 10-cv-20496-JLK (S.D. Fla. Aug. 5, 2013).

Class Action Fairness Act of 2005, Pub. L. No. 109-2, 119 Stat. 4 (2005).

Class Action Settlement Agreement and Release at § III.B.3, Exhibit A to Memorandum of Points and Authorities in Support of Plaintiff's Unopposed Motion for Preliminary Approval of Class Action Settlement, Kimberly Birbrower v. Quorn Foods, Inc., No. 2:16-cv-01346 at 16–18 (C.D. Cal. Feb. 26, 2017).

Court Awarded Attorney Fees, 108 F.R.D. 237, 247 (1985).

Discover Bank v. Superior Court, 36 Cal. 4th 148, 163 (2005) *abrogated by* AT&T Mobility LLC v. Concepcion, 563 U.S. 333.

Doyle v. MasterCard Int'l Inc., No. 16-04270 (2d Cir. Jul. 6, 2017).

Ebner v. Fresh, Inc., 838 F.3d 958 (9th Cir. 2016).

Ellinghaus v. Educ. Testing Serv., No. 2:15-cv-03442 (E.D.N.Y. Sep. 30, 2016).

Eno v. M & I Marshall & Illsley Bank, No. 10-cv-22730-JLK (S.D. Fla. Aug. 2, 2013).

Eubank v. Pella Corp., 753 F.3d 718 (7th Cir. 2014).

Fair Debt Collection Practices Act, 47 U.S.C. § 1692k (2012).

Fairness in Class Action Litigation and Furthering Asbestos Claim Transparency Act of 2017. H.R. 985, 115th Cong. (2017).

Fears v. Wilhelmina Model Agency, Inc., No. 02-4911, 2005 WL 1041134 (S.D.N.Y. May 5, 2005).

Federal Arbitration Act, 9 U.S.C. § 2 (2012).

Fed. R. Civ. P. 23(a)(4), 23(c)(2)(B), 23(c)(2)(B)(v), 23(e), 23(f), 23(g)(1), 23(g) (1)(A), 23(h).

Fernandez v. Merrill Lynch, No. 15-22782 (S.D. Fla. Nov. 28, 2017).

Firestone Tire & Rubber Co. v. Risjord, 449 U.S. 368, 374 (1981).

Gokare P.C. v. Fed. Express Corp., No. 11-CV-02131 (W.D. Tenn. 2012).

Gomez v. Jelly Belly Candy Co., No. ED-CV-1700575-CJCFFMX, 2017 WL 2598551 (C.D. Cal. June 8, 2017).

Gutierrez v. Wells Fargo Bank, N.A., No. C 07-05923 WHA, 2015 WL 2438274 (N.D. Cal. May 21, 2015).

Gutierrez v. Wells Fargo Bank, N.A., 730 F. Supp. 2d 1080, 1140 (N.D. Cal. 2010), *aff'd in part, rev'd in part and remanded sub nom.*, Gutierrez v. Wells Fargo Bank, NA, 704 F.3d 712 (9th Cir. 2012).

Hanrahan v. Britt, 174 F.R.D. 356 (E.D. Pa. 1997).

Harris v. Associated Bank, N.A., No. 10-cv-22948-JLK (S.D. Fla. August 2, 2013).

Harris v. Time, Inc., 237 Cal. Rptr. 584 (Cal. Ct. App. 1987), *modified* (May 21, 1987).

Hilao v. Estate of Marcos, 103 F.3d 767 (9th Cir. 1996).

Hill v. Gateway 2000, Inc., 105 F.3d 1147 (7th Cir. 1997).

In re Amino Acid Lysine Antitrust Litig., 918 F. Supp. 1190 (N.D. Ill. 1996).

In re AT&T Corp., 455 F.3d 160 (3d Cir. 2006).

In re Baby Prod. Antitrust Litig., 708 F.3d 163 (3d Cir. 2013).

In re Bridgestone/Firestone, Inc., Tire Prods. Liab. Litig., 288 F.3d 1012 (7th Cir. 2002).

In re Checking Account Overdraft Litig., No. 1:09-md-02036 (S.D. Fla. 2011).

In re Checking Account Overdraft Litig., 830 F. Supp. 2d 1330 (S.D. Fla. 2011).

In re Compact Disc Minimum Advertised Price Antitrust Litig., No. MDL 1361, 2005 WL 1923446.

In re Deepwater Horizon, 739 F.3d 790 (5th Cir. 2014).

In re Fannie Mae Sec Litig., No. 1:04-cv-01639 (D.D.C.).

In re High-Tech Employee Antitrust Litig., No. 5:11-CV-02509 (N.D. Cal.).

In re Johnson & Johnson Derivative Litig., 900 F. Supp. 2d 467 (D.N.J. 2012).

In re Nat'l. Football League Players' Concussion Injury Litig., 307 F.R.D. 351, 388 (E.D. Pa. 2015), *amended sub nom. In re* Nat'l Football League Players' Concussion Injury Litig., No. 2:12-MD-02323-AB, 2015 WL 12827803 (E.D. Pa. May 8, 2015).

In re Nat'l Football League Players' Concussion Injury Litig., 821 F.3d 410 (3d Cir.), as amended (May 2, 2016).

In re Nat'l Football League Players' Concussion Injury Litig., No. 2:12-MD-02323-AB, (E.D. Pa. May 8 2018).

In re Oil Spill by the Oil Rig "Deepwater Horizon" in the Gulf of Mexico, 910 F. Supp. 2d 891 (E.D. La. 2012), *aff'd sub nom.*

In re Oil Spill by the Oil Rig "Deepwater Horizon" in the Gulf of Mexico, No. 2:10-md-02179 (E.D. La. 2012).

In re Oracle Sec. Litig., 131 F.R.D. 688 (N.D. Cal.), modified, 132 F.R.D. 538 (N.D. Cal. 1990).

In re Oracle Sec. Litig., 132 F.R.D. 538 (N.D. Cal. 1990).

In re PaineWebber Ltd. Partnerships Litig., 999 F. Supp. 719 (S.D.N.Y. 1998).

In re Rhone-Poulenc Rorer Inc., 51 F.3d 1293 (7th Cir. 1995).

In re San Juan Dupont Plaza Hotel Fire Litig., No. MDL-0721, 2010 WL 60955 (D.P.R. Jan 7, 2012).

In re Subway Footlong Sandwich Mktg. & Sales Practices Litig., 316 F.R.D. 240 (E.D. Wis. 2016).

In re Subway Footlong Sandwich Mktg. & Sales Practices Litig., 869 F.3d 551 (7th Cir. 2017).

In re Synthroid Mktg. Litig., 264 F.3d 712 (7th Cir. 2001).

In re Synthroid Mktg. Litig., 325 F.3d 974 (7th Cir. 2003).

In re TFT-LCD (Flat Panel) Antitrust Litigation, No. 3:07-md-01827 (N.D. Cal.).

In re Volkswagen "Clean Diesel" Mktg., Sales Practices, & Prod. Liab. Litig. No. 3:15-MD-02672 (N.D. Cal.).

In re Volkswagen "Clean Diesel" Mktg., Sales Practices, & Prod. Liab. Litig., No. 2672 CRB (JSC), 2017 WL 1352859 (N.D. Cal. Apr. 12, 2017).

In re Volkswagen "Clean Diesel" Mktg., Sales Practices, & Prod. Liab. Litig., 229 F. Supp. 3d 1052 (N.D. Cal. 2017), *enforcement granted*, No. 2672 CRB (JSC), 2017 WL 914066 (N.D. Cal. Mar. 6, 2017).

In re Washington Pub. Power Supply Sys. Sec. Litig., 19 F.3d 1291 (9th Cir. 1994).

Kansas v. Crane, 534 U.S. 407 (2002).

Kirk Dahl et al. v. Bain Capital Partners LLC, No. 1:07-cv-12388 (D. Mass.).

Laster v. AT&T Mobility LLC, 584 F.3d 849 (9th Cir. 2009), *rev'd sub nom.* AT&T Mobility LLC v. Concepcion, 563 U.S. 333 (2011).

Lindsey v. Normet, 405 U.S. 56 (1972).

Lindy Bros. Builders of Phila. v. Am. Radiator & Standard Sanitary Corp., 487 F.2d 161 (3d Cir. 1973).

McDaniel v. Cty. of Schenectady, No. 04CV0757GLSRFT, 2007 WL 3274798 (N.D.N.Y.).

McKinley v. Great W. Bank, Docket No. 10-cv-22770-JLK (S.D. Fla., Aug. 2, 2013).

Mills v. Capital One, N.A., No. 14 CIV. 1937 HBP, 2015 WL 5730008 (S.D.N.Y. September 30, 2015).

Newman v. Schiff, 778 F.2d 460 (8th Cir. 1985).

Notice of Proposed Class Action Settlement, Heather Starks v. Jimmy John's, LLC, No. BC501113 (Cal. Sup. Ct.).

Pa. R.R. v. United States 111 F.Supp. 80 (D.N.J. 1953).

Pearson v. NBTY, Inc., 772 F.3d 778 (7th Cir. 2014).

Pergament v. Frazer, 93 F. Supp. 13 (E.D. Mich. 1950), *aff'd sub nom.*, Masterson v. Pergament, 203 F.2d 315 (6th Cir. 1953).

Pincus v. Starbucks Corp., No. 16-cv-04705 (N.D. Ill. Oct. 14, 2016).

Printz v. United States, 521 U.S. 898 (1997).

Private Securities Litigation Reform Act of 1995, Pub. L. No. 104-67, 109 Stat. 737 (1995).

Ramah Navajo Chapter, v. Jewell, No. 1:90-CV-957 (D.N.M.).

Redman v. RadioShack Corp., 768 F.3d 622 (7th Cir. 2014).

Reynolds v. Beneficial Nat'l Bank, 288 F.3d 277 (7th Cir. 2002).

Robert Scott v. Serv. Corp. Int'l, No. BC421528 (Cal. Sup. Ct.).

Rules Enabling Act. 28 U.S.C. §§ 2071–77 (2012).

Schulte v. Fifth Third Bank, 805 F. Supp. 2d 560 (N.D. Ill. 2011).

Silverman v. Motorola Sols., Inc., 739 F.3d 956 (7th Cir. 2013).

Spark v. MBNA Corp., 157 F. Supp. 2d 330 (D. Del. 2001), *aff'd*, 48 F. App'x 385 (3d Cir. 2002).

Staton v. Boeing Co., 327 F.3d 938 (9th Cir. 2003).

Strumlauf v. Starbucks Corp., No. 16-CV-01306-YGR, 2018 WL 306715 (N.D. Cal. Jan. 5, 2018).

Swanson v. Citibank, N.A., 614 F.3d 400 (7th Cir. 2010).

Telephone Consumer Protection Act, 47 U.S.C. § 227(b)(3)(B) (2012).

Tennille v. W. Union Co., No. 09-CV-00938-MSK-KMT, 2013 WL 6920449 (D. Colo. Dec. 31, 2013).

Tennille v. W. Union Co., 785 F.3d 422 (10th Cir. 2015).

Troester v. Starbucks Corp., 680 F. App'x 511 (9th Cir. 2016).

Wallace on Behalf of Ne. Utilities v. Fox, 7 F. Supp. 2d 132 (D. Conn. 1998).

Wal-Mart Stores, Inc. v. Dukes, 564 U.S. 338 (2011).

Webster Eisenlohr, Inc. v. Kalodner, 145 F.2d 316 (3rd Cir. 1944).

Williams v. Rohm & Haas Pension Plan, 658 F.3d 629 (7th Cir. 2011).

Wolfgeher v. Commerce Bank, N.A., No. 10-cv-22017-JLK (S.D. Fla. Aug. 2, 2013).

Index